4TH EDITION

TRADE MATTERS

ENGLISCH FÜR GROSS- UND AUSSENHANDELSKAUFLEUTE

von
Michael Benford
Isobel Williams

sowie
Sandra Haberkorn und Sabine Steeg-Hintermeier

unter Mitarbeit der Verlagsredaktion

Cornelsen

TRADE MATTERS

Verfasser/in: Michael Benford, Bochum
Isobel Williams, Berlin
Verfasserinnen KMK-Seiten: Sandra Haberkorn und Sabine Steeg-Hintermeier, Wiesbaden
Berater/innen: Marc Engels, Erkelenz; Sandra Haberkorn, Wiesbaden; Alexandra Köpf, Ulm; Bianca Sonnenschein, Erkelenz; Martin Wippersteg, Essen
Projektleitung: Andreas Goebel
Verlagsredaktion: Kari-ann Warnakulasuriya
Außenredaktion: James Abram
Redaktionelle Mitarbeit: Verena Groß, Katarina Hlavata, Christine House, Oliver Busch (Wörterverzeichnisse)
Bildredaktion: Gertha Maly, Christina Scheuerer
Layoutkonzept: finedesign, Berlin
Gesamtgestaltung und technische Umsetzung: vitaledesign, Berlin
Umschlaggestaltung: vitaledesign, Berlin
Coverfoto: Shutterstock / Red ivory
Illustrationen: Oxford Designers & Illustrators

Erhältlich sind auch:
Handreichungen für den Unterricht mit MP3-CD und Online-Zusatzmaterialien
ISBN 978-3-06-451639-7

Soweit in diesem Lehrwerk Personen fotografisch abgebildet sind und ihnen von der Redaktion fiktive Namen, Berufe, Dialoge und Ähnliches zugeordnet oder diese Personen in bestimmte Kontexte gesetzt werden, dienen diese Zuordnungen und Darstellungen ausschließlich der Veranschaulichung und dem besseren Verständnis des Inhalts.

www.cornelsen.de

Die Webseiten Dritter, deren Internetadressen in diesem Lehrwerk angegeben sind, wurden vor Drucklegung sorgfältig geprüft. Der Verlag übernimmt keine Gewähr für die Aktualität und den Inhalt dieser Seiten oder solcher, die mit ihnen verlinkt sind.

1. Auflage, 1. Druck 2018

Alle Drucke dieser Auflage sind inhaltlich unverändert und können im Unterricht nebeneinander verwendet werden.

Druck: Mohn Media Mohndruck, Gütersloh

ISBN 978-3-06-451637-3
ISBN 978-3-06-451638-0 (E-Book)

PEFC
PEFC/04-31-1033

PEFC zertifiziert
Dieses Produkt stammt aus nachhaltig bewirtschafteten Wäldern und kontrollierten Quellen.

www.pefc.de

Vorwort

Trade Matters 4th edition ist eine Neubearbeitung des bewährten Englisch-Lehrwerks für Groß- und Außenhandelskaufleute und wurde für die Ausbildung in Berufsschulen sowie die innerbetriebliche Aus- und Weiterbildung konzipiert.

Das Lehrwerk setzt Englischkenntnisse voraus, die dem Niveau B1 des Europäischen Referenzrahmens *(Common European Framework of Reference)* entsprechen. Es deckt die Themen der aktuellen Lehrpläne der Bundesländer für Englisch in der Berufsschule konsequent ab.

Trade Matters 4th edition besteht aus zwölf Units, die flexibel einsetzbar sind. Jede Unit umfasst vier abgeschlossene Lernsituationen, die jeweils in einer Doppelstunde bearbeitet werden können. Eine Unit ist wie folgt aufgebaut:

Foundation: Diese Doppelseite bietet Ihnen mit Grundwissen und elementarem Themenvokabular einen Einstieg in das Thema der Unit.

Part A/B: Diese stark berufsbezogenen ausgerichteten Module können je nach Umfang der Inputmaterialien jeweils zwei bis vier Seiten umfassen. Hier werden fachspezifische Schwerpunkte der Unit mithilfe authentischer und aktueller Materialien behandelt.

Communication: Berufliche Kommunikation steht im Fokus des abschließenden *Communication*-Teils. Ein „Das kann ich"-Kästchen – eine Checkliste zur Selbstevaluation – rundet die Unit ab und ermöglicht es den Lernenden, über ihren persönlichen Lernerfolg zu reflektieren.

Alle Lernsituationen sind so konzipiert, dass sie ausgelassen oder zu einem anderen Zeitpunkt behandelt werden können. Somit berücksichtigt die Modulstruktur einer jeden Unit die organisatorische Vielfalt des Englischunterrichts und schafft größtmögliche Flexibilität im Unterricht.

Besonderer Wert wird in diesem Lehrwerk auf **Handlungsorientierung** und direkten Berufsbezug gelegt: Jedes Modul beginnt mit einer branchenspezifischen *Situation* und führt über handlungs- und kompetenzorientierte Lernschritte zu einem Handlungsprodukt. Dieses Lernziel ist jeweils zu Beginn des Moduls mit einem Pfeil gekennzeichnet und ermöglicht so eine schnelle Orientierung.

Unterschiedliche Aktions- und Sozialformen ermöglichen zudem den Einsatz von kooperativen Lernformen und fördern **eigenverantwortliches Lernen**.

Um der Heterogenität der Auszubildenden gerecht zu werden, finden sich zahlreiche Aufgaben zur **Binnendifferenzierung** in den Units. Diese sind mit einem Strich unter der Aufgabenziffer gekennzeichnet und verweisen auf editierbare Kopiervorlagen in den Handreichungen, die alternative Bearbeitungsmöglichkeiten für die jeweilige Aufgabe zur Verfügung stellen.

Zur Vorbereitung auf die **KMK-Prüfung** Stufen II und III werden anhand von sechs Unterrichtseinheiten und einer kompletten Musterprüfung prüfungsrelevante Materialien und Aufgaben angeboten und so eine systematische Prüfungsvorbereitung ermöglicht.

Grundlegende grammatikalische Strukturen werden durchweg im **situativen Kontext** vermittelt, ergänzt durch eine systematische Grammatikübersicht im Anhang und Übungsmaterialien in den Handreichungen. Zur Erweiterung des berufsrelevanten Wortschatzes werden Themenwortschätze im Anhang angeboten sowie eine umfangreiche *Unit word list* mit allen neuen Wörtern in chronologischer Reihenfolge wie auch eine *A-Z word list* mit allen neuen Wörtern in alphabetischer Reihenfolge. Außerdem im Anhang finden Sie berufsbezogene *Useful phrases,* die eine effektive berufliche Kommunikation erleichtern plus eine Aufstellung der Incoterms.

Sämtliche Audiomaterialien finden Sie in den Handreichungen für den Unterricht und darüber hinaus geben kurze **Videos** passend zu den Themen kurze Einblicke in das spätere Berufsleben und vermitteln Fachwissen in motivierender Form. Diese Materialien und die dazugehörigen Arbeitsblätter stehen den Lehrkräften online zur Verfügung.

Der Verlag, die Autoren sowie die Berater und Beraterinnen wünschen Ihnen viel Erfolg und Freude mit *Trade Matters 4th edition.*

Table of contents

1 Working conditions

FOUNDATION: My apprenticeship

Situation: You are an apprentice at Orbit Group AG, a large consumer electronics wholesaler whose working language is English. The company is looking for new international trainees.
→ **You write a description of your apprenticeship for the trainee section of the website.**

1 Describing two apprenticeships

Your line manager asks you to write an English description of your apprenticeship for the website, so you look online for some examples.

A 2)) **Read and listen to what Sophie says, then copy and complete the chart.**

Hello. My name is Sophie, I'm 19 years old. I'm from Bremen. I left school last year with A levels in English, German and Mathematics. I work at Import/Export GmbH where I'm training to be a management assistant in wholesale and foreign trade. My apprenticeship lasts for three years. I'm doing a work-based apprenticeship. I work in the office from 9 to 5 and do block release at vocational school every three months. I get a small salary from the company. It's not much, but I still live with my parents, so I don't have expenses like rent or food. My colleagues are great and help me a lot. I'd like to work in one of the company's foreign branches one day.

1 school qualifications		
2 training company		
3 name of apprenticeship		
4 details of apprenticeship	– length	
	– type	
	– hours in company	
	– time at vocational school	
5 who pays her living expenses		
6 hopes for the future		

B 3)) **Listen to Robert describing his training and answer these questions.**

1 What are Robert's school qualifications?
2 Where does he work?
3 What will Robert be when he qualifies?
4 How long does his apprenticeship last?
5 What type of training course is he doing?
6 How is his training divided between the office and vocational school?
7 Who pays for Robert's course?
8 What does Robert hope for the future?

2 Talking about your apprenticeship

You talk about your apprenticeship with your colleagues.

Work with a partner from a different training company. Ask and answer questions about your apprenticeship. Use ideas from exercise 1 to structure your conversation.

› *Useful phrases: Describing apprenticeships, page 186*

Asking for information

Who do you work for?
What is the name of your company?
Where is the company located?
How many employees does your company have?

› *Grammar: Questions and short answers, page 154*

3 Reading about the dual education system

You also read online about Germany's dual system of vocational training.

Read the text then answer the FAQs below it.

Most students in Germany complete their school education between the ages of 15 and 18. After that, some of them enter a dual training scheme at a vocational college. With this scheme, an apprentice gets job experience at work and theoretical knowledge of their profession at school.

An apprenticeship usually lasts between 24 and 36 months, depending on the profession. Apprentices spend 50 to 70 per cent of their time working in companies and the rest of the time in the classroom. Depending on the profession, an apprentice may do day release or block release.

The employer is responsible for the apprentice's training and education. They give the apprentices a special apprenticeship contract. The contract protects the apprentice from being fired during the training programme.

Gaining a vocational college qualification gives young workers good chances in their future lives. The qualification standards are the same throughout the whole of Germany, which means that the degree is recognized by every company. Even though the German qualification is not recognized in some countries, the fact that someone has trained in Germany is often enough to get them a good position abroad.

FAQs
1. I would like to work in commerce. How can a dual training scheme help me?
2. Why do some apprenticeships last longer than others?
3. How will my time be split between in-company training and vocational school?
4. My friend is doing block release and I am doing day release. Why aren't we doing the same thing?
5. Who is responsible for my training?
6. Can my employer stop my training before I've finished my apprenticeship?
7. I might have to move to a different town after I qualify. How will my qualification help me find a new employer?
8. I would like to work abroad. How will my qualification help me get a job?

4 Writing about your apprenticeship

It is time to write about your apprenticeship for the trainee information page on your company website.

Write a short description of your training. Give your name, age and say where you are from. Then structure the rest of your description as below. Write about 150 words.

- your school qualification
- where you work
- what you are training to be
- a short explanation of the dual system
- a short description of your apprenticeship (block/day release; hours in the office / at school)

› *Thematic vocabulary: Training and apprenticeships, page 200*
› *Useful phrases: Describing apprenticeships, page 186*

PART A: Working conditions at my company

Situation: Orbit Group AG, a large consumer electronics wholesaler, encourages its employees to work at its branches all over the world. You attend a seminar in the UK about working conditions.
→ **You make a poster about working conditions at your training company in Germany.**

1 Describing ideal working conditions

The trainer first tells you to brainstorm some ideas about your ideal working conditions.

A Choose the ten most import factors from the word cloud and add ideas of your own.

medium-sized company
subsidized travel
hot desking
smart clothes
small company
quiet office
overtime
open-plan office
canteen
big company
flexitime
customer contact
shift work
business English
company smartphone
company car
dress code
busy office
home office
job-sharing

B Discuss your list with a partner. What points do you agree and disagree on? Give reasons.

C Conduct a class survey and find the five most important points. Explain why they are important to you.

Agreeing and disagreeing

In my opinion, / I think a busy office is really important.
– I agree with you. / Yes, I think you're right.
– I disagree / don't agree. I think … is more important.

2 Comparing conditions

You listen to two other seminar participants, Lisa and Lukas, answering interview questions about their individual working conditions.

A 4 Listen to the two interviews and make notes on the following points:

- the size of the company
- current department
- total number of apprentices
- working hours, breaks, overtime
- dress code
- business trips
- employees' availability outside working hours
- facilities and benefits offered by the company
- job prospects at the company

B Find an apprentice in your class from another company or department and interview each other about your working conditions. Use the list of points above.

› *Grammar: Questions and short answers, page 154*
› *Thematic vocabulary: Training and apprenticeships, page 200*

3 Looking the part

Like many companies, Orbit Group AG has a dress code for its office staff.

A **Study the dress code and use it to explain which of the appearances (1–8) below would be acceptable and which not. Describe what is and isn't allowed.**

Orbit Group AG dress code

	allowed		not allowed	
	male	female	male	female
clothes	– suit – jacket & trousers – shirt & tie	– suit / trouser suit – jacket, skirt & blouse – dress	– shorts – loud colours – denim of any colour	– shorts – short skirts – low-cut tops
shoes	– black/brown shoes	– flat or low-heel shoes	– flip-flops / trainers	
piercings, tattoos, jewellery, etc.		– one pair of earrings	– visible body piercings or tattoos – excessive jewellery – heavy make-up	

B **How would your boss react if you or your colleagues dressed in this way? Have a class discussion about the importance of a dress code in the workplace.**

1

2

3

4

5

6

7

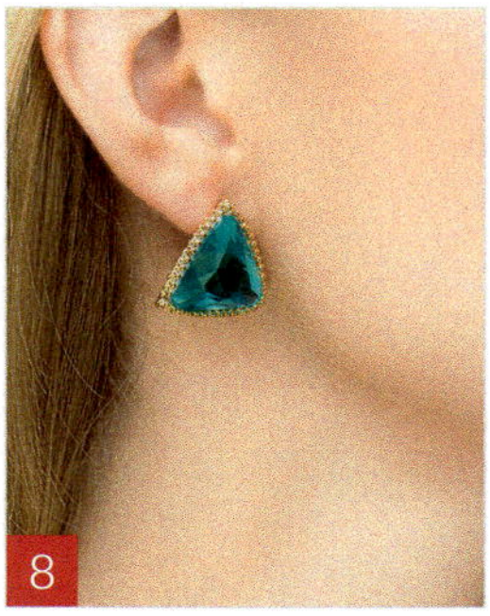
8

4 Describing your working conditions

Now it is time to describe the working conditions in your training company.

Working in small groups, create a poster about the working conditions (in your department/company) and present it to the class. Use your answers to the interviews in exercise 2B and add ideas of your own.

PART B: Working conditions abroad

Situation: Orbit Group AG, a large consumer electronics wholesaler, sends you to an international seminar about training and working conditions in different countries.
→ **You discuss the advantages and disadvantages of the dual system of vocational training in Germany with other apprentices.**

1 Comparing working conditions

You attend the seminar and the trainer gives you a diagram about how much paid free time to expect when working in different countries.

A **With a partner, use the list below to guess the names of the countries, giving reasons for your answers.**

Austria • Germany • Greece • Japan • UK • USA

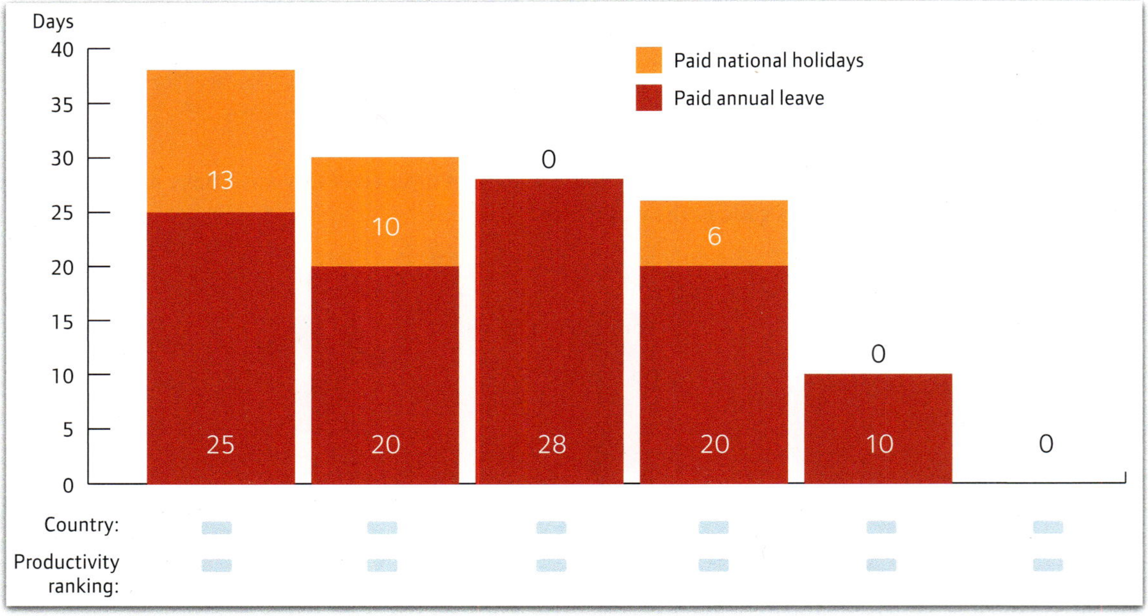

B 5 **Check your answers by listening to what the trainer says about the countries. Put them in order of productivity (1–6).**

C 5 **Listen again and complete the phrases from the dialogue with the words you hear.**

1 … the only country in which employers ___ pay their employees for national holidays and annual leave.
2 … they are ___ to last in our diagram …
3 Germany has the second ___ number of paid days off work …
4 Which of these two ___ pay its employees for 28 days' annual leave …?
5 Sorry, it's the UK in ___ place followed by …
6 ___ Greece, which has the … productivity.

D **Does anything surprise you about the data? Discuss it with your partner and the class.**

> **Expressing obligation**
>
> A German company **has to** give its employees paid annual leave.
> German employers **have to** pay their employees on national holidays.
> An American company **doesn't have to** give its employees paid annual leave.
> American employers **don't have to** pay their employees on national holidays.

› *Grammar: Modals and their substitutes, page 158*

2 Describing your training

Two seminar participants, Selina from the US and Daniel from the UK, tell your group how they are preparing for a career in commerce.

Hi, I'm Selina Gonzales, I'm 19 and I've always wanted to work in commerce. I left school at 18 with a High School Diploma, I speak Spanish and I'm doing a 2-year associate's degree course in business administration at Rockland Community College in New York State. My final grade will be based on my coursework.
In my fourth semester, I'll do an internship at a company. Studying at a 2-year college from home is a lot cheaper than going to a 4-year college in a different city. I live at home for free and get help from my folks with the tuition fees, too. I also have time to work part-time in a convenience store, so I won't be in debt when I graduate. With my associate's degree I can either get a good job or do a bachelor's degree. My career goal is to be a buyer in the clothing industry.

I'm Daniel Chandler, I'm 19 and I left school last year with two A-levels. I wanted to learn about commerce and I didn't like the idea of going to uni and getting into debt, so I'm earning money by doing a work-based intermediate apprenticeship in business administration at Southampton Trading Ltd. I have an assessor from Eastleigh College, and she regularly visits me at my workplace. She talks to my line manager and gives me homework, which I upload to my electronic portfolio. My employer pays my college fees. There's no time limit or final examination because my grades are based on my assessor's reports and my coursework. I hope to complete the apprenticeship next year and then do an advanced apprenticeship with day release at Eastleigh College. This will take me another year and improve my chances of a better job, but my long-term goal is to have my own business one day.

Infobox

Nach Abschluss der Sekundarstufe II (evtl. mit *High School Diploma* [gleicht dem dt. Abitur]) besuchen viele nordamerikanische Schüler/innen ein *community college*. Dies stellt eine zweijährige Bildungseinrichtung zur Berufsausbildung und Vorbereitung auf ein Hochschulstudium dar. Der durch den Besuch eines *community college* erworbene Abschluss nennt sich *associate's degree*, und kann zum Erwerb eines *bachelor's degree* (Bachelorabschluss) angerechnet werden. Letzteres wird i. d. R. nach einem vierjährigen Studium an einer Hochschule erlangt. In Nordamerika ist eine Lehre (*apprenticeship*) im europäischen Sinne fast ausschließlich nur in technischen Berufen möglich.

Work with a partner and use the two texts and the notes below to role-play a conversation with Selina (US) and then with Daniel (UK) in which you both talk about your training.

- introductions
- academic qualifications
- current course/job
- finance
- assessment/grades
- future plans

Talking about the future

I'll do an internship.
I **won't be** in debt
Will you **study**?

› *Grammar: Future with will and going to, page 155*

3 Comparing different training systems

The vocational training systems in industrialized countries vary greatly.

A **Take a few minutes to list the pros and cons of the German dual system. Think about:**

- how you get theoretical/practical training
- your experience at your company/college
- vocational training in other countries (e.g. UK, USA or a country you know about)

B **Make a list of pros and cons on the board and have a discussion about the dual system.**

COMMUNICATION: Introductions and small talk

Situation: You work for Orbit Group AG, a large consumer electronics wholesaler.
→ **You look after a visitor from England until your supervisor, Ms Müller, is ready to meet him.**

1 Introducing yourself and others to colleagues

The Human Resources department at Orbit Group stores information about its employees on computerized personnel files.

A 6)) **Listen to the people introducing themselves. Copy and complete the entries in your notebook.**

Name: Martyna Nowak
Age: ___ 1
Place of birth: Poland
Job description: ___ 2

Name: Halil Özdemir
Age: ___ 3
Place of birth: ___ 4
Job description: training supervisor

Name: Deema Mansour
Age: ___ 5
Place of birth: Syria
Job description: ___ 6

Name: Robert Klein
Age: 21
Place of birth: ___ 7
Job description: ___ 8

Name: Canan Tolon
Age: ___ 9
Place of birth: Turkey
Job description: ___ 10

Name: Alexei Melnyk
Age: 29
Place of birth: ___ 11
Job description: ___ 12

B **You have three minutes to introduce yourself to the other people in the class.**

My name is …
I'm … years old.
I was born in …
I'm a/an …

Introducing yourself

I'm Sophie. I'm **from** Bremen. (NOT: I'm ~~coming~~ from Bremen.)
I work **at** ABC Import/Export. (NOT: I work ~~by~~ ABC Import/Export.)
I'm **an** office manager. / I'm **a** management assistant. (NOT: ~~My job is …~~)

C **Introduce one of the people you met to the rest of the class.**

This is …
He's/She's … years old.
He/She was born in …
He's/She's a/an …

› *Useful phrases: Making introductions page 186*

2 Making formal introductions

A Work with a partner. Introduce yourself in a formal way to your partner (a visitor).

B Now formally introduce your partner to another pair. › *Useful phrases: Making introductions, page 186*

3 Making small talk

A In groups, choose suitable topics for small talk in business. Say which topics you should avoid.

holidays · your city/town · religion · the journey to the meeting place · illnesses · sport · politics · the weather · pay · where someone works

B Match the questions (1–5) to the possible responses (a–e).

1 Is this your first time in Berlin?
2 How is your hotel?
3 It's lovely weather, isn't it?
4 How was your journey?
5 Where are you based?

a Yes. It's fantastic. We've been very lucky this year.
b Very nice. I travelled by train this time.
c Yes. I've heard that it's a very interesting city.
d Fine. I have a good view from the window in my room.
e In Scotland. In Edinburgh, in fact.

4 Meeting and greeting the visitor

Now it is time to meet the visitor. You know that the person Ms Müller is expecting is called Mr Brown.

A Work in groups of three. Complete the dialogue. Then close your books and practise the dialogue.

You	*Excuse*[1] me. *Are you*[2] Mr Brown?
Visitor	Yes, I am.
You	I'm (*own name*). ___[3] do you do? ___[4] to Orbit Group.
Visitor	Thank you. It's ___[5].
You	I'm afraid Ms Müller has been held up, but she'll be here in a few minutes. ___[6] your coat?
Visitor	Yes, thank you. Here you are.
You	___[7] you like something to drink?
Visitor	Yes, please. I'd like a cup of coffee with milk and sugar.
You	Here you are. Is this your ___[8] in Germany?
Visitor	No. I've been here before, but only on holiday.
You	Oh. Here's Ms Müller now. Mr Brown, ___[9] Ms Müller.
Ms Müller	___[10] morning, Mr Brown. Sorry to keep you waiting.
Visitor	No problem. Your assistant has been looking after me very well.

Offering help/refreshments

Can I take your coat?
Would you like something to drink?
Would you like some tea or coffee?

› *Useful phrases: Showing visitors around the company, page 188*

B Write your own dialogue and practise it in your group.

DAS KANN ICH (Unit 1)

- Eine kurze Beschreibung meiner dualen Ausbildung auf Englisch erstellen. (Foundation)
- Ein englisches Plakat über die Arbeitsbedingungen im Ausbildungsbetrieb gestalten. (Part A)
- Die Vor- und Nachteile des dualen Ausbildungssystems auf Englisch diskutieren. (Part B)
- Englischsprachige Besucher/innen empfangen und jemandem vorstellen. (Communication)

2 My workplace

FOUNDATION: In the office

Situation: You work in the Administration department of a large manufacturing company. As your department is moving to new offices next week, your line manager asks you to make an inventory of the office equipment before you move.

→ **You make an inventory of the equipment in your office.**

1 Thinking about office activities

Before you start your inventory, you think about some of the things you have to do in the office.

A **Study the photos (1–6). What are the people doing?**

1

2

3

4

5

6

B **What equipment do you work with regularly?**
What do you (not) enjoy doing?

I use the computer every day. I have to key in data. I enjoy doing that.

Talking about likes and dislikes

I **like making** / **to make** photocopies.
I **prefer working** / **to work** at the computer.
I **enjoy meeting** customers. (NOT: I enjoy ~~to meet~~ …)
I don't **enjoy writing** emails. (NOT: I don't enjoy ~~to write~~ …)

› *Grammar: Verb + infinitive or -ing form, page 156*

2 Comparing types of offices

On your way to work, you listen to a podcast from Alisha Warner, an office consultant.

> Today, I'd like to compare two very different types of offices: the small office and the open-plan office.

VIDEO 1

Watch the video for more information about different types of office.

A 7 **Listen and answer the questions.**

1. What is the main purpose of an office environment?
2. What is the benefit of working in a small office?
3. How are the work spaces divided in a lot of open-plan administration offices?
4. Why do some employees dislike this kind of office?
5. What are the two advantages of working at a shared table?
6. What are the pros and cons of hot-desking?
7. According to Alisha, why should employees always feel happy and comfortable at their place of work?

B **What type of office do you prefer to work in? Explain your reasons, using words from the list if necessary.**

concentrate on work · quiet · light and airy · loud/noisy · spacious

3 Identifying equipment for meetings

The equipment in the current meeting room has to be handled with care during the move. Your line manager has taken photos so he can check that the equipment is in order when it arrives at the new premises.

A **Study the photos and decide what the things are.**

1

2

3

4

5

6

B **What equipment is in the meeting room at your place of work?**

4 Writing an inventory of your office equipment

Now it is time to write an inventory of your office equipment.

Work in a small group. Sit around a table with a large sheet of paper. Write "Inventory of office equipment" in the middle as a title.

Step 1 List the types of equipment you have in your office and meeting room on your corner of the sheet.
Step 2 Discuss your list with the rest of your group. Make a tally list.
Step 3 Use your tally list to write an inventory of the equipment to be taken to the new office premises.
Step 4 Show your inventory to the class.

PART A: An organization chart

Situation: You are getting some work experience at Cantec GmbH, a canning machinery manufacturer in Essen. You are expecting some English-speaking visitors to the company so you study the organization chart.

→ **You draw an organization chart of your training company.**

1 Understanding an organization chart

The chart shows the management, the heads of department and the numbers of staff and apprentices.

Cantec GmbH

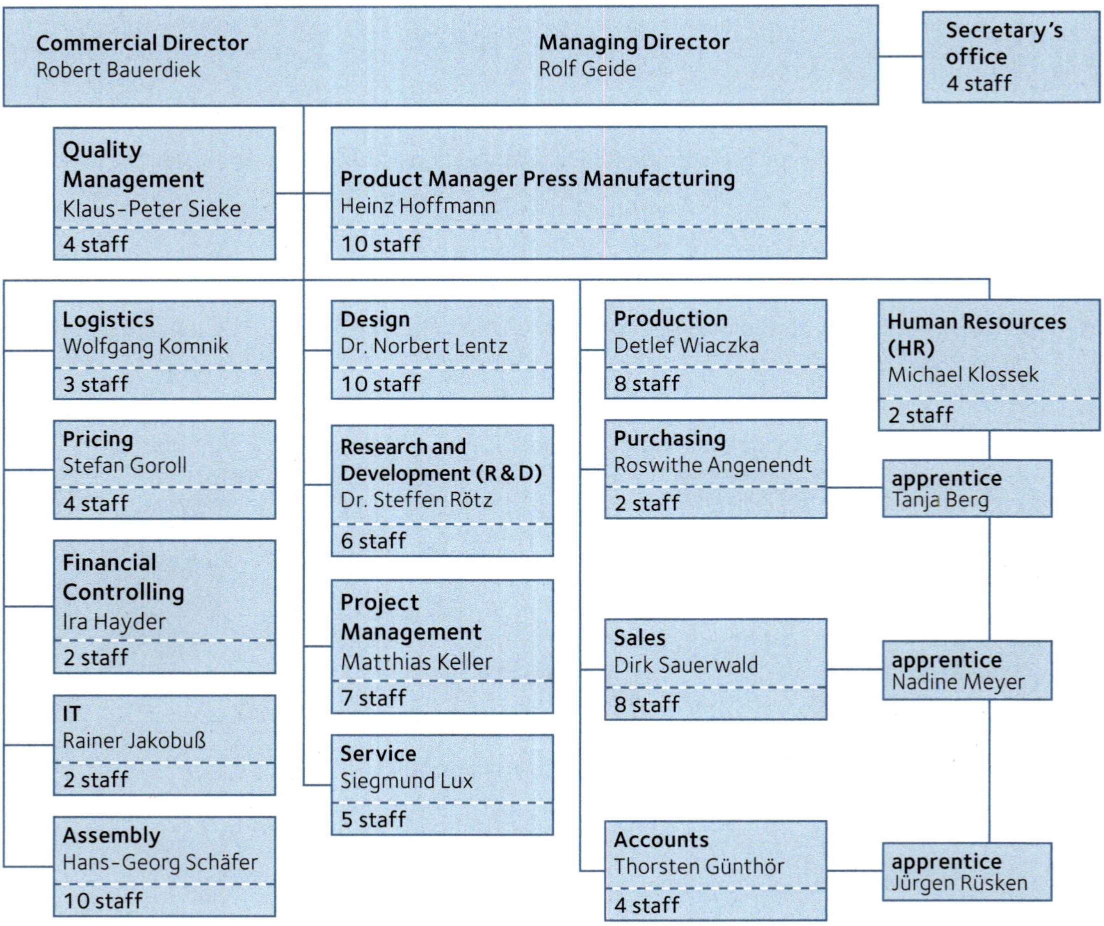

A **Find a department in the chart for each of the descriptions below.**

1 We work out how much the customer's order will cost.

2 We monitor how much money the company makes and spends.

3 We put the machines together here.

4 We buy the components needed for an order.

5 We find new products and improve existing ones.

6 We're responsible for employing and training people.

B **Decide whether the following statements about the organization chart are true or false. Correct the false statements.**

1 Michael Klossek buys in parts for customer orders.
2 Robert Bauerdiek und Rolf Geide are in charge of the company.
3 Dr Steffen Rötz coordinates people, materials and equipment.
4 Thorsten Günthör deals with invoices.
5 Heinz Hoffmann visits potential customers and makes them offers.
6 Rainer Jakobuß is responsible for computer hardware and software.

C **Who reports to whom? Use the organization chart to complete the statements.**

The designers report to ___[1] and the production engineers report to ___[2]. All the heads of department report to two people - ___[3], the ___[4] Director and ___[5], the ___[6] Director. The apprentices all report to ___[7] because he's the Head of ___[8]. They also report to their heads of department. Tanja Berg, for example, also reports to ___[9] because she's the Head of ___[10].

2 Talking about your company

Four Cantec employees are talking about their jobs.

A 8 **Use the information you hear and the organization chart to find out their names, positions and tasks.**

B 8 **Listen again and complete the sentences with the words you hear.**

1 The people in my department are ___ for a whole contract.
2 Our responsibilities ___ supervising work at customers' sites.
3 My job also ___ going to trade fairs.
4 I'm in ___ of planning.
5 This ___ analysing our sales figures.
6 I really ___ doing my job.
7 My work ___ understanding what materials are needed.

C **Use your answers to exercise 2B to complete the following description.**

I'm in the Logistics department and I ___[1] working there because my work is different every day. Logistics basically ___[2] arranging for goods to be transported to the customer and often ___[3] speaking English. My boss is ___[4] for running the whole department, but I'm in ___[5] of arranging shipments to Scandinavia.

3 Creating your company's organization chart

Now it is time to create an organization chart for your training company.

Work in small groups and draw an organization chart of your company, either as a poster or with suitable software, and present it to the class. Explain who you and the other apprentices in your company report to.

› *Thematic vocabulary: Job titles, page 200; Company departments, page 200*

Describing your company

The management is responsible for **running** the company.
I'm in charge of **arranging** shipments.
My work includes/involves/entails **speaking** English.

› *Grammar: Gerunds, page 157*

PART B: Job profiles

Situation: You work for Möbeltech GmbH in Igelsberg. Peggy Murphy, an Irish work experience student, asks you for help with an assignment.
→ **You create profiles of departments and jobs at your training company.**

1 Describing departments

Peggy has to write job profiles for the apprentice file. She first visits eight of the company's departments and makes notes on them.

A **Match four of the names in the box to the departments in the photos.**

Accounting • Human Resources (HR) • Export • Marketing • Production • Purchasing • Quality Assurance • Sales

1

2

3

4

B **Translate Peggy's notes about six of the departments she visits into German.**

1 choose the best suppliers
2 determine salaries and benefits
3 handle all payments and receipts
4 keep to standards and norms
5 maintain and repair equipment
6 monitor products and performance
7 plan the use of manpower and machinery
8 produce financial reports
9 obtain shipping documents
10 recruit, train and promote staff
11 arrange for goods to be shipped abroad
12 visit suppliers' plants

C **Match her notes (1–12) with six of the departments from the list in exercise 1A above.**

D **With a partner, discuss the work of the remaining two departments and write a description of what they do. Compare your ideas with those of other pairs. Do you agree?**

› *Thematic vocabulary: Job titles, page 200; Company departments, page 200*
› *Useful phrases: Describing jobs and responsibilities, page 186*

2 Describing jobs

Peggy now interviews some employees and writes down what they say about their jobs.

A 9 **Guess the missing words in the extracts from six of Peggy's interviews then listen to the recording and check your answers. Which departments do the employees work in?**

1 Most of our work ___ negotiating the best possible terms with suppliers.
2 I'm basically ___ for finding the best person for the job.
3 I'm in ___ of public relations.
4 Working in my department ___ understanding customs regulations.
5 It's my ___ to make sure that we sell as many of our products as possible.
6 We ___ the whole manufacturing and delivery process from beginning to end.

B 9 **Listen again, write down more facts about the work of the six departments, then expand your notes into whole sentences. Compare them with your neighbour's. Have you missed anything?**

C **Study the project manager's description of her job and use some of the words to complete what the accounting manager says. Make any necessary changes.**

Project manager

My job means taking responsibility for a whole project. A few months ago, I was in charge of an order from a Norwegian hotel chain and I was responsible for supplying the furniture for six new hotels in Oslo. The project involved working closely with the production manager and meeting the customer's deadlines. I personally oversaw the design of the furniture to the customer's specifications, and the production manager co-ordinated the manpower and machinery needed for the job.

Accounting manager

I'm in ___[1] of the whole accounting department, so I'm personally ___[2] for everything that happens there. I ___[3] its daily operations, and my work often ___[4] working closely with project managers. I also have overall ___[5] for ___[6] deadlines for financial reports, which ___[7] getting the data ready in good time and ___[8] the manpower needed to do the job.

3 Creating a job profile

Now it's your turn to describe your department and the work you do there.

A **Working in small groups, make notes on your department's work and responsibilities, e.g. as a mind map or flow chart, and then write a short text about it, but without naming the department.**

B **Put the texts on the blackboard/walls of your classroom and read what they say. Guess which department each text describes.**

› *Thematic vocabulary: Job titles, page 200; Company departments, page 200*
› *Useful phrases: Describing jobs and responsibilities, page 186*

Describing how often something happens

I **often** go to Scandinavia.
My department **sometimes** organizes training courses.
We **always** make sure our standards are kept to.

› *Grammar: Adverbs of frequency, page 158*

COMMUNICATION: Telephoning

Situation: You are doing a work placement at the UK subsidiary of Hamm Maschinenbau GmbH.
→ **You call a customer and leave a message.**

1 Leaving a voicemail message

Your line manager, Niklas Hartmann, has left you a note asking you to call a customer, Mr Dalton at Esher Engineering, or to leave him a message if he isn't in the office.

A First read the telephone phrases (a–i) and put them in the right order for a phone call or voicemail message.

a Could you ask … (*name*) to call me back / call … ?
b Good morning/afternoon.
c I'd like to speak to/leave a message for … (*name*).
d I'm calling on behalf of … (*name*).
e It's about the …
f My/His/Her number is …
g Thank you. Goodbye.
h The details are as follows: …
i This is … (*name*) from Hamm Engineering UK Ltd.

· Phone Esher Engineering to confirm the service checks on their lathes.
· Say that you're calling on my behalf.
· Ask to speak to Roger Dalton. He's the factory manager.
· Tell him that two maintenance technicians will be at the factory at 8.30 on Tuesday, 7 June.
· All checks should be completed by 12.30 at the latest.
· If you only get voicemail, ask Mr Dalton to call me back to confirm the date and time.
· Give him my mobile number (07261 299510). Thanks.

B Work with a partner. Use the phrases (a–i) and the notes above to leave a voicemail message for Mr Dalton. Record your message on your smartphone and play it back to your partner.

2 Understanding voicemail

Mr Dalton was out when you called yesterday and this morning, when you come into the office, you find he has left a message. You pass it on to your line manager, but make three mistakes.

10 Listen to the recording and find the mistakes in your version of Mr Dalton's message.

While you were out

Caller: Mr Roger Dalton, Esher Engineering

Mr Dalton says that our technicians can't check the lathes on Tuesday, 7 June but they can come on Wednesday, 8 June from 7–12 or on Friday, 10 June after 1 o'clock. Please call his secretary on 0044 1372 454022 to confirm one of the dates.

3 Taking phone calls

Before phoning some clients, you check that you know some frequently-used telephone expressions.

A Work with a partner and decide how you would say the German phrases (a–j) in English.

a Bleiben Sie bitte dran.
b Der Anschluss ist besetzt.
c Ich stelle Sie durch.
d Das habe ich nicht verstanden. Könnten Sie es bitte wiederholen?
e Buchstabieren Sie bitte Ihren Namen.
f Möchten Sie mit jemand anderem sprechen?
g Ich versuche, Sie zu verbinden.
h Möchten Sie eine Nachricht hinterlassen?
i … (Name) ist im Moment nicht da.
j Wie ist Ihr Name bitte?

B 11 Listen to Niklas Hartmann's phone call to Esher Engineering and check your answers.

C What extra elements are in the English phrases that are missing in the German?

4 Making a phone call

You are back in Germany now and your line manager asks you to phone an English-speaking client.

A **Work with a partner and use the instructions to make a phone call in English.**

> **Giving telephone numbers**
>
> Say each digit separately, except for double digits, e.g. 01233455 = "oh (*AE*: zero) one two double-three four double-five".

Partner A: Ferdinand/Megan Pretorius
Bloemfontein Steel Ltd, South Africa

- Nehmen Sie das Telefongespräch auf Englisch entgegen (Begrüßung, Firmenname, Ihr Name).
- Der Anschluss von Dr Botha ist besetzt. Ob der/die Anrufer/in jemand anders sprechen möchte?
- Sie versuchen, den/die Anrufer/in mit Frau Smit zu verbinden und erklären, dass diese im Moment nicht erreichbar ist. Fragen Sie, ob der/die Anrufer/in eine Nachricht hinterlassen möchte?
- Bitten Sie den/die Anrufer/in, seinen/ihren Namen zu buchstabieren.
- Fragen Sie nach der Handynummer.
- Notieren Sie die Nummer und machen Sie einen Fehler beim Wiederholen.
- Schließen Sie das Gespräch höflich ab.

Partner B: You (own name)
Hamm Maschinenbau GmbH, Germany

- Stellen Sie sich vor und sagen Sie, dass Sie mit Dr Botha sprechen möchten.
- Äußern Sie die Bitte, mit Hannah Smit verbunden zu werden.
- Ja, Dr Botha möchte Sie auf Ihrem Handy anrufen. Es ist wichtig.
- Buchstabieren Sie Ihren Vor- und Nachnamen.
- Geben Sie Ihre Handynummer mit Ländervorwahl (+49 …) an.
- Korrigieren Sie den Fehler.
- Schließen Sie das Gespräch höflich ab.

B **Now improvise a typical telephone dialogue with an English-speaking client who calls the company where you are doing your apprenticeship and wishes to speak to somebody who is not available. Include a message, a telephone number and a name to be spelt.**

› *Useful phrases: Telephoning, page 187; Taking telephone calls, page 187*

DAS KANN ICH (Unit 2)

- Eine Bestandsliste der Büroausstattung auf Englisch erstellen. (Foundation)
- Die Struktur meines Ausbildungsbetriebes auf Englisch beschreiben. (Part A)
- Meine Arbeit und meine Abteilung auf Englisch beschreiben. (Part B)
- Eine/n englischsprachige/n Kunden/Kundin anrufen; eine Nachricht hinterlassen. (Communication)

KMK Exam practice 1

1 Produktion: Stufe II

Situation: Der Blog *Worldwide Apprenticeships* sammelt Ausbildungsberichte von jungen Auszubildenden aus aller Welt. Ihr Unternehmen unterstützt diese Initiative, da es für Sie während Ihrer Ausbildung auch die Möglichkeit gibt, an einem Austauschprogramm mit anderen Auszubildenden aus dem Ausland teilzunehmen. Sie werden gebeten, einen persönlichen Bericht zu schreiben.

Aufgabe: Schreiben Sie einen Bericht, der folgende Punkte beinhaltet:

- Fakten über die Firma (Standort(e), Produkte/Dienstleistungen, Mitarbeiter/innen, Abteilungen und Tätigkeiten)
- Ausbildung im Dualen System (Ausbildungsfirma/Berufsschule/Prüfungen)
- Arbeitsbedingungen (Arbeitszeiten, Urlaub, Möglichkeiten der Fortbildung, Verdienstmöglichkeiten, besondere Angebote der Firma)

2 Hörverstehen: Stufe I

Situation: One of your tasks every morning is to listen to the voicemail messages customers have left on your department's answering machine.

12 **Task: Listen to the telephone messages and write memos for your colleagues including the following information:**

- date and time of call
- who the message is for
- who the message is from, including the company
- message for colleague
- caller's contact details

3 Interaktion: Stufe II

Work with a partner. Partner A: Look here. Partner B: Look at File 1 on page 134.

Situation: Sie arbeiten für die Schmitt & Otte GmbH in Fulda. Ihre Firma handelt mit Sportartikeln aus den USA. Sie befinden sich in der Ausbildung und wurden von Ihrem Chef gebeten, einen englischen Praktikanten / eine englische Praktikantin zu begrüßen. Sie lernen Steve/Sue Mosley kennen, der/die für sechs Monate in Ihrer Firma arbeiten und Sie in den ersten beiden Wochen in der Exportabteilung begleiten wird.

Aufgabe: Gestalten Sie in Partnerarbeit einen Dialog mit Hilfe der folgenden Punkte:

- Begrüßen Sie Ihr Gegenüber. Betreiben Sie Small Talk.
- Fragen Sie nach der Firma Ihres Gesprächspartners / Ihrer Gesprächspartnerin.
- Geben Sie Auskunft über Arbeitsabläufe (Arbeitszeiten, Pausen usw.) und über alles was Ihr/e Gesprächspartner/in wissen möchte.
- Geben Sie Auskunft über das deutsche Ausbildungssystem.
- Geben Sie Tipps zur Freizeitgestaltung und zu Wochenendaktivitäten.
- Beraten Sie Steve/Sue bezüglich der Unterkunft (Nachfrage Personalbüro, eventuell Unterbringung in Wohngemeinschaft mit anderen Azubis, Fahrgemeinschaft).

4 Mediation: Stufe II

Situation: Sie arbeiten für Wenzel und Gabler, eine Firma, die Bremsscheiben für die Automobilindustrie vertreibt. Ihre Firma exportiert weltweit. Ihr Vorgesetzter, Herr Becker, ist zu einem Firmenevent bei der Versicherung TAP (Colchester, UK) eingeladen, die das Factoring Ihrer Firma betreut. Er gibt Ihnen eine Übersicht, die er im Internet gefunden hat und bittet Sie, ihn bei der Vorbereitung auf diesen Besuch zu unterstützen. Er möchte sich über die Teammitglieder und ihre Aufgaben informieren.

Aufgabe: Kopieren und vervollständigen Sie die Tabelle für Herrn Becker, indem Sie die wichtigsten Informationen eintragen.

Responsibilities at TAP

CEO: Ms Emily Rosenberg
The CEO is responsible for all the company's internal and external activities. In cooperation with the Board of Directors, the CEO establishes and maintains the framework standards for the company. The CEO monitors the directors and establishes instruments of successful management.

Regional Director: Mr Cliff Hedgebond
Regional directors have overall responsibility for helping agents in local branches. They support their agents to achieve their objectives and help them to meet their responsibilities.

Development Manager: Ms Cary Braid
DMs are responsible for strategy goals in cooperation with Regional Directors. They ensure that the work in the subsidiaries is compliant with and meets the objectives laid down in the company's guidelines.

Financial Director: Mr Robert Hunt
FCs are licensed to give detailed advice on all financial product lines of the company and they supervise the financial transactions. FDs are responsible for all overseas transactions. They are also in charge of tax and revenues.

Customer Care Manager: Mr Ben Miller
The manager of this section controls and trains the employees in the call centre and sets up and evaluates the written correspondence concerning the customers. He is also responsible for identifying the training needs of call centre agents to ensure that all staff have the skills and knowledge to deal with the customers effectively.

Human Resources Director: Mr Regis Colen
The HR Director deals with all questions of recruitment, redundancies, pension schemes and apprenticeships. He initiates the annual evaluation that is obligatory for all members of staff and reports the results to the CEO.

Position:	Englische Anrede, Vor- und Nachname:	Hauptaufgaben / Verantwortlich für: (in Stichworten)
CEO/Geschäftsführerin	*Ms Emily Rosenberg*	- *interner/externer Auftritt der Firma*

3 My company

FOUNDATION: Types of companies

Situation: The company where you are doing your apprenticeship now has many international business partners, so it decides to add more information in English to its website.
→ **You create a timeline of your company for its English website.**

1 Analysing a timeline

You surf the internet and find an article about Richard Branson, a famous British businessman.

Read the text and complete the timeline (1–8) on page 25.

In 2018, Richard Branson, the inventor of the Virgin brand, was worth $5 billion and his empire included around 400 companies all over the world. His first business venture was in 1959 at the age of nine when he planted Christmas trees on some land near his home in London. He planned to sell them at the age of 18 and move to Bali with the profits. Technically speaking, he was a sole trader because he did not intend to share the profits with anybody, he was his own boss and he had unlimited liability, meaning he bore all the risk. Rabbits ate his Christmas trees and he lost everything.

In 1968, he started again as a sole trader selling records by mail order under the brand name Virgin. He took business away from conventional record stores by offering much lower prices. In 1972, he set up a record company with unknown bands such as the Sex Pistols and Boy George. Such artists were more of a risk, so he made it into a private limited company (Virgin Records Ltd), because its members were only liable to the extent of their investment and did not risk losing their personal wealth, e.g. when fighting broke out at the Sex Pistols' concerts.

Branson added more private limited companies to the Virgin Group and also founded an airline, Virgin Atlantic, in 1984. Later, when he needed a large amount of money to finance his airline, he formed a public limited company called The Virgin Group plc and sold its shares on the stock exchange. However, as the chairman of a public limited company, he disliked the obligation to tell his shareholders what he was doing and to show a short-term profit, so he later bought back all the shares for £200 million and made his company into a private limited company again. In 1993, he entered the railway business and won franchises for major routes by undercutting British Rail. Two years later he founded Virgin Money offering financial services in the UK, Australia and South Africa. In 1999, he launched a new, cheaper mobile phone service in the UK called Virgin Mobile, which now operates in 15 countries.

Richard Branson is also famous for spectacular adventures, including space travel with Virgin Galactic, founded in 2004. However, before tourists can book a voyage for $250,000 per person, there are still many barriers to overcome, as was clearly shown when one of his spacecraft crashed on a test flight killing the pilot. After that, Branson's next business ventures were less spectacular: a chain of healthcare clinics opened in the UK in 2008, and Virgin Hotels was launched two years later in Florida. Branson still hits the headlines with activities such as motor racing, gas balloon racing, drones, robotics and TV shows.

Richard Branson timeline

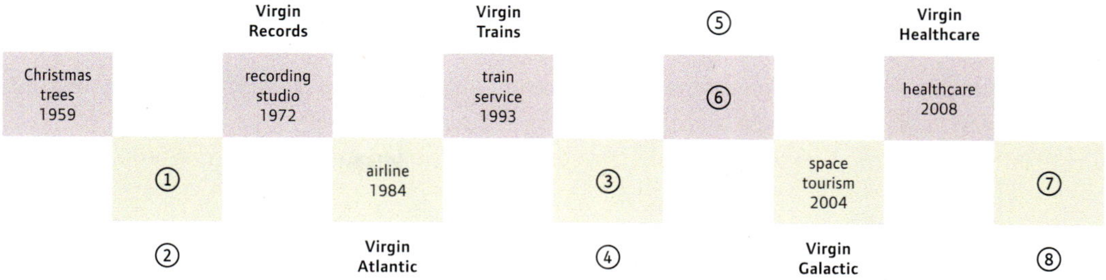

2 Describing your company

You research the different types of company that Richard Branson founded and find these explanations.

Three ways to do business

Sole trader	UK: Private limited company (Ltd)* US: Limited liability company (LLC)	UK: Public limited company (plc) US: Corporation (Corp/Inc)
– The company belongs to the sole trader. – The sole trader takes decisions alone. – He/She gets all the profit. – He/She could lose everything.	– The company belongs to a closed circle of members. – The members decide what is best for the company. – The members share the profits. – The members can only lose the money they have invested.	– The company belongs to the shareholders (members of the public). – The directors decide what is best for the company and the shareholders. – The shareholders share the profits. – The shareholders can only lose the money they paid for the shares.

* In South Africa, Australia and New Zealand: Proprietary limited company (Pty Ltd)

Study the explanations of the three different ways to do business and complete the sentences with the correct information.

1 The person who bears most risk is ___.
2 A private limited company is owned by ___.
3 A sole trader has ___ freedom to make decisions.
4 A shareholder in a plc gets ___ of the profit.
5 Members of the public can buy shares in ___.
6 Bankruptcy is a serious risk for ___.

Describing types of company

A public limited company belongs to the shareholders, **who** share the profits. Shareholders can only lose the money **that/which** they paid for the shares if the company goes bankrupt.

› *Grammar: Relative clauses, page 156*

3 Creating a timeline

Your line manager asks you to prepare a timeline for your company's English website.

A **Work in small groups, if possible with people from the same company. Search your company's website for data and visual elements. Find out who bears the risk at your company and include this in your timeline. (If your company is not suitable, choose another local company.)**

B **When you have collected enough material, sketch out your timeline on a large sheet of paper. Add suitable images and graphics to make it visually appealing.**

C **Complete your timeline and hang it on the wall. Do a gallery walk and give each other points for design, clarity and information. Choose the timeline that gets its message across best.**

› › *Thematic vocabulary: Company organization, page 201*

PART A: Showing visitors around

Situation: You are getting some work experience at Cantec GmbH, a medium-sized engineering company in Essen that exports canning technology all over the world

→ **You take English-speaking visitors on a guided tour of your training company.**

1 Preparing for visitors

As Cantec GmbH often has visitors from abroad, your line manager asks you to prepare an English version of the layout of the company.

Study the diagram and use the words in the box to complete the labelling.

accounting · assembly · design · finance · human resources · managing director · material delivery · pricing · production · project management · purchasing · quality assurance · research and development · sales · showroom

Third floor

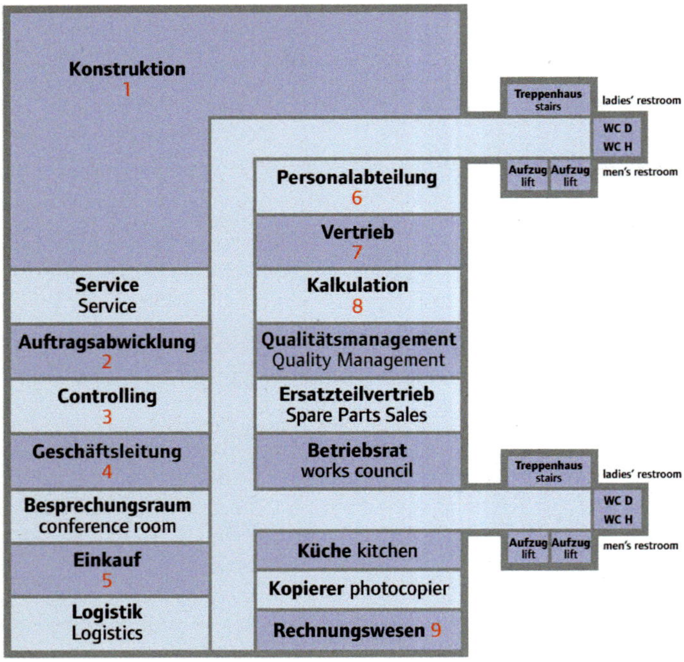

Ground floor

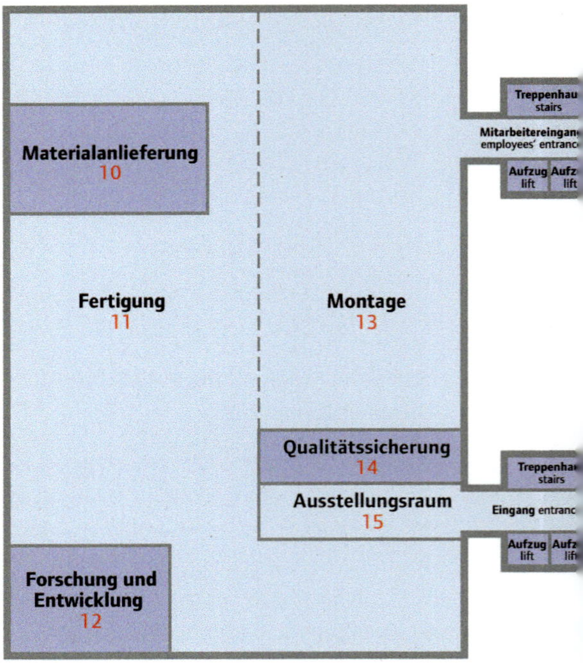

2 Following a tour around a company

To make sure you know suitable English phrases for giving a guided tour, you join two tours around Cantec for visitors from abroad.

A 13 **Listen to the two tours and write down the following information:**

- who the visitor(s) is (are)
- the starting point of the tour
- the departments visited
- the finishing point

Infobox

BE: lift	*AE:* elevator	*Aufzug*
second floor	third floor	*2. OG*
first floor	second floor	*1. OG*
ground floor	first floor	*Erdgeschoss*

B 13 **Read the extracts from the first tour below and guess the missing words. Then listen to the recording again to check your answers.**

1 We are ___ to welcome you to our company.
2 We very much hope you ___ your stay here.
3 Are there any ___ before we begin?
4 In that case, we'll ___ here in the conference room.
5 I'll now ___ you down the corridor to the design department.
6 The gentleman ___ the left of the window is Dr Lenz.
7 Our next ___ is the Quality Management department.
8 It's ___ to go downstairs to the factory to see how our machines are built.
9 Here you can ___ how our production lines are put together.
10 Well, that ___ our tour.

Giving directions

to the left/right of …
between (the) … and (the) …
next to (the) …
opposite (the) …
upstairs/downstairs
to take the lift/elevator/escalator/stairs to the … floor

C **With a partner, practise taking (a) visitor(s) on two or three tours of Cantec's offices and factory. Include the following points in your tour:**

- choose a starting point, two departments on each floor and a finishing point
- greet the visitor(s) politely
- introduce yourself (full name and position)
- offer to answer questions
- add your own ideas
- finish the tour politely

VIDEO 2

Watch the video to see another company tour.

Begin like this: *Good morning and welcome to … . My name is … . I'm … . If you have any questions …*

3 Writing a website post

The Managing Director asks you to write a short article about the Chinese delegation's visit to Cantec for the company website.

13 **Listen to the first tour again and write a short text including the following information:**

Chinese company:	China Tomato, Xinjiang, north-west China
Representatives:	Managing director Wang Wei and three colleagues
Details of visit:	Importance of canning technology for farmers in China / presentation / tour of company (names of German colleagues and their departments / machines seen in factory) / tour of Essen

Talking about the past

A delegation from China **visited** our company last week.
First of all, we **took** them on a tour of our offices.

› *Grammar: Simple past, page 154*

Begin like this: *Last week we were delighted to welcome a delegation from …*

4 Taking visitors on a tour of your company

Now it's time for you to take some English-speaking visitors on a tour of your own training company.

A **Work in small groups from the same training company. Prepare a plan of your company and label the departments in English.**

B **Find people in your class from another company and use your plan to show them around. Make sure you cover the same points in your tour as in exercise 2C.**

› *Useful phrases: Showing visitors around the company, page 188*
› *Thematic vocabulary: Company departments, page 200*

PART B: A company profile

Situation: You are getting some work experience at Cantec GmbH, a canning machinery manufacturer in Essen. A delegation from China is visiting the company.
→ **You give a presentation in English about your company to visitors from abroad.**

1 Preparing presentation slides

The Sales Director asks you to find suitable slides to use in a presentation for the visitors.

A **You create six slides (A–F). Match them with the headings in the list below.**

can manufacturing process · company data · factory interior · final slide · parent company · world market

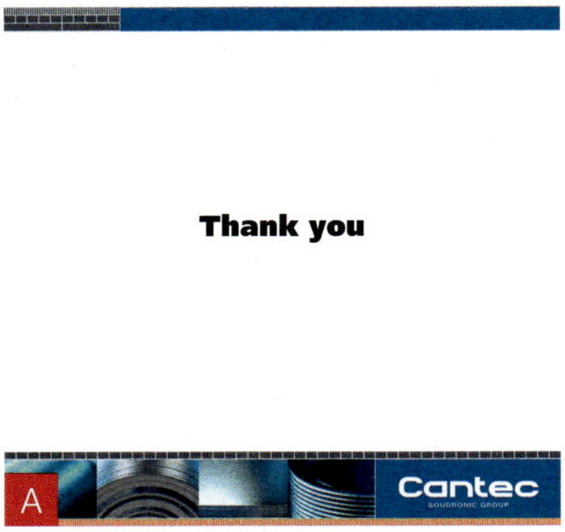

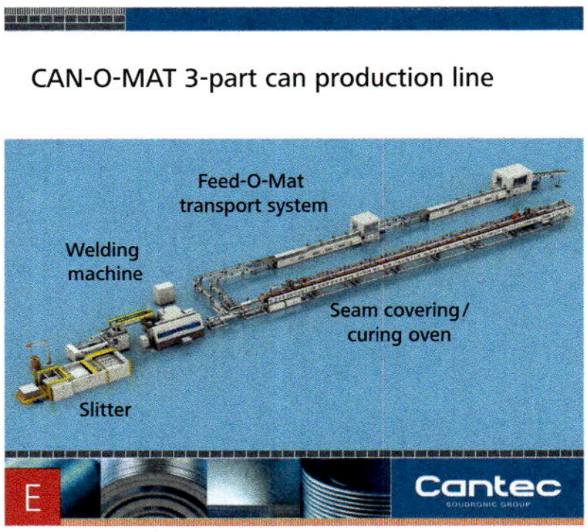

B **With a partner, decide in what order the slides should be shown.**

C **14 Listen and write down the order in which the Sales Director describes the slides. Is it the same?**

Describing repeated actions

We **export** 98% of our products.
We **transport** all the components to our customers.
We **assemble** them on site.

› *Grammar: Simple present, page 154*

2 Writing a handout

Each visitor from abroad will receive a handout including a profile of Cantec GmbH.

A 14 **Listen again and make notes on the company and its products under the following headings:**

- name, location, company statistics, parent company
- products/services, customers
- factory, machinery

B **Use your notes to write a profile of the company to add to the handout for the visitors.**

› *Useful phrases: Describing companies, page 188*

VIDEO 3

Watch the video to see another company presentation.

3 Structuring a presentation

Before you write your presentation about your own company, you think about some of the phrases you can use to guide the audience.

Group the expressions that the Cantec Sales Director uses in her presentation under the headings below.

Welcoming the audience	Introducing your topic	Structuring your presentation	Moving to the next point	Describing visuals	Dealing with questions	Conclusion
Good morning, …	…	…	…	…	…	…

- … and will then move on to …
- As you can see from this slide, …
- Good morning, ladies and gentlemen and welcome to …
- I'd like to begin by giving you a presentation about …
- I'll be happy to answer any questions you may have.
- I'll start with …
- I work in the … department.
- Many thanks for listening.
- My name is …
- Now if you'd like to ask any questions, I'd be delighted to answer them.
- Now, let's move on to our next point.
- That was a brief overview of …
- The next thing I'd like to show you is …
- Then at the end …
- This next slide shows …

4 Preparing a presentation

Now it is time to prepare a short presentation about your own training company.

Work with a partner and prepare a presentation about your training company. You can use the following presentation aids:

- a (large colourful, illustrated) poster
- slides or transparencies (maximum of 8 slides)
- some of the company's products
- your own idea(s)

Follow the steps in Communication (pages 30–31) to help you.

› *Useful phrases: Giving presentations, page 188; Thematic vocabulary: Company organization, page 201*

COMMUNICATION: A short presentation

Situation: Some trainees from the UK are soon going to start work at your company.
→ **You give a short presentation to the new trainees about your work.**

1 Thinking about the contents of a presentation

Your line manager gives you a list of points you should include in your talk.

what the company does · your department · what you do

A Work with a partner. Read the list and decide together what you would like to add to your line manager's list above. Make notes.

B Compare your notes with another pair and decide on the final points you will cover. Make a mind map.

C Agree on the order you will present the contents. Make a numbered list. Write the name and date of your talk at the top of the list.

Presentation to new trainees: 08.07.20..
1 *Introduction (self/the company)*
2
3

2 Writing the presentation

A Use your mind map and the list from exercise 1 to write your text. Follow this structure.

Introduction	– Say in a few words what you are going to talk about.
Main part	– Use one paragraph for each topic. – Use signposts to move from one subject to the next.
Conclusion	– Summarize the main ideas. – Invite questions from the audience.

B Check the text together for clarity and correctness as follows.

- Is the information in the text correct? If not, correct it.
- Is the spelling and grammar correct? Use your dictionary and the list of phrases on page 29.

3 Making a prompt card

A presentation comes across best when the presenter looks at the audience and speaks naturally. As it is difficult to do either of these things when you read from a text, you should make yourself a prompt card.

A Follow the steps below.

- Highlight important words and phrases in your text.
- Copy the words and phrases onto an index card.
- Include signposts to structure the ideas.

- manufacturing company
- workshop
- apprentice ...

B Practise your presentation in your group, using only your prompt card.

4 Giving a presentation

Your presentation will be a success if you study the tips below.

Divide the tips into *Before/During/After the presentation*.

Tips for a great presentation

- **A** Always face your audience!
- **B** Decide what visual aids are best for your topic (objects, transparencies, posters, etc.)
- **C** Decide when it is best to give out handouts (before, during or after the presentation).
- **D** Do not overload transparencies or slides with information.
- **E** Do not speak for too long before handing over to your partner.
- **F** Find out about any cultural differences (e.g. attire, gestures and body language).
- **G** Give your contact details (e.g. email, website, business card) if appropriate.
- **H** Make eye contact and do not turn your back on the audience to point to the screen.
- **I** Offer to answer any questions the audience may have.
- **J** Practise with a partner before giving the presentation to your audience.
- **K** Prepare hand-held prompt cards with key words.
- **L** Speak slowly and freely only using your prompt cards.
- **M** Start by explaining what the presentation is about.
- **N** Welcome the audience and introduce yourself/yourselves.

5 Giving your presentation

It is time to give your presentation and to give each other feedback.

A **Decide who is going to speak first in your group. When it is your turn, stand up, look directly at the audience and smile. Then speak freely and clearly using your prompt card. Ask for questions at the end.**

B Give each other feedback using this feedback sheet. Give points from 1 to 3. (1 point = needs improvement, 2 points = good, 3 points = very good)

› *Useful phrases: Giving presentations, page 188*

Presentations feedback		Points
Content	you covered all the necessary points	
	you used examples to support your points	
Structure	your talk was easy to follow	
	you used useful phrases to structure your talk	
	you summarized the main ideas in your conclusion	
Presentation	you smiled and looked friendly	
	you spoke clearly and freely	
	you looked at the audience when you spoke	
Dealing with questions	you dealt with questions in a friendly manner	
	you answered all the questions clearly	
Overall score for the presentation		/30

DAS KANN ICH (Unit 3)

- Einen informativen Zeitstrahl über meine Firma auf Englisch erstellen. (Foundation)
- Englischsprachige Besucher/Besucherinnen durch meinen Ausbildungsbetrieb führen. (Part A)
- Meinen Ausbildungsbetrieb englischsprachigen Besuchern/Besucherinnen präsentieren. (Part B)
- Eine kurze Präsentation über meine Arbeit für neue Auszubildende halten. (Communication)

4 Presenting a product

FOUNDATION: Contact with customers

Situation: You work in the Export Sales department of Orbit Group AG, a consumer electronics wholesaler. New apprentices are starting this week and some of them don't speak German very well. Your line manager asks you help provide information for them in English.

→ **You make a fact sheet showing how you interest your customers in your products and how they get to the end consumer.**

1 Making your products known to customers

First of all, you brainstorm some ideas for the fact sheet with your colleagues.

A Work in groups and study the pictures. Which of these activities does your company use to make its products known? Describe them.

B What activities (if any) have you been involved in? What did you do?

Talking about things you have done in the past

I **updated** the customer information page of the website **two weeks ago**.
I **worked** at my company's booth at a trade fair **last year**.
I **have never been involved in** anything like this for my company.

› *Grammar: Simple past, page 154; Present perfect, page 155*

2 Getting the product to the customer

Your line manager also gives you this text to read to help you prepare the fact sheet.

Indirect and direct distribution channels

How does a product get from the manufacturer to the customer? When a product changes hands several times before reaching the final consumer, we talk about indirect distribution.

Let's start with the retailer. Think about a high-street store or a supermarket. These stores, which sell everyday consumer goods, are often in the neighbourhood or only a short drive away so they are easy to reach. A lot of people prefer to shop locally rather than ordering something online because they don't want to wait for the goods to be delivered.

Wholesale companies buy large amounts of goods in bulk from the manufacturer, then they sell on these goods to the retailer, who will buy smaller quantities of the goods. Wholesalers store the goods they've bought in warehouses before they sell them to retailers. Some wholesalers also sell their products directly to the public.

The middleman, or agent, helps with negotiations between the manufacturer and the seller. Agents are useful to a manufacturer because they have a network of contacts. They often speak a foreign language, which is especially useful for people in the import-export market.

A company that sells directly to consumers through direct mail, a catalogue of its own products or an internet platform is using a direct distribution channel.

Using these channels, manufacturers can sell their products directly to the consumer without going through a retailer, a wholesaler or an agent. Cutting these people out of the picture saves the manufacturer money.

Read the text and note down the following points:

1 two places where a retailer does business
2 two reasons why some people prefer to shop locally rather than online
3 two customers that wholesalers sell their products to
4 two reasons why agents are useful to manufacturers
5 three direct distribution channels
6 how direct distribution benefits the manufacturer

3 Creating a fact sheet

Now you produce your fact sheet for the new international apprentices.

A **Work with someone who works at the same company as you. Make notes on the following points:**

- what your company sells or distributes
- how the company comes into contact with its customers
- the distribution channels your company uses

B **Decide how you are going to present the information above, then make your fact sheet. Try to keep it as simple as possible. Here are some ideas.**

- Use a photo collage to show your products.
- Write a list of how your company makes your customers aware of its products.
- Make a flow chart showing your distribution channels: *manufacturer* → ... → ...

› *Thematic vocabulary: Business partners and traders, page 201*

PART A: Sales talk

Situation: You are an apprentice in the Sales department at TopLine Sanitär, a major German wholesaler of bathroom fixtures and fittings. Your company always has a booth at the Installatie Vakbeurs trade fair in the Netherlands, and this year you join the sales team.
→ You conduct a sales conversation with a customer.

1 Connecting with customers

The Sales Director tells you that selling has a lot to do with personality and technique.

A Take this simple personality test to find out if you are a good salesperson.

On a scale of 1 (strongly disagree) to 7 (strongly agree), give yourself points for each of the following statements. Add up your score and then look at the answers on page 36.

1. I am the life and soul of the party.
2. I talk a lot.
3. I don't stay in the background.
4. I talk to a lot of different people at parties.

Discuss your results in a group. Are you good at selling? Why (not)?

B Next you discuss sales techniques. Choose the best options in the situations below.

1 When a customer is looking at the products on display, it's best to greet them and say …
- **a** "What are you looking for?"
- **b** "Have you seen our new product?"
- **c** "Let me know if you need any help."

2 When a customer shows interest in a particular product, you should …
- **a** begin by discussing prices and any possible discounts.
- **b** give the customer detailed information about the product.
- **c** find out exactly what the customer needs.

3 If a customer shows interest in an item that is still wrapped, you should …
- **a** unwrap it and give it to the customer.
- **b** unwrap it, hold it up and explain all its features clearly.
- **c** not unwrap it but give the customer some sales material about it.

4 If the customer needs time to think about the item on offer, you should …
- **a** explain that you will sell the item to someone else if the customer waits too long.
- **b** tell the customer that there is no great hurry and ask them how much time they need.
- **c** promise to put the item aside for 24 hours but sell it to someone else if the chance arises.

Discuss your answers in your group. Do you all agree?

2 Trying out sales techniques

The Sales Director is busy with a potential customer, so you listen to how some other colleagues deal with visitors to the stand.

mixer tap

A 15 **Listen to the three sales dialogues and make notes on the following points in each case.**

1 How does the salesperson greet the potential customer?
2 How much does each person talk?
3 Does the salesperson find out what the customer wants?
4 Is the customer interested in more information?
5 Do you think the salesperson will make a sale? Why (not)?

B 15 **Listen to the third dialogue again and use the words you hear to complete the sentences below.**

1 ___ let me know if you need any help.
2 Let me do that for you, ___.
3 Is it for private or ___ use?
4 We have all these items ___ stock.
5 We're offering ___ a 20% discount on the catalogue price if they order this week.
6 Delivery is from stock and we give a five-year ___.
7 How long did you say the special offer was ___ for?
8 Any company that ___ an order by Friday will get a 20% discount.

shower enclosure

C **This dialogue between the Sales Director and a regular customer has got mixed up. Re-arrange it in the right order. The first one has been done for you.**

Customer	Sales Director
A Good afternoon, Mr Pattberg. Yes, it's nice to be back.	G Anything particular I can do for you, or would you prefer to look around?
B That's it for the time being.	H Certainly. Dr Sharma. You'll get our offer today. Is there anything else I can do for you?
C Well, we're currently modernizing flats and houses all over Europe and we're looking for bathrooms fixtures and fittings.	I I see what you mean. How about this mixer tap from our Classic line? Is this more what you were looking for? It's been very popular for a long time now.
D Yes, it's very modern, but I'd rather have something more timeless because we don't want it to look old in ten years' time.	J Good afternoon, Dr Sharma. Nice to see you again.
E Yes, that's more like it. Could I see the whole set?	K In that case, I think we have what you're looking for, Dr Sharma. Our Free Flow line is very popular at the moment and it has a very modern look to it. This is the mixer tap for the washbasin.
F Yes, the Classic line is more what we're looking for. Could you send me an offer for 50 sets? We can talk about the extras later.	L Yes, certainly. Here's the basic set and some extras – a massage shower head and a thermostatic mixer.

1 J, 2 ...

D **Practise the dialogue with a partner.**

› *Useful phrases: Advising customers, page 189*

Asking polite questions

Could you send me an offer for 50 sets?
Anything particular I can do for you, or **would** you prefer to look around?

› *Grammar: Modals and their substitutes, page 158*

3 Using your sales techniques

A customer from Scotland is visiting TopLine Sanitär's stand at the Installatie Vakbeurs trade fair and is enquiring about a product.

Role-play the conversation with a partner using the following prompts.

VIDEO 4

Watch the video to see more about sales talk.

Partner A
Mitarbeiter/in bei TopLine Sanitär

Begrüßen Sie den Kunden / die Kundin.

Fragen Sie, ob er/sie Hilfe braucht oder sich nur umschauen möchte.

Reagieren Sie freundlich.

Fragen Sie, ob die Armaturen für den privaten oder gewerblichen Gebrauch verwendet werden sollen.

Zeigen Sie und dann geben Sie ihm/ihr das *Free Flow Standard*-Modell.

Zeigen Sie dem Kunden / der Kundin das *Free Flow de luxe*-Modell.

Es ist aus leichtem Metall, sehr strapazierfähig und momentan auf Lager; Lieferzeit 10 Tage, solange der Vorrat reicht. Fragen Sie, ob er/sie ein Angebot haben möchte.

Er/Sie wird das Angebot bis Ende der Woche erhalten.

Fragen Sie, ob Sie ihm/ihr sonst noch helfen können.

Schließen Sie das Gespräch freundlich ab.

Partner B
Kunde/Kundin von Dundee Trading, Schottland

Reagieren Sie freundlich auf die Begrüßung.

Sie wollen sich im Moment nur umschauen.

Erkundigen Sie sich nach ein paar Minuten nach Waschtischarmaturen.

Sie möchten die Armaturen für den privaten Gebrauch nutzen.

Sie finden das Modell zu schwer. Fragen Sie, ob er/sie etwas Leichteres hat.

Reagieren Sie positiv auf dieses Modell und bitten Sie um mehr Informationen.

Fordern Sie ein Angebot über 100 Stück an und geben Sie ihm/ihr Ihre Karte.

Bedanken Sie sich.

Sie haben keine weiteren Wünsche. Schließen Sie das Gespräch freundlich ab.

Answers: Part A, exercise 1A

Score	Personality	Suitability as a salesperson
23–28	You are an extrovert.	Your will only achieve average sales figures because you will put off customers by being overconfident and overexcited.
15–22	You are an ambivert, (part extrovert, part introvert).	You will achieve very good sales figures because you will know when to be enthusiastic and when to listen carefully to what the customer is saying.
1–14	You are an introvert.	You will only achieve average or below-average sales figures because you won't be able to show real enthusiasm for your company's products and services.

PART B: A product presentation

Situation: You are an apprentice in the Sales department at BodyLine Fischer GmbH, a sports equipment wholesaler. Your company has a showroom for its trade customers, and some English-speaking visitors have been invited to see what you have on offer.

→ **You give a presentation in English about your company's latest products.**

1 Preparing your presentation

The Sales Director tells you to present the eight new products shown on your company's website in a suitable way.

What would you say about each of these products? Match the speech bubbles (1–8) below with the illustrations (A–H).

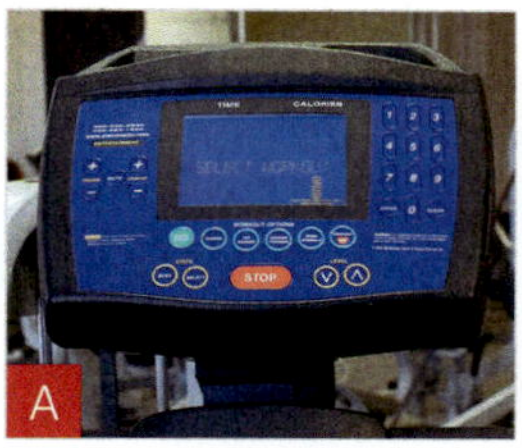
A
console

B
energy snacks/drinks

C
exercise ball

D
exercise mat

E
rowing machine

F
trampoline

G
treadmill

H
weight bench

1 Help yourselves!

2 It's designed to be used flat or at a 45° angle as you can see here.

3 The important feature here is that it trains your whole body in a comfortable sitting position.

4 They come in four thicknesses.

5 They're available in five different sizes and colours.

6 This is the heavy-duty model for up to 150 kg.

7 This machine has a special slow-start feature for extra safety.

8 It has lots of new features, including media streaming and internet connectivity.

2 Listening to a presentation

The visitors arrive and your colleague Hannah Klein gives them a full presentation of the company's latest products.

A 16 **Listen to the recording and write down how each of the products (A–H) on page 37 is presented.**

B 16 **Listen again and complete the sentences with the words you hear.**

1 You'll get a catalogue on our ___ range at the end of the morning.
2 We also have some ___ of our latest energy drinks and snacks for you.
3 For this I need a volunteer! Is anybody willing to ___ it out?
4 They also require next to no ___.
5 They are made of the very best, extremely ___ materials.
6 He's going to ___ some of our other new products.
7 This model is ___ both for home use and in the gym.
8 I'd now like to round off the morning with a video on our new ___ console.

C One of the trade customers sends a text message about the presentation to his boss in Hong Kong. Use your answers to exercise 2B to fill in the gaps. Make any necessary changes.

Mr Wang: I've just seen a presentation of BodyLine's new products. They ___[1] two new exercise machines with consoles that are very ___[2] and also a trampoline that is ___[3] for use anywhere. The machines require very little ___[4] and the materials used are extremely ___[5], which explains the 10-year guarantee. I ___[6] out the treadmill myself and also tested some ___[7] of their new drinks and snacks. I liked them and I'm sending you details of their ___[8] range as a PDF. Regards, Lee

3 Advising customers

After the presentation some of the visitors ask Hannah Klein for advice about which products to buy.

A Match the sentence parts below to complete her advice.

> My company has a chain of gyms and we're going to offer Pilates classes. What sort of exercise mats do I need?

> Well, for Pilates they don't need to be very thick, so I would recommend using our thinner Studio 2 mats.

1 If I were you, …
2 I would advise you …
3 I would recommend …
4 You should …
5 I would suggest that …

A offer your customers exercise balls in different sizes and colours.
B equipping one room with thick mats for floor exercises.
C you buy a range of mats in different thicknesses.
D to install a lot of easy-to-use exercise machines.
E I'd have an area with a row of benches and mirrors on the walls.

B Now use the expressions in 3A to put these sentences into English.

1 An Ihrer Stelle würde ich dickere Gymnastikmatten kaufen.
2 Ich empfehle, unsere Gymnastikbälle zu benutzen.
3 Ich rate Ihnen, Rudergeräte zu kaufen.
4 Ich schlage vor, einen Raum mit Hantelbänken auszustatten.
5 Sie sollten mehr Abendkurse anbieten.

> **Giving advice**
> **If I were you, I would/wouldn't** use this machine.
> You **should/shouldn't** train every day.

› *Grammar: Conditional sentences, page 156; Modal verbs and their substitutes, page 158*

4 Writing an invitation

Your company is having an open day, so you post an invitation on your website and add a link to it in all emails to your business partners.

INVITATION TO OUR OPEN DAY

Come and see our products, meet our team, relax and enjoy the fun.
We have a great programme of events for you, and the kids will have a great time, too!

Programme

10.00 a.m.	Snack and chat
10.30 a.m.	Guided tour
11.30 a.m.	Product demo 1
1.00 p.m.	Barbecue
2.30 p.m.	Product demo 2
4.00 p.m.	Prizes for lucky winners

For kids

Bouncy castle
Coco the Clown
Face-painting
Games, games, games
Mario the Magician
Lucky draw

Form small groups and write an invitation for an open day at your company.

- Add the name of your company and the date, time and location.
- Make a list of the different types of products or services offered by your company and choose (a) suitable way(s) of presenting them.

5 Presenting your company's products

You give a presentation of one of your company's products at the open day.

A **Either bring in a product sold by your company, or use an image, for example from your company's website. Make a list of the features you want to explain and look up any technical terms that you might need.**

B **Use the role-card to prepare and write out a dialogue between a wholesaler and a potential buyer at your company's open day.**

Partner A: Wholesaler	Partner B: Potential buyer

– Introduce yourself (name, position).
– Present the product to the buyer. Include …
  – its most important features
  – price, including discounts
  – delivery period
  – after-sales service
  – any extra guarantee(s) given
  – how to order (e.g. online, order form, sales representative, over the phone, etc.)
  – your own ideas
– Answer the customer's questions.
	– Introduce yourself and your company.
	– Ask the wholesaler about the product.
	– After the presentation, ask questions on 4 or 5 of the following points:
	  – size(s)
	  – colour(s)
	  – new feature(s)
	  – material(s) used
	  – competitors' prices (same, lower?)
	  – your own ideas

C **Practise performing the dialogue with your partner. Then perform the dialogue in front of the class (without notes). Make a video if possible. When you have finished, swap roles and do it again.**

COMMUNICATION: Emails

Situation: You are getting work experience in the Sales department of Technical Tools Ltd, a supplier to the technical trades. Your line manager asks you to take care of a customer enquiry.
→ **You write an email to a customer.**

1 Giving email addresses over the phone

You check the English for some of the symbols that appear in email addresses.

A Match the symbols (1–6) to the words (a–f).

1 +	**4** -	**a** at	**e** plus
2 _	**5** .	**b** dot	**e** number
3 @	**6** 3	**c** hyphen	**f** underscore

B 17)) **Listen to your line manager and a customer on the phone. Which email addresses are correct?**

1
a tm.martin@technical-tools.de
b tmmartin@technical_tools.de
c tm.martin@technical_tools.de

2
a maryannbrown@5+5_services.net
b mary-anne-brown@5+5services.net
c maryann-brown@5+5services.net

C Work with a partner. Partner A: Look here. Partner B: Look at File 2 on page 134.

Dictate these email addresses to Partner B. Check B's answers.

1 DavidMcCarthy+list@net.us
2 sergei-nikitin@com.ru
3 your own email address
4 the email address of your firm or another email address you often write to

Can you spell that, please?

Could you repeat that, please?

2 Writing a subject line

The first indication of what is in an email is the subject line. This must state clearly what the email is about.

A Work with a partner. Study the subject lines (1–6) below and find an email which …

1 is a request for information.
2 gives information about a meeting.
3 asks for assistance.
4 contains new information.
5 announces a change of plan.
6 is a covering letter for a brochure.

a	**Subject:**	Need your help with English
b	**Subject:**	New venue for event on Saturday
c	**Subject:**	Flyer (attached)
d	**Subject:**	Meeting 25.03. Starting time?
e	**Subject:**	Update on project
f	**Subject:**	Agenda

B With your partner, write suitable subject lines for the following emails (1–6).

1 Sorry, I would like to change the date of the meeting to Friday 12 July.
2 Could you send me information about the presentation, please?
3 I am on holiday from 21.03 till 04.04 inclusive and will answer emails when I return.
4 I am writing to confirm your application for a stand at the Technical Trades Fair. The stand number is C208.
5 As promised, here is the link to the website www.tipsformails.com.
6 This is just to let you know that I am interviewing a new export clerk at 12.30.

3 Writing a reply to an email enquiry

Your line manager gives you the enquiry below and asks you to reply by email.

From r-johnson@rjbl.co.uk

To: sales@techtool.co.uk

Subject: **Enquiry for Phillips screwdrivers and screws**

Dear Sir or Madam

We have studied your catalogue on the internet and are interested in your Phillips screwdrivers (catalogue number SP 492876) and your slotted screwdrivers (catalogue number SS 8592201).
We would like to order 100 of each type of screwdriver.
We would also like to order 1,000 boxes of Phillips screws and 1,000 boxes of slotted screws.
Please let us know if you have these items in stock.

Yours faithfully
Robert Johnson

Robert Johnson Building Ltd

Use a suitable greeting and subject line and reply to Mr Johnson. Include the following points:

- Thank him for his enquiry.
- Say that the screwdrivers and the screws are in stock.
- Say you will dispatch them next week.
- Say that you look forward to doing business with him in the future.
- Use the correct complimentary close.

Using polite language in emails

Could and *would like* are more polite than phrases with *can*, *need* or *want*.
~~Can~~ you let me know by Monday? → **Could** you let …
I ~~need~~ the information today. → I **would like** the …
We ~~want~~ to have a meeting. → We **would like** to …

› *Useful phrases: Writing emails, page 189*

Salutation and complimentary close in emails

If you do not know the name of the person you are writing to, begin your email with *Dear Sir or Madam*.
If you do not know your business partner well, use a formal salutation and complimentary close.

	Salutation	Complimentary close	
Formal (to unknown person)	Dear Sir or Madam	Yours faithfully	
Formal (to person whose name you know)	Dear Mr/Ms Smith	Regards Best regards	Best wishes Yours sincerely
Less formal	Dear Paul / Hi Paula Good morning, Paul	Regards Best regards	Best wishes All the best

DAS KANN ICH (Unit 3)

- Ein Informationsblatt über meine Firma und ihre Betriebswege auf Englisch erstellen. (Foundation)
- Ein Verkaufsgespräch mit einem Kunden / einer Kundin auf Englisch führen. (Part A)
- Ein Produkt meiner Firma auf Englisch präsentieren. (Part B)
- Die E-Mail eines britischen Kunden auf Englisch beantworten. (Communication)

KMK Exam practice 2

1 Hörverstehen: Stufe II

Situation: The American-based company CCA Clothing is about to open a new branch in a nearby town. Their stores sell second-quality clothes and accessories as well as remainders. You work for the wholesaler Fair Flowers and Promotional Gifts Ltd, which has received a request for some products from CCA Clothing. Your boss has arranged a telephone call with the Public Relations Officer of CCA and asks you to make notes.

18 **Task: Listen to the telephone call and make notes about what action needs to be taken.**

2 Leseverstehen: Stufe II

Situation: Sie arbeiten in einem Textilunternehmen in Kassel. Ihre Firma möchte sich auf dem britischen Markt weiter etablieren und sucht dafür einen Logistikpartner vor Ort. Für ein Meeting sollen mehrere infrage kommende Unternehmen zunächst vorgestellt werden. Um einen ersten Überblick zu erhalten, arbeiten alle Teammitglieder mit Übersichten. Sie bearbeiten die Firma Logotech International.

Aufgabe: Lesen Sie den Text und füllen Sie die Tabelle unten stichwortartig auf Deutsch aus.

Logotech International

Logotech International is a privately-owned international distribution and trading company. The company has been highly successful in international trade for over 15 years. The company's main activities are sourcing, distributing and selling fashion articles from overseas markets.

Logotech started out as a family business in 2003 when its core business was suppling fashion stores around the Midlands in the UK. Since then, the company has grown rapidly and now employs over 200 people. The head office is situated in Chorley (UK) with an overseas subsidiary in Mumbai, India and two large warehouses in Manchester and Liverpool. The location is easily accessible via major motorways, two nearby airports (Liverpool, Manchester) and a port in Liverpool.

The company is well established and has highly-professional sales, marketing, warehousing and distribution operations. Consequently, Logotech International's retail customers now range from outlet centres to major supermarkets and department stores all over Great Britain. TKMix, H-store, G&N and Darlington are just some of their customers.

At the moment, the company is building a large logistics centre at the port of Liverpool which is due to open in about three months. A further milestone was the purchase last year of a freight forwarding company with an impressive fleet of over 30 trucks and lorries. With its experience, knowledge and capital, the company intends to grow further and ensure the success of its suppliers and customers.

Name der Firma		Verkehrstechnische Anbindung	
Hauptsitz		Lagerhaltungsmöglichkeiten	
Zweigstellen		Kunden	
Unternehmensform		Lieferkapazitäten	
Gründungsjahr		Aktuelle Aktivitäten	
Anzahl der Angestellten			

3 Mediation: Stufe II

Situation: Sie bereiten sich auf ein Auslandspraktikum bei einem Unternehmen für Sanitärbedarf in Bath (UK) vor. Sie fertigen sich eine Übersicht an, die Ihnen helfen soll, einen ersten Überblick über die Handelspartner des Praktikumsbetriebs zu gewinnen.

Aufgabe: Führen Sie die Tabelle fort, indem Sie die wesentlichen Informationen aus dem Text stichwortartig auf Deutsch in die Tabelle einfügen.

Types of traders

Getting a product to the market requires an effective marketing channel for companies that manufacture durable goods and other products. A supply chain typically features various middlemen between the manufacturer and the consumer. The most common links in the supply chain are distributors, wholesalers and retailers.

Distributors

Distributors have a business relationship with the manufacturers that they represent. Many distributors maintain exclusive buying agreements that limit the number of participants or enable distributors to cover a certain territory. The distributor becomes the manufacturer's direct point of contact for prospective buyers of certain products. However, distributors rarely sell a manufacturer's goods directly to consumers. Due to the very large amount of each product they have on hand or are able to acquire from manufacturers, distributors tend to work with wholesale representatives that will buy large quantities of one product. Depending on the product, they can also help in providing product information, technical support and after-sales service to their customers.

Wholesalers

Wholesalers buy a large quantity of products directly from distributors. High-volume purchase orders typically improve a wholesaler's buying power. Many distributors provide discounts for a certain number of items purchased or the total amount spent on merchandise. Wholesalers acquire all types of merchandise, ranging from phones, televisions and computers to bicycles, clothing, furniture and food. Wholesalers have a very strong interest in selling the goods as fast as possible, as storage space is a very costly factor.

Retailers

Retailers consist of small and large businesses that sell products directly to consumers. To realize a profit, retailers search for products that coincide with their business objectives, and find suppliers with the most competitive pricing. In a supply chain, retailers often have the largest profit margin. This profit margin can be reduced due to the costs of store rental or the number of employees. Online retailers are obviously less affected by these factors. Generally, a retailer can buy small quantities of an item from a wholesaler.

Vertragshändler/Distributoren	Großhändler	Einzelhändler
- *repräsentieren Hersteller, zu denen sie eine Geschäftsbeziehung unterhalten*	- *kaufen große Produktmengen direkt von Vertriebshändlern*	- *kleine und große Unternehmen, die direkt an Endverbraucher verkaufen*

5 Marketing strategies

FOUNDATION: Market research tools

Situation: You work in the office of Go For It!, a sportswear wholesaler based in Dublin, Ireland. The company specializes in exercise equipment and sportswear for women. Go For It! is thinking about its options for collecting customer data.
→ **You write a memo with your recommendations for collecting customer data.**

1 Collecting customer data

You talk to your Irish colleagues about different ways of finding out information about your customers.

1

2

3

4

Work in groups and discuss the following questions. Make lists and report back to the class.

1 How do companies collect information about customers?
2 What information does a customer disclose when taking part in any of the activities?
3 What benefits or privileges does a customer have when they take part in the activities above?

2 Reading about market research

Before you write your recommendations, you check what you know about market research.

Why do market research?

Market research helps companies to find out about customer satisfaction and to predict how customers might react to a new product on the market.

Desk or field research?

Primary research, which is gathering data directly from the customer, is one way to collect information. The other type of research is done by analysing data that has already been collected and published, for example, statistics or studies. This is called desk research.

Tools for field research

Companies use things like loyalty cards or online questionnaires for field research. Every time a cashier swipes a loyalty card across the scanner at the checkout, every time somebody answers a questionnaire in the street or does an online survey, a company somewhere is gathering data about its customers.

Two types of information the company asks for

Companies are interested in two types of data. The first is personal data, e.g. name, age, address, etc.; the second is purchasing history, e.g. the items or services that a customer buys.

Customer Relationship Management (CRM)

CRM is a strategy for managing all a company's relationships and interactions with current, future and potential customers and for storing all this data in one place, normally a powerful database in the cloud. Cloud-based data systems can be accessed anywhere and at any time, making it possible for all sales personnel to receive updated information instantly, e.g. by smartphone, laptop or desktop computer. In this way, sales teams can work more efficiently and boost overall productivity by improving customer satisfaction and customer loyalty.

Targeting specific customers

Using data collected in the CRM system, a company's sales team can customize its marketing strategies and advertising for a particular type of customer. Rather than waste money on a one-size-fits-all advertising campaign for a particular product or service, the sales team can break down the market into segments and target each one individually, using e.g. social media to reach younger people, and flyers and digital signage for trade fair visitors.

Read the text above and make notes in German on the following:

1 die Gründe, weshalb Firmen Marktforschung betreiben
2 den Unterschied zwischen Desk- und Field-Research
3 die Datenarten, die Firmen interessieren
4 die Vorteile von Customer Relationship Management
5 die Vorteile von Marktsegmentierung

3 Writing a memo with recommendations

Now you write your recommendation for a good method for collecting customer data.

Work with a partner from the same training company. Discuss the methods for collecting customer data, then decide on a good option for your firm and your specific target group. Write a memo with your recommendation to your line manager.

- Summarize the most important information from the text.
- Make a recommendation: *Our recommendation is as follows: ...*
- Give reasons for your recommendation: *The reasons we believe ... are as follows: ...*

› *Thematic vocabulary: Sales and marketing, page 201*

PART A: A marketing strategy for a new product line

Situation: Your company, Textil-Vertrieb Mahler GmbH, wants to add a line of environmentally-friendly clothing to its product range. The production company calls in an international marketing consultant for advice, and you take part in the meeting.
→ **You make suggestions to improve your company's marketing strategy.**

1 Discussing the product

At the meeting with the marketing consultant, you discuss the first new product, an environmentally-friendly unisex jacket.

Study the product brief and match the sentence halves.

Product brief

Product	Unisex jacket
Product name	??
USPs (unique selling propositions)	made of – recycled water bottles (PET) – Fair Trade organic cotton
Target group	socially-responsible consumers
Market	Europe and beyond
Distribution	– online – stationary trade?
Sizes	XS, S, M, L, XL, XXL
Price(s)	??

1 The jackets can be worn by …
2 Customers outside Europe …
3 The jacket will be available in …
4 The unique selling propositions will attract …
5 This product might also be sold …

a six different sizes.
b in shops.
c socially-responsible consumers.
d both men and women.
e will also be able to buy the jacket.

2 Discussing the product

The consultant, Mary Garcia, is talking about the factors to consider before launching the product.

A 19 **Listen to her presentation and write down the four Ps of the marketing mix.**

B 19 **Listen again. Copy the table and make notes on what Mary Garcia says about each of the four Ps.**

First P:	1 2 3	Third P:	1 2
Second P:	1 2	Fourth P:	1 2

3 Reading about YouTube marketing

Mary Garcia mentions marketing your new line on YouTube. You do some research and find an infographic on search engine optimization (SEO).

Keywords

Nothing is more important than choosing the right keywords to describe your video. Good keywords get you more internet traffic and increase your viewer conversion rate, so choose them carefully!
If you're marketing wooden furniture, a generic keyword like "furniture" will put you up against big players like IKEA. Instead, use long-tail (specific) keywords like "fitted pine kitchen furniture" to guide potential customers to your video.

Video description

You have a maximum of 800 words in your video description and only the first 25–30 will be visible in your YouTube search results, so place your most important keywords, your site's URL, your blog, your social media and your YouTube channel at the beginning.

Video title

Use the most relevant keywords in your video title, as close to the beginning as possible. Keep it under 66 characters because that's how much you see on the search engine's results page (SERP), e.g. of Google. Include the word "video" to direct traffic to YouTube.

Tags

These help your video to rank higher on the SERP. YouTube's tag box has space for a maximum of 500 characters, and experts recommend that you use three types of tag: **specific tags**, which are one-word keywords closely linked to your video (e.g. cupboard, pine, fitted); **compound tags**, which are two or more words describing your video (but without "grammatical" words like is, that, when, etc.), e.g. Scandinavian design, custom-made; **generic tags**, i.e. non-specific words describing general categories, e.g. furniture, wooden, modern.

A **Sort the words in the box into generic and specific tags. There are ten matching pairs.**

advertising · beef · carrots · clothes · electricity · energy · food · hamburger · jingle · meat · metal · pizzeria · restaurant · rowing · shirt · sport · steel · train · transport · vegetable

Generic	*Specific*
advertising ...	*jingle* ...

B **The production company makes a video showing the new jacket and how it is made. Working in small groups, think of the following items for the video:**

- 2 or 3 long-tail keywords
- a video title (max. 66 characters)
- a video description (25–30 words)
- 6 tags (2x specific, 2x compound, 2x generic)

C **Compare your results with those of other groups and discuss them in class.**

4 Discussing market research results

Before the product launch, you interview people in the street to decide on the price of the new jacket. Here is what some of them said.

A €200 is my limit, but for that it has to look great and last more than a couple of years.

B €30 for a jacket? Is it made with slave labour?

C €50? It can't be any good at that price and how much of that is helping the environment?

D €250 for a jacket? You must be kidding! Or is it a designer jacket?

E €150 is a reasonable price for a good jacket and it will help the environment at the same time.

A **Use their answers (A–E) to make at least five sentences about different prices. Use the table below to help you.**

If	the price is/isn't above/below we (don't) advertise it for we (don't) ask for (at least) we (don't) sell it at	[price],	people some people a lot of people most people nobody	will/won't

be able to afford it. believe it's a good product. expect a designer jacket. expect the jacket to last longer. feel they're helping the environment. think it's made with slave labour. think it's good/poor quality. (want to) buy it.

Explaining consequences

If we **ask** for €30, people **will think** it's poor quality.
If we **don't ask** for at least €100, people **won't believe** it's a good product.

› *Grammar: Conditional sentences, page 156*

B **Discuss with a partner what you think the best pricing strategy for the jacket should be. Present your ideas to the class and give reasons for your opinion.**

5 Marketing your company's products

The company where you are doing your apprenticeship decides to review its marketing strategies.

A **Work in small groups from the same training company. Choose one or more of your company's products and make notes on the following tasks:**

- analyse the current marketing mix (the four Ps)
- consider ways of optimizing sales by changing the marketing mix

B **Present your ideas to the class.**

› *Thematic vocabulary, Sales and marketing, page 201*

PART B: An advertising strategy

Situation: Your company, Textil-Vertrieb Mahler GmbH, is using an international marketing consultant to help launch a new type of eco-friendly jacket with the production company. The jacket is made from recycled plastic bottles and Fair Trade organic cotton.
→ **You help to devise an advertising strategy for a new product/line for your company.**

1 Reviewing advertising strategies

The consultant sends your company some literature about the different ways of advertising a product.

A Match the different ways of advertising (A–L) to the definitions (1–12) in the diagram.

- A branding
- B celebrity endorsement
- C guerrilla advertising
- D niche advertising
- E old media
- F online advertising
- G pop-up shop
- H public relations (PR)
- I social media
- J stealth advertising
- K testimonials
- L YouTube

Possible advertising strategies

for the *Honesty* line?

1. Facebook, Twitter, Instagram, etc.
2. creating a unique name and image of a product
3. interactive video channel
4. internet, apps and QR codes
5. TV, radio, cinema, newspapers, magazines, etc.
6. reports from satisfied customers
7. secretly paying people to promote products
8. giving money to a good cause
9. support from a famous person
10. targeted advertising
11. temporary retail outlet
12. unconventional activities in public

B With a partner discuss which four ways you would use to advertise the new eco-friendly jacket.

C When you have finished, discuss your ideas in class. Can you agree on the four best ways to advertise the new product?

› *Thematic vocabulary, Advertising strategies, page 201*

2 Launching the campaign

The advertising campaign for the new unisex jacket is agreed and starts with an event in the city centre. A BBC radio reporter is covering the event and interviewing your boss, Ben Kaiser.

A **20))) Listen to the broadcast. Which forms of advertising from exercise 1A are used or are mentioned by Ben Kaiser?**

old media – radio report, ...

B **20))) Listen again and complete the sentences below with the words you hear.**

1 Last year, ___ of the bottles were thrown away and ended up in the oceans.
2 Today is Day 1 of our 'Save The Oceans' ___ .
3 Would you have recycled those 25 plastic bottles if you ___ heard about this event?
4 My trip ___ have been possible if Textil-Vertrieb Mahler hadn't offered to sponsor me and my team.
5 If it hadn't been for Textil-Vertrieb Mahler's sponsorship, you ___ have done it.
6 You can see Timo's progress down the Rhine on his YouTube ___ .

C **Make more sentences about the event as in exercise 2B (3–5) and the example.**

1 The bottles were thrown away and ended up in the oceans.
→ If the bottles hadn't been thrown away, they wouldn't have ended up in the oceans.
2 The company launched the product in the rush hour and maximized attention.
3 The company sponsored a good cause and improved its image.
4 The company offered a special deal for one day and attracted hundreds of people.
5 There was a celebrity at the launch, so the media came.
6 A camera team videoed the event, so people were able to see it online.
7 The video went viral, and the company sold thousands of jackets in a short time.

Talking about past possibilities

If people **had understood** the problem, they **would have recycled** earlier.
If they **hadn't had** a sponsor, they **wouldn't have videoed** the event.

› *Grammar: Conditional sentences, page 156*

D **Use words from the broadcast to complete the reporter's article on the BBC's website.**

Surfing sensation at central station

How many of us realize that ___ [1] of plastic bottles are thrown into the world's oceans every year? Textil-Vertrieb Mahler, a German clothing wholesaler in Dusseldorf, plans to do something about the problem of plastic water bottle ___ [2], and that's why they have a new jacket on the market made from 25 ___ [3] plastic bottles. The ___ [4] price is 150 euros, but when the product was ___ [5] at Dusseldorf's busy central station last week, people could pay for it by recycling 25 plastic bottles.

When I arrived, a long queue had formed outside their ___ [6] shop and they were joined by Germany's top surfer, Timo von Struck. He plans to paddle down the Rhine, which is over 1,200 km long, on a ___ [7] made of plastic bottles and collect plastic ___ [8] all the way to help stop the destruction of our oceans and waterways.

3 Creating a brand

Mary Garcia, the marketing consultant, underlines the importance of creating a brand and gives you and Ben Kaiser a list of five key points to consider.

Study the diagram and the extract from Ben's email reply to Mary Garcia. Find the information in his email that corresponds to each of the five points.

1 Image	2 Customers	3 Slogan	4 Logo	5 Colours
Find the words that describe your company best.	Describe the people you are selling to.	Find a catchphrase that says it all.	Design a logo with a clear message.	Choose the colours that suit your products.

Hi Mary

Thanks for the information on branding. We've had a think about it and have come up with the following ideas:

We think that a simple drawing of a handshake in pale green and blue tones with the caption "Clothes with a conscience" best shows our priorities.

The many likes that we have received on Facebook recently show that our clientele have a sense of social responsibility and understand that we are an environmentally conscious, honest and transparent company.

What do you think?

Best wishes
Ben

4 Devising an advertising campaign

The company where you are doing your apprenticeship plans to bring out a new product/line and forms a team to choose the best advertising strategy.

A **Work in groups from the same training company. Use the list in exercise 1A (page 49) to review your company's current advertising strategies. How successful are they?**

B **Devise an advertising campaign to launch the new product/line. Think of how you will attract and keep the public's attention.**

C **Present your ideas to the class. Would they work? Have a class discussion about them.**

› *Useful phrases: Giving presentations, page 188*
› *Thematic vocabulary: Advertising strategies, page 201*

COMMUNICATION: Graphs and charts

Situation: Your union representative is speaking at an international conference next week.
→ **You prepare notes on some graphic information that he can use in his talk.**

1 Describing graphs

You refresh your knowledge of the English expressions for describing graphs.

A **Match the names in the list to the graphs (a–c). There is one name more than you need.**

bar chart · line graph · pie chart · table

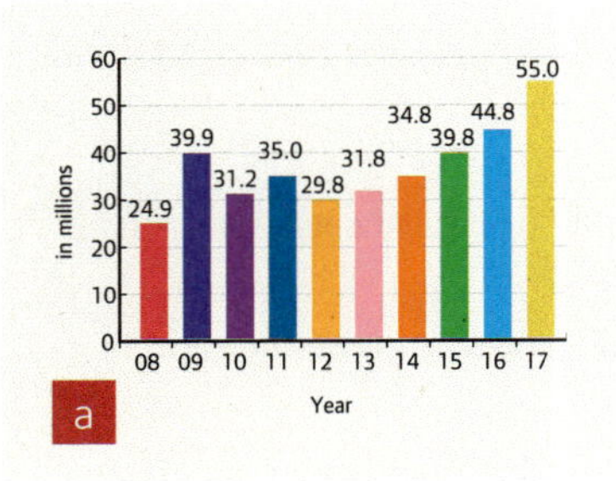

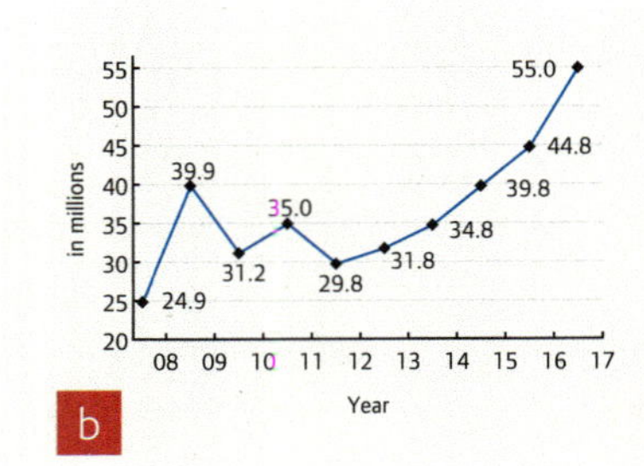

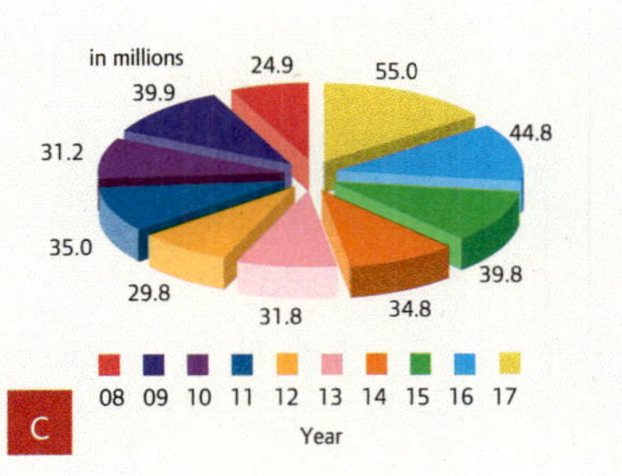

B **Match the words/phrases (1–12) to the graphs (a–h). For some graphs, several expressions can be used.**

1 to remain constant / stay the same
2 to go up / down
3 to increase / the increase
4 to hit a maximum / minimum
5 to flatten out / level off
6 to decrease / the decrease
7 to drop / the drop
8 to rise / the rise
9 to fluctuate / the fluctuation
10 to fall / the fall
11 to climb / the climb
12 to peak / the peak

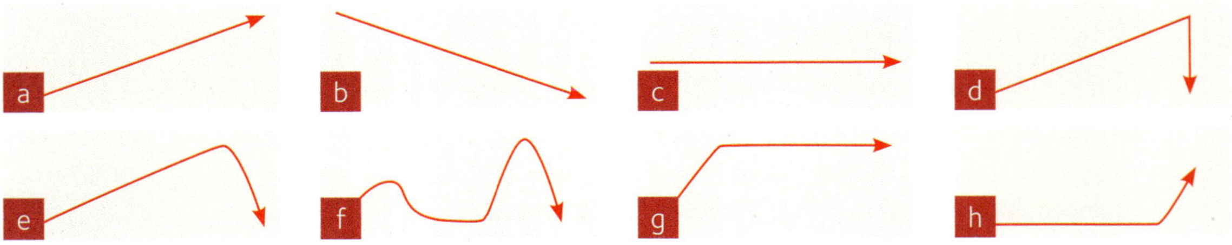

C **Work with a partner.** Partner A: **Look here.** Partner B: **Look at File 12 on page 140.**

Describe this line graph to Partner B. Partner B will draw it. Check Partner B's graph when you have finished. › *Useful phrases: Describing graphs, page 190; Thematic vocabulary: Describing graphs, page 202*

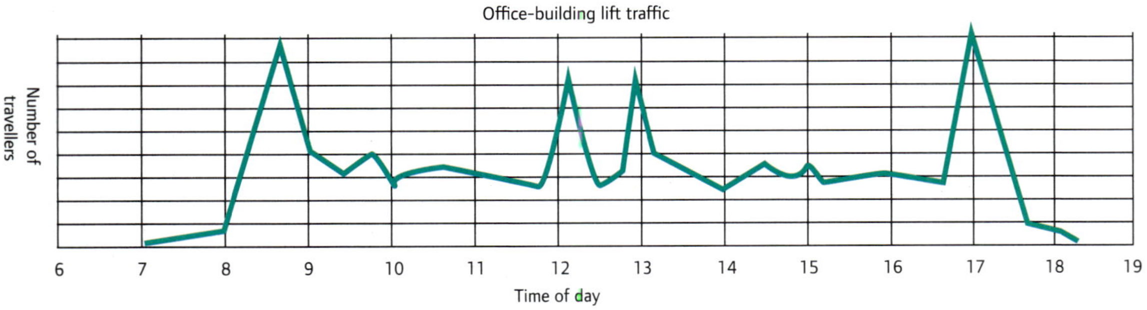

2 Talking about figures

At the conference, your union representative uses a table to describe sales of technical products worldwide in the last financial year.

A 21)) **Listen and decide which of the tables is being presented.**

A

Quarterly sales (millions of euros)				
Area	Q. I	Q. II	Q. III	Q. IV
UK	10.3	11.4	8.2	10.5
Germany	8.9	9.3	8.6	7.1
E. Europe	0.2	0.8	1.7	3.6

B

Quarterly sales (€ m)			
Q. I	Q. II	Q. III	Q. IV
10.3	11.4	8.2	10.3
8.0	8.3	8.1	6.2
0.3	0.9	3.8	4.5

C

Quarterly sales (€ m)			
Q. I	Q. II	Q. III	Q. IV
10.3	11.4	8.2	10.7
8.2	7.4	8.0	9.5
0.5	1.6	2.3	2.3

B **Work with a partner. Choose one of the tables and describe the sales figures for Germany or Eastern Europe. Your partner should say which table you are describing.**

3 Describing a table

Your union representative would like to compare and contrast average working hours in Germany with conditions in other countries. You have found the following table.

	Working hours per week	Working day*	Lunch break
Germany	41.1	07.30/08.30–16.00/17.30	30–45 mins (12.00–13.30)
France	37.9	08.00–18.00	60 mins (12.00–14.00)
GB	41.4	08.00/09.00–17.00/18.00	60 mins (12.00–14.00)
Scandinavia	39.1	08.00–16.00	30 mins (11.30–12.00)
USA	40+	08.00–17.00+	30 mins (12.00–13.00)

* The working day: Blue-collar workers in some countries begin work one hour earlier than white-collar workers.

A **Work with a partner. Study the table and write notes, using the following headings:**

Introduction

The table shows information about …

A Working hours per week

The shortest working hours per week are to be found in …

B Working day

In Germany, most people begin work between 7.30 and 8.30 and finish …

C Lunch breaks

People in France and Great Britain have the longest …

B **Work in groups. Discuss what type of graph(s) you could use to present the data on working hours.**

DAS KANN ICH (Unit 5)

- Empfehlungen für eine neue Marktforschungsstrategie auf Englisch schreiben. (Foundation)
- Verbesserungen zur Vertriebsstrategie der eigenen Firma auf Englisch erarbeiten. (Part A)
- Eine Werbekampagne für ein neues Produkt auf Englisch vorstellen. (Part B)
- Notizen anhand einer Grafik auf Englisch erstellen. (Communication)

6 Meetings and negotiations

FOUNDATION: Preparations for a meeting

Situation: You work in the Hamburg branch of a British company, Fleming Imports Ltd. The company is interested in buying cocoa beans from Grano de Cacao, a farmers' co-operative in Bolivia. After a first video conference, two representatives are coming to Hamburg to negotiate a contract.
→ You send out the agenda to the people who are going to attend the meeting.

1 Preparing for a meeting

First of all, you think about what you have to do to prepare for the meeting that is coming up.

Copy the mind map below and add more ideas of your own.

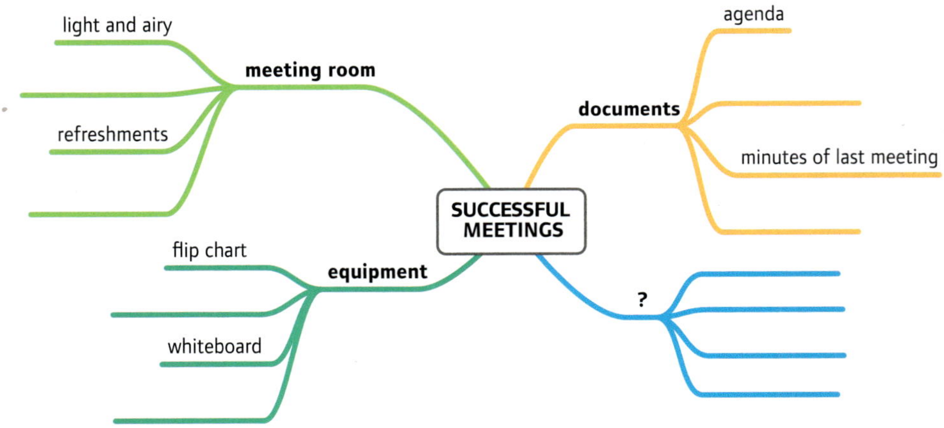

2 Making a to-do list

Your colleagues Penny Jones and Niklas Behringer have received a memo from Mary Brown, the CEO's personal assistant, asking them to prepare for the meeting with the representatives of Grano de Cacao.

Fleming Imports Ltd, Hamburg branch **Memo**

To Penny Jones, Niklas Behringer **Date** 20 December 20..
From Mary Brown, PA to CEO **Ref.** MB/OAs

Subject Meeting with representatives from Grano de Cacao, Bolivia on 20 January 20..

Please make all the necessary arrangements in good time for the meeting.

22 **Listen to them discussing the details of the meeting, and make a list of what needs to be done.**

Before the meeting
… the number of participants … a suitable room and equipment (data projector, flipchart, etc.) …
On the day of the meeting
…
After the meeting
…

Making a to-do list

Anything else we **should do** before the day of the meeting?
We **need to make** a name tag for each participant.
We **have to make sure** each place in the conference room has everything the participants need.

› *Grammar: Modals and their substitutes, page 158*

3 Writing an agenda

You and Niklas discuss the agenda for the meeting with Mary Brown, the CEO's PA.

23 **Listen and write down what is planned for each time listed on the agenda.**

Fleming Imports Ltd, Hamburg Branch

Meeting with Grano de Cacao representatives **Date:** 20 January 20..

Participants:

Fleming Imports Ltd
Jenny Fleming, CEO
Mary Brown, PA to CEO
Helen Clark, Warehouse Manager
Tom Baker, Purchasing Manager

Grano de Cacao
Carmen de Luña, Director
Miguel Reyes, Legal Adviser

Agenda

9.30 – 10.00 a.m.	…
10.00 a.m. – 12.00 noon	…
12.00 – 12.30 p.m.	…
12.45 – 1.45 p.m.	…
2.00 – 4.30 p.m.	…
4.30 – 5.00 p.m.	…

4 Writing an email

After you and Niklas talk to the CEO's PA, you email the agenda and documents to all the participants.

Write the email to all the participants, including the following points:

- the date, time and place of the meeting
- the agenda
- the tour of the warehouse
- a car to take the visitors from the airport to their hotel
- an invitation for the guests to an evening meal when they arrive
- attachments: all the documents needed for the meeting

› *Useful phrases: Writing emails, page 189*
› *Thematic vocabulary: Meetings and presentations, page 202*

PART A: An international meeting

Situation: Your company, Brewery-2-Brewery GmbH in Gelsenkirchen, exports brewing equipment all over the world. You are in the export sales team and attend the next international sales meeting.
→ You take part in a works council meeting about flexitime.

1 Preparing for a sales meeting

The Export Sales Director, Sarah Bonrath, has emailed details of the meeting to the participants in advance.

Find the words in her email that match the definitions below.

From: Sarah Bonrath <sarah.bonrath@btwob.com>
Subject: Agenda for sales meeting on 26 June 20..
Attachment(s): Presentation

Dear all

I hope you are all well.

I'm sure you will remember that our last meeting was postponed because some of the participants were unable to attend, so I have scheduled our meeting for 9 a.m. on 26 June.

The items on the agenda are as follows:

1 Presentation (Rajiv Mittal, Mumbai, India)
2 Current order situation
3 Deliveries
4 Installing and operating equipment
5 AOB

As always, the minutes of the meeting will be emailed to you one day later.

Best regards

Sarah Bonrath
Export Sales Director

1 extra points discussed at the end of a meeting
2 the points to be discussed at a meeting
3 a record of all the things said or decided at a meeting
4 to go to (a meeting)
5 to change to a later date
6 to choose a date

2 Attending a meeting

The meeting takes place as planned, but some changes have been made to the agenda.

A **24)) Listen to the meeting and write down the new items on the agenda in the correct order. Which point is not discussed?**

B 24 In preparation for taking part in meetings yourself, you make a list of useful phrases. Listen again and fill in the missing words.

Taking part in meetings

Starting the meeting
Good morning everybody and welcome to …
The first item on today's ___[1] is …

Introducing yourself
I'm … / My name is …

Asking someone to speak
Would you go ___[2], please?
Can you give us a brief update?

Asking for reactions
Would anyone like to ___[3] or ask a question?
Are there any issues?

Starting a new topic
Let's ___[4] on to the next topic, which is …
The next point is …

Asking to speak
Could I just say that …?
Can I ___[5] in on that?

Agreeing and disagreeing
I ___[6] agree with … (name).
Yes, I agree.
(I'm afraid) I don't agree with … (name).
I agree up to a point, but …

Promising action
I'll ___[7] that on to …
We'll get back to you.

Finishing the meeting
Let's ___[8] up the meeting with …
Well, that would seem to be it.

3 Checking the minutes of a meeting

The next day you receive the minutes of the meeting. You check the facts against your own notes and notice that there are five mistakes.

Study the minutes, find the mistakes and correct them. Listen to the recording again, if necessary.

Brewery-2-Brewery GmbH

Minutes of sales meeting on 26 June 20..

Attendees: Sarah Bonrath (Germany), Wen Fang (Singapore), Donald Masters (UK), Rajiv Mittal (India)

1: New agent
Ms Wen Fang from Singapore Trading joined Brewery-2-Brewery as an agent six months ago.

2: Presentation
Rajiv Mittal gave a presentation called "Beer in Mumbai" and said that the figures were not positive.

3: Current order situation
Donald Masters described how his orders were up 10% on last year.
Wen Fang was unable to give any information about sales figures.
Rajiv Mittal stated that his orders were up 5% on last year.

4: Deliveries
Donald Masters reported that deliveries were punctual 95% of the time, which was better than last year (75%).

5: Complaints
Donald Masters complained that some of the equipment had arrived dirty due to poor packing.

AOB
The finance department will contact Rajiv Mittal about travel expenses next week.

4 Taking part in a meeting

Now you take part in a works council meeting and write the minutes of the meeting.

Work in groups of six. Partners A and B: Look here. Partners C and D: Look at File 4 on page 135. Partners E and F: Look at File 5 on page 136.

Situation:
Brewery-2-Brewery is an American-owned company and has 20 employees in the office and 15 in the warehouse. At the last works council meeting, many employees were in favour of introducing flexitime. Today, there is a meeting between the American General Manager and the employees to discuss it.
Attending the meeting are:

- the General Manager (Partner A)
- the Human Resources Manager (Partner B)
- the Works Council Representative (Partner C)
- an office worker (Partner D)
- a warehouse employee (Partner E)
- an apprentice wholesaler (Partner F)

VIDEO 5

Watch the video to see more about meetings.

	Office	Warehouse
Working hours	7.30 a.m. – 3.30 p.m.	Early shift: 6.00 a.m. – 2.00 p.m. Day shift: 10.00 a.m. – 6.00 p.m.
Break	9.30 a.m. – 9.45 a.m.	15 minutes taken flexibly
Lunch break	12.00 noon – 12.45 p.m.	

A Use your role card below and the expressions in exercise 2B to conduct a meeting and come to a decision.

Partner A: General Manager

Your opinion on flexitime is neutral and you will decide on the basis of the arguments you hear.

- start the meeting, introduce yourself and ask the participants to introduce themselves
- explain that the meeting is about introducing flexitime
- ask the Works Council Representative to explain why some people want it
- ask if there are any questions
- consult with the HR Manager and come to a decision

Partner B: Human Resources Manager

You are against flexitime because there must always be at least two employees in the warehouse to load and unload lorries early in the morning and late in the afternoon. You would also like to introduce shift work in the office to guarantee the necessary paperwork for the lorries all day.

- introduce yourself
- explain your position
- answer the questions
- consult with the General Manager and come to a decision

› *Useful phrases: Taking part in meetings, page 190*

B When you have finished, write the minutes of the meeting.

› *Thematic vocabulary: Meetings and negotiations, page 202*

Talking about the past

Donald Masters **described** his sales figures.
Rajiv Mittal **gave** a presentation.
He **stated** that his orders **were** up.

› *Grammar: Simple past, page 154; Reported speech, page 157*

PART B: Hosting foreign suppliers

Situation: You work for Kaiser Trading SE, a food and non-food wholesaler for traders throughout Europe. Your company's annual suppliers' meeting is now taking place in Munich.
→ **You meet a supplier to negotiate new terms of business.**

1 Negotiating using the direct approach

Before the meeting, Kaiser Trading's Purchasing Director sends an email to a Romanian clothing manufacturer explaining that new terms will need to be negotiated.

Dear Mr Popescu

I enclose an invitation to our annual suppliers' meeting next month and look forward to speaking to you again in person.

In view of the stiff competition in the global denim and jeans market, we are reviewing all suppliers' contracts in order to reduce costs and remain competitive. We would therefore welcome your suggestions how your prices can be reduced significantly.

At the same time the market for low-priced denim is rapidly expanding, so we wish to consider how you can increase production to keep up with this trend and discuss your suggestions at our meeting.

Please let me know, should you be unable to attend.

Best wishes
Annika Wenzel

Purchasing Director

Kaiser Trading SE

A Read the email and answer the questions.

1 How do we know that Annika Wenzel and the supplier have met before?
2 How many suppliers' contracts are going to be discussed?
3 What suggestions is Mr Popescu expected to make at the meeting?
4 What are the current trends in the denim market?
5 What is the worst-case scenario for Mr Popescu?

B 25 Listen to the first version of the dialogue in which the Purchasing Director uses the direct approach to negotiating. Answer the questions.

1 What three important changes does Annika Wenzel want?
2 How much time does the supplier get to consider the new terms?
3 How do you think the supplier feels after this discussion?

C 25 Listen again and write down the exact wording of the questions Annika Wenzel asks Mr Popescu about the three important changes.

- *Can you ...?*
- *Will your company ...?*
- *Will you ...?*

2 Negotiating using the indirect approach

Annika Wenzel also uses the indirect approach to negotiating.

A **26** **Listen to a second version of her conversation with Mr Popescu and complete the sentences.**

1 Our ___ are 10% ___ than us. Do you see what I mean?
2 We are thinking of ___ 20% more from your ___.
3 We can ___ you with more machines if you can find more ___.
4 We need a ___ delivery period of 30 ___.
5 I ___ that you use Road Train GmbH. Here's their ___.
6 Would you like some time to ___ about the new ___?

How do you think the supplier feels after this discussion?

B **Work with a partner and practise asking for better terms using the direct and the indirect approach.**

Goods or services	Acceptable range
packing charge per (machine)	€20–25
extra guarantee (computer)	12–24 months
quantity discount on 100 units (T-shirts)	3–5%
sale or return agreement (books)	3–6 months

Can you provide … at … per machine?

We can pay a little more for … if you can …

3 Negotiating better conditions

The Croatian company Kolar Leather is a supplier for Kaiser Trading SE. Today you are going to negotiate with one of the directors of Kolar Leather to obtain better conditions for your company.

Role-play the conversation, using the language box below and the prompts on page 61.

Small talk	
I hope you're well. … is such a beautiful city!	The weather is so good today! Did you have a good trip/flight?
Main negotiating points	
Direct approach Are you prepared to …? Can you reduce the price by … (e.g. €20)? Will you increase … (e.g. production) by …? Are you able to guarantee … (e.g. delivery)? Do you accept these terms?	**Indirect approach** We need to talk about … … is a problem for us. … (e.g. our competitors) are …% cheaper. We're thinking of ordering more/less … We need a maximum/minimum of … How much/many more … can you produce?
Time factor	
Direct approach Let's get down to business. I have a lot of meetings/appointments today. I need an answer now. The next supplier is waiting.	**Indirect approach** Please take your time. Shall we take a break (for coffee/lunch)? Have you had enough time to think about …?
Offering help	
We can help you with … We can give you … if you can …	I suggest that you …

› *Useful phrases: Negotiating, page 191*

Partner A:
Sie (eigener Name), Kaiser Trading

Betreiben Sie Small Talk.

Sie müssen über die Preise sprechen, denn die Konkurrenz ist 5 % billiger.

Einer Ihrer Lieferanten in Split schließt gerade seine Firma und verkauft sein gesamtes Inventar. Vielleicht hat er ein Stromaggregat. Sie schlagen vor, dass Herr/Frau Horvat dort anruft und geben ihm/ihr die Telefonnummer des Besitzers.

Sie schlagen vor, eine Kaffeepause zu machen.

Pause

Sie freuen sich und fragen, ob er/sie die Preise reduzieren kann.

Sie freuen sich über diese Lösung und beenden höflich das Gespräch.

Partner B:
Ivan/Nina Horvat, Kolar Leather

Betreiben Sie Small Talk.

Sie haben technische Probleme in Ihrer Werkstatt. Sie könnten Ihre Kosten um 5 % reduzieren, wenn Sie ein neues Stromaggregat (*electricity generator*) hätten. Aber das können Sie sich nicht leisten, denn Stromaggregate sind sehr teuer.

Sie bitten um Zeit, die Firma anzurufen.

Pause

Sie haben den Besitzer angerufen und kaufen ihm ein fast neues Stromaggregat günstig ab.

Wenn die Maschine gut ist, können Sie Ihre Preise in drei Monaten um 5 % reduzieren.

Sie beenden höflich das Gespräch.

4 Role-play: A negotiation competition

You are going to role-play a situation in which a wholesaler negotiates with a supplier. You will get points for the results of your negotiations and will find out who is the better negotiator!

Work with a partner.
Partner A (wholesaler): Look at File 6 on page 137.
Partner B (supplier): Look at File 7 on page 138.

› *Useful phrases: Negotiating, page 191*

COMMUNICATION: Arrangements for meetings

Situation: You work at Top Mode Großhandel GmbH in Dusseldorf. The company is exhibiting at a trade fair in Glasgow next week.
→ **You rearrange the date and time of a meeting for your line manager.**

1 Setting up a meeting with a client

Your English line manager, Paul Smith, asks you to arrange a meeting with a customer. He gives you the following instructions.

> *Pls. get in touch with Mary Doyle at InFashion Ltd, Dublin; set up a mtg. to present our denim jackets. Ms Doyle wants to discuss some details before ordering.*
> *Suggest we meet at FunFashion trade fair in Glasgow: 26 April, morning any time until 12.30 p.m.; or 27 April, betw. 12.30 and 6.30 p.m. Need about 3 hrs.*
> *Ask which day is suitable (pls. book room for mtg.).*
> *Thanks.*
> *Paul*

Telling the time in English-speaking countries

When telling the time in English, use the short forms, *a.m.* and *p.m.*

a.m. *(ante meridiem)* = between midnight and midday
p.m. *(post meridiem)* = after 12.00 noon

In English-speaking countries the twenty-four hour clock is generally only used for timetables.

Work with a partner. Complete the email to Ms Doyle using words and phrases from the notes above.

From: trainee@topmode.de
To: m.doyle@infashionltd.ie
Subject: **Meeting with Paul Smith to discuss our denim jackets**

Dear Ms Doyle

Paul Smith of Top Mode has asked me ___[1] with you in order to ___[2] a meeting. Mr Smith would like to ___[3] our denim jackets and ___[4] some details with you before you place your order.

Mr Smith will be at the FunFashion trade fair in Glasgow next week, so he ___[5] either of the following dates: 26 April at any time in the ___[6] until 12.30 p.m. or 27 April between 12.30 and 6.30 p.m.

He thinks that the meeting will take about ___[7]. Please let me know if either of these dates ___[8].

I hope to hear from you by tomorrow as I need time to ___[9] a room for the meeting.

Yours ___[10]

Giving dates, days and times

at 6 p.m., **at** lunchtime, **at** the weekend
on Monday, **on** 21 June
in the morning/afternoon/evening, **in** January, **in** 2017

2 Rearranging a meeting

Two days before the meeting, Mary Doyle phones to rearrange it. Paul answers the phone.

A 27)) **Listen to the call. Why is Mary rearranging the meeting? What are the new arrangements?**

B 27)) **Listen again. Which phrases do you hear?**

1 **a** I'm sorry to call at such short notice. **b** I'm sorry to have to trouble you.
2 **a** I'm afraid I have to cancel our meeting. **b** I'm afraid I have to reschedule our meeting.
3 **a** Something has come up and, unfortunately, I can't get out of it. **b** I'm sorry, but I've got another meeting at that time.
4 **a** Can you come later on the same day? **b** Do you have another time in mind?
5 **a** Could we postpone the meeting until Friday at the same time? **b** How would Friday at the same time suit you?
6 **a** I apologize for the trouble. **b** I'm sorry to have inconvenienced you.

3 Confirming the details of a rearranged meeting

Paul asks you to send an email on his behalf to Mary Doyle, confirming the new details of their meeting.

Write the email, stating the new date and time of the meeting. Start and end the email with a suitable salutation and complimentary close.

› *Useful phrases: Writing emails, page 000*

4 Role-play: Changing arrangements

Because Paul is now meeting Mary Doyle on Friday, he has to postpone his breakfast meeting with a business associate, Jane Duncan, on that day. He asks you to make a new arrangement with Jane.

Work with a partner. Partner A: Look here. Partner B: Look at File 8 on page 139.

Role-play a phone call with Jane Duncan. Explain Paul's situation and use details from his itinerary below to suggest a new date and time for a meeting with Jane Duncan, e.g. for lunch or dinner.

ITINERARY –	Wed 25th – Sat 28th		
Wed 25	Flight LH 134 07.20 → Glasgow (arr. 08.40)		Dinner: Hans Treder 19.00 (Wallace Restaurant)
Thur 26	~~Meeting: Mary Doyle 9.30–12.30~~	Meeting: Martin O'Leary, Irish Wool, Ltd 14.00–16.00	
Fri 27	Working breakfast: Jane Duncan 7.00–9:30 Meeting: Mary Doyle 9.30–12.30	Meeting: Karin Wood, KW-Shoes, Ltd14.00–18.00	Buffet: Glasgow Retail Trade Association 19.00–22.30
Sat 28	Golf: Harry Jones 11.00		Flight LH 918 19.15 → Dusseldorf (arr. 22.25)

› *Useful phrases: Making arrangements, page 192*

DAS KANN ICH (Unit 6)

- Die Tagesordnungspunkte für ein Meeting erstellen und per E-Mail verteilen. (Foundation)
- An einer Betriebsratssitzung zum Thema gleitende Arbeitszeit teilnehmen. (Part A)
- Neue Lieferbedingungen mit einem Lieferanten auf Englisch aushandeln. (Part B)
- Einen neuen Termin für ein Meeting mit einer Geschäftspartnerin finden. (Communication)

KMK Exam practice 3

1 Produktion: Stufe III

Situation: Your company is planning to hold a conference on the digital transformation of the wholesale trade in a conference centre and hotel near your headquarters. One possible location is the Black Forest Convention Centre, which your company has used for similar events in the past. The new City Seminar Hotel near to your headquarters is also being considered this year.
You have already visited the City Seminar Hotel with a team and have received an attractive offer, including accommodation and complete conference services. In addition, you have also requested a customer satisfaction evaluation from an independent review website.
You have been asked to present the City Seminar Hotel and compare it with the Black Forest Convention Centre at the next team meeting.

Task: Write a script for your presentation. Start with a suitable introduction, explain why the meeting is taking place, compare the two locations using the information in the table and charts, and end the presentation properly.

Black Forest Convention Centre

Location	Black Forest, beautiful surroundings; 50 km from company; Hotel 5 km from convention centre
Meeting rooms	meeting rooms ranging in size from single meeting room to combined meeting rooms of 10,000 square feet
Equipment	state-of-the-art conference facilities and equipment
Specialties	spa with indoor pool, sauna, gym
Ratings/reviews	Awarded "European leading conference hotel star": good experiences in the past 5 years by our company

City Seminar Hotel

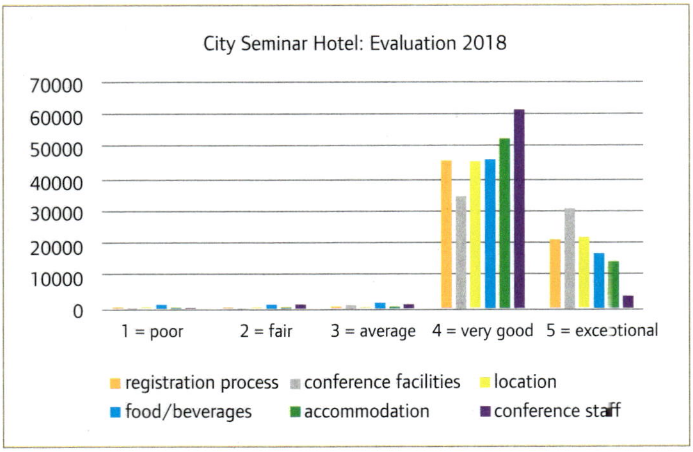

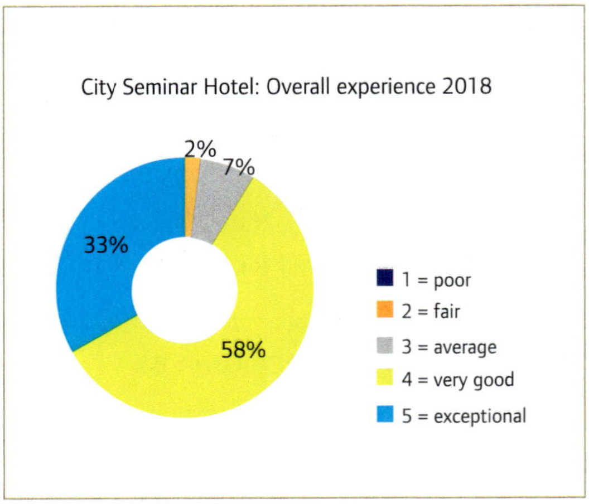

2 Produktion: Stufe II

Situation: You have given your presentation and have now been asked to write a recommendation for the Managing Director.

Task: Write an email to the Managing Director recommending where to hold the conference. Give reasons for your decision.

3 Hörverstehen: Stufe II

Situation: Sie hören ein *brainstorming meeting* bei der Firma Food Business Solutions Limited, UK. Drei Mitarbeiter/innen der Marketingabteilung (Mr Warden, Leiter der Abteilung, Claudine, seine Assistentin, und Stephanie, eine Praktikantin aus Deutschland) besprechen den neuen Internetauftritt.

28 **Aufgabe: Hören Sie sich die Diskussion an und füllen Sie die Tabelle aus.**

Datum der Einladung	
Ziel der Besprechung	
Höhe des Budgets	
Wen/Was möchten Sie erreichen?	
Vorgeschlagene Lösungen	
Was beinhaltet Pressewerbung?	
Was umfasst ihre Datenbank?	
Aktuelle Aktivitäten	

4 Produktion: Stufe II

Situation: Sie arbeiten für die Firma Zweirad Zatopek, einen Dortmunder Großhändler für Fahrräder, Fahrradbekleidung und -zubehör. Die Firma unterhält auch eine Niederlassung in Reading, UK. Kurz vor ihrem Urlaub schickt Ihre Chefin Ihnen eine E-Mail.

Aufgabe: Verfassen Sie eine E-Mail an die englischen Kollegen und Kolleginnen, wie von Ihrer Chefin unten gebeten.

Hallo

Bitte kümmern Sie sich während meines Urlaubs um die äußerst wichtige Besprechung am 6. Oktober hier in Dortmund.

- Einladung an alle Abteilungsleiter/innen
- Themen: neuer Firmenname, Verkaufsbericht, schlechter Auftritt auf der diesjährigen Pariser Fahrradmesse
- Dauer: mindestens 5–6 Stunden!

Bieten Sie den Kollegen/Kolleginnen Hilfe bei der Reiseorganisation an, da wir etwas spät mit der Einladung zum Treffen dran sind. Seien Sie höflich aber bestimmt – alle Abteilungsleiter/innen müssen dabei sein!

Vielen Dank
Emilia

7 International trade fairs

FOUNDATION: Preparations for a trade fair

Situation: You work in the Marketing department of BS Electronics GmbH, a German subsidiary of an international company. You are preparing for the ElectroTech trade fair in Dublin.
→ **You discuss promotion giveaways and choose two for your stand.**

1 Planning your exhibition stand

There is a lot to be decided before you can book a stand, so your line manager calls a planning meeting.

Work in groups. Brainstorm ideas about what you need for your stand under the headings below.

Interaction with visitors to the stand
- *up-to-date business cards*

...

Marketing materials
- *brochures and flyers*

...

Refreshments for staff and visitors

...

Other ideas

...

2 Choosing the location of your stand

Your team also has to decide on the location of the stand in the exhibition hall. You listen to the audio descriptions on the information page of the trade fair website.

A 29 **Listen to the audio descriptions and make notes to complete the chart.**

Type of stand	Location	Benefit	Rental fees
Row stands	*open onto the aisle*	*visitors walk past each stand as they go along the aisles*	*the cheapest stands to rent*
Corner stands	*at the end of a row; open onto* ...	*both aisles* ...	*higher than* ...
End of block stands	...	...	...
Island stands	...	...	...
Outdoor stands	...	...	...

B **Compare and contrast the stands on page 67 with a partner. Which one might your own training company rent at a trade fair? Give reasons.**

› *Grammar: Comparatives and superlatives, page 157*

The type of stand you choose will depend on its position to neighbouring stands or how they open onto the aisles. Click for audio description.

Row stands

Corner stands

End of block stands

Island stands

Outdoor stands

3 Deciding on promotion giveaways

Your line manager would like you to think about the type of giveaways to have on the stand.

A **Read the text below and make notes on the following aspects:**

- the benefits of giveaways
- the qualities giveaways should have

Why promotion giveaways are important

What are the most important things on your stand at a trade fair? Surprising as it may seem, it's not your sales literature or your business cards but your giveaways.

Promotional items are a major key to attracting people to your stand – and they improve your corporate image. Giveaways help people to see your company in a positive way and they make them more likely to consider your products or services.

For this reason, it's important to hand out top-quality products that have a practical use. Think of giveaways that will be immediately useful to visitors to the fair: tote bags, pens, hand sanitizers, water bottles or coffee in reusable to-go beakers. Some of the most useful trade fair giveaways are ones that will be used every day, such as LED keychain flashlights, phone chargers and sticky notes.

Make sure your giveaway shows your company logo. Remember: it won't help you if users can't immediately link the giveaway to your brand.

B **Using information from the text above, or your own ideas, put your top five giveaways in order of priority.**

			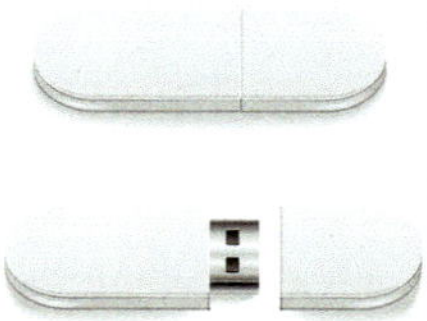	?
anti-stress ball	chocolate drops	USB charger	memory stick	your ideas

C **Discuss your choice of giveaways with a partner and then with the class. Choose two giveaways to have on your stand at the trade fair.**

› *Thematic vocabulary: Trade fairs, page 202*

PART A: Commissioning a stand

Situation: You work for the trade fair team at Ökobau Müller GmbH in Freiburg. Your company will be exhibiting its products at the next Architecture and Building Expo in Dublin.

→ **You commission a suitable stand and arrange catering for an on-stand event.**

1 Identifying types of stand

You look at a number of exhibition stand companies online, in particular Booth-Tech Ltd from Dublin.

Read the descriptions of the three types of stand and think about which one(s) would be most suitable for Ökobau Müller. Give reasons for your choice.

Exhibit with Booth-Tech Ltd

About to launch a new product? Trying to raise brand awareness? Need a space to demonstrate and discuss your products with a video loop in the background? Whatever the purpose of your stand, Booth-Tech will find the perfect solution with all the features you need. Visit us at www.booth-tech.ie or call +353 1416 6614.

Choose from three types of stand:

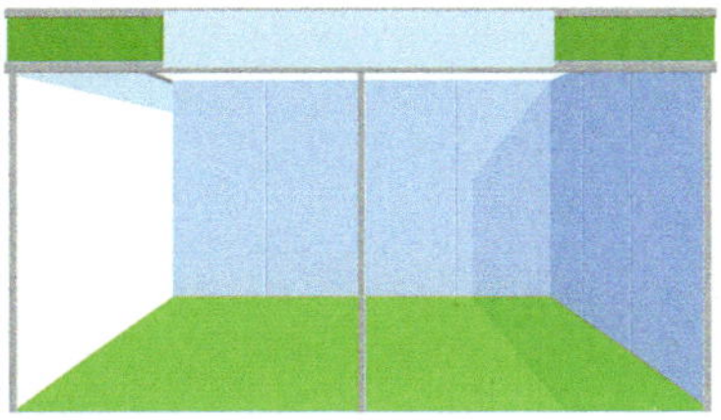

1 Shell scheme
- box-shaped aluminium frame-work with posts at each corner
- assembled in minutes
- suitable for multiple use
- can be made to fit into your vehicle

2 Modular
- simple combination of 1, 2 or 3 wall panels and a floor
- assembled in minutes
- suitable for multiple use
- can be made to fit into your vehicle

3 Bespoke
- any shape, size, style
- unique to your company
- made to your specifications
- planned with 3D visualization

2 Discussing the requirements

Your line manager, Lena Richter, calls Dermot Kennedy at Booth-Tech Ltd to discuss the stand.

A 30 **Listen to their conversation and make notes on the points below.**

1 purpose of stand
2 size of stand
3 features on stand
4 division of space
5 single/multiple use
6 type of stand

B 30 **Listen again and complete the sentences with the words you hear.**

1 In that case, I would ___ having a larger stand.
2 And I would also ___ having some literature racks.
3 I would strongly recommend ___ one, so you can store your valuables.
4 I suggest that you ___ the other 25 square metres 50/50.
5 I would recommend that you have an ___ stand.
6 We always recommend ___ a shell scheme stand if you're exhibiting at different locations.

VIDEO 6

Watch the video to see more about designing a stand.

3 Designing the stand

Booth-Tech Ltd sends Lena Richter some suggestions for the layout of the stand.

A **Read the email and use the highlighted words from it to label the diagram of a stand.**

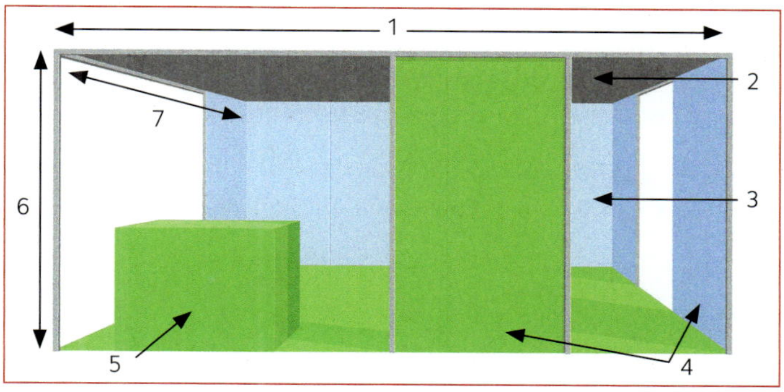

To:	lena.richter@oekobau-mueller.de
From:	d.kennedy@booth-tech.ie
Subject:	Stand layout

Dear Ms Richter

With reference to our phone call yesterday regarding a display stand, I am sending you some examples to help you with your decision.

We make stands with closed, semi-closed or open sides, with or without a roof and counter. Using infill panels along the sides and a backdrop will give you more space for advertising, but open sides will make your stand more accessible to visitors. The dimensions of the stands shown are 4m x 10m x 5m (height/width/depth). The video screen can be placed anywhere you choose.

Please send us a sketch of what you require and details of the vehicle you will be using to transport the stand. We will then create a 3D visualization, adapt it as necessary and make you a firm offer.

We look forward to hearing from you soon.

Best regards
Dermot Kennedy

B **Use the language box to describe one of the two layouts to a partner. Guess the stand described.**

1 (prices starting at €2,500)

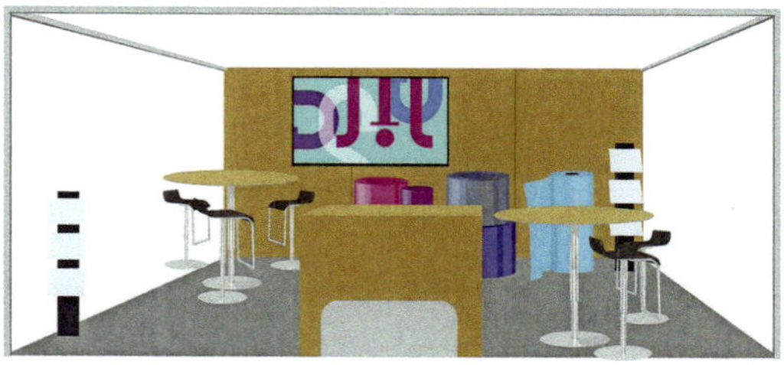

2 (prices starting at €3,000)

Describing a trade fair stand

on the left/right
on the left/right-hand side/panel/wall
at the top/bottom / in the middle
at the back/front
in the (left/right-hand) corner

between / next to / behind / in front of
with/without a roof
open/closed/semi-closed side(s)
an infill panel / a backdrop with (photos/ descriptions/diagrams/data)

4 Planning an on-stand event

Your team plans an on-stand networking event with drinks and snacks at 4 p.m. on both days of the exhibition. 50 visitors have confirmed by email that they will attend over the two days.

A **With a partner, use the brochure below to put together a menu for 25 visitors. You have a budget of €1,200 for a 3-hour event on the first day of the trade fair.**

O'Reilly's Catering Ltd

Let us cater for your event, so you can sit back and enjoy it! Here's just a small selection from our hospitality pack. Bespoke menus available on request. Call us on +353 1419 8000.

Please note:
Minimum 20 covers.
All menus include waiting staff for a maximum 2-hour period.
Any service required in addition to this time is chargeable at €20 per hour.

BEVERAGES

Freshly brewed tea and coffee	€1.80
Fruit and herbal teas and decaffeinated coffee	€1.80
Still and sparkling water (500 ml)	€1.85
Selection of fruit juices (1 litre)	€4.50
Fruit smoothies (200 ml)	€2.20
Smithwick's red ale (500 ml)	€4.50
Guinness (330 ml)	€3.50

Full wine list available on request.

savoury bites
€4.75 p.p.

canapés
€9.95 p.p.

finger buffet
€17.75 p.p.

fork buffet
€19.95 p.p.

B **Now you phone through your order to O'Reilly's Catering.**

Partner A: **Look at File 9 on page 139.** Partner B: **Look at File 10 on page 140.**

5 Commissioning a stand for your company

Your training company requires a stand for trade fairs/exhibitions in English-speaking countries.

Work in groups and do the following tasks:

Either:
1 Discuss and then draw a sketch of a suitable stand to show your company's goods/services.
2 Role-play a phone call to an exhibition stand company in which you ask questions about the six points listed in exercise 2A.

Or:
1 Put together a menu for an on-stand event at a trade fair.
2 Role-play a phone call to a catering company in which you order food and drinks for the event.

Making suggestions/recommendations

I (would) **suggest having** a larger stand.
I (would) **recommend having** some literature racks.
I (would) **suggest** (that) **you split** the other 25 square metres 50/50.
I (would) **recommend** (that) **you have** an island stand.
Why don't you order a finger buffet?
Have you considered having savoury bites?

› *Grammar: Gerunds, page 157*

› *Useful phrases: Advising customers, page 189*

PART B: Promoting your company

Situation: Your company, Compact Living GmbH, is a wholesaler of space-saving furniture. You are going to be on your stand at the 100% Design Show in London, where visitors are expected from all over the world.

→ **You practise how to present your company and its products to visitors from different cultural backgrounds.**

1 Understanding different cultures

As you are expecting visitors to your stand from all over the world, you do some research into business etiquette in different countries.

A **Do this cultural awareness quiz. Complete the sentences with the most suitable answer (a, b or c).**

1 When meeting French business people, it is best to avoid … .
- **a** personal questions
- **b** eye contact
- **c** humour

2 During negotiations with an Italian delegation, one of the team keeps taking phone calls. This is because they … .
- **a** are not interested in your offer
- **b** want to make you feel uncomfortable
- **c** are probably talking to their boss and it would be rude not to answer

3 The best way to be successful with Brazilian business partners is to … .
- **a** show anger
- **b** build relationships
- **c** stress deadlines

4 In Finland people are respected for their … .
- **a** modesty
- **b** patience
- **c** intelligence

5 At the end of a meal in a Russian's home, you should … .
- **a** eat everything on your plate
- **b** leave a little food on your plate
- **c** take your plate to the kitchen

6 Which part of a person's body should you not touch in Thailand?
- **a** head
- **b** hand
- **c** shoulder

7 You know an Egyptian businessman but not his wife. When you meet her for the first time, you should … .
- **a** greet her and offer her your hand
- **b** wait for her to introduce herself to you
- **c** wait for the businessman to introduce her to you

8 What is the most commonly-spoken language in the UK after English?
- **a** Urdu
- **b** Polish
- **c** Portuguese

9 If there is a period of silence when in a meeting with a Japanese business person, you should … .
- **a** ask what is wrong
- **b** break the silence
- **c** wait

10 Who makes decisions in Chinese companies?
- **a** the team
- **b** the managing director
- **c** a manager

B Work with a partner. Look at the Illustrations by Yang Liu, a Chinese businesswoman living and working in Berlin, about the cultural differences between Germany (blue) and China (red).

Punctuality

View of superiors

Approaching new things

Problem-solving

Source: Yang Liu Design, Berlin

Write at least two sentences to describe each contrast. Compare your results with those of other members of the class and find more examples.

C Discuss any experience you have had of trading partners from different cultures with a partner and then with the class.

VIDEO 7

Watch the video to see more about dealing with different cultures.

2 Adapting to different cultures

Several business people from different countries visit your stand on the first day of the fair and make appointments to come back later. They are interested in your folding tables.

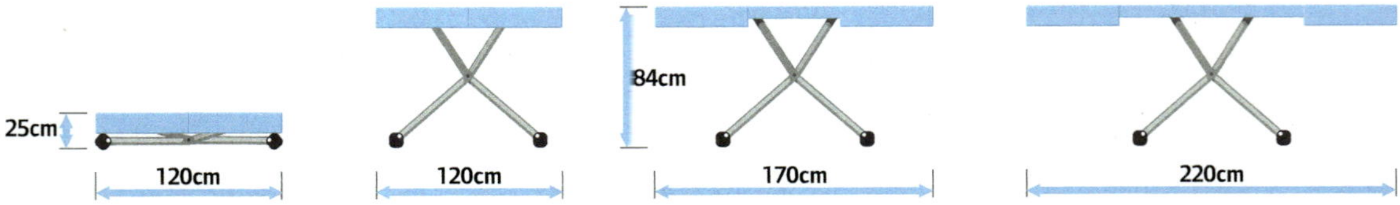

A 31 Listen to the conversations with a Japanese, an Italian and an American business person and make notes on the following points:

- small talk (and topics)
- the focus of the conversation
- the time needed to make a decision
- interruptions during the meeting
- who makes decisions
- any other differences

B Work in small groups. Use the points listed above and ideas of your own to discuss how negotiations are conducted between German business partners. Discuss your ideas with the class.

3 Dealing with foreign customers

Your company, Compact Living GmbH, has a stand at the Heim+Handwerk trade fair in Munich.

A Role-play a conversation with a Japanese business partner using the following prompts.

Partner A: Mitarbeiter/in bei Compact Living GmbH

Partner B: Kunde/Kundin, Nagoya Trading, Japan

A: Begrüßen Sie den Kunden / die Kundin freundlich. Sie freuen sich, ihn/sie wiederzusehen.

B: Reagieren Sie freundlich.

A: Betreiben Sie Small Talk. Bieten Sie etwas zu trinken an.

B: Sie möchten nur ein Glas Mineralwasser.

A: Fragen Sie, ob er/sie mehr über den Tisch wissen möchte.

B: Fragen Sie, aus welchen Materialien der Tisch gemacht werden kann und bitten Sie, die technischen Zeichnungen zu sehen.

A: Erklären Sie, dass die Tische aus Birkenholz (*birchwood*), Mahagoni (*mahogany*) oder Faserplatten (*fibreboard*) gemacht werden und geben Sie ihm/ihr die technischen Zeichnungen.

B: Schauen Sie sich die Zeichnungen kommentarlos für mehrere Minuten an. Fragen Sie anschließend, wie schwer der Tisch aus Mahagoni ist.

A: Er wiegt 15 kg. Fragen Sie, ob er/sie andere platzsparende Möbel aus Mahagoni ansehen möchte.

B: Sagen Sie, dass Sie die anderen Möbel vielleicht später ansehen werden.

A: Fragen Sie, ob er/sie weitere Informationen benötigt.

B: Sie möchten wissen, ob die Tische auch mit höhenverstellbaren Beinen (*height-adjustable legs*) lieferbar sind.

A: Dies wäre gegen Aufpreis (*at an extra charge*) möglich. Fragen Sie, ob Sie ihm/ihr ein Angebot zuschicken sollen.

B: Das könnte er/sie vielleicht später machen. Bedanken Sie sich für die Informationen.

A: Sie haben zu danken. Sagen Sie, dass er/sie vor Ende der Messe gerne wieder vorbeischauen kann.

B: Sie werden evtl. wieder vorbeischauen und sagen „auf Wiedersehen" auf Deutsch.

A: Schließen Sie das Gespräch freundlich ab.

› *Useful phrases: Advising customers, page 189*

B Adapt the instructions in exercise 3A to create similar conversations with customers from Italy and the USA, or any other countries you know. Perform your conversations in front of the class.

COMMUNICATION: Business trips

Situation: You work in the Export Sales department of GlasKlar Großhandel GmbH in Berlin. The company manufactures glass bottles and jars for the food industry. You and your line manager, Maria Weber, are going to attend a conference in London.
→ **You hire a car at a hotel reception.**

1 Booking the flights

Maria Weber has a friend who works at British Airways. She calls her to find out about flights to and from London.

32)) **Listen to their conversation and complete the details of the flights.**

Flight	Date	Departure	Arrival	Details
BA ___[1]	April ___[2]	Berlin Tegel ___[3]	London Heathrow ___[4]	___[5] flight ___[6] class 2 aisle seats
BA ___[7]	April 23	London Heathrow ___[8]	Berlin Tegel ___[9]	___[10] flight ___[11] class 2 seats same row; one ___[12] seat

2 Finding hotel accommodation

The conference centre is 20 minutes away from the airport. Maria asks you to find a hotel online which might be suitable.

Read the text and explain the main features of the hotel to Maria in German.

Crown Palace 4-star hotel

Welcome to the Crown Palace Hotel.

Our modern hotel offers first-class accommodation and business facilities. The spacious, air-conditioned rooms have internet access and a desk. All rooms feature a flat screen TV. The rooms are fitted with minibars, and tea and coffee-making equipment.

The 4-star Crown Palace has a gym with an indoor pool and sauna.

Our breakfast buffet includes a wide range of vegan options.

Our stylish restaurant is open daily from 7 till 10.30 p.m.

Our well-stocked bar is open from 11 till 11 and our lounge serves non-alcoholic drinks and snacks 24 hours a day.

24-hour front desk
Free Wi-Fi available throughout the hotel
100% smoke-free

Our shuttle bus to Heathrow airport runs every 20 minutes.

The Crown Palace is less than a 30-minute drive away from Thorpe Park, Windsor Castle and the Chiltern Hills Nature Reserve. The university town of Cambridge is only 1.5 hours away.

3 Checking in at a hotel

When you arrive at the hotel, there are three guests in front of you at reception. You listen to the receptionist talking to them.

1 Giovanni Rossi

2 Mary McGregor

3 Yusuf Zuabi

A 33 **Copy the table. Listen to the guests as they check in and fill in the missing information.**

	What questions do the guests ask?	What information does the receptionist give?
Giovanni Rossi	1	2
Mary McGregor	3	4
Yusuf Zuabi	5	6

B **Work with a partner. Role-play a short conversation at the reception. Ask and answer questions about some of the following, or use your own ideas:**

air conditioning · meeting room · taxi to the airport · Wi-Fi

4 Role-play: Hiring a car

Your return flight is in the early evening, so you and Maria decide to take a look at the countryside outside London before you travel back to Berlin. You talk to the receptionist for advice.

Work with a partner. Partner A: Look here. Partner B: Look at File 3 on page 134.

Partner A
You are the guest at the hotel. Ask the receptionist for information about hiring a car for the day. Ask about the following:
- where you can hire a car
- the cost of a hire car
- the mileage (included? car returned full or empty?)
- the type of insurance cover; excess in case of accident/damage
- where to pick up / return the car

You decide to book a car for Monday 23 April, 8 a.m. You will pay for it with your Visa card.

› *Thematic vocabulary: Business trips, page 202*

DAS KANN ICH (Unit 7)

- Die passenden Werbegeschenke für einen Messeauftritt suchen. (Foundation)
- Einen Messestand in Auftrag geben und das Catering für ein Event organisieren. (Part A)
- Ein Beratungsgespräch mit einem Kunden / einer Kundin auf Englisch führen. (Part B)
- Ein Mietauto an einer Hotelrezeption in England buchen. (Communication)

8 Enquiries, terms of delivery and payment

FOUNDATION: Finding a new supplier

Situation: You work for AllesMöbel GmbH, a German furniture wholesaler. The company has decided to expand its range of office furniture. Your line manager asks you to look for prospective suppliers at home and abroad.

→ **You collect information for your line manager from an English text.**

1 Finding new suppliers

You think about different sources for getting information about suppliers.

A Work in small groups. Talk about how to find out about prospective suppliers and their goods.

B In your group, collect reasons why your company might need a new supplier. Exchange your findings in class.

2 Choosing a supplier

Your line manager sends you a link to a podcast describing what to look for in a good supplier.

A **Before you listen, match the German translations (1–8) to the English expressions (a–h).**

1 Anbieter	a a good deal
2 Bonitätsprüfung	b value for money
3 ein gutes Angebot	c defect
4 Fehler	d open-account terms
5 offenes Zahlungsziel	e payment in advance
6 Preis-Leistungs-Verhältnis	f solvency
7 Vorauszahlung	g vendor
8 Zahlungsfähigkeit	h credit check

B 34 Now listen to the podcast and complete the notes with the missing words or phrases.

Points to consider	Choosing a supplier
1 Prices	a the lowest price is not always ___ b don't jump at an offer just because ___ c check the whole ___ before you choose
2 Quality of the goods	a find out if a new supplier can consistently provide ___ b ___ from other clients might be useful. c be careful with ___ recommendations from the internet
3 Warranties	a the most common deals with the product being free from ___ when it leaves the supplier b the buyer has to make a claim within ___
4 Terms and conditions	a it's important that you know your ___ b how are the responsibilites and ___ for transport of the goods shared? c a new supplier might ask for ___ until your relationship is established
5 Reliability of supplier	a it is important to find out about the ___ of the supplier b if you don't do this, you might put your business ___ c search the internet for a company that will do a ___ for you

C Work in groups. Rank the points the speaker suggests in order of importance. Compare and discuss your rankings in class.

3 Collecting information about ethical and environmental aspects

A link from the podcast leads you to the following text. You think your line manager will also want to consider the aspects mentioned in the text before she decides on a new supplier.

List the most important information in the text in German for your line manager.

Choosing a new supplier?

Don't forget to look into the ethical and environmental aspects

Two very important questions you should always ask before you decide on a supplier are: "Is this company ethical in the way they treat their employees?" and "How much do we know about this supplier's attitudes to the environment?"

Regarding the first question, it makes sense to look into the physical environment in which employees work. Do these meet health and safety regulations of the country where the goods are produced? Are employees free to form trade unions, and do they have the right to collective wage bargaining? What is the reputation of the country of origin of the goods as far as human rights are concerned? Is there sexual discrimination? Is there any suspicion that your prospective supplier uses forced labour or child labour?

As far as environmental issues are concerned, are your supplier's production methods sustainable? Are their processes environmentally friendly? Do they comply to standards and regulations? Don't forget. You can always do your bit for the environment if you buy from a domestic supplier. That way, you will avoid long shipping distances and keep your carbon footprint down.

PART A: Enquiries

Situation: You work in the Logistics department of AgriTrade South Africa Pty Ltd, a company that exports fruit and vegetables all over the world.
→ You send enquiries to a number of suppliers.

1 Contacting suppliers

As sweet corn goes rotten after a short time, the company decides to set up its own canning facility near Cape Town and to look for a source of canning equipment. One enquiry is to Cantec GmbH, an engineering company in Essen.

To:	Dirk Sauerwald, Sales Director <dirk.sauerwald@cantec.com>
From:	luke.booysen@agritrade.co.za
Subject:	Enquiry about canning technology

Dear Mr Sauerwald

We note from your company's website that you sell fully-integrated can body production lines and we are most interested in your CAN-O-MAT system for three-piece cans.

We are a leading producer and exporter of sweetcorn in South Africa with excellent business contacts all over the country and beyond. Until now we have bought empty cans from Europe, but in order to cut costs for transportation and storage we are looking for a supplier of canning technology, so we can set up our own can-making facility. Initially, we will require approx. 250 million cans per year, diameter 99–119 mm.

Please send us a favourable quotation for a CAN-O-MAT production line, including details of your terms of delivery and payment.

How soon can you deliver?

References are available on request.

We look forward to hearing from you soon.

Yours sincerely

Luke Booysen
Logistics Director

AgriTrade South Africa Pty Ltd, 150 Main Rd, Paarl, 7646, South Africa
Tel. +27 (0) 21 860 1800 Fax. +27 (0) 86 528 0473
Email: info@agritrade.co.za www.agritrade.co.za

Study the email and match the sentence halves.

1 AgriTrade is a South African …
2 Dirk Sauerwald works for a German …
3 The South African company plans …
4 The CAN-O-MAT production line will …
5 Luke Booysen wants Cantec to send him …
6 AgriTrade asks for details of …

a Cantec's terms of delivery and payment.
b a quotation for a CAN-O-MAT system.
c produce about 250 million cans per year.
d producer of sweetcorn.
e to make its own cans instead of buying them.
f engineering company called Cantec.

2 Structuring an enquiry

Before you write further enquiries, you check the standard structure used.

A Use words from the list on the right to translate the enquiries checklist (1–6) into German.

Enquiries checklist

1 source of address
2 description of your company
3 reason for your enquiry
4 your requirements:
- quotation
- sales material
- price list
- discounts
- samples
- terms of delivery and payment
- delivery
- representative's visit

5 references
6 polite ending

(Preis)angebot · Beschreibung Ihrer Gesellschaft · Grund für Ihre Anfrage · höfliche Schlussformel · Ihr Bedarf · Liefer- und Zahlungsbedingungen · Lieferung · Muster / Probe(n) · Preisliste · Quelle der Anschrift · Rabatte · Referenzen · Verkaufsmaterial · Vertreterbesuch

› *Useful phrases: Writing enquiries, page 192*

B Study the email from AgriTrade (on page 78) and make a list of the points on the checklist that it includes.

C Match the phrases below with headings from the checklist and then translate them into German.

1 We would be grateful if a representative could call on us.
2 If your products meet our requirements, we will place a substantial order.
3 Please also let us know if you are able to provide samples.
4 You have been recommended to us by ...
5 We would welcome a favourable quotation for these items, including all discounts granted.

3 Enquiring on the phone

Dirk Sauerwald at Cantec in Essen sends an initial proposal for a CAN-O-MAT production line to AgriTrade. Your boss, Luke Booysen, then phones him to discuss further details of the proposal.

CAN-O-MAT production line

35 **Listen to their telephone conversation and make notes on the following points.**

- delivery period
- training
- price
- payment
- after-sales service

4 Role-play: Telephoning foreign suppliers

Before he makes a decision on the canning facility, Luke Booysen asks you to contact another canning equipment manufacturer.

Work with a partner. Partner A and Partner B: Look at File 13 on page 141.

PART B: Understanding terms of delivery and payment

Situation: You have just started work in the Purchasing department of MegaKauf Großhandel GmbH, which wholesales goods imported from all over the world. You are attending a seminar about international trade as part of your training.

→ **You consider terms of delivery, payment and insurance in transit for individual suppliers.**

1 Looking at terms of delivery

The seminar starts by looking at five of the eleven International Commercial Terms (Incoterms®) used by buyers and sellers all over the world.

A Find the German equivalent in the list for each Incoterm (1–5) in the diagram.

geliefert Zoll bezahlt (benannter Bestimmungsort) • frei an Bord (benannter Verschiffungshafen) • frachtfrei versichert bis (benannter Bestimmungsort) • frachtfrei bis (benannter Bestimmungsort) • ab Werk (benannter Lieferort)

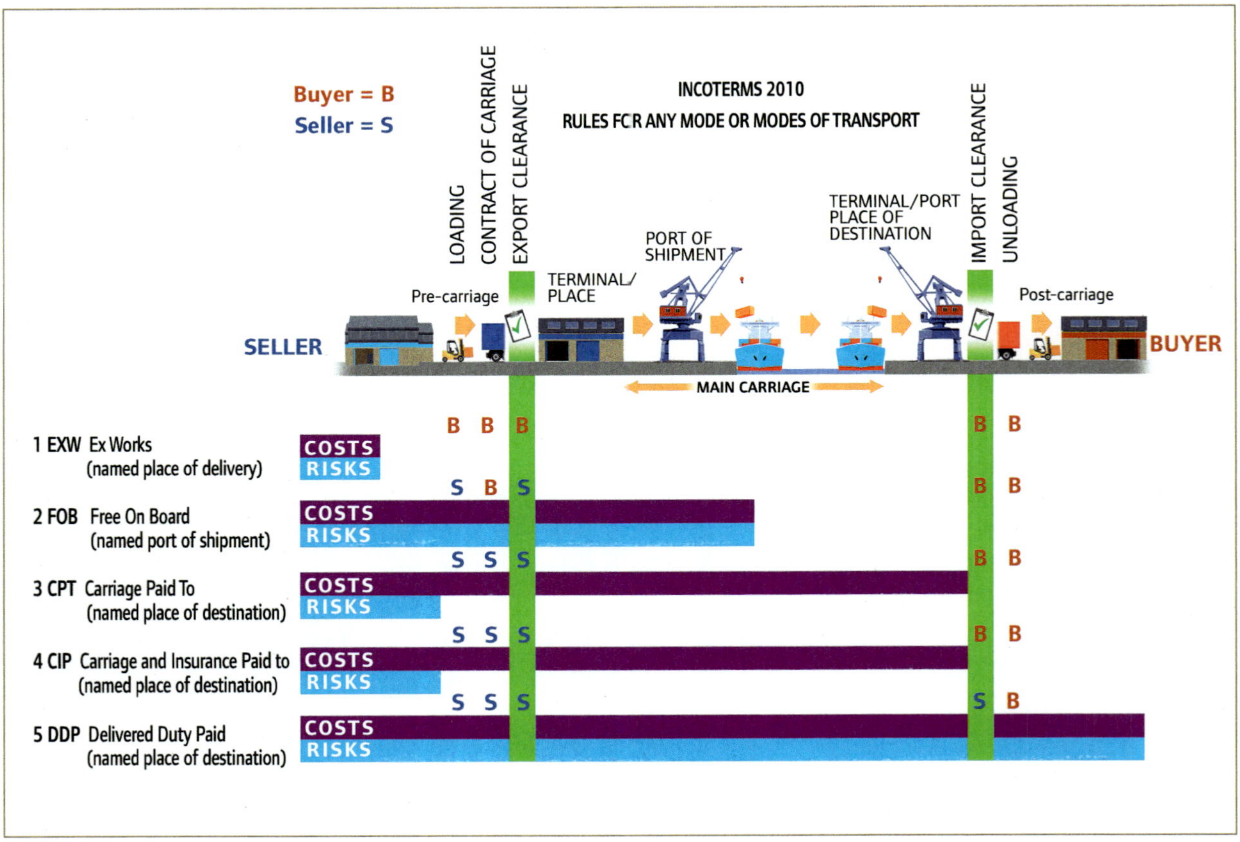

B **With a partner, study the seminar handout (on page 81) about the five Incoterms and then explain who is responsible for the highlighted factors in the following situations (1–5).**

1 **EXW** A German importer in Frankfurt buys a consignment of fruit from a Spanish exporter in Valencia. (loading, export clearance, main carriage)

2 **FOB** A Chinese exporter in Nanjing near the port of Shanghai sells a consignment of clothing to a German importer in Bielefeld. (export clearance, cost of main carriage)

3 **CPT** A German exporter in Cologne sells a consignment of farming machinery to a Portuguese importer in Lisbon. (loading, risk during main carriage)
4 **CIP** A German importer buys a consignment of floor tiles from an Italian exporter. (risk during main carriage, unloading)
5 **DDP** A New Zealand exporter in Wellington sells a consignment of seafood to a German customer in Berlin. (import clearance, unloading)

Incoterms: information sheet

Transport (carriage) costs
When a seller supplies goods using an Incoterm beginning with the letter E or F, this means that they do not pay for the main carriage. In the case of EXW, the seller only makes the goods available at their premises (e.g. factory, warehouse, etc.).

With F terms, the seller only pays for transport of the goods to a convenient location, e.g. a port, an airport or a train station not too far away. In the case of FOB, the seller has the goods loaded on a ship at the port of shipment.

For the seller, C terms include loading and the cost of the main carriage to the destination but not unloading at the destination.

D terms cover all transport costs until the goods have reached their destination.

Risk
E and F terms mean less risk for the seller. In the case of EXW, the seller bears no risk outside their premises. With an F term, the seller bears the risk until the goods have been handed over to the first carrier, e.g. are on board a ship at the port of shipment. With CPT and CIP, the risk to the seller is the same because it passes to the buyer when the goods have been collected by the first carrier. With CIP, the seller also insures the goods for the main carriage but no longer bears any risk when they have been handed over to the first carrier.

D terms cover all risks until the goods have reached their destination.

Import and export clearance
With ten of the eleven Incoterms, export clearance (e.g. export licences, documentation) is arranged and paid for by the seller. The exception is EXW. With ten of the eleven Incoterms, import clearance (e.g. customs duty, import licences and documentation) is arranged and paid for by the buyer. The exception is DDP.

C **Copy the table into your book and complete it for the Incoterms FCA, DAP, DAT, FAS, CFR and CIF. Refer to the full list of Incoterms on pages 183-185.**

	Main carriage		Seller bears risk	
	paid	unpaid	including main carriage	excluding main carriage
FCA		✓		
DAP				

2 Choosing the right Incoterm

As part of the seminar, you listen in to some phone calls to foreign suppliers.

A 36)) **Listen to three of the calls and identify the Incoterm and the place agreed in each case.**

1 electricity generators
2 garden furniture
3 LED displays

› *Incoterms, page 183*

B 36)) **Listen again and note which Incoterm was discussed but not chosen in each case.**

3 Looking at terms of payment

The next topic discussed at the seminar is terms of payment. Payment can be made with or without the help of shipping documents.

A **First use the words in the list on the right to find the German equivalents of the terms of payment (a–f). Then put the terms of payment in order of preference for the seller.**

Payment without shipping documents

a 10 days 2%, 30 days net
b 30% with order, 70% on completion
c cash on delivery
d cash with order (CWO)
e open account terms with monthly/quarterly settlement
f payment in advance (TT)

Barzahlung bei Auftragserteilung · gegen Nachnahme · offenes Zahlungsziel mit monatlicher/vierteljährlicher Abrechnung · Vorauszahlung/Vorkasse (telegrafische Überweisung) · Zahlung innerhalb 10 Tagen abzüglich 2 % Skonto oder innerhalb 30 Tagen netto · 30 % bei Auftragserteilung, 70 % bei Fertigstellung

› *Terms of payment, page 185*

B **Study the text and put the stages of the transaction (A–J) in the diagram in the order in which they take place (1–10).**

Payment with shipping documents

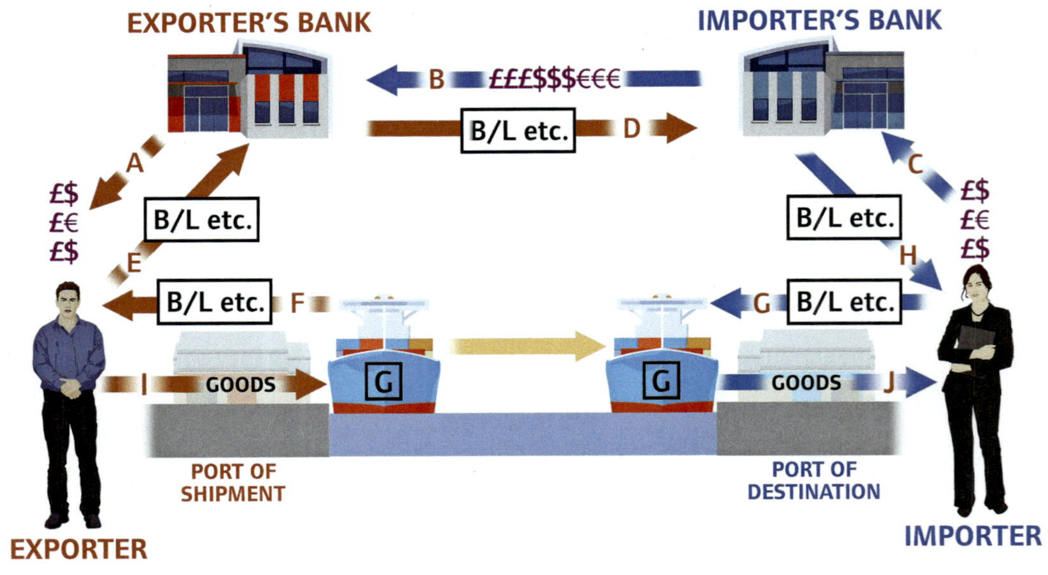

Payment by irrevocable and confirmed documentary letter of credit (simplified)

Payments using shipping documents are based on the principle that the holder of the shipping documents can take possession of the goods. The shipping documents include the commercial invoice, the insurance certificate and either the bill of lading (sea), air waybill (air) or consignment note (road or rail). In international trade, payment is very often made by letter of credit (L/C).
With payment by irrevocable and confirmed documentary letter of credit, the exporter's bank guarantees to buy the documents from the exporter if they are exactly as agreed. It then sells them to the importer's bank, which sells them to the importer.

The following (simplified) example is for sea transport (see diagram). It uses a bill of lading, which is both a document of title (ownership), a contract of carriage and a receipt for the goods.

1 The exporter gives the goods to the shipping company and they are loaded onto a ship.
2 The exporter receives a bill of lading (B/L), showing he has title to the goods.
3 He gives the B/L, the commercial invoice and the insurance certificate to his bank.
4 The bank inspects the documents and, if they are in order, pays the exporter.
5 The exporter's bank now has title to the goods and sells them to the importer's bank.
6 The importer's bank pays the exporter's bank and now has title to the goods.
7 The importer's bank sells the documents to the importer.
8 The importer pays the importer's bank and now has title to the goods.
9 The importer gives the documents to the shipping company at the port of destination.
10 The shipping company gives the importer the goods.

Payment by documentary credit is safe but expensive because both banks charge fees for their services.

› *Terms of payment, page 185; Thematic vocabulary: Shipping documents, page 203*

4 Looking at case studies

The seminar trainer gives you some examples of previous transactions and asks you to suggest suitable terms in each case.

A Choose a suitable Incoterm + place in the following situations.

1 A Spanish company in Valencia buys some heavy road construction machinery from a German company in Duisburg. The buyer requires the exporter to bear all the costs and risks for the goods to their destination, including unloading the machinery at the terminal in Valencia.
2 A German manufacturer near Bielefeld receives an order for 200 tractors from a buyer in Nairobi, Kenya. The goods are to be sent by sea to the Port of Mombasa. The German manufacturer is only prepared to transport the goods to Hamburg and load them on board a ship.
3 An Argentinian beef exporter in Buenos Aires, Argentina sends a consignment of meat by ship from the Port of Buenos Aires to the Port of Rotterdam. The exporter bears the transport costs to the port of destination and also pays for the meat to be insured while it is on board the ship.
4 A German exporter in Dresden is only prepared to load the goods on board the carrier's vehicle at his premises and provide any documents needed.

Infobox

Incoterms including insurance
The Incoterms CIF and CIP require the seller to insure the goods for the main carriage for 110% of their value.

› *Incoterms, page 183*

B Choose a suitable term of payment in these situations.

1 A supplier normally gives the buyer a month to pay but offers a two per cent discount for payment within ten days.
2 A manufacturer will only sell the goods to the buyer if the manufacturer is guaranteed payment by a bank in his country.
3 A reliable customer placing regular orders is allowed to pay every three months.
4 A manufacturer requires almost a third of the sum agreed when the order is placed and the rest when the goods have been manufactured.

› *Terms of payment, page 185*

COMMUNICATION: The layout of business letters

Situation: You work at MedEquip GmbH, a Berlin-based wholesaler of medical supplies and equipment for hospitals and clinics. This week you are helping out in the Sales department.
→ **You write an offer to a new customer in the UK.**

1 Reading an English business letter

Your line manager gives you a letter of enquiry from a new customer.

A **Study the layout and match the parts (1–12) of the letter on page 85 to the labels below (a–l).**

a address/letterhead	**d** copies	**g** inside address	**j** signature block
b body of the letter	**e** date	**h** reference initials	**k** subject line
c complimentary close	**f** enclosure	**i** salutation	**l** attention line

B **Make notes (in German) about all the information that Linda Lambert asks for.**

2 Writing an English business letter

Your line manager asks you to write an offer to Ms Lambert at the Dryden Medical Clinic.

A **Complete the letter with suitable words and phrases from the list.**

confirmation · deal with · delivery · discount · enclosing · enquiry · guaranteed · look forward to · offer · packed · price · this date

Dear Ms Lambert

Thank you for your ____[1] about theatre monitors We are pleased to send you the following ____[2]:

One (1) 32" OT-HD monitor. ____[3]: €2700.00.

We can deliver within two weeks of ____[4] of your order. Terms of ____[5] are DAP your clinic.

This offer is valid for two weeks from ____[6]. If you place your order within one week, we can also offer a 2% ____[7]. All of our monitors are ____[8] for two years.

We will ____[9] your order carefully and quickly. The monitor will be ____[10] in an aluminium container for transport.

I am ____[11] a copy of our latest catalogue and price list and ____[12] future orders.

Yours sincerely

B **Write the complete offer, using the correct layout for a business letter, a suitable salutation and complimentary close, today's date, etc.**

› *Useful phrases: Writing business letters, page 193*
› *Thematic vocabulary: Commercial correspondence, page 203*

➔ Salutation and complimentary closes in letters

	Salutation	Complimentary close
to a firm	Dear Sir or Madam	Yours faithfully *(BE)*
		Yours very truly / Cordially yours *(AE)*
to a person	Dear Mr/Ms Brown Dear Sharon/Martin	Yours sincerely *(BE)*
		Sincerely yours / Best personal regards *(AE)*

1 Dryden Medical Clinic
17 Dryden Street
London SE9 2BS
+44 (0)20 129546783
info@drydenclinic.com

2 29 April 20..

3 Our ref: LL/DC

4 MedEquip GmbH
Rudower Straße 250
12489 Berlin
GERMANY

5 For the attention of the Sales Manager

6 Dear Sir or Madam

7 Enquiry about operating theatre monitors

8 We have seen your advertisement in this month's editon of the trade magazine "Medical Business". We see that your company sells medical hardware.

We are a large outpatient clinic in London. We are planning to update our operating theatres and are interested in high-definition operating theatre monitors. We would like to place a trial order for one 32" OT-HD monitor. If the product is suitable, we may place further orders.

Please let us have details of your terms of delivery and payment. We would also like to know what type of packaging you use to protect the monitor during transport.

Many thanks for your attention to our enquiry. We look forward to hearing from you soon.

9 Yours faithfully

10 Dryden Medical Clinic

Linda Lambert

Linda Lambert
Clinic Manager

11 cc Dr Alice Black

12 Enc: Information pack "Dryden Medical Clinic"

DAS KANN ICH (Unit 8)

- Eine begründete Lieferantenauswahl treffen. (Foundation)
- Schriftliche und telefonische Anfragen auf Englisch erledigen. (Part A)
- Die passenden Zahlungs- und Lieferbedingungen für internationale Geschäfte aussuchen. (Part B)
- Ein schriftliches Angebot für eine englische Firma erstellen. (Communication)

KMK Exam practice 4

1 Leseverstehen: Stufe II

Situation: Ihre Firma ist als internationaler Großhändler für Büroprodukte oft auf Fachmessen vertreten, um neue Kunden zu akquirieren. Sie haben eine Einladung von Farook International Stationery (FIS) zur Paperworld Middle East erhalten. Ihr Chef bittet Sie, als Entscheidungsgrundlage für eine mögliche Teilnahme die wichtigsten Informationen über die Messe und FIS zusammenzutragen.

Aufgabe: Lesen Sie den Text und fassen Sie die wichtigsten Informationen auf Deutsch tabellenartig zusammen.

Paperworld Middle East

Farook International Stationery (FIS) has been there from the beginning. As the United Arab Emirates' (UAE) biggest manufacturer of stationery and office supplies, the company was naturally one of the first companies to exhibit at the Paperworld Middle East trade fair when it started in 2011 and is now one of its official launch partners. The annual trade fair for industries dealing in stationery, paper and other office supplies, aims to stimulate business opportunities throughout Africa and the Middle East and will be welcoming over 300 exhibitors at this year's fair, which takes place from 27 February to 1 March. The fair is a platform for firms to present an array of different products and services ranging from traditional supplies for schools and offices, arts and crafts materials and writing implements to environmentally-friendly paper-based products, toys, gifts and games.

The trade fair has proven a great success becoming increasingly popular with international players – the first year attracted 4,420 buyers yet in 2017 this had already risen to 6,443 buyers from over 93 different countries. This achievement can be attributed to the Paperworld brand, which is well received all over the globe, but also to its Dubai location which makes it easily accessible for international markets and a great way to access the emerging markets in the nearby regions.

Farook International Stationery's continued support of the trade fair has of course also been a big factor in the success of the event. FIS started out back in 1980 as a retailer and wholesaler of stationery but had moved into the manufacturing side of the business by 1990. Since then it has gone a long way in making customers think of high-quality goods when they see the stamp 'Made in the UAE', building up a good product range and customer base and now exporting 10 product lines to over 90 countries worldwide. These are displayed in their 14 showrooms, 13 of which are in the United Arab Emirates, with the last one in Oman, along with 12 stationery brands from other international companies.

PAPERWORLD

Art der Messe	
Standort	
Anzahl der Aussteller	
Gründungsjahr der Messe	
Termin/Dauer der Messe	
Beispiele für angebotene Produkte	
Enwicklung der Anzahl internationaler Käufer	

Farook International Stationery

Art der Firma	
Weitere Daten und Fakten über die Firma	
Aktuelle Aktivitäten	

2 Interaktion: Stufe III

Work with a partner. Partner A: Look here. Partner B: Look at File 11 on page 140.

Situation: Your company has a stand at an international trade fair and you are responsible for welcoming the customers and guests. Some customers have been given appointments, but due to some delays, they have to wait for a short time. You entertain the customers while they are waiting and help out with any problems that may occur.

Aufgabe: Role-play a conversation at the trade fair stand with Partner B. Be prepared to ask and answer questions. You may have to use your imagination and make up possible answers. Use the ideas below to help you.

- Introduce yourself and explain the situation.
- Offer refreshments and engage in small talk (three topics) with the guest.
- Reassure the guest if he/she gets annoyed about waiting.
- Try to find a solution for the customer (possible offers: internet access, information material, voucher for lunch?)

3 Mediation: Stufe III

Situation: Im Rahmen eines Auszubildendenaustauschs zwischen internationalen Standorten Ihrer Firma erwarten Sie im kommenden Monat einen Auszubildenden aus Kanada, der vier Wochen im Einkauf mitarbeiten soll. Ihr Ausbilder bittet Sie daher, aus folgendem Artikel eine Checkliste auf Englisch zu erstellen, welche Aspekte bei der Lieferantenauswahl grundsätzlich zu berücksichtigen sind.

Aufgabe: Lesen Sie den Text und erstellen Sie eine Checkliste auf Englisch.

Lieferantenauswahl

In einer globalen Welt werden die Auswahlmöglichkeiten bei Lieferanten immer größer, der Preisdruck aber auch. Worauf sollte man also bei der Lieferantenauswahl achten?

Natürlich ist der Preis immer noch häufig das entscheidende Kriterium. Günstige Produktpreise und Rabatte oder lange Zahlungsziele tragen dazu bei, die Kosten zu senken. Ein wesentlicher Aspekt ist aber auch, dass die Produkte von guter Qualität und makellos sein sollten. Falls es dennoch einmal zu Problemen wegen eines falschen, kaputten oder fehlerhaften Produkts kommen sollte, sollte der Lieferant eine Entschädigung oder Ersatzlieferung anbieten.

Grundsätzlich ist es wichtig, dass Liefertermine eingehalten werden und der Lieferant immer lieferbereit ist. Vorteilhaft ist hier sicher, wenn ein Lieferant in Standortnähe seinen Sitz hat und keine langen Lieferwege zurückzulegen sind.

Nicht alle Kriterien sind für alle Unternehmen wichtig oder gleichwertig. Der Lieferant sollte flexibel auf Kundenwünsche eingehen und diese gegebenenfalls auch schnell umsetzen. Besonders bei anspruchsvolleren Produkten sind Beratung, Service und Freundlichkeit der Mitarbeiter/innen Aspekte, die berücksichtigt werden sollten. In der heutigen Zeit beschäftigen sich immer mehr Betriebe mit Umweltaspekten, wie z. B. umweltfreundliche und nachhaltige Produkte und Entsorgungs- und Recyclingangebote.

9 Submitting an offer

FOUNDATION: Replies to customer enquiries

Situation: You work in the Sales department of a hiking and outdoor equipment wholesaler. Your company uses templates for making offers in different languages.
→ **You write an offer to a prospective customer.**

1 Looking at different types of offers

Your line manager gives you a list of types of offers in German and asks you to key in the English translations.

A Translate the English expressions (1–8) using the German expressions from the list on the right.

Types of offer

1 firm offer
2 legally binding
3 quotation
4 solicited offer
5 subject to confirmation
6 unsolicited offer
7 valid while stocks last
8 without obligation

(Preis-)Angebot • gültig solange der Vorrat reicht • bindend/verbindlich • unverbindlich • unverlangtes Angebot • verbindliches Angebot • verlangtes Angebot • vorbehaltlich einer Bestätigung

B Use one of the English words or phrases to complete the sentences.

1 All prices are quoted *without obligation.*
2 Another company was able to offer a lower ___ for the cost of the work.
3 Contracts are ___ agreements between two or more parties.
4 It looks as if the ABC company doesn't want to do business with us. They didn't respond to the ___ we sent them last month.
5 Our offer is non-binding and ___ .
6 Our ___ will remain open as long as stocks last.
7 These special conditions are ___ .
8 You send a ___ in response to a customer enquiry.

2 Replying to an enquiry

Your company has received an enquiry from Mike Baird, a retailer of trekking equipment in the UK. Your line manager asks you to complete the reply to the enquiry.

Replace the German sentences and expressions (1–10) in the letter below with the correct English phrases.

Dear Mr Baird

Enquiry about our range of backpacks

With reference to your enquiry of 12 December 20.., we are pleased to hear that (*Sie sich für unsere Produkte interessieren*) ___1 and are planning to include them in your range.

As requested, (*fügen wir unseren aktuellen Katalog bei*) ___2. We are pleased to inform you that everything is (*derzeit auf Lager*) ___3.

(*Wir möchten diese Gelegenheit wahrnehmen*) ___4 to draw your attention to the latest addition to our range, the Ultra-Light backpack, a 50-litre backpack which weighs less than 1 kilo. (page 4)

Our prices are quoted (*ab Werk*) ___5 and our terms are (*2,5 % Skonto bei Zahlung innerhalb von 10 Tagen*) ___6.

(*Wir erledigen Aufträge sofort*) ___7 and guarantee an efficient and reliable service.

We feel sure that (*ein Probeauftrag*) ___8 will convince you of the quality of our goods.

Please do not hesitate to contact us (*falls Sie weitere Einzelheiten benötigen*) ___9. We look forward to hearing from you soon.

Yours sincerely

(your name)

(*Anlage*) ___10: catalogue

› *Useful phrases: Writing offers, page 194*

3 Writing an offer

Your line manager asks you to write an offer in reply to an enquiry for windproof jackets from Charles McAdam, Mountain Range, 13 Highland Way, Perth PH1 1TS, Great Britain, a retailer of mountaineering equipment.

Write the offer to Mr McAdam using your line manager's points below. Remember to begin and end your letter politely.

- *reference to enquiry (give today's date) and interest in product*
- *price list*
- *all items in stock; immediate delivery guaranteed*
- *details of terms of delivery and payment (DAP Perth)*
- *all products made in Germany*
- *suggestion for trial order*

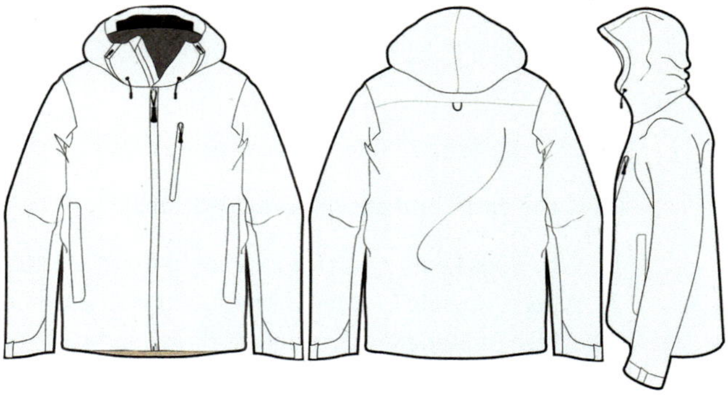

› *Thematic vocabulary, Business transactions, page 203*
› *Useful phrases: Writing offers, page 194*

PART A: Offers

Situation: You work in the Sales department at MegaKauf Großhandel GmbH in Dusseldorf. Your company receives an enquiry from Murphy's Homecare Ltd, a chain of DIY stores with branches all over Ireland.

→ **You write an email to confirm the details of an offer to the customer.**

1 Making an offer

Your line manager, Leonie Hartmann, writes to Luke O'Connor, the Purchasing Director at Murphy's Homecare.

To:	Luke O'Connor, Purchasing Director <luke.oconnor@murphys-homecare.ie>
From:	Leonie Hartmann, Sales Director <leonie.hartmann@mgk.de>
Subject:	Your enquiry dated 20 October 20.. about charcoal barbecues
Attachment(s)	greber_ch_bbq.pdf

Dear Mr O'Connor

Many thanks for the above-mentioned enquiry.

We are a major distributor of high-quality products and have an excellent reputation throughout Europe and North America. A brochure with our Greber charcoal barbecues is attached for your information and to download details of our entire range together with our export price list, please visit our website at www.megakauf-gh.com.

As agreed in our telephone conversation this morning, we will be pleased to supply you with 200 Greber Smoker charcoal barbecues. Our price of €15,000 is quoted FCA Dusseldorf. Our terms of payment for an initial order are CWO or, with favourable references, 10 days 3%, 30 days net. Delivery will be made approx. 6 weeks after receipt of order.

Please do not hesitate to contact us if you require further details.

We look forward to receiving your order.

Best regards
Leonie Hartmann
Sales Director

MegaKauf Großhandel GmbH, Oberkasseler Str. 200, 40545 Düsseldorf, Germany

› *Incoterms, page 183; Terms of payment, page 185*

Read the email and answer the questions.

1 Why does Leonie Hartmann write to Murphy's Homecare Ltd?
2 Where, outside Europe, is MegaKauf also well known for their products?
3 Which of MegaKauf's products does Leonie Hartmann send Murphy's Homecare more detailed information about?
4 Where will the goods be collected if Murphy's Homecare accept MegaKauf's offer?
5 How much of the price of the goods will Murphy's Homecare need to pay if they cannot give favourable references?
6 How long will Murphy's Homecare need to wait before they receive their order?

2 Structuring an offer

When you write offers, you can usually follow a simple structure.

Use words from the list on the right to translate the offers checklist (1–8) into German.

Offers checklist

1 reference to enquiry
2 description of your company/goods/services
3 sales material
4 price
5 terms and discounts
6 delivery
7 polite ending
8 enclosure(s) (*letter*) / attachment(s) (*email*)

Anlage(n) • Beschreibung Ihrer Firma/Waren/Dienstleistungen • Bezug auf Anfrage • Geschäftsbedingungen und Rabatte • höfliche Schlussformel • Lieferung • Preis • Verkaufsmaterial

› *Useful phrases: Writing offers, page 194*

3 Making an offer on the phone

The barbecues sell well in Murphy's Homecare's DIY stores and now customers are also enquiring about gas barbecues. Luke O'Connor contacts Leonie Hartmann to ask what MegaKauf can offer.

A 37 **Listen to the dialogue and say if the statements are true or false. Correct the false statements.**

1 Leonie Hartmann offers Luke O'Connor a new barbecue that has just come on the market.
2 It has no special features apart from a lid and two wheels.
3 Murphy's Homecare have a warehouse near Dublin.
4 MegaKauf can deliver door to door.
5 Luke O'Connor is not pleased with the delivery period.

B 37 **Listen again and make notes on points 1–6 in the offers checklist above.**

Reference to enquiry – email *Description of goods/services – ...* ...

4 Evaluating an offer

During her conversation with Luke O'Connor, Leonie Hartmann mentions three Incoterms.

A **Look at pages 183–185 and answer the questions below for each of the three Incoterms: FCA, CIF and DAP.**

1 Who pays for the main carriage?
2 Who packs the goods?
3 Who chooses the freight forwarder/vessel?
4 When does the risk pass from the seller to the buyer?
5 Who pays for damage to the goods during the main carriage?
6 Who pays for unloading the goods at their destination?

B **Explain which Incoterm Luke O'Connor accepts and why.** › *Incoterms, page 183*

5 Confirming the offer

Leonie Hartmann asks you to write to Luke O'Connor to confirm the details of the offer.

A 37 **Listen again or use your notes from exercise 3B to make a checklist of MegaKauf's offer.**

B **Use your notes to write an email from MegaKauf to Murphy's Homecare with all the details of the offer.**

› *Useful phrases: Writing offers, page 194; Thematic vocabulary: Business transactions, page 203*

PART B: Comparing offers from different suppliers

Situation: You work in the Purchasing department at MegaKauf Großhandel GmbH in Dusseldorf. The Purchasing Director asks you and your colleagues to contact four manufacturers of garden furniture whose products she saw at the Ambiente trade fair in Frankfurt.

→ **You compare the offers and recommend a supplier.**

1 Contacting a supplier via chat

The Purchasing Director wants offers for 20 garden sets (table and four chairs), and she gives you a checklist to fill in for each supplier. First you use the chat function of Alibaba.com to contact Pretty Lotus Furniture in Shenzhen, China.

A **Read through the chat, copy the checklist on page 95 and fill in the details.**

MegaKauf: Hello, this is MegaKauf in Dusseldorf, Germany.

Anna He: Hello. This is Pretty Lotus Furniture. My name is Anna. How can I help you?

MegaKauf: Good morning, Anna. We saw your garden set no. VBCT 990 in Frankfurt and need more information.

Anna He: Yes, it is very popular. What would you like to know?

MegaKauf: Is the price of €480 an FOB price?

Anna He: Yes, FOB Shenzhen.

MegaKauf: Is there a minimum order quantity?

Anna He: Yes, 5 sets.

MegaKauf: Thank you. What is the transit time from the Port of Shenzhen to Dusseldorf Central Station?

Anna He: 35 days from the Port of Shenzhen to Bremen then one more day to Dusseldorf.

MegaKauf: Thanks. And the charge for Shenzhen to Dusseldorf?

Anna He: One moment please (*pause*) Using our shipping agent, it is €1,200 for a *20' GP container to Dusseldorf Central Station. One container holds a maximum of 20 sets. Do you want 20 sets?

MegaKauf: Perhaps. How much are 20?

Anna He: 20 sets cost €9,600.

MegaKauf: Plus €1,200 for transport to Dusseldorf. The import tax and customs duty on €10,800 is about 26% so that comes to (*pause*) €2,808. The total cost would be €13,608.

Anna He: Yes, and that's a very good price.

MegaKauf: OK, but what are your terms of payment?

Anna He: TT – 30% with order, 70% before loading.

MegaKauf: Thanks. How long is your guarantee?

Anna He: 2 years.

MegaKauf: Do you offer a quantity discount?

Anna He: We have a good price and nobody is cheaper than us.

MegaKauf: Thanks. I'll be in touch again soon.

Anna He: Thank you. I will send you photos of all our products via Alibaba. Have a nice day.

MegaKauf: Thanks, you too.

*20' GP – 20-foot general purpose container

B Read through the chat again and answer the questions.

1 How did MegaKauf find out about Pretty Lotus Furniture's products?
2 Who will pay for the main carriage if MegaKauf accepts the price of €480 per unit FOB Shenzhen?
3 How will the furniture be transported to Bremen?
4 How much more than the basic price of €9,600 will the garden furniture cost if MegaKauf decides to buy 20 sets?
5 How much of the total price will MegaKauf have to pay before the goods are shipped?
6 What does Anna promise to do after the chat?

C You contact several companies to get the best shipping rates for the garden furniture. Use words from the chat to complete the email below. Make any necessary changes.

Dear Elaine

I would like to know your ___ 1 for shipping a 20' ___ 2 container of furniture from the ___ 3 of Shenzhen to Dusseldorf Central Station, Germany. Our supplier's terms of delivery are ___ 4, so we require sea transport for the main carriage. Can you offer a ___ 5 time of less than 35 days?

Would you also handle payment of customs ___ 6 and import ___ 7 on our behalf? We have contacted a number of shipping ___ 8 with the same request and hope to hear from you in the very near future.

Best regards

2 Reading an email offer

Your colleague Emil Partmann receives an email from a Finnish supplier, FinDesign Oy, in Oulu, Finland. He then collects additional information on transport costs in a chat with a freight forwarder.

A Study the offer and add the details to your checklist.

To:	emil.partmann@megakauf-gh.com		
From:	miika.virtanen@findesign.fi		
Subject:	Your enquiry about Artek+ garden sets	Attachment(s)	fin-design_outdoors.pdf

Dear Mr Partmann

Many thanks for the above-mentioned enquiry, which we received this morning.

We are a major manufacturer of outdoor furniture with many satisfied customers throughout Europe and beyond. Our current catalogue is attached for your information.

As regards the goods requested, we are pleased to submit the following quotation:

Product:	Artek+ garden set
Unit price:	€650
Terms of delivery:	FCA Oulu Station
Terms of payment:	CWO or L/C
Guarantee:	4 years
Quantity discount:	2% as from 50 sets

If regular orders are placed with our company, open account terms may be granted.

We feel sure that a trial order will convince you of the quality of our products and look forward to doing business with you. Please do not hesitate to contact us if you require further details.

Yours sincerely

Miika Virtanen

B Read through the chat and add details of the transport charges to your checklist.

FREIGHT RATE QUOTES • FREIGHT RATE QUOTES • FREIGHT RATE QUOTES •

Emil Partmann 24-May-20.. 7:10

Please let us have quotes for transporting the following from Oulu Train Station, Finland to Dusseldorf Central Station, Germany:
- 20 sets of garden furniture; 1,750 kg; approx. 30 m^3
- 1 set of garden furniture; 87.50 kg; approx. 1.50 m^3

24-May-20.. 7:11 Raj Pragasam

Understand. Thank you. Our rate for 1,750 kg in closed wagon is €1,200. For 87.50 kg in shared container it is €400. Delivery period 4 days. Local charges applicable at both ends.

Emil Partmann 24-May-20.. 7:12

Thanks. Will be in touch.

24-May-20.. 7:13 Raj Pragasam

My pleasure!

3 Contacting suppliers by phone

Finally, your colleague phones Intermobili in Milan, Italy and Projardin in Metz, France.

38 **Listen to the two dialogues and add the details for both companies to your checklist.**

Manufacturer / 20 x Garden sets	Pretty Lotus Furniture, Shenzhen, China	FinDesign, Oulu, Finland	Intermobili, Milan, Italy	Projardin, Metz, France
Unit price				
Minimum order quantity				
Incoterm				
Transit time				
Extra transport costs				
Sub-total				
Import taxes				
Total				
Terms of payment				
Guarantee				
Quantity discount				

4 Comparing the offers

Your company, Megakauf Großhandel GmbH, has its own fleet of lorries and vans. You and your colleagues review the offers.

A **Work in groups of four. Use the data from your checklist and first compare the four Incoterms. Discuss the following points:**

- Who pays for the main carriage in each case?
- What extra transport costs are there for the buyer?
- Where is the risk transferred from the seller to the buyer?

B **Next compare the terms of payment and any discounts. Check the terms offered for …**

- an initial order
- regular orders

C **Now compare the prices and work out the total cost (i.e. price, minimum order quantity, transport costs, taxes, discounts) for each of the four suppliers. Each team member chooses one of the four suppliers and works out the price for …**

1 the smallest possible order
2 20 garden sets
3 1,000 garden sets

D **What other factors are important when making your final choice of supplier? Discuss your ideas in your team and report back to the class.**

E **Now write a report for your Purchasing Director. Use all the data to recommend the best supplier and give reasons for your choice.**

COMMUNICATION: Clarifying information on the phone

Situation: You work in the Sales department of Marx Kitchens plc, a wholesaler of kitchen equipment in Birmingham. Your line manager sometimes has to clarify details of offers and orders.
→ **You telephone a supplier to sort out a misunderstanding.**

1 Completing a reply to an enquiry

Due to an error, some details are missing from an offer to a prospective customer, John Jamieson. He phones your department and discusses the problems with your line manager, Mary Hamilton.

A **Work with a partner. Decide together who says what, your line manager or the customer.**

1 I'm sorry to hear that.
2 Shall we go through the details together?
3 I would like to have everything sorted out as soon as possible.
4 The most important information is missing.
5 How much is the discount?
6 I think I have all the information I need now.
7 I really must apologize for the problems.
8 I'm so sorry that you've had to go to all this trouble.

B **39 Listen and check your answers.**

C **39 Listen to the call again and complete the missing details with numbers and expressions from the list. There are three more items than you need.**

3 · 6 · 10 · 15 · 50 · cash with order · CIF · DDP · delivered from stock · do not include · include

Dear Mr Jamieson

Thank you for your enquiry of 24 April. We are pleased to note that you are interested in our products.

Our terms of delivery are within ___ [1] weeks, ___ [2] Liverpool.
Orders of fewer than ___ [3] items can usually be ___ [4].

Please note that on bulk orders of more than ___ [5] items, we grant a quantity discount of ___ [6] %.

For new customers, we prefer ___ [7].

As requested, we attach our latest catalogue. Please note that prices ___ [8] VAT (see our terms and conditions, page 6).

We look forward to doing business with you.

Yours sincerely
Jennifer Smith
Sales Department

2 Correcting the details of an order

A few days later, Mr Jamieson sends an order. As there are some errors in the order form, Mary Hamilton phones Mr Jamieson.

A **40 Listen to the call. What two important details has Mr Jamieson omitted on the order form (page 97)? What mistake has he made in his final calculation?**

B **Re-write the order form, including the missing details and the new total price.**

Dear Ms Hamilton

I refer to our recent telephone conversation. I would like to order the following items:

10 microwave ovens and 25 electric kettles

I attach your order form as requested and look forward to receiving the goods.

Yours sincerely
John Jamieson

Quantity	Item number, description and colour	Unit price	Total
10	Microwave oven	£180	£1,800
25	Electric kettle	£27	£ 675
			£2,475
		3% discount on bulk order	£ 74.25 -
		Total price	£2,400.75

3 Role-play: Checking details before placing an order

Last month, while visiting a trade fair, the Purchasing Manager attended a presentation on aluminium kitchen tables. Before deciding whether to add the tables to the company's range of products, she asks you to check some details with the manufacturer, Top Tables.

Work with a partner. Partner A: Look here. Partner B: Look at File 21 on page 146.

You work for Marx Kitchens. Call Top Tables to check the details of the product and the terms of delivery. Use the Purchasing Manager's notes on the right.

Top Tables, presentation, 22 Feb.

Aluminium kitchen tables
Size Large – 1000 x 755
Price €1,000, EXW
Terms of payment: 1/3 with order, 2/3 30 days after delivery
Customer discount: 5%
Delivery to be made immediately on receipt of order

› *Useful phrases: Clarifying details on the phone, page 195*

Checking information on the phone

A: We can deliver everything by Thursday.
B: Thursday. **Right**.
A: My address is 23 Fairfield Gardens.
B: **Sorry. Did you say** 23 or 33?

A: My number is 0171 452869. (Can you just read that back to me?)
B: I'll just read that back to you. 0171 452869.

DAS KANN ICH (Unit 9)

- Ein Kaufangebot an eine/n Kaufinteressent/in auf Englisch schreiben. (Foundation)
- Die Details eines Angebots per E-Mail auf Englisch bestätigen. (Part A)
- Verschiedene Angebote vergleichen und eine Kaufempfehlung schreiben. (Part B)
- Die Details einer Bestellung mit einem Kunden / einer Kundin auf Englisch klären. (Communication)

10 An order

FOUNDATION: Introduction to a contract of sale

Situation: You work in the Sales department of Michelsen Teekontor GmbH, a tea importer in Bremen. One of your duties is preparing contracts of sale in English using a template.
→ **You check a standard English contract for a new customer.**

1 Understanding a contract of sale

Your line manager asks you to put together a contract of sale for a new customer in Ireland.

A Match the German paragraph headings from the list on the right with their English equivalents (1–10) in the checklist.

Contract of sale checklist

1 Sale of goods
2 Purchase price
3 Terms of payment
4 Seller's representations
5 Delivery of goods / Shipping
6 Refund and cancellation policy
7 Force majeure
8 Representations
9 General
10 Termination of contract

Angaben des Verkäufers • Allgemeine Bedingungen • Darstellungen • Einkaufspreis • höhere Gewalt • Lieferbedingungen/Versand • Rückvergütung und Stornierungsbedingungen • Vertragsbeendigung • Warenverkauf • Zahlungsbedingungen

B Match the extracts from an English contract (a–j) with the German translations (1–10) on page 99.

a Each Party promises the other Party that it has the authority to enter into this Contract and to perform all of its obligations under this Contract.

b If one of the Parties chooses to end the Agreement prior to product delivery, the Buyer is responsible for paying for all work and costs incurred up until that date.

c ... the Buyer shall pay for and accept from the Seller the "Goods" listed at such prices as agreed by the Parties in this Agreement.

d ... the Buyer shall pay to the Seller the purchase price of €... .

e The Buyer will be assumed to have accepted the Goods unconditionally unless a claim that a Good is defective is made within ... days from the date of delivery.

f The Party whose performance has been interrupted by such circumstances shall use every reasonable means to resume full performance of this Agreement as promptly as possible.

g The Seller assumes responsibility for the Goods, and all risk of damage, loss, or delay of the Goods, until the Goods are delivered to or collected by the Buyer.

h The Seller has full right, power, and authority to sell the Goods.

i To change anything in this Contract, the Buyer and the Seller must agree to the change in writing and sign a document showing their Contract.

j Unless otherwise stated, payment for the Goods is due within … days of the date of the Seller's invoice.

1 Alle Vertragsänderungen müssen vom Käufer und Verkäufer schriftlich und durch Unterzeichnen des Vertrags vereinbart werden.
2 Der Käufer ist willens, die Güter vorbehaltlos zu akzeptieren, es sei denn, dass innerhalb von … Tagen nach Lieferung eine Reklamation erfolgt, dass eine Ware mangelhaft ist.
3 Der Käufer wird dem Verkäufer den Kaufpreis in Höhe von € … entrichten.
4 Der Käufer wird die vom Verkäufer angeführten „Güter" zu den Preisen bezahlen und akzeptieren, die von den Vertragsparteien in diesem Vertrag vereinbart wurden.
5 Der Verkäufer hat vollumfänglich das Recht, die Macht und die Autorität, die Güter zu verkaufen.
6 Der Verkäufer übernimmt die Verantwortung für die Güter sowie alle Risiken durch Beschädigung, Verlust oder Verspätung der Güter bis zu dem Zeitpunkt, zu dem die Güter dem Käufer geliefert oder von ihm abgeholt wurden.
7 Die Vertragspartei, deren Leistungsdurchführung durch solche Umstände unterbrochen wurde, wird jede angemessene Maßnahme ergreifen, die volle Durchführung dieses Vertrags so schnell wie möglich fortzusetzen.
8 Falls eine der Parteien beschließt, die Vereinbarung vor Produktlieferung zu beenden, ist der Käufer verantwortlich für die Bezahlung aller bis zu diesem Datum angefallenen Arbeiten und Kosten.
9 Soweit nicht anderweitig vereinbart, ist die Bezahlung der Güter innerhalb von … Tagen nach Rechnungsdatum fällig.
10 Jede Vertragspartei sichert der anderen Partei zu, dass sie befugt ist, den Vertrag zu schließen und sämtliche Verpflichtungen zu erfüllen, die sich aus diesem Vertrag ergeben.

C **Find the English equivalents of the underlined words in the German translations.**

D **Now match the extracts (a–j) to the paragraph headings in the contract of sale checklist (page 98).**

2 A contract for a new customer

Michelsen Teekontor GmbH has prepared a contract for a new customer, Fine Teas Ltd, in Dublin. Your line manager asks you to check it.

Each of the following statements about the contract is wrong. Correct the statements.

1 If the contract is cancelled before the goods are delivered, Michelsen has to pay for everything that has been done up to the date of cancellation.
2 Fine Teas has to accept the goods and pay the price for them that Michelsen has decided.
3 As soon as the goods have been delivered, Fine Teas must send a written statement to Michelsen saying that the goods have been accepted. If Fine Teas does not do this, Michelsen will believe that Fine Teas has rejected the consignment.
4 Fine Teas Ltd has to carry all the risks during transport of the goods to their premises.
5 Fine Teas Ltd must pay for the goods by cash before they are dispatched.

PART A: Placing and acknowledging orders

Situation: You work in the Purchasing department at MegaKauf Großhandel GmbH in Dusseldorf. Your company sells fair-trade leather goods made in Pakistan. As the goods are selling well, you now want to place large orders regularly.
→ You negotiate terms with a supplier, then place an order for goods.

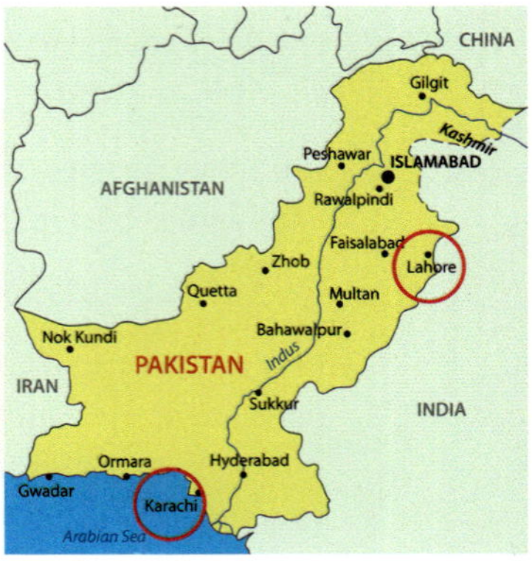

1 Reviewing current terms

Study the last order that your colleague, Sven Maier, placed with A.P. Leather International in Lahore, Pakistan.

To: nasir.mahmood@ap-leather.com.pk **16 December 20..**
From: sven.maier@mkg.de
Subject: Order for leather garments **Attachment(s):**

Dear Mr Mahmood

Having seen your offer on the internet and spoken to you on the telephone, we now wish to place an order for the following goods:

Quantity	Description	Article no.	Unit price	Total
100	Men's fashion jacket	MFJ-303	US$30.00	US$3,000.00
100	Men's fashion pants	MFF-304	US$25.00	US$2,500.00
100	Ladies' fashion jacket	LFJ-603	US$25.00	US$2,500.00
100	Ladies' fashion pants	LFP-604	US$20.00	US$2,000.00
			Total price	**US$10,000.00**

Terms of delivery: EXW Lahore, Pakistan within 30 days after receipt of order
Terms of payment: 25% with order, 75% before loading by transfer to your a/c at Allied Bank Limited
Packing: Container, *LCL, palletized

Transport and insurance of the goods from Lahore to Dusseldorf via the ports of Karachi and Bremen will be arranged by us.

We look forward to receiving your confirmation of order and advice of dispatch in the near future and trust the goods will arrive punctually and in good condition.

Yours sincerely

Sven Maier
Purchasing Department

MegaKauf Großhandel GmbH
Oberkasseler Str. 200, 40545 Düsseldorf, Germany

*LCL = less than a container load. See diagram page 101.

Work with a partner and discuss how the terms of delivery and payment could be improved and any other changes that could be made in MegaKauf's favour. Discuss your ideas with the class.

2 Negotiating better terms

Your colleague, Sven Maier, phones Nasir Mahmood at A.P. Leather International to negotiate better terms and to place an order.

A **41 Listen to the dialogue and note down the following information:**

- the terms of the last order
- the terms that MegaKauf want
- the terms agreed
- the validity of the new agreement

B **Has Sven Maier negotiated the new terms you expected?**

20' General Purpose Container
Capacity: 33.2 m³ / 1,172 ft³
Max. payload: 30,250 kg / 66,578 lbs
FCL: full container load
LCL: less than a container load (groupage consignment)

Symbols and abbreviations

'	foot (*pl* feet)	m³	cubic metre(s)
"	inch(es)	ft³	cubic foot (*pl* feet)
kg	kilo(s)	lb(s)	pound(s)

› *Conversion tables, page 204*

3 Acknowledging an order

The Pakistani supplier confirms the new terms, but when they send their acknowledgement of MegaKauf's next order, some of the details are wrong.

Study the email and compare it with your notes from exercise 2A. Find the three errors in the email.

To: sven.maier@mkg.de
From: nasir.mahmood@ap-leather.com.pk
Subject: Confirmation of your order no. FWL 68D for 6,000 leather garments dated 02 January 20..

Dear Mr Maier

We are pleased to confirm the above-mentioned order for delivery FCA Lahore, (FCL or LCL) 30 days after receipt of order, payment of USD150,000.00 to be made 1/3 with order, 1/3 on delivery and 1/3 30 days after delivery.

We look forward to doing further business with you.

Yours sincerely

Nasir Mahmood
Export Sales Director
A.P. Leather International

4 Structuring an order

An order usually covers some or all of the points in the checklist.

A **Use words from the list below to translate the orders checklist (1–8) into German.**

Angaben über die bestellten Waren / Dienstleistungen · Anlage(n)/Anhang/Anhänge · Bestätigung / Versandanzeige · Bezug auf Angebot · höfliche Schlussformel · Internationale Handelsklausel · Liefertermin/-zeit · Lieferung · Preis(e) und Rabatt(e) · Verpackung · Versand · Versicherung · Zahlung

› *Useful phrases: Writing orders, page 195*

Orders checklist

1 reference to offer
2 details of goods/services ordered
3 price(s) and discount(s)
4 delivery
  - Incoterm
  - delivery date/period
  - transport
  - packing
  - insurance
5 payment
6 acknowledgement / advice of dispatch
7 polite ending
8 enclosure(s) (*letter*) / attachment(s) (*email*)

B **Choose 12 of the 16 headings in the list to complete the order below.**

article no. · cash discount · delivery · description · insurance · packing · payment · quantity · quantity discount · size · subtotal · total · total price · trade discount · transport · unit price

___1	___2	___3	___4	___5
100	HQ printer	HQ3000	€60.00	€6,000.00
250	Quickchip laptop	QC99	€100.00	€25,000.00
			– 30% ___6	– €9,300.00
			___7	€21,700.00
			+ 20% *VAT	€4,340.00
			___8	**€26,040.00**

___9: DAP buyer's premises by 30 June 20..
___10: Sturdy cartons
___11: 2% 10 days, 30 days net after receipt of invoice
___12: By road

*value added tax = *Mehrwertsteuer*

Infobox

Structuring an order or acknowledgement
If you are writing about **two or more** items, use a table with headings (see exercise 4B) to make your order easy to understand. If you are only writing about **one** item, just use headings:

Article:	Ladies' fashion jacket
Article no.:	GPS3000
Quantity:	100
List price:	€25.00

Writing prices

Currency symbol first
No space
Comma where there is a point in German
Point where there is a comma in German

€10,500.50

5 Placing an order

Your line manager in the Purchasing department asks you to place an order for terracotta tiles with Ceramica Lombardia, a manufacturer of tiles in Perugia, Italy. You phone them, then send a written order.

A **Work with a partner. Partner A: Look at File 17 on page 144. Partner B: Look at File 15 on page 142.**

B **Now place your order (see exercise 5A) in writing. Include the following points in your order:**

- heutiges Datum
- Ansprechpartner/in: Herr Antonio / Frau Arianna Rossetti (a.rossetti@ceramica-lombardi.it), in der Verkaufsabteilung
- Bezug auf Telefongespräch
- Bestellung unsererseits mit Auftrags-Nr. VBIT97 von 500 m^2 Terracotta Fliesen vom Typ TCT90, Stückpreis 25,00 € pro qm und 500 m^2 Terracotta Fliesen vom Typ BIT75, Stückpreis 20,00 € pro qm
- Lieferbedingungen: CPT Düsseldorf auf Paletten, volle Containerladung, per Lkw innerhalb von 30 Tagen nach Auftragseingang
- Versicherung von Perugia nach Düsseldorf wird von uns übernommen
- Zahlungsbedingungen: Barzahlung bei Auftragserteilung
- Bitte um Auftragsbestätigung und Versandanzeige
- Hoffnung auf pünktliche Lieferung der Ware in gutem Zustand
- Aussicht auf weitere Aufträge, wenn die Ware sich gut verkauft
- höfliche Schlussformel

› *Useful phrases: Writing orders, page 195*

PART B: Shipping an order

Situation: You work in the Export Sales department of Brewery-2-Brewery GmbH in Gelsenkirchen. Your company has received an order for microbrewing equipment from Harpoon Brew Supply Inc. in Bedford, Massachusetts, USA.

→ You fill in an application form for a documentary letter of credit.

1 Reviewing shipping documents

First you look at an overview of the documents typically needed for an international transaction.

Document	German	Features
1 Bill of lading (B/L) – sea transport	Konnossement	– document of title (negotiable – ownership is transferable) – receipt for the goods – contract of carriage – 'clean' if the goods are in apparent good order and condition – 'foul' if the goods are not in apparent good order and condition
2 Air waybill – air transport	Luftfrachtbrief	– not a document of title (non-negotiable – ownership is not transferable) – receipt for the goods – contract of carriage
3 Consignment note – rail or road transport	Frachtbrief	– not a document of title (non-negotiable – ownership is not transferable) – receipt for the goods – contract of carriage
4 CMR document / truck waybill	Lastwagen-frachtbrief	– not a document of title (non-negotiable – ownership is not transferable) – receipt for the goods – contract of carriage – printed in three languages
5 Multi-modal B/L – sea, air, rail or road transport	multimodales Konnossement	– can be a document of title (negotiable or non-negotiable) – receipt for the goods – contract of carriage
6 Insurance certificate	Versicherungs-schein	– proves that the goods are insured – used in a documentary credit transaction
7 Certificate of origin	Ursprungs-zeugnis	– shows where the goods are from – issued by a chamber of commerce in the exporter's country – used to assess customs duties
8 Commercial invoice	Handels-rechnung	– request for payment – shows the price the buyer has to pay for the goods
9 Pro-forma invoice	Proforma-Rechnung	– not a request for payment – shows how much the buyer will have to pay for the goods
10 Packing list	Packliste	– contains details of the goods (number of packages, weights, dimensions)
11 Bill of exchange (draft)	Wechsel (Tratte)	– the buyer can pay by accepting or paying a bill of exchange

Study the list of documents on page 103 and complete the following sentences with the correct answer.

1 If the bill of lading is 'clean', the goods … .
  a are not dirty **b** show no sign of damage **c** are perfect in every way

2 Ownership of the goods can be transferred by selling … .
  a the bill of lading **b** the air waybill **c** the consignment note

3 An air waybill, a consignment note, a CMR document and a bill of lading have … .
  a one feature in common **b** two features in common **c** three features in common

4 When several modes of transport are combined, goods are sent using … .
  a one transport document **b** separate transport documents **c** a consignment note

5 The amount of customs duty to be paid when goods are imported is calculated using … .
  a the insurance certificate **b** the packing list **c** the certificate of origin

6 The pro-forma invoice shows how much a product … .
  a cost **b** costs **c** will cost

7 The packing list shows … .
  a the price and value of the goods **b** the size and weight of the goods **c** the quality of the goods

8 A bill of exchange is … .
  a a contract of carriage **b** a receipt for the goods **c** an instrument of payment

2 Presenting the right documents

Harpoon Brew Supply Inc. agrees to pay by irrevocable and confirmed documentary letter of credit (L/C) opened by the buyer at their bank in the US, payable to the seller at their bank in Germany.

A Read the application form on the opposite page and answer the questions.

1 What is the name of the buyer?
2 What is the name of the seller?
3 What is the name of the buyer's bank?
4 What is the name of the seller's bank?
5 When is the deadline for presentation of the shipping documents to the seller's bank?
6 What currency is the price stated in?
7 How do we know that the load cannot be split into parts or loaded from one ship to another?
8 What are the ports of shipment and destination?
9 What is the Incoterm and the port of destination for this shipment?
10 What documents must Brewery-2-Brewery GmbH present to their bank in order to receive payment?

B Find the English equivalents of the following German words and expressions in parts 1–10 of the letter of credit application form. They are in the same order.

1 Auftraggeber/in
2 eröffnen
3 unwiderruflich
4 avisierende Bank
5 zugunsten
6 Begünstigte/r
7 gültig bis
8 eine Tratte ziehen
9 Teillieferung
10 Umladung

Bank of Massachusetts

Application and Agreement for Commercial Letter of Credit

TO: Bank of Massachusetts, N.A. ("Bank of Massachusetts")

A. Application — File No. FGBGT 98

1. Applicant Name & Address (guarantor for Letter of Credit) requests Bank of Massachusetts to issue an irrevocable letter of credit as follows ☑ Full text teletransmission ☐ Courier

Harpoon Brew Supply Inc., 44 Crosby Drive
Bedford, MA 01730, USA

2. Advising Bank Name & Address: (if left blank, the Bank of Massachusetts Banking Center will be used)

Deutsche Bank, Von-Oven-Straße 12–16,
45879 Gelsenkirchen, Germany

3. For Account of Party / Named Applicant on the Letter of Credit (Name & Address, if different from Applicant):

4. In favor of (Beneficiary Name & Address):

Brewery-2-Brewery GmbH
Karl-Meyer-Straße 100, 45884 Gelsenkirchen, Germany

5. Expiration Date. Drafts to be drawn on and presented to the negotiating or paying bank on or before:

March 31, 20..

6. Amount: (EUR72,000.00) seventy-two thousand and 00/00

Put in figures and words. For example: ($10,000) Ten thousand and 00/00

Currency: EUR ▾ ____________ (if left blank, U.S. dollars) **Tolerance** 0% ▾

7. Covering: 100 **% of invoice value.** (Full invoice value unless otherwise specified.)

8. Available by drafts: ☑ Sight ☐ ____ Days Sight ☐ ____ Days Date (being the date of the transport document)
Drafts to be drawn on Bank of Massachusetts or Bank of Massachusetts' correspondent, at Bank of Massachusetts' option.

9. Partial Shipment: ☐ Permitted ☑ Not Permitted

10. Transshipment: (Not applicable to Air Shipments or Multimodal Transport Shipments.) ☐ Permitted ☑ Not Permitted

11. Transferable Letter of Credit? ☐ Yes ☑ No

12. Shipment/Dispatch/Taking in Charge From/At	Latest shipment Date	For Transportation To	Final Destination
North Sea port	March 31, 20..	Port of Boston, MA	Bedford MA, USA

13. Merchandise to be described in invoice as (omit unnecessary details and specify price basis below):
Complete Microbrewery 1000 liters per brew 2-vessel brewhouse in stainless steel

14. Shipping Terms / Price Basis (check one): ☐ FCA ☐ FOB ☑ CFR ☐ CIF ☐ Other: BLANK ▾

15. Documents Required (check applicable boxes below):
☑ Commercial Invoice in 3 original(s) and 3 copies.
☑ Packing List in 3 original(s) and 3 copies.
☑ Certificate of Origin in 3 original(s) and 3 copies.
☑ Negotiable Marine/Air Insurance Policy or Certificate for at least 110% invoice value in duplicate, effected by ☑ Buyer ☐ Seller
Including coverage for: ☐ War Risk ☑ All Risks ☐ Other Risks (specify):
☑ Transport Documents: ☑ Marine B/L ☐ Multimodal B/L ☐ Air Waybill ☐ Truck B/L ____ Other
Presented in: ☑ Full Set ☐ 2/3 ☐ 1/3 ____ Copy
Consigned to / the order of ____ (if left blank, consigned to applicant)
Marked Notify Applicant
Marked Freight: ☐ collect ☑ prepaid
☐ Other documents:

16. Special Instructions to be included in the Letter of Credit (unless otherwise stated):
All bank charges (other than those of Bank of Massachusetts) are for the account of the Beneficiary. Discount charges, if any, are for the account of the Beneficiary. All documents are to be sent by the negotiating/paying bank to Bank of Massachusetts in one cover by courier or registered mail.
☐ Other instructions:

17. Special Instructions to Bank of Massachusetts:

18. Documents must be presented to the negotiating or paying bank no later than: 21 days after date of transport document (on board validation applicable for ocean shipment) but within the validity of the Letter of Credit. (Will be 21 days if left blank.)

☑ If this box is marked, Applicant authorizes Bank of Massachusetts to effect payment of any sums due under this Application and Agreement by means of debiting Applicant's account with Bank of Massachusetts set forth below. This authorization does not affect the obligation of Applicant to pay such sums when due, if there are insufficient funds in such account to make such payment when due, or if Bank of Massachusetts fails to debit the account, and this authorization does not affect any setoff rights of Bank of Massachusetts at law or in equity. Applicant's account number with Bank of Massachusetts is 7340001524 .

3 Understanding the terms of an L/C

Harpoon Brew Supply Inc. now has a problem with the order and contacts Brewery-2-Brewery GmbH to request a change of plan.

A 42 **Listen to the telephone dialogue between your colleague, Louisa Schneider, in Gelsenkirchen and Kevin King of Harpoon Brew Supply Inc. Note down the following information:**

- the buyer's problem
- what the buyer wishes Brewery-2-Brewery to do to solve the problem
- the changes that Brewery-2-Brewery can make under the terms of the L/C
- the financial consequences of the buyer's problem for Brewery-2-Brewery
- the solution suggested by Brewery-2-Brewery

B **Louisa Schneider expects that Kevin King will need help transferring the microbrewery to its new destination, so she asks you to write an email to Nancy Kline, Brewery-2-Brewery GmbH's agent in New York, to explain the situation. Describe the buyer's problem and explain what can and can't be done to help him.**

To: n.kline@brewery-2-brewery-usa.com
From: name.surname@brewery-2-brewery-de.com
Subject: Harpoon Brew Supply Inc.

Hi Nancy

Thanks for your email. This is the background to Kevin King's request ...

› *Useful phrases: Writing emails, page 189*

4 Shipping goods

Kevin King asks Nancy Kline in New York to help him ship the microbrewery to its new destination, so she contacts Lopez Catering in Philadelphia to discuss arrangements. She then calls Kevin King back and explains the details to him.

A 43 **Listen to their telephone conversation and decide if the following statements are true or false. Correct the false statements.**

1. Lopez Catering has agreed to buy the microbrewery.
2. The microbrewery is now at the port of Boston.
3. All the financial formalities have been dealt with.
4. The microbrewery will be finally unloaded at the port of Philadelphia.
5. Nancy Kline suggests sending the goods by road.
6. The microbrewery is packed in six containers.
7. It would take about a week to transport the goods from Boston to Pennsylvania by sea.
8. Nancy Kline will send Kevin King a contract for him to sign.

B 43)) **Listen again and complete the sentences with the words you hear.**

1 Kevin: You mean you can ___ it?
2 Nancy: You now need to get on to your bank and transfer ___ to Lopez Catering.
3 Nancy: The buyer pays for ___ at the port of destination.
4 Nancy: Then the goods will have to be ___ at the port of Boston.
5 Kevin: Would it not be easiest just to send the ___ from Boston to Philadelphia by ship?
6 Nancy: ___ is not allowed.
7 Nancy: But that's without ___ and you would still need to have the containers picked up.
8 Kevin: Well, as Lopez Catering wants ___ delivery, that sounds like the best option.
9 Nancy: It would cost $2,160 for delivery ___.
10 Kevin: What's the delivery time ___ ?
11 Nancy: That's the freight ___ I would recommend.
12 Nancy: They will send you a contract of ___.

C **List the terms of delivery (Incoterms) mentioned in the recording then explain why the term chosen is most suitable in this case.**

› *Incoterms, page 183*

VIDEO 8

Watch the video to see more about orders and shipment.

5 Applying for a letter of credit

Brewery-2-Brewery GmbH has received an order for a microbrewery from a new Irish chain of restaurants called The Dining Experience with its headquarters in Cork. Payment has been agreed by irrevocable and confirmed documentary letter of credit, to be opened through an Irish bank. Today you receive a phone call from Megan Connolly in Cork. She asks you to help her fill in the application form because she has never done this before and does not want to make any mistakes. She emails you the form from the Commercial Credit Bank and you enter the necessary data for her.

Use the following information to complete the application form for the letter of credit (see File 16 on page 143).

Auftraggeber ist The Dining Experience, 22 Shandon Street, Clarke's Bridge, Cork T23 V2TO, Irland (Sachbearbeiter/in: Ms Megan Connolly, Tel. +353 21 429 5555, Fax +353 21 429 6666). Begünstigter ist Brewery-2-Brewery GmbH, Karl-Meyer-Straße 100, 45884 Gelsenkirchen, Germany (Sachbearbeiter/in: Ms Louisa Schneider, Tel. +49 209 177 8253, Fax +49 209 177 8254).

Das Akkreditiv lautet über 55.000,00 EUR +/– 0 % und ist bis 31. März 20.. gültig. Das Akkreditiv soll durch die avisierende Bank bestätigt werden, wobei sämtliche Gebühren zu Lasten des Auftraggebers gehen.

Die Sendung wird in Gelsenkirchen übernommen und zum Hafen Cork gebracht. Teillieferungen und Umladungen sind nicht erlaubt. Letztes Verladedatum ist 10. März 20.. und die Lieferbedingungen sind CIF Cork.
Bei den einzureichenden Dokumenten handelt es sich um die Handelsrechnung und drei Kopien; Packliste und drei Kopien; Ursprungszeugnis, das den deutschen Ursprung der Ware bestätigt; voller Satz reiner Bordkonnossemente mit dem Vermerk „Fracht bezahlt"; Versicherungszertifikat für den vollen CIF-Wert der Sendung zzgl. 10 %.
Die Sendung besteht aus sechs Holzkisten (*wooden crates*) mit Brauereiausrüstung.

› *Incoterms, page 183; Terms of payment, page 185*
› *Thematic vocabulary: Shipping documents, page 203*

COMMUNICATION: Enquiries, offers and orders

Situation: You work at MedEquip GmbH, a Berlin-based wholesaler of medical supplies and equipment for hospitals and clinics.
→ You write an enquiry and an order to a supplier; you send an offer to a customer.

1 Checking language for enquiries

You check that you know suitable English phrases for writing a letter of enquiry.

Match the phrases and sentences from a German letter of enquiry (a–i) to the English equivalents (1–9).

> **TIP**
> You will find similar phrases in the model letter on page 85.

- **a** Wir haben Ihre Anzeige … gesehen.
- **b** Wir sind ein/eine … in Deutschland.
- **c** Wir haben vor, …
- **d** Wir interessieren uns …
- **e** Wir möchten eine Probebestellung … aufgeben.
- **f** Wenn die Dienstleistungen Ihrer Firma unsere Voraussetzungen erfüllen, …
- **g** Bitte nennen Sie uns Einzelheiten …
- **h** Die … Bank wird Ihnen gerne Referenzen zukommen lassen.
- **i** Wir freuen uns, bald von Ihnen zu hören.

1. If the product is suitable …
2. … *(name of bank)* will be happy to supply references.
3. Please let us have details …
4. We are a … *(type of firm)* in Germany.
5. We are interested in …
6. We are planning …
7. We have seen your advertisement …
8. We look forward to hearing from you soon.
9. We would like to place a trial order …

2 Writing an enquiry for medical monitors

MedEquip GmbH is looking for a new supplier of operating theatre monitors. Jan Dube, the Purchasing Manager, asks you to write a letter of enquiry to a manufacturer in Scotland. Before you write the letter, you make some notes in English.

Write a letter of enquiry to MML using the notes below. Add today's date and your own reference numbers. Remember to use the correct salutation, subject line and complimentary close.

› *Useful phrases: Writing enquiries, page 192*
› *Thematic vocabulary: Business transactions, page 203*

> **TIP**
> The letter on page 85 will help you with the layout and address.

Enquiry to MML – Medical Monitors Ltd, Unit 5, Silverbank Industrial Estate, Ferry Road, Edinburgh EH4 2EF, United Kingdom – details from their website

- *who we are; what we do*
- *expanding our range of operating theatre monitors*
- *trial order for one 32" OT-HD monitor*
- *confirmation that monitor is completely sealed, dustproof and waterproof (DIN-Norm EN60601)?*
- *further orders if trial order satisfactory*
- *terms of delivery / payment?*
- *reference: Triodod Bank, Berlin*
- *look forward to early reply*
- *cc: Jan Dube*

3 Writing an offer for wheelchairs

The Sales Manager took a call from a customer in Ireland today. She gives you her notes and asks you to write an offer in reply.

Anruf: Ms Helen O'Meara, Administrator, Toll Road Hospital, Dublin 4J, Irland
Anfrage: E-Chair BP075 (battery-powered wheelchair)
Menge: 10
Lieferbedingungen: DAP Dublin
Zahlungsbedingung: 1/3 bei Bestellung, 2/3 bei Lieferung
Lieferzeit: 2 Wochen nach Bestellung
Preis: 2.320,00 EUR / Rollstuhl
Mengenrabatt: 2,0 %
Katalog und aktuelle Preisliste

Read the notes then write the offer using the prompts below.

- thank customer for the enquiry (today's date)
- thank her for interest in your products
- confirm details of product and price
- state terms of delivery and payment
- enclose price list and catalogue as requested
- express hope that you will hear from her soon

› *Useful phrases: Writing offers, page 194*

4 Writing an order for an operating theatre monitor

Neil McCain, the Sales Manager of Medical Monitors Ltd in Edinburgh, replies to your enquiry (see exercise 2). Jan Dube, your Purchasing Manager, is happy with the offer and asks you to write the order.

Write the complete order using Jan Dube's notes and a suitable complimentary close.

› *Useful phrases: Writing orders, page 195*

- *Mr McCain für Angebot danken*
- *Bestellung: ein 32" OT-HD OP-Saal Bildschirm*
- *Bestätigung des Preises: £ 2700,00*
- *Bestätigung der Lieferbedingungen: DAP Berlin*
- *Zahlungsbedingung: CWO*
- *Aussicht auf weitere Bestellungen*
- *höfliche Schlussformel*

DAS KANN ICH (Unit 10)

- Einen englischen Kundenvertrag verstehen und überprüfen. (Foundation)
- Verbesserte Bedingungen aushandeln und eine Bestellung aufgeben. (Part A)
- Ein Antragsformular für ein Akkreditiv auf Englisch ausfüllen. (Part B)
- Eine Anfrage, ein Angebot und eine Bestellung auf Englisch verfassen. (Communication)

KMK Exam practice 5

1 **Leseverstehen: Stufe II**

Situation: Sie arbeiten für eine internationale Firma in Frankfurt, die auch eine Niederlassung in York hat. Die Geschäftsleitung plant Weiterbildungskurse für die englischen Mitarbeiter/innen und hat bereits eine Schulungsakademie vor Ort ausgewählt. Die Frage, wie man die Kurse anbieten will, ist noch nicht geklärt. Ihr Abteilungsleiter hat Sie nun beauftragt, die zwei Kursarten zu vergleichen.

Aufgabe: Lesen Sie die Kursbeschreibungen. Kopieren und vervollständigen Sie anschließend die Tabelle soweit wie möglich.

Individual training

No matter what level you are at, our courses will give you the skills and expertise you need to gain a competitive advantage in the challenging and complex world of export, import and international trade. We evaluate your personal level and start from there, thus guaranteeing the best progress.

- Courses cover a wide range of international trade topics
- Three levels of learning: Introductory, Operational, Management
- One-to-one teaching
- Small classes of no more than 5 people possible – but not from the same company
- Taught in evening classes by quality-assured experts in the subject matter
- Individual work pace
- Focus on yourself, your needs and your goals, work with maximum concentration
- Costs: £75 per 90-minute session
- Costs may be partially tax-deductible

In-house training

Companies are increasingly seeking in-house training because of its flexibility, convenience and cost-effectiveness. Choosing the right training provider is the key to helping your employees and organization achieve their goals and receiving a strong return on your investment.

- Convenience – as courses are timed to suit your required dates
- Less disruption to work schedules, adaptable to work shifts
- Tailor-made for company needs
- Recognized as tax-deductible
- All skill levels possible, heterogeneous groups are given customized solutions
- Value for money – charges are per event rather than per person (30–35 people in a course), approx. £650
- Time savings – all the work involved in designing the training activity
- Comfort and relaxation among familiar colleagues
- Strengthens teams within company

Aspekt	Einzelschulung	Inhouse-Training
Inhalte/Themen?		
Größe der Lerngruppen?		
Lernniveaus?		
Kosten?		
Wann finden die Kurse statt?		
Qualifikation der Trainer/innen?		
Wie werden die Kurse zusammengestellt?		
Gibt es steuerliche Abschreibungsmöglichkeiten?		
Vorteile in sozialer Hinsicht?		

2 Produktion: Stufe II

Situation: Ihre Firma entschließt sich für ein Inhouse-Training. Dabei sollen die nachfolgenden Aspekte geklärt werden.

Aufgabe: Verfassen Sie eine E-Mail-Anfrage unter Berücksichtigung der folgenden Punkte:

- Zeitraum: Oktober oder November nächsten Jahres
- Themen müssen noch genau mit Geschäftsleitung abgesprochen werden, zwecks Terminabsprache bitte Herrn Fischer telefonisch kontaktieren (0353-1-477184)
- Etwa 60 Teilnehmer/innen in zwei Gruppen
- Einstufungstest vorab möglich? Dann Gruppen eventuell nach Leistungsstand aufteilen
- Kurse sollen nachmittags liegen, allerdings nicht montags und freitags
- Samstag möglich? Extrakosten?
- Welche räumliche Ausstattung muss die Firma bereitstellen?

3 Hörverstehen: Stufe II

Situation: Sie machen ein Praktikum bei einem englischen Großhändler für Zubehör von Motorrädern und Fahrrädern. Für die einzulagernden Waren ist das firmeneigene Außenlager an seine Kapazitätsgrenzen gestoßen. Sie sind dem Lagerleiter zugeteilt und sollen Lösungsmöglichkeiten erarbeiten. In diesem Zusammenhang stellt Ihnen ihr Kollege Tom telefonisch seine Rechercheergebnisse dar.

44 **Aufgabe: Hören Sie sich das Gespräch an und machen Sie sich Notizen im Formular.**

	Lager 1	Lager 2
Lage		
Platz/Kapazität		
Kosten		
Verfügbarkeit		
Zusätzliche Informationen		
Kontaktdaten		

11 Problems and complaints

FOUNDATION: Making and dealing with complaints

Situation: You work for Kelvin Kitchen Appliances Ltd, a UK wholesaler of kitchen appliances. The company has had a lot of complaints recently and has lost some customers as a result.
→ **You explain to a new German trainee how to handle complaints properly.**

1 Different ways to complain

You talk to other apprentices about different reasons for complaining.

Work in groups. Describe the last time you made a complaint to a company. What was the problem? How did you make your complaint? What did you do? How did the company react?

2 Making suggestions for improving service

Your line manager has put together a diagram showing the types of complaints the company has received in the last three months. She sends round a memo asking for suggestions how to make improvements.

In the last three months, we have had a lot of complaints about our deliveries (see pie chart).

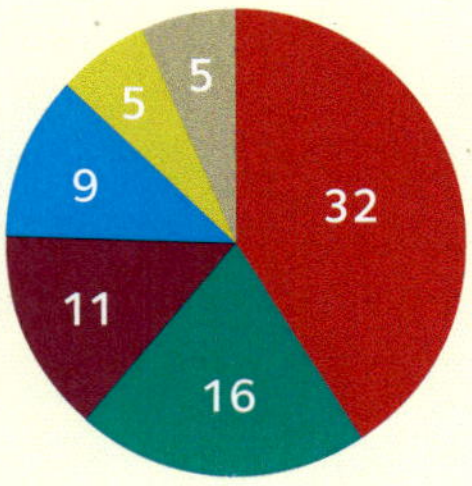

- late delivery
- mistake in the invoice
- parts of delivery missing
- wrong (or no) paperwork included
- goods damaged on arrival
- wrong goods delivered

These numbers are far too high and we have lost customers. If we can't improve our service, we will lose more. The only way to keep our customers satisfied is to make sure that our products arrive in good condition and on time.

Please send us your feedback on why these things have happened and your suggestions how we might avoid them in future.

A **Talk in groups about what the pie chart shows. Compare and contrast the findings.**

B **Discuss who or what might be responsible for each of the problems. Say how things might be improved. Use your ideas to write a short memo for your supervisor.**

Comparing figures

The majority of complaints were (about) …
… made up …% of the complaints.
There were **fewer** complaints about …
The **fewest** complaints related to …
… is/was **the same as** … / **higher/lower than** …

› *Grammar: Comparatives and superlatives, page 157*

3 Making a complaint

Sometimes Kelvin Kitchen Appliances have problems with consignments from their suppliers. Your line manager describes two ways to make complaints.

45 **Listen and complete the notes your line manager has made for her talk.**

Making a telephone complaint	*Making a complaint in writing*
1 *Before you make the call:* ___	5 *Start:* ___
2 *The start of the call:* ___	6 *Body of the letter:* ___
3 *During the call:* ___	7 *Suggestions:* ___
4 *Follow up:* ___	8 *Conclusion:* ___

4 Mediation: Complaint management

Your line manager wants to make sure that a new trainee from Germany knows the company's policy on dealing with complaints.

Read the text and make a German summary of the most important points for the new trainee.

Taking customer complaints seriously

In a recent study on customer satisfaction carried out by *Business Matters* magazine, people were asked to say what they had expected and what they experienced when making complaints. The results might give some companies a lot to think about.

At the top of the list of expectations, with 93% of the interviewees stating that these things were important to them, were:
1) an acknowledgement of the complaint, and
2) the wish to be taken seriously.

As far as the first expectation was concerned, 81% of the people who took part in the survey said that they had received an acknowledgement. As for being taken seriously, however, only 5% felt that the person who took their complaint listened to them and showed them respect. Similarly, over 67% of complainants expected someone to get back to them, but only 5% were contacted as promised.

65% of the customers who completed the survey expected an apology for the inconvenience they had been caused, but only 35% actually received one. Thanks for bringing the problem to the attention of the company was given in only 25% of the cases.

Saying thank you is cheap. Reimbursement, which was expected by 17.5% of the customers who complained, was given in only 10% of the cases, while other forms of compensation were only given in 2.5% of the cases. 40% of the complainants registered no satisfactory response.

What should companies learn from this survey? Customers who complain expect to be acknowledged and taken seriously; they would like an apology for their inconvenience and a thank you for pointing out the problem. Reimbursement or compensation of some sort came low on the list of complainants' expectations and, not every complainant was reimbursed. In 40% of the cases, there was no satisfactory response. Is it any wonder that companies lose customers?

Make sure that you don't disappoint your customers and drive them away. Take complaints seriously, apologize for the mistake and make sure that you do what you promise to do.

› *Thematic vocabulary, Complaints, page 204*

PART A: A complaint about faulty goods

Situation: You work in the Purchasing department of MegaKauf Großhandel GmbH. Several months ago, you bought a consignment of smoke alarms from Safety First Ltd, an Irish manufacturer, but have since received complaints from several of the retailers who bought them.

→ **You complain to a manufacturer and respond to a customer's complaint.**

1 Writing a complaint

Your colleague, Tamara Beck, has written to the Sales Director of Safety First Ltd in Dublin.

To:	fiona.murphy@safety-first-ltd.ie <Fiona Murphy, Sales Director>
From:	tamara.beck@mkg.de
Subject:	Order no. VBF900 for 5,000 EW1 smoke alarms dated 12 May 20.. — Attachment(s): photos_smoke_alarm.gif

Dear Ms Murphy

The above-mentioned smoke alarms were delivered on 12 June 20.. and forwarded to various customers all over Europe.

When they opened the boxes, they discovered that some were without batteries and mounting screws and others did not work when tested and were discoloured.

We enclose photographs of these items for your information.

Please explain why our order was so poorly executed.

Whatever the case may be, you will appreciate that we cannot sell these articles and must therefore ask you to replace the entire consignment, as these goods are needed urgently.

We feel sure you will understand that our future business relationship will depend on how this matter is dealt with.

We expect to hear from you in the very near future.

Yours sincerely
Tamara Beck

Purchasing Department
MegaKauf Großhandel GmbH
Oberkasseler Str. 200, 40545 Düsseldorf, Germany

Read MegaKauf's complaint and match the sentence halves.

1 MegaKauf bought the smoke alarms from …
2 MegaKauf sold the smoke alarms to …
3 The retailers discovered that …
4 The colour of some of the alarms …
5 Tamara Beck wants …
6 Megakauf wants the manufacturer to …
7 Megakauf will only place further orders …
8 Tamara Beck expects the manufacturer …

a had also changed.
b an explanation from the manufacturer.
c retailers in different European countries.
d if a satisfactory solution is found.
e some alarms were incomplete and/or faulty.
f to deal with the matter immediately.
g replace all the smoke alarms.
h an Irish manufacturer called Safey First Ltd.

2 Structuring a complaint

Most complaints have a similar structure.

Use words from the list on the right to translate the complaints checklist (1–7) into German.

Complaints checklist

1 Reference to goods
2 Description of problem
3 Request for explanation
4 Consequences for the buyer and seller
5 Request for action
6 Polite ending
7 Enclosure(s) (*letter*) / Attachment(s) (*email*)

Anlage(n)/Anhang/Anhänge · Bitte um Ergreifung geeigneter Maßnahmen · Bitte um Erklärung · Bezug auf Waren · Darstellung des Problems · Folgen für Käufer und Verkäufer · höfliche Schlussformel

› *Useful phrases: Making complaints, page 196*

3 Dealing with a telephone complaint

Tamara Beck receives a phone call from Gunner Kristoffersen in the Purchasing department of a Danish DIY chain that bought a consignment of EW1 smoke alarms from MegaKauf.

A 46 **Listen to the dialogue and note down the following information.**

1 warranty
2 guarantee
3 terms of payment
4 what the retailer wants
5 possible consequences for Megakauf
6 deadline set by the retailer for a solution

Infobox

Warranty and guarantee

German law distinguishes between **warranty** (*Gewährleistung*) and **guarantee** (*Garantie*). Goods bought in Germany come with a statutory warranty period of 24 months, during which the seller must rectify any defects. If a defect is noticed during the first six months, it is assumed that the goods were faulty at the time of purchase unless the seller can prove the opposite. If a defect is noticed later, the buyer must prove that the goods were faulty at the time of purchase. Under German law, a guarantee is an additional, voluntary promise made by the seller or manufacturer, e.g. to replace or repair a machine during and/or after the warranty period. A guarantee cannot replace the 24-month warranty period. It is usually offered by the manufacturer.

B 46 **Listen to the dialogue again and complete the sentences with the words you hear.**

1 Gunner: We're extremely ___ with the smoke alarms.
2 Gunner: Some of the alarms are ___, meaning that they don't work when tested.
3 Gunner: Others are ___, and in some of the boxes, the batteries and mounting screws are ___.
4 Gunner: And let me point out that the alarms are still ___ warranty …
5 Tamara: We're ___ sorry to hear that, Mr Kristoffersen.
6 Tamara: I ___ you we'll find a solution as soon as possible.
7 Tamara: I ___ understand, Mr Kristoffersen.
8 Gunner: We expect you to replace the whole consignment free of ___.
9 Gunner: If we don't get replacements, we'll return the whole consignment carriage ___ and ___ all future orders.

C **Find the phrases in exercise 3B to match the German expressions below.**

1 in der Gewährleistungszeit
2 Ich versichere Ihnen
3 Ich habe volles Verständnis dafür
4 unfrei
5 äußerst unzufrieden
6 verfärbt
7 kostenlos
8 fehlerhaft

VIDEO 9

Watch the video to see more about complaints.

4 Replying to a written complaint

Your boss, Hannah Schmidt, responds to the Danish DIY chain's complaint by email.

A Arrange the parts of her email (A–H) in the correct order.

A Yours sincerely

B We look forward to doing further business with you.

C Since hearing from you, we have contacted the manufacturer and discovered that there was an error in their Quality Control department.

D Replacements for the faulty appliances will be delivered to you carriage paid within 48 hours.

E I hope this solution will find your approval and would ask you to accept our apologies for the inconvenience caused.

F I have just been informed of your phone call regarding the above-mentioned consignment of smoke alarms and am dismayed to hear that the goods are unsatisfactory.

G Hannah Schmidt
Purchasing Director
MegaKauf Großhandel GmbH

H Dear Mr Kristoffersen

B Find two ways of saying sorry or expressing regret (*Bedauern*) in the email.

› *Useful phrases: Responding to complaints, page 197*

5 Complaining and responding to a complaint

MegaKauf Großhandel GmbH recently bought some microwave ovens from a Swedish manufacturer, Scantech AB, Stortorget 95, 25114 Helsingborg, Sweden, and sold them on to a number of retailers all over Europe. However, you are now receiving complaints about the poor quality of the goods.

A Write a letter or an email on behalf of your Purchasing Director, Ms Hannah Schmidt, to Mr Patrik Berglund (p.berglund@scantech-ab.se), the Export Director at Scantech AB. Include the following points:

- heutiges Datum
- Bezug auf Auftrag Nr. GBST12 über 1.000 Mikrowellenherde Typ MW 99 von vor drei Monaten
- Ware vor zwei Monaten erhalten und Einzelhändlern überall in Europa zugestellt
- inzwischen mehr als ein Dutzend Beschwerden von unzufriedenen Kunden eingegangen (siehe Anlagen)
- Geräte unzuverlässig, denn Lebensmittel oft nur halb gar
- Bitte um Erklärung
- unfreie Rücksendung der Geräte an den Hersteller
- nachdrücklicher Hinweis auf umgehenden kostenlosen Ersatz, da Geräte noch in der Gewährleistungszeit
- unverzügliche Bearbeitung der Angelegenheit erwartet
- Fortsetzung der Geschäftsbeziehung von der Regelung der Beschwerde abhängig
- höfliche Schlussformel

› *Useful phrases: Making complaints, page 196*

B Work with a partner. Partner A and Partner B: Look at File 19 on page 145.

PART B: A complaint about a quarterly statement

Situation: You work in the Accounting department at MegaKauf Großhandel GmbH. Your company's terms of payment with Sligo Potteries, an Irish supplier of tableware, are open account terms with quarterly settlement.

→ You clarify some discrepancies in a quarterly statement with the supplier and ask for the statement to be corrected.

1 Checking terms and prices

On March 20, MegaKauf notices a special offer for crockery on the Irish supplier's website and immediately orders 50 dinner services and 50 teapots together with some other items.

A **Study the special offer and work out the total price of the crockery ordered.**

B **At the beginning of April, MegaKauf receives the following statement for the first quarter, but there are some discrepancies. Check the statement and find the three errors.**

Sligo Potteries Ltd — 200 Jinks Ave, Abbeyquarter North, Sligo, F91 X5EH, Ireland

Statement no. MK9031 — **Date** 31 March 20..

Date	Quantity	Description	Article no.	Unit price (€)	Total (€)
9 Jan 20..	10	Galway steak knife set	SN75	30.00	300.00
26 Feb 20..	25	Abbey cutlery set	CS250	100.00	2,500.00
20 Mar 20..	50	Shamrock dinner service	SDS100	95.00	4,750.00
20 Mar 20..	50	Shamrock teapot	STP50	18.00	900.00
20 Mar 20..	10	Sláinte champagne flute	CF 22	5.00	50.00
				Total	**8,500.00**

C **How much has MegaKauf been overcharged by?**

2 Writing about payment

Most emails and letters about payment have a similar structure.

Payments checklist (buyer)

1 Reference to invoice/statement
2 Reference to payment of invoice/statement, as appropriate
3 Reference to discrepancies/errors/amendments, as appropriate
4 Polite ending
5 Enclosure(s) (*letter*) / Attachment(s) (*email*)

Anlagen(n)/Anhang/Anhänge · Bezug auf Begleichung der Rechnung/Abrechnung · Bezug auf Rechnung/Abrechnung · höfliche Schlussformel · Bezug auf Unstimmigkeiten/Irrtümer/Änderungen

Use words from the list to translate the payments checklist (1–5) into German.

3 Querying a statement

Your colleague, Rita Ronstadt, in the Accounting department at MegaKauf contacts the supplier about the statement.

To:	rory.kelly@sligo-potteries.ie <Sales Director>		
From:	rita.ronstadt@mkg.de		
Subject:	Your statement no. MK9037_Q1 dated 31 March 20..	Attachment(s)	MK9037_Q1.pdf

Dear Mr Kelly

Thank you for the above-mentioned statement for goods received last quarter.

Having checked it against our own records, we must point out that you have not included our credit note for €498 dated 15 January 20.. . In addition, the 50 Shamrock tea services and teapots in your clearance sale have been incorrectly charged and you have also omitted to include the special discount of 25% granted on orders for 50 items or more.

You have therefore overcharged us by a total of €2,210.50.

We are returning your statement and would request you to amend it. As soon as we have received the new statement we will remit the sum owing.

Please do not hesitate to contact us should you have any queries.

Best regards
Rita Ronstadt

Accounting Department
MegaKauf Großhandel GmbH

A Find the English equivalents of the following German terms in the email.

1 berichtigen
2 Aufzeichnungen
3 belastet
4 Fragen
5 gewährt
6 Gutschrift
7 (mit etw) abgeglichen
8 überweisen
9 versäumt
10 zu viel berechnet

B Use information in the email to answer the following questions.

1 What period of time does the statement cover?
2 How many errors are there in the statement?
3 Which company is owed €498?
4 What must a customer do to qualify for a clearance sale quantity discount?
5 What action does MegaKauf want Sligo Potteries to take after receiving this email?
6 How much less does MegaKauf expect to pay?

4 Clarifying a statement

Sligo Potteries contact MegaKauf to explain the statement.

A 47 **Listen to the telephone conversation between Rory Kelly and Rita Ronstadt and write notes to explain the following:**

- the procedure for including a credit note with an order
- why the Shamrock crockery was wrongly charged
- the solution suggested by the Irish supplier

B Use your notes to explain what went wrong to a partner.

› *Grammar: Simple past, page 154; Reported speech, page 157*

C 47 **Listen to the telephone conversation again and complete the sentences with the words you hear.**

1 Sorry about the ___ with the prices and so on, but ...
2 The €498 was for goods ___ to us last year, ...
3 That meant we would ___ €498 from your next order.
4 ... so that's why it was ___ from your statement.
5 I've ___ that as well and I've found out what went wrong.
6 ... the Shamrock line sells well over here, so we ordered ___.
7 You didn't click the button on the website to ___ your order and get your special price ___.
8 ... our software was programmed to ___ the reduction on all orders placed via the button on the website.
9 I'll send you an email with a special link to your ___.
10 I'm glad we were able to ___ it all out.

5 Responding to a query

Rory Kelly emails Rita Ronstadt straight away.

Use your answers to exercise 4C to complete his email. Make any necessary changes.

Dear Ms Ronstadt

As promised in our phone call just now about our statement for the last quarter, I have ___[1] the matter and ___[2] out the ___[3]. A credit note for goods that you ___[4] to us last year was ___[5] and some items were also wrongly charged, meaning that all in all you were overcharged by a total of €2,210.50.

Please therefore use the following link to access your ___[6] and ___[7] your order for Shamrock crockery again, including the code for the credit note that you received from us last year.

http://www.sligo-potteries/ie/account_amend?token=8e4a666

Our accounting system will then automatically ___[8] you a 25% ___[9] on the crockery and ___[10] €498 from the total amount of the statement for the last quarter.

An amended statement will then be sent to you ___[11] for payment.

We apologize for the inconvenience and look forward to doing further business with you.

Best regards

6 Dealing with discrepancies

When checking recent invoices and statements, you find some discrepancies and then deal with them.

A **Work with a partner.** Partner A: **Look at File 20 on page 146.** Partner B: **Look at File 23 on page 148.**

B **When checking the statement for the last quarter sent to MegaKauf by a Scottish supplier of skiing equipment (Winter Gear Ltd, 222 Grampian Road, Aviemore PH22 1RH, UK), you notice some discrepancies. Write a letter or an email to the supplier to query the statement.**

- Datum: 5. April 20..
- Ansprechpartnerin: Ms Sheena Murray (E-Mail: s.murray@wintergear.org), Accounts Director
- Bezug auf Abrechnung Nr. GBST/375 vom 2. April 20.. über € 31.550,00
- falscher Nachlass bei Positionen 1 und 2 für Skischuhe (*skiing boots*), nur 15 % statt der versprochenen 50 % gewährt
- Gutschrift Nr. RBM/6 vom ... (15. des vergangenen Monats) über € 185,00 nicht berücksichtigt
- falsch berechnete Abrechnung liegt bei
- Bitte um berichtigte Abrechnung über € 25.065,00
- Überweisung des entsprechenden Betrags nach Erhalt der korrigierten Abrechnung
- höfliche Schlussformel

› *Useful phrases: Making complaints, page 196*

COMMUNICATION: A telephone complaint

Situation: You work at MedEquip GmbH, a Berlin-based wholesaler of medical supplies and equipment.
→ **You deal with a telephone complaint.**

1 Dealing with complaints on the telephone

Your line manager gives you a list of English phrases for dealing with complaints and tells you to keep it by the phone in case English-speaking customers call.

Match the headings (1–5) to the phrases (a–j). There are at least two phrases for every heading. Some phrases match more than one heading.

1 Apologizing
2 Asking for information
3 Reacting to information
4 Action
5 Ending the call

› *Useful phrases: Responding to complaints, page 197*

a Can I just check with you that I've understood everything?
b Could you tell me what it's about, please?
c Could you give me the order number, please?
d I'll have a replacement sent out as soon as possible.
e I'm sorry to hear that.
f Is there anything else I can do for you today?
g Just a moment while I write that down.
h Oh, no. That doesn't sound at all good.
i Thank you for your call. Once again, I'm sorry that there was a problem.
j We're prepared to replace the goods at our expense.

2 Dealing politely with customers

A new customer, Jerzy Adamczyk, calls to complain about a trial order of operating theatre monitors. Your colleague, Melissa Wolf, takes the call. She is not very polite.

A 48 **Listen to the phone call and decide how you would improve it. Make a list.**

B 49 **Now listen to how Melissa should have dealt with the phone call with Jerzy Adamczyk. Which (if any) of your improvements does she make?**

TIP

Making / Dealing with complaints on the phone
Give your name clearly at the start of the call and write down the name of the person you are speaking to immediately. If necessary, check the spelling of the name.

3 Complaining to a supplier

MedEquip GmbH ships many orders in special containers made by Sheffield Metal, a company in England. The latest consignment has not arrived, so your line manager phones to complain about the delay in delivery. Jeanette Hogg answers the phone.

A **Look at the phrases (a–h) below and decide who says what – the caller or the person taking the call. (There are four phrases for each speaker.)**

a delivery was promised
b How can I help you?
c I will do my best
d it's an order for
e the exact details
f the order number?
g to enquire about my order
h We can't fulfil our orders

B **When you have finished, match the phrases (a–h) with the gaps (1–8) in the text to complete the transcript of the phone call.**

Jeanette Good morning. Sheffield Metal, Sales Department. Jeannette Hogg speaking.
Max Good morning. This is Max Jahn from MedEquip in Germany.
Jeanette Good morning, Mr Jahn. ___[1]
Max I'm calling ___[2] for containers for medical equipment. The order was sent almost one month ago, on 18 April, and ___[3] by 3 May but, so far, nothing has arrived.
Jeanette Oh. I'm sorry to hear that. Could you give me ___[4]
Max Yes. It's DF54736.
Jeanette DF54736. Just a moment, please. I'll check. I'm sorry, Mr Jahn. I don't seem to have any record of your order. Can I just check that I've understood everything? The order number is DF54736 and you ordered the containers on 18 April. Could you give me ___[5] of the order, please?
Max Yes, ___[6] your aluminium containers for medical equipment.
Jeanette Aluminium containers for medical equipment. Mr Jahn, I'll have to speak to my colleague to find out what the problem is. Can I get back to you later?
Max Well, yes. But I hope it won't take long. ___[7] until we have your containers.
Jeanette Yes. I realize that, Mr Jahn. I'm very sorry about this and ___[8] to get back to you as soon as possible.
Max Many thanks for your help, Ms Hogg.

C **50 Now listen and check your answers.**

4 Role-play: Dealing with a telephone complaint

Now you make and deal with a telephone complaint.

A **Work with a partner.** Partner A: **Look here.** Partner B: **Look at File 18 on page 144.**

Partner A
You work for MedEquip GmbH in Berlin. You take a call from a customer in the UK who makes a complaint. Before you begin, prepare a sheet for taking notes as follows:

- Date
- Name of customer, company
- Order number of goods
- Date of delivery
- Nature of the complaint
- What you agree with the caller

While you are waiting for Partner B to call, check that you know how to deal with complaints in English (exercises 1 and 2).

› *Useful phrases: Telephoning, page 187; Responding to complaints, page 197*

B **When you have finished the phone call, change roles and do it again using different details.**

C **When you have played both parts, write up the notes you made as Partner A as a memo for your supervisor.**

DAS KANN ICH (Unit 11)

- Einem Kollegen / Einer Kollegin die wichtigsten Punkte eines englischen Textes auf Deutsch erklären. (Foundation)
- Sich bei einem Hersteller beschweren; auf eine Beschwerde auf Englisch antworten. (Part A)
- Ungereimtheiten bei einer Abrechnung auf Englisch aufklären. (Part B)
- Mit telefonischen Beschwerden auf Englisch richtig umgehen. (Communication)

12 A job application

FOUNDATION: Where do I go from here?

Situation: You are nearing the end of your course and are thinking about applying for a work placement abroad. You start to think about what you have learned in your apprenticeship and where you might work when you have qualified.

→ **You write a description of your apprenticeship for a European job agency.**

1 Listening to newly-qualified trainees

You listen to an interview with three newly-qualified trainees. They are talking about the jobs they do and where they would like to find a permanent position.

Customer services specialist

Marketing assistant

Office management assistant

A 51 **Listen and say what the speakers liked best about their apprenticeship.**

1 Who enjoyed learning from experienced people?
2 Who liked the mixture of going to vocational college and doing practical work?
3 Who enjoyed going to meetings?

B 51 **Listen again and complete the table with the missing information.**

Name	What I do at work	I'd like to …
Maren	*respond to customers' ___ [1] and guide them through the ___ [2]*	___ [3]
Garry	*analyse ___ [4] and write ___ [5], help with ___ [6]*	___ [7] *and become* ___ [8]
Delon	*support ___ [9]* *anything from writing ___ [10] to organizing ___ [11]*	___ [12] *where I can* ___ [13]

2 Thinking about your skills

You think about the skills you have learned during your apprenticeship.

A What do you enjoy most about your apprenticeship? What skills are you learning? How do you learn and develop these skills. First make notes on your own.

B Now talk to a partner about the skills you are learning.

C Now compare your ideas with another pair and make a list of the skills you are all learning, for example, working with spreadsheets, keying in data, etc. (Keep this list; you will need it for Part A).

Talking about skills; thinking about possibilities

I **can** analyse customer feedback and sales data.
I'**m able to** work on my own.
They **might be able to** get a job in the UK.
You **could** look for work in the financial sector.

› *Grammar: Modals and their substitutes, page 158*

D Report your ideas to the class. In class, make a list in English of the different job titles in your field, e.g. wholesale assistant. How can you use the skills you are learning in your preferred area of work?

3 Doing internet research

You search the internet for job opportunities in Europe.

A Work with a partner. Do internet research to find suitable career prospects in Europe. Make a poster, webpage or PowerPoint presentation showing job offers and companies in your sector. Present your ideas to the class.

B If you make posters, pin them to the wall and do a gallery walk. Rank the posters using the categories below. Give points from 1–5 for each category.

headline · design · photos/pictures · content · overall effect

4 Reading about the Europass

While you are doing your research online, you come across the European Skills Passport (Europass). You decide to use it to collect your own personal details for applications and your CV.

Download the Europass and start to complete it with your details. (Your teacher has the correct URL.)

INFO

The European Skills Passport (Europass)

This is a standardized CV and language document that can be created online or on your own computer. Potential employers throughout Europe can clearly see your skills and qualifications.

The following sections might be of particular interest to you:

- **Language Passport** – a self-assessment tool for language skills and qualifications;
- **Europass Mobility** – a record of skills acquired during a learning experience in a European country;
- **Certificate Supplement** – a description of skills acquired by holders of vocational training certificates.

5 Describing your apprenticeship

You have contacted an EU job agency asking for help in looking for work experience in Europe. The agent for Germany asks you to write a short description of your apprenticeship in English for the agency file.

Write a short description of your apprenticeship. Before you begin, think about the aspects you should include, e.g. type of training, skills you learned, qualifications you gained, and make notes.

PART A: Applying for a job abroad

Situation: The company you work for is interested in taking on trainees from other countries.
→ **You write a job advertisement in English for the position you are leaving.**

1 Finding a job

Before you write the advertisement, you think about how you got started in your current position.

Work in groups. Talk to colleagues about how you got started in your job. Make notes and report back to the class.

Where did you find out about your job?

How did you apply for the job?

What qualifications did you have when you applied?

2 Two interesting jobs

Your line manager would like to place an advertisement for your position on an international recruitment agency website. You check the website to get ideas for your advertisement.

Study the two advertisements on page 125. What details in them can you use when you write the advertisement for your job? Think about the following aspects:

- the type of employer
- what the company is looking for
- what the requirements are
- what the company offers
- how to apply

www.international-recruitment.com/training/office

Trainee Export Clerk

International freight forwarding company, Hamburg, Germany

As an export clerk, you will prepare airline waybills, complete export customs entries and classify goods. You will also deal with general administrative work, including invoicing and correspondence.

Requirements:
- min. school leaving certificate
- basic knowledge of MS Office, Excel and Outlook
- fluent German and English and one other language

You should have good written skills and good communication skills.
You should also be a quick learner.

Training period: 3 years, dual system, day release at vocational college 2 days a week

Possibility of being taken on full-time after completing your training.

Please submit your application with Ref. number TExCl_14387 here

www.international-recruitment.com/training/office

Trainee Customer Services Specialist in Industry

Manufacturing company, Essen, Germany

Your training in the workplace includes dealing with enquiries, offers and orders, advising customers and doing market research. You will also prepare and take part in visits to trade fairs and exhibitions.

Requirements:
- a recognized school leaving certificate
- good mathematical skills
- fluent German and English

You should be an accurate worker and be able to work without supervision.
Training takes place over 36 months, including six weeks' block release twice a year.
In the workplace, you will receive continuous support from experienced employees.
Opportunities for follow-up education and promotion within the company.

Please submit your application with Ref. number TCsSp_10732 here.

3 Writing an advertisement for the recruitment agency website

Now you write the advertisement for your current position for the recruitment website.

A **Begin with the job title and the training location, then include information about what the successful candidate will do, etc.**

B **When you have finished, pin your advertisement on the wall and do a gallery walk. Which advert describes your apprenticeship most accurately? Which one sounds like an interesting option for prospective trainees?**

› *Useful phrases: Describing jobs and responsibilities, page 186*

PART B: Interviews

Situation: You have been shortlisted for a position as a German-speaking customer sales representative with a British company.
→ **You prepare for and practise a telephone interview and a face-to-face interview.**

1 Choosing the right candidate

Jennifer Winters, Head of Human Resources at the British company Trade International plc, carries out telephone interviews with candidates who have applied for the job of customer sales representative.

A **52 Listen to the interviews and copy and complete the table below.**

	Interview 1	Interview 2	Interview 3
Name			
Present employer			
Strengths			
Weaknesses			
Why this job?			
Future plans			
Own questions			

B **Discuss the interviews and say which of them were good or bad examples. What did the candidates do right/wrong? Which of the three candidates is the best role model for your own telephone interview?**

2 Preparing for a telephone interview

To further prepare yourself for your telephone interview, you read these tips.

Read the text and note down in German the most important tips for your telephone interview.

TIPS FOR YOUR TELEPHONE OR SKYPE INTERVIEW

Be prepared!
- Before the interview you should gather a copy of the job description along with a copy of your letter of application, your CV and your references, and write a list of questions you want to ask the interviewer and a list of your strengths.
- Pin these documents to the wall so that you can check them during the call without having to flick through piles of paper.

On the day of the call
- Place a notebook and a couple of pens beside the phone so you can take notes during the interview.
- Make sure the room you are in is quiet.
- If it is a telephone interview, use a landline where possible. If you have to use your mobile phone, make sure it is fully charged and that you take the call in a place where reception is good.
- If it is a Skype interview, dress as you would for a face-to-face interview so that you make a good impression. Remember to check that the microphone and video camera on your computer are working before the interview.

During the call
- Concentrate and stay focused. Listen carefully and reply to the interviewer appropriately.
- Be professional and polite. At the end of the call, you can ask, "Do my qualifications meet the company's needs?" However the interview goes, always end with "Thank you for your call." The last few words of a conversation are often the ones that people remember, so always leave a good impression at the end.

3 Role-play: Practising a telephone interview

You and a colleague decide to practise a telephone interview together.

Asking for clarification on the telephone

I'm sorry, could you say that again?
So, if I understand you correctly, …
I don't quite understand what you mean by …

› *Useful phrases: Telephoning, page 187*

A Work with a partner.

Partner A: You are the interviewer. Look at File 24 on page 148.
Partner B: You are an applicant for the position. Look at File 14 on page 142.

B With your partner, prepare a dialogue and role-play a telephone interview.

4 Preparing for a face-to-face interview

You listen to a podcast in which an expert gives tips on how to handle face-to-face job interviews.

A What is the expert likely to say? With a partner, brainstorm a list of expressions you might hear and make notes under the headings below.

Here are a few expressions from the podcast to start you off.

VIDEO 10

Watch the video to see more about interviews.

Stage 1: Greetings and introductions
arrive at the interview on time

Stage 2: Small talk
talk about the weather

Stage 3: The main part of the interview
talk about yourself

Stage 4: Questions from the candidate
do background research into the company before the interview

Stage 5: Further arrangements and the end of the interview
ask when you can expect to hear from the company again

B 53 Now listen and check. How many of your expressions did you hear?

5 Practising for an interview

You and your colleague decide to practise the main part of an interview together.

A First of all, study the list of common interview questions (File 22 on page 147) and how to answer them.

B Work with a partner.

Partner A: Choose one of the job advertisements you read in Part A (page 125) and tell your partner which one you have chosen. Think about the questions the interviewer might ask and how you might answer. Make notes.

Partner B: Study the job advertisement your partner has chosen. Make a list of questions you might ask.

C When you are both ready, role-play the job interview. When you have finished, change roles if you wish.

COMMUNICATION: A CV and a covering letter

Situation: You find out online about the documents which you will need for job applications.
→ **You study an English CV and covering letter and write a job application.**

1 Reading a website about CVs

You find an interesting website with tips, but the headings have got mixed up.

Work with a partner. Read the tips (1–9) and match them to the headings (a–i).

a Education and training	**d** Personal details	**g** Work experience
b Hobbies and interests	**e** References	**h** Contact details
c Personal statement	**f** Key skills	**i** Further skills

www.internationalCVs_Technical

TIPS for writing your CV

International CVs

Your CV is a summary of your abilities, work experience, education and qualifications. There is no set format for a British CV but you should keep it short, using clear headings to guide the reader.

1 Give your name and address, telephone number(s) (home/mobile) and email address.

2 This should be a short message that grabs the attention of the reader. Use note form. This helps to keep your CV focused and direct, for example: *Motivated (wholesale) management assistant with experience in German trade industry.*

3 Here you can summarize your skills and experience which are relevant to the job you are applying for.

4 As a general rule, CVs should be in reverse chronological order, listing the most recent position first. For each position, you should provide the dates of the start and end of employment, the employer's name and address, the job title, the main duties and responsibilities and achievements.

5 Give a brief description of qualifications (school, academic and/or professional). Give the names of schools or colleges in reverse chronological order.

6 Here you should write about common skills gained throughout your education and work experience, such as languages, IT skills, good maths skills or a full, clean driving licence. These skills are of interest for any employer.

7 This feature is optional, but could provide something more personal to discuss at an interview. Be careful about what you write; a dangerous sport or *socializing with friends* may not be what an employer wants to hear!

8 Write your date of birth and nationality under this heading.

9 Due to data protection laws, candidates should not provide referees' names, addresses or any other contact details on CVs, but should state that details are available on request. Always ask your referees' permission before you give someone their contact details.

2 Analysing a CV

You also find an example of a British-style CV online.

Study the CV below. What differences can you find between this CV and a German CV?

MARTIN BIENEK
Am Kattenkamp 236, 33611 Bielefeld, Germany
Landline: (+49) 521 394677
Mobile: (+49) 176 3628419
Email: martin.bienek43@gmx.com

PERSONAL STATEMENT
Mobile and flexible apprentice management assistant in wholesale and foreign trade, in final year of 3-year course, seeking position abroad.

KEY SKILLS
Accountancy, Economics
Microsoft Word, Excel
Native speaker of German
Excellent spoken and written English
Good spoken and written Polish

WORK EXPERIENCE

June 20..	Assistant in information office, London Tourist Board Became skilled at dealing with enquiries and interacting with visitors from all over the world.
July 20..	4-week work placement at Metro AG, doing general office work

EDUCATION AND TRAINING

Since 20..	3-year apprenticeship at Vocational College, Bielefeld, Germany
June 20..	*Abitur* (Final examination similar to A-Levels) Main subjects: English, Computer Studies
20..–20..	Primary and secondary education in Bielefeld

FURTHER SKILLS
Full driving licence
First aid certificate

HOBBIES AND INTERESTS
Athletics, football
Training local junior football team

PERSONAL DETAILS
Date of birth: 06 April 20..
Nationality: German

REFERENCES
Available on request

3 Analysing a covering letter

Martin has applied for a job as a management assistant in wholesale and foreign trade at a food wholesaler in Ireland.

Read Martin's covering letter on the opposite page and match the parts (1–5) with explanations from the list.

- **a** asking the employer to invite you for an interview
- **b** reference to details on your CV
- **c** reference to the position
- **d** saying why the applicant is applying for the position
- **e** stating why the applicant is the best person for the job

4 Writing: An application for a job abroad

You find the following advertisement in a trade magazine and decide to apply for the position.

Prepare your CV and write your application.

German-speaking

Junior Management Assistant

in Export

Location: Dublin, Republic of Ireland
Salary: 21,000 euros to 23,000 euros depending on experience

Job description: duties include
- frequent contact with customers both face-to-face and on the phone
- taking orders, making offers and controlling dispatch of goods

We are looking for:
- relevant vocational school leaving certificate
- basic knowledge of MS Office
- fluent German and English

You should be:
- confident and personable
- keen to learn
- flexible

What we offer:
- an excellent working atmosphere
- optional language training courses
- good chances of promotion

Please submit your CV together with a covering letter to:
Ms O'Brien, Human Resources, 22 Grand Canal Harbour, Dublin 2, D02 A342

› *Useful phrases: Writing covering letters, page 199*

Am Kattenkamp 236, 33611 Bielefeld, Germany
Phone: (+49) 521 394677, Mobile: (+49) 176 3628419
Email: martin.bienek43@gmx.com

20 April 20..

Scott Traders Ltd
Silverbank Industrial Estate
DUBLIN
D11 D4E2
IRELAND

Attn. Mr Haig, Human Resources Director

Dear Mr Haig

Management assistant in wholesale and foreign trade

1 With reference to your advertisement Ref. No. 17673 on the internet, I would like to apply for the post described.

2 I am very interested in the job you are offering as I feel sure it will give me the opportunity to develop both personally and professionally. I am particularly keen to work in a position which allows me to apply my skills on a daily basis.

3 As you can see from the enclosed CV, by June of this year I will have completed the final year of a three-year apprenticeship at a Vocational Training College in Bielefeld, Germany. I will then be a fully-qualified management assistant in wholesale and foreign trade.

4 As I have practical skills and experience, am flexible and mobile and speak fluent English, German and Polish, I believe I will be a strong member of any team I join and will benefit your company.

5 My CV is enclosed and I am available for an interview at short notice.

I would very much appreciate it if you would consider my application and hope that you will grant me an interview.

I look forward to hearing from you soon.

Yours sincerely

M. Bienek

Martin Bienek

Encl.

DAS KANN ICH (Unit 12)

- Eine Beschreibung meiner Ausbildung auf Englisch verfassen. (Foundation)
- Eine Stellenanzeige auf Englisch schreiben. (Part A)
- Mich auf ein Bewerbungsgespräch auf Englisch gut vorbereiten. (Part B)
- Bewerbungsunterlagen auf Englisch richtig verfassen und gestalten. (Communication)

KMK Exam practice 6

1 Interaktion: Stufe III

Task: Work with partner. Use the role cards to role-play a telephone call between a wholesaler (Partner A) and a customer (Partner B).

Partner A

Situation: You work in the Purchasing department of Work & Business, a textile wholesaler. Last month you ordered overalls from a new supplier which were due last week but only arrived today. The warehouse has sent you a report saying that the delivery is not up to standard. Since you need the delivery for customer orders, the matter is quite urgent and you are not satisfied. With the help of the report and the order confirmation, you call the supplier to make a complaint and to find out what can be done.

Order confirmation: Miller Workwear

Order No. 245-9876-A34		
QTY	Product	price/unit
100	Overall 7010 green	38.14
500	Overall 9870 black	34.45
800	Overall EXTRA XD	47.89

Report from warehouse: Work & Business

Order No. 245-9876-A34 from Miller Workwear		
100	Overall 7020 green	*wrong article!*
400	Overall 9870 black	*100 items missing!*
800	Overall EXTRA XD	*see below*
Notes: *One box with the overalls arrived crushed, at least 50 overalls are therefore stained.*		

Partner B

Situation: You work for Miller Workwear, a manufacturer who specializes in the design and production of high quality workwear. You receive a call from a new customer who you really want to keep as a customer. Work & Business is a wholesaler for workwear and might order large quantities in the future. Unfortunately, there were some problems with the delivery. With the help of the order confirmation and the report from the shipping department below, you try to clarify things and to find a solution. Offer compensation when necessary.

Order confirmation

Order No. 245-9876-A34		
QTY	Product	price/unit
100	Overall 7010 green	38.14
500	Overall 9870 black	34.45
800	Overall EXTRA XD	47.89

Report from shipping department

Order No. 245-9876-A34 Delivery # FG78-II89
100 Overall 7020 green *Article No. has changed, identical with 7010* 400 Overall 9870 black *Couldn't send all, not enough in stock, additional delivery maybe in 3 days.* 800 Overall EXTRA XD *Everything OK*
Notes: *Got a call from forwarding agent, one parcel was accidentally damaged by driver. We should send invoice to the forwarding agent for damages.*

2 Produktion: Stufe III

Situation: Sie arbeiten für Biba-International in Reading. Ihre Firma hat eine Lieferung von Weckern in Eiform von Rosewater Ltd in Manchester erhalten. Aus der Warenannahme erhalten Sie untenstehendes Annahmeformular. Die Wecker werden dringend für einen wichtigen Kunden (Farstadt) für den Osterverkauf benötigt. Fragen Sie nach einer schnellen Lösung.

Aufgabe: Verfassen Sie einen Beschwerdebrief an Biba-International.

Ihre Adresse: 32 Industry Road, Reading, RG2 7PS
Ansprechpartner und Adresse von Rosewater Ltd: Mr John Rochester, Sales Manager, Rosewater Ltd, 11 Lower High St, Manchester, M3 3ER

<table>
<tr><td colspan="2">Order No: 45672</td><td colspan="2">Date of Order: 11/01/20..</td><td colspan="2">Delivery Note: 657/34</td></tr>
<tr><td colspan="2">Consignment received on: 13/03/20..</td><td colspan="2">Freight Forwarder: –</td><td colspan="2">Delivery provider: UPS</td></tr>
<tr><td colspan="2">Visual inspection: Parcel damaged on outside</td><td colspan="2">Possible reasons for outside damage: rough handling</td><td colspan="2">Inspected by: A.H.</td></tr>
<tr><td>Missing Items: –</td><td colspan="2">Surplus Items: –</td><td colspan="2">False Items: –</td><td>Broken Items: 8</td></tr>
<tr><td colspan="6">Short description: Glass dials of alarm clocks in parcel 2 (marked EasCL012) broken, all 8 clocks damaged</td></tr>
</table>

3 Produktion: Stufe III

Situation: Sie absolvieren Ihre Ausbildung in der Daimler Niederlassung in Hofheim und sind daran interessiert, ein Praktikum in der Zweigstelle in Abu Dhabi zu machen. Der Leiter der Exportabteilung unterstützt Ihr Vorhaben. Er bittet Sie, ein Bewerbungsanschreiben anzufertigen, welches er an die Personalleiterin international, Frau Julie McArthur, weiterleiten will. Nach Ihrem Gespräch mit ihm finden Sie am nächsten Tag eine Notiz auf Ihrem Schreibtisch.

Aufgabe: Fertigen Sie ein Bewerbungsanschreiben an.

Hallo,
nach unserem gestrigen Gespräch habe ich ein paar Tipps für Sie bezüglich Ihres Bewerbungsschreibens. Ihr Brief sollte Folgendes enthalten:

- *Bezug auf mich*
- *Gründe, warum Sie nach Abu Dhabi möchten*
  a) *beruflich: große Niederlassung; Möglichkeit, sich weiterzuentwickeln*
  b) *persönlich: Interesse an arabischen Ländern; Vater Bauingenieur / Familie hat einige Jahren im Oman gelebt*
- *Gründe, warum Sie für die Stelle geeignet sind (nennen Sie mindestens zwei „soft skills", Frau McArthur legt darauf sehr großen Wert)*

Vergessen Sie nicht, Ihr Schreiben angemessen und höflich zu beginnen und zu beenden!

Viel Glück!

P Partner files

FILE 1: Exam practice 1, exercise 3, Interaktion

Partner B

Sie sind Steve/Sue Mosley, ein englischer Praktikant / eine englische Praktikantin aus Manchester. Dort arbeiten Sie für ein großes Logistikzentrum (Wesley Logistics), welches europaweit beliefert. Ihre Firma plant auch in Deutschland und Frankreich Niederlassungen aufzubauen. Sie absolvieren ein sechsmonatiges Praktikum in Fulda bei der Firma Schmitt & Otte, die mit Sportartikeln aus den USA handelt. Heute ist Ihr erster Tag.

Gestalten Sie in Partnerarbeit einen Dialog mithilfe der folgenden Punkte:

- Machen Sie sich bekannt. Betreiben Sie Small Talk.
- Geben Sie Auskunft zu Ihrer Firma und nennen Sie Gründe, warum Sie nach Deutschland gekommen sind.
- Fragen Sie nach einer Kantine und wo Sie zuerst eingesetzt werden.
- Sie möchten wissen, wie das deutsche Ausbildungssystem funktioniert.
- Informieren Sie sich über Freizeitgestaltung und Aktivitäten am Wochenende.
- Schildern Sie Ihre derzeitige Unterbringung (weit außerhalb von Fulda, sehr einsam, schlechte Anbindung an Nahverkehr). Erkundigen Sie sich nach anderen Unterbringungsmöglichkeiten.

FILE 2: Unit 4, Communication, exercise 1C

Partner B

Dictate these email addresses to Partner A. Check A's answers.

1 beatrice-kuhn@berlin_tools.de
2 Hamish.MacPherson@net.uk
3 your own email address
4 the email address of your firm or another email address you often write to

FILE 3: Unit 7, Communication, exercise 4

Partner B

You are the hotel receptionist.

You begin the conversation. Greet the guest by name and ask how you can help.

You have the following information about hire cars:
- Hire car available through hotel. Hotel has 5% discount with Hertz. Small car, £50 a day, unlimited mileage.
- Insurance included, customer pays 15% ("excess") in case of accident.
- Pick up at hotel; return at Hertz counter, Heathrow.
- Payment is by credit card.

You need to know what time the guest needs the car and when it will be returned. Offer a receipt and wish the guest a pleasant day with the car.

FILE 4: Unit 6, Part A, exercise 4A

Partners C and D

Situation:
Brewery-2-Brewery is an American-owned company and has 20 employees in the office and 15 in the warehouse. At the last works council meeting, many employees were in favour of introducing flexitime. Today, there is a meeting between the American General Manager and the employees to discuss it. Attending the meeting are:

- the General Manager (Partner A)
- the Human Resources Manager (Partner B)
- the Works Council Representative (Partner C)
- an office worker (Partner D)
- a warehouse employee (Partner E)
- an apprentice wholesaler (Partner F)

	Office	Warehouse
Working hours	7.30 a.m. – 3.30 p.m.	Early shift: 6.00 a.m. – 2.00 p.m. Day shift: 10.00 a.m. – 6.00 p.m.
Break	9.30 a.m. – 9.45 a.m.	15 minutes taken flexibly
Lunch break	12.00 noon – 12.45 p.m.	

A **Use your role card below and the expressions in exercise 2B to conduct a meeting and come to a decision.**

Partner C: Works Council Representative

You are in favour of flexitime for the office staff because a lot of the employees need time, e.g. for their children, older relatives, visits to doctors, etc. You would like core time from 9.00 a.m. to 3.00 p.m. with flexible breaks. You don't think that flexitime is a good idea for the warehouse.

- introduce yourself
- explain that flexitime was suggested at the last works council meeting
- ask the other three employees to explain their position and then explain yours
- ask the HR manager a question (invent)

Partner D: office worker

You are married with two children (7 and 9). You would like to start work in the office after 8.00 a.m. after you have taken the children to school. Your husband is a lorry driver and leaves home at 5 a.m., so he can't help. When your children are ill, you also need to take them to the doctor's in the morning. You would be happy to make up for a late start by working later in the afternoons when your mother can help out with the children.

- introduce yourself
- explain your position
- ask the HR manager a question (invent)

FILE 5: Unit 6, Part A, exercise 4A

Partners E and F

Situation:

Brewery-2-Brewery is an American-owned company and has 20 employees in the office and 15 in the warehouse. At the last works council meeting, many employees were in favour of introducing flexitime. Today, there is a meeting between the American General Manager and the employees to discuss it. Attending the meeting are:

- the General Manager (Partner A)
- the Human Resources Manager (Partner B)
- the Works Council Representative (Partner C)
- an office worker (Partner D)
- a warehouse employee (Partner E)
- an apprentice wholesaler (Partner F)

	Office	Warehouse
Working hours	7.30 a.m. – 3.30 p.m.	Early shift: 6.00 a.m. – 2.00 p.m. Day shift: 10.00 a.m. – 6.00 p.m.
Break	9.30 a.m. – 9.45 a.m.	15 minutes taken flexibly
Lunch break	12.00 noon – 12.45 p.m.	

A **Use your role card below and the expressions in exercise 2B to conduct a meeting and come to a decision.**

Partner E: warehouse employee

Your priority is not to be on early shift (6.00 a.m. – 2.00 p.m.) for more than two weeks in a row. If flexitime can guarantee this, you will be in favour of it. You don't mind starting early or finishing late.

introduce yourself
- explain your position
- ask the HR manager a question (invent)

Partner F: apprentice wholesaler

You and a lot of other apprentices would like to have flexitime because if you stay out late one night, you can start later the next morning without getting into trouble. You don't like starting work at 6 a.m. but you don't mind working until 6.00 p.m.

- introduce yourself
- explain your position
- ask the HR manager a question (invent)

FILE 6: Unit 6, Part B, exercise 4

Partner A: Wholesaler (own name)

The company where you are doing your apprenticeship has heard of a new supplier of your best-selling product[1]. You have arranged a meeting with the supplier (Partner B) to discuss placing a small initial order.

[1]Choose from: bicycles • car radios • coffee machines • electric drills • kitchen chairs • rucksacks • suitcases • T-shirts • your own idea. Agree with Partner B what the product is.

Use the table below to negotiate an order covering the following points:

- **quantity:** you only wish to test a few customers' reactions to the product at the moment
- **discount:** try to get a discount, e.g. an initial order discount or an introductory discount
- **terms of payment:** you want the maximum time to pay
- **delivery period:** you would like the goods as soon as possible

Try to get as many points as possible, but do not show your partner your scoring system.

At the end of the negotiation, use the table to work out your score.

Wholesaler's score sheet			
Quantity[2]	**Discount**	**Terms of payment**	**Delivery period**
10 Score: 25 points	5% Score: 25 points	90 days Score: 25 points	2 days Score: 25 points
20 Score: 20 points	4% Score: 20 points	60 days Score: 20 points	7 days Score: 20 points
30 Score: 15 points	3% Score: 15 points	30 days Score: 15 points	30 days Score: 15 points
50 Score: 10 points	2% Score: 10 points	30% with order, 70% on delivery Score: 10 points	60 days Score: 10 points
100+ Score: 5 points	1% Score: 5 points	in advance Score: 5 points	90 days Score: 5 points

[2]Adapt the quantity to your product as appropriate, e.g. 100 bicycles, 1,000 T-shirts, etc.

Questions and negatives

Can you reduce the price? Yes, we **can**. / No, we **can't**.
Will you give a guarantee? Yes, we **will**. / No, we **won't**.
Do you accept the terms? Yes, we **do**. / No, we **don't**.

› *Grammar: Questions and short answers, page 154*

FILE 7: Unit 6, Part B, exercise 4

Partner B: Supplier (John/Joanne Taylor)

You are a salesman/woman for a company in Ireland that has been exporting its products[1] very successfully to a large number of customers for more than 20 years. You meet a new wholesaler (Partner A) to discuss the terms of a first order.

[1]Agree with Partner A what the product is.

Use the table below to negotiate an order covering the following points:

- **quantity:** try to sell as many as possible
- **discount:** your prices are already very competitive
- **terms of payment:** new customers normally pay CWO (cash with order)
- **delivery period:** the product is in great demand and your regular customers have priority

Try to get as many points as possible, but do not show your partner your scoring system.

At the end of the negotiation, use the table to work out your score.

Supplier's score sheet			
Quantity[2]	**Discount**	**Terms of payment**	**Delivery period**
100+ Score: 25 points	1% Score: 25 points	in advance Score: 25 points	90 days Score: 25 points
50 Score: 20 points	2% Score: 20 points	30% with order, 70% on delivery Score: 20 points	60 days Score: 20 points
30 Score: 15 points	3% Score: 15 points	30 days Score: 15 points	30 days Score: 15 points
20 Score: 10 points	4% Score: 10 points	60 days Score: 10 points	7 days Score: 10 points
10 Score: 5 points	5% Score: 5 points	90 days Score: 5 points	2 days Score: 5 points

[2]Adapt the quantity to your product as appropriate, e.g. 100 bicycles, 1,000 T-shirts, etc.

Questions and negatives

Can you reduce the price? Yes, we **can**. / No, we **can't**.
Will you give a guarantee? Yes, we **will**. / No, we **won't**.
Do you accept the terms? Yes, we **do**. / No, we **don't**.

› *Grammar: Questions and short answers, page 154*

FILE 8: Unit 6, Communication, exercise 4

Partner B

You are Jane Duncan, a business associate of Paul Smith.

Role-play a phone call with Paul Smith's assistant (Partner A). Use your itinerary to arrange a new time for a meeting with Paul.

ITINERARY – **Wed 25th – Sat 28th**			
Wed 25	Flight BA 8954 → Glasgow (arr. 13.40)	14.00 – 17.00 Fashion show	
Thur 26	~~7.00 – 9.30 Working breakfast: Paul Smith~~ 10.00 – 12.30 Presentation: New Styles	14.00 – 16.00 Meeting: Kirstie Adam, Fashion Futures	
Fri 27	9.15 – 12.45 Meet Gerry Maddox to discuss contract	Meeting: John King, 14.00 – 18.00	Buffet: Glasgow Retail Trade Association 19.00 – 22.30
Sat 28	Shopping	Flight BA 3627 13.15 → London	

› *Useful phrases: Making arrangements, page 192*

FILE 9: Unit 7, Part A, exercise 4B

Partner A

You work for Ökobau Müller GmbH.

Call O'Reilly's Catering Ltd (Partner B) and place an order for the on-stand event using the information on your role card.

- Stellen Sie sich vor (Vor- und Nachname, Firma) und beschreiben Sie kurz Ihr Anliegen (Ort, Uhrzeit).
- Geben Sie Ihre Wünsche für das Buffet an.
- Sie gehen von drei Stunden aus.
- Sie brauchen das Buffet nur einmal am 6. Oktober.
- Fragen Sie, wie viel das Buffet in etwa kosten wird.
- Das Buffet kostet mehr als erwartet. Fragen Sie, warum.
- Entscheiden Sie, ob Sie das Angebot annehmen oder nicht.
- Bitten Sie ggf. um ein schriftliches Angebot per E-Mail (name.surname@oekobau-mueller.de).
- Schließen Sie das Gespräch höflich ab.

FILE 10: Unit 7, Part A, exercise 4B

Partner B

You are Liam/Lauren Kelly of O'Reilly's Catering Ltd.

Partner A will call you to discuss an order for an event at a trade fair. Deal with Partner A's requests using the information on the role card.

- Answer the phone (company, first name).
- Ask for details: number of guests; snacks; drinks.
- Recommend the fork buffet (very popular, etc.).
- Ask how long the buffet is expected to last.
- Explain that there will be a service charge for the third hour.
- Ask how often the client wants the buffet.
- Work out the total price and add 5%.
- Explain that food and labour prices have risen by 5%.
- Send a written offer if requested.
- Finish the conversation politely.

FILE 11: KMK Exam practice 4, exercise 2, Interaktion

Partner B

You are the Sales Manager for a large foundry (= *Gießerei*) in Hungary. You have an appointment with a manager from Billing & Sons at an international trade fair. You arrive at their stand on time.

Role-play a conversation at the trade fair stand with Partner A. Be prepared to ask and answer questions. You have to use your imagination and make up possible answers. Use the ideas below to help you.

- Introduce yourself and say that you are expected, show understanding if you have to wait.
- Ask for a different refreshment and engage in small talk with the company representative.
- Show annoyance that nothing is happening.
- Accept one of the offers that the representative makes.

FILE 12: Unit 5, Communication, exercise 1C

Partner B

Describe this line graph to Partner A. Partner A will draw it. Check Partner A's graph when you have finished.

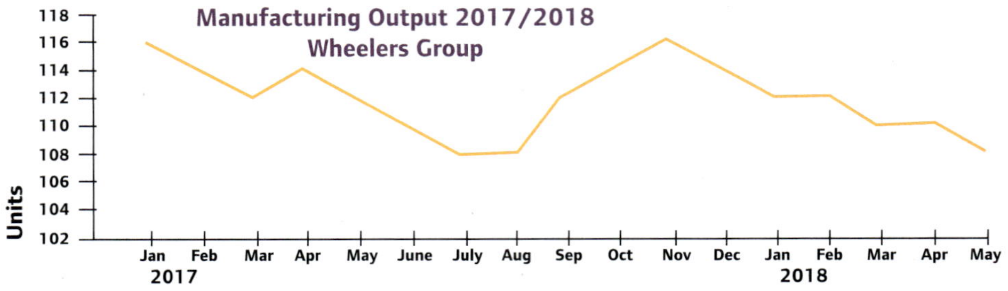

FILE 13: Unit 8, Part A, exercise 4

Partners A and Partner B

Role-play a telephone conversation between AgriTrade South Africa Pty Ltd and an American supplier, using the following prompts.

Partner A: Hersteller Glen/Glenda Jackson, CanLine Inc., Atlanta, Georgia	Partner B: Kunde/Kundin Sie (eigener Name), AgriTrade, Südafrika
Nehmen Sie den Anruf freundlich entgegen.	
	Stellen Sie sich und Ihr Unternehmen vor. Die amerikanische Firma ist Ihnen von Stellenbosch Trading, SA empfohlen worden.
Sie freuen sich und fragen, für welches Produkt er/sie sich interessiert.	
	Laut Website stellt die amerikanische Firma Dosenfertigungslinien her. Fragen Sie, ob auch eine Lieferung nach Südafrika möglich wäre.
Erklären Sie, dass Sie normalerweise den amerikanischen Markt mit Fertigungslinien beliefern und ausländische Kunden mit leeren Dosen versorgen, aber es wäre sicherlich möglich, eine ganze Fertigungslinie zu exportieren.	
	Fragen Sie nach den Lieferbedingungen für eine solche Linie.
Sie liefern Linien immer ab Werk.	
	Fragen Sie, ob er/sie auch Verpackung für den Seetransport zur Verfügung stellen kann.
Danach ist nie gefragt worden, aber Sie finden sicherlich eine Lösung.	
	Fragen Sie, ob er/sie Ihnen behilflich sein könnte, einen geeigneten Spediteur für den Transport der Anlage nach Südafrika zu finden.
Sie werden sich erkundigen.	
	Fragen Sie nach den Zahlungsbedingungen.
30 % im Voraus und 70 % bei Fertigstellung.	
	Fragen Sie nach dem Kundendienst.
Sie liefern Ersatzteile und bei Problemen schicken Sie eine/n Techniker/in. Dies wäre sicherlich für Südafrika möglich. Fragen Sie, ober er/sie weitere Fragen hat.	
	Sie haben keine weiteren Fragen und schließen das Gespräch höflich ab.
Schließen Sie das Gespräch höflich ab.	

FILE 14: Unit 12, Part B, exercise 3A

Partner B

There is a job vacancy at Trade International plc. Jennifer/John Winters, Head of Human Resources, calls an applicant for a telephone interview.

You are the applicant. Work with Partner A and role-play the telephone interview. You begin by answering the phone.

- Introduce yourself.
- Say that this is a suitable time for phone call.
- Talk about your CV.
- Describe yourself from your own point of view and from that of your colleagues.
- Give examples of how you are a team player.
- Describe your hobbies.
- Describe your strengths and weaknesses.
- Give reasons for choosing this career.
- Describe what you expect from the job.
- Justify why you should be chosen for the job.
- Ask any questions you may have.

Swap roles when you have finished.

FILE 15: Unit 10, Part A, exercise 5A

Partner B

You work in the Export Sales department of Ceramica Lombardi in Perugia, Italy.

Role-play a telephone call with a customer (Megakauf Großhandel GmbH) in Dusseldorf, using the information on your role card.

Seller: Antonio / Arianna Rossetti, Ceramica Lombardi, Perugia, Italien

- Nehmen Sie den Telefonanruf auf Englisch entgegen (Begrüßung, Firmenname, Ihr voller Name).
- Reagieren Sie sehr positiv und fragen Sie, wie viel der Ware der Kunde / die Kundin möchte.
- Erklären Sie, dass 500 m^2 einer halben Containerladung entsprechen. 1.000 m^2 wären eine volle Containerladung und viel günstiger.
- Es sind FCA Preise einschl. Verpackung auf Paletten.
- Sie sind gerne bereit, dem Kunden / der Kundin mit dem Transport der Ware zu helfen. Fragen Sie, ob er/sie die Ware lieber mit der Bahn oder per Lkw geliefert haben möchte.
- Sie können den Spediteur (*forwarder*) Sardelli Logistics empfehlen.
- Eine halbe Containerladung mit Lieferung CPT Düsseldorf per Lkw kostet 1.300 €. Eine volle Containerladung kostet 1.650 €. Der Kunde / Die Kundin muss die Ware selbst versichern.
- Zahlungsbedingungen: Barzahlung bei Auftragserteilung
- Lieferung 30 Tage nach Auftragseingang
- Danken Sie für den Auftrag, erklären Sie, dass Sie ihn jetzt schriftlich (*in writing*) brauchen und fragen Sie nach dem Namen und der E-Mail-Adresse des Kunden / der Kundin.
- Erkundigen Sie sich, ob noch weitere Fragen bestehen.
- Danken Sie für die Bestellung und verabschieden Sie sich.

FILE 16: Unit 10, Part B, exercise 5

Application for Irrevocable Documentary Credit

To: COMMERCIAL CREDIT BANK

*Indicates mandatory information to be provided

Applicant Full Name & Address*: *(Importer)*

Contact Person:

Tel: Fax:

Debit Account No.*: 6 9 2 - 2 7 4 - 8 5 1 - 3

Beneficiary Full Name & Address*: *(Exporter)*

Contact Person:

Tel: Fax:

Amount of Letter of Credit*

Amount and Currency (in words)

Currency and Amount (in figures) / . Tolerance +/- %

Expiry Date*: / /
D D M M Y Y Y Y
(LC will expire in Beneficiary's country)

☐ LC To Be Confirmed By Advising Bank

Confirmation Charge To Be Paid By: ☐ Beneficiary ☐ Applicant

All Other Bank's Charges Including Reimbursement If Any For Account Of*: ☐ Beneficiary ☐ Applicant

Shipment From: Shipment To:

Partial Shipment Allowed ☐ Yes ☐ No

Transhipment Allowed ☐ Yes ☐ No

Latest Shipment Date: / /
D D M M Y Y Y Y

Incoterm Place

Documents Required

Commercial Invoice ☐ plus ☐ copies.

Packing List ☐ plus ☐ copies.

Certificate of Origin ☐ evidencing goods of origin.

☐ For shipment by sea, full set of original clean "on board" bills of lading / ☐ multimodal or combined transport documents. marked ☐ freight prepaid ☐ freight collect and notify ____

☐ Air waybill, marked ☐ freight prepaid ☐ freight collect and notify ____

☐ Original CMR/Truck waybill marked ☐ freight prepaid ☐ freight collect ____

☐ Other transport documents (please specify) ____

☐ If CIF/CIP: Insurance policy/certificate for full CIF/CIP value plus ☐ 10 %

☐ If FOB etc: Insurance covered by applicant/buyer

Goods (brief description including quantity without excessive detail)

FILE 17: Unit 10, Part A, exercise 5A

Partner A

You work in the Purchasing department of Megakauf Großhandel GmbH in Dusseldorf.

Role-play a telephone call with a supplier (Ceramica Lombardi) in Perugia, Italy, using the information in the role card.

Buyer: Sie (eigener Name), Einkauf, MegaKauf Großhandel GmbH, Düsseldorf

- Stellen Sie sich vor (Ihr voller Name, Firmenname, Ort) und sagen Sie, dass Sie Terracotta Fliesen Typ TCT90 und BIT75 bestellen möchten.
- 250 m^2 von jeder Sorte, evtl. mehr.
- Danken Sie für die Auskunft und sagen Sie, dass laut Webseite der Firma die Großhandelspreise 25 € pro qm (*per square metre*) für Typ TCT90 und 20 € for Typ BIT75 betragen. Sind die Preise ab Werk oder FCA?
- Sie möchten die Ware nach Düsseldorf transportieren lassen. Kann der/die Verkäufer/in Ihnen damit helfen?
- Sie möchten die Ware per Lkw bekommen. Kann der/die Verkäufer/in einen Spediteur (*a forwarder*) empfehlen?
- Danken Sie dem/der Verkäufer/in und fragen Sie nach den Frachtsätzen (*freight rates*).
- Danken Sie für die Information und fragen Sie nach den Zahlungsbedingungen.
- Lieferzeit?
- Sie möchten 1.000 m^2 Fliesen bestellen, d. h. 500 m^2 von jeder Sorte.
- Geben Sie Ihren vollen Namen und Ihre E-Mail-Adresse an (E-Mail: vorname.nachname@mkg.de).
- Sie haben keine weiteren Fragen. Sie werden Ihre Bestellung gleich per E-Mail abschicken.
- Bedanken und verabschieden Sie sich.

FILE 18: Unit 11, Communication, exercise 4A

Partner B

Role-play a telephone complaint using the prompts below.

You are the customer. Before you begin, make some notes as follows:

- the name of your firm (e.g. London City Clinic)
- the order number
- the date of delivery (e.g. yesterday)
- the problem (e.g. damaged/wrong goods, delay in delivery)
- what you hope from Partner A (e.g. rebate; immediate delivery by express carrier at no charge to your company/hospital)

When you are ready, call Partner A and begin the call.

FILE 19: Unit 11, Part A, exercise 5B

Partners A and Partner B

The Purchasing Director at Simplex Household Appliances in Dublin, Ireland, phones MegaKauf because he/she has received complaints from customers about the MW99 microwave ovens.

Work with a partner and role-play the phone call using the instructions below.

Partner A: Eigener Name, Einkauf, MegaKauf Großhandel GmbH, Düsseldorf	**Partner B: Liam/Lena O'Brien, Einkaufsleiter/in, Simplex Household Appliances, Dublin, Irland**
Nehmen Sie den Anruf auf Deutsch entgegen.	Stellen Sie sich auf Englisch vor und fragen Sie, ob Sie das Gespräch auf Englisch führen können.
Schalten Sie auf Englisch um und fragen Sie freundlich, wie Sie dem/der Anrufer/in helfen können.	Es handelt sich um die eine Sendung Mikrowellenherde vom Typ MW99. Sie erhalten Beschwerden von Kunden, weil die Geräte fehlerhaft sind.
Drücken Sie Ihr Bedauern aus und fragen Sie nach der Auftrags-Nr. und dem Datum.	Auftrags-Nr. VBIB94 vom … (vor einem Monat)
Sie finden den Auftrag im System. Bitten Sie den/die Anrufer/in, das Problem genauer zu beschreiben.	Ihre Kunden erzählen Ihnen, dass die Lebensmittel oft nur halbgekocht sind.
Erklären Sie, dass der Fehler inzwischen bekannt ist. Ein falsches Bauteil (*component*) wurde in einigen Geräten benutzt.	Wie dem auch sei, Sie brauchen dringend Ersatz. Fragen Sie, wann Sie damit rechnen können.
Ersatz wird umgehend geschickt ohne zusätzliche Kosten für den Kunden / die Kundin.	Danken Sie Ihrem/Ihrer Gesprächspartner/in für die schnelle Lösung.
Entschuldigen Sie sich für die Unannehmlichkeiten und fragen Sie, ob Sie sonst noch etwas für den Kunden / die Kundin tun können.	Es handelte sich nur um das eine Problem.
Schließen Sie das Gespräch freundlich ab.	Schließen Sie das Gespräch freundlich ab.

› *Useful phrases: Telephoning, page 187*

FILE 20: Unit 11, Part B, exercise 6A

Partner A

MegaKauf receives an incorrect invoice for outdoor equipment from a supplier in the UK.

You work for Cumbria Equipment Ltd. Role-play a telephone conversation with MegaKauf GmbH (Partner B), using the following prompts.

Partner A (seller)
Bill/Jill Knightley, Director of Accounting, Cumbria Equipment Ltd, UK

- Nehmen Sie den Telefonanruf auf Englisch entgegen (Firmenname, Begrüßung, Ihr voller Name).
- Sie finden die Rechnung im System und fragen, um was es geht.
- Bitten Sie den/die Anrufer/in um einen Moment Zeit, während Sie kontrollieren.
- Erklären Sie, dass nur die pinkfarbenen Rucksäcke im Angebot waren, nicht aber die gelben. Entschuldigen Sie sich dafür, dass die pinkfarbenen falsch in Rechnung gestellt wurden. Sie haben dem Kunden / der Kundin € 250,00 zu viel berechnet.
- Fragen Sie, ob der Kunde / die Kundin damit einverstanden ist, eine Gutschrift über € 250,00 zu akzeptieren.
- Bedanken Sie sich und schließen Sie das Gespräch freundlich ab.

FILE 21: Unit 9, Communication, exercise 3

Partner B

You work in the Sales department at Top Tables. You take a call from an assistant in the Purchasing department at Marx Kitchens and clarify the details of a new product.

Answer the call with your own name. Before you begin, read the details below.

Product: Aluminium kitchen tables

Sizes: medium 1000 x 755
large 1500 x 900

Prices: medium €1,000
large €1,850

Quoted: DDP London

New customer terms of payment: COD

New customer discount: 3%

Delivery: up to 30 days after receipt of order.

› *Useful phrases: Clarifying details on the phone, page 195*

FILE 22: Unit 12, Part B, exercise 5

Common interview questions	Tips
... about yourself – Tell us about yourself. – How would you describe yourself? – What are your hobbies? – What are your strengths and weaknesses?	– Be honest. Show that you are able to use your strengths and indicate that you are working on your "weaknesses".
– Tell us about a mistake you made in the past and how you handled it.	– Be positive. Even if a mistake was made, remember to say that you learned from it.
– What question would you not like us to ask you?	– Say that you hope they do not ask you about a particular department / task as you do not yet have much experience in that department/area. Keep it simple and say something positive.
... about your education, work experience and skills – Why did you choose to train at vocational college? – What responsibilities did you have / do you have during the work placement? / at work? – Please tell me about your present job. – What have you learned in your present job that you think will help you in the position you're applying for with us?	– Talk about the aspects of your education, work experience and skills that are relevant for the job in question. – Talk about a particular project or task which you did successfully.
... about what you know – What languages do you speak? – What computer software are you familiar with?	– Answer honestly. – Be honest. Don't say you know MS Office if you only learned Word, PowerPoint and Excel.
... about your motivation – Why did you apply for this job? – Why do you want to work for this company? – Why do you think you would be a good candidate for this job? – What would you like to achieve in the next five/ten years?	– Show that you have researched the company and know what the job is about. – Stress the positive aspects of the company and the job. – Talk about realistic goals and describe how you would like to progress with your career.
Questions you can ask the interviewer	
– I would like to continue improving my skills. What courses does the company offer? – What kind of training is given to new employees? – Who would I report to? – What are the prospects for promotion? – What are the next stages of the selection process? – When could I start?	

FILE 23: Unit 11, Part B, exercise 6A

Partner B

MegaKauf receives an incorrect invoice for outdoor equipment from a supplier in the UK.

You work for MegaKauf. Role-play a telephone conversation with the supplier (Cumbria Equipment Ltd: Partner A), using the following prompts.

Partner B (*buyer*)
Sie (eigener Name), Rechnungswesen, MegaKauf, Düsseldorf, Deutschland

- Stellen Sie sich vor (Ihr voller Name, Firmenname, Ort) und sagen Sie, dass Sie wegen Rechnung Nr. RS4230 vom ... (*Datum vom 28. des vergangenen Monats*) über € 11.000,00 anrufen.
- Der Preis für die Posten (*items*) 2 und 5 ist falsch. Es handelt sich um eine Bestellung für gelbe und pinke Rucksäcke vom Typ Arctic 27, die im Angebot waren, aber es ist der normale Preis von € 55,00 statt € 50,00 pro Stück berechnet worden. Man hat Ihnen € 500,00 zu viel berechnet.
- Sie sind gerne bereit, ein paar Minuten zu warten.
- Reagieren Sie höflich und bitten Sie um eine berichtigte Rechnung.
- Akzeptieren Sie die vorgeschlagene Lösung und schließen Sie das Gespräch freundlich ab.

FILE 24: Unit 12, Part B, exercise 3A

Partner A

There is a job vacancy at Trade International plc. Jennifer/John Winters, Head of Human Resources, calls an applicant for a telephone interview.

You are Jennifer/John Winters. Work with Partner B and role-play the telephone interview. Partner B answers the phone and begins.

- Introduce yourself.
- Suitable time for phone call?
- Ask the candidate to talk about his/her CV.
- How would the candidate describe himself/herself?
- How would the candidate's colleagues describe him/her?
- Is the candidate a team player? Examples?
- Hobbies?
- Strengths and weaknesses?
- Reason for deciding to train as ...
- Expectations of the job?
- Why should this particular candidate be chosen?
- Questions?

Swap roles when you have finished

KMK Mock exam: Stufe II

Schriftliche Prüfung

Zeit:	120 Minuten
Hilfsmittel:	allgemeines zweisprachiges Wörterbuch
Maximale Punktzahl:	100 Punkte

Im Rahmen der schriftlichen Prüfung werden die Aufgabenanteile für die drei Kompetenzbereiche wie folgt gewichtet:

Rezeption	**40 %**
Produktion	**30 %**
Mediation	**30 %**

Im Folgenden werden vier Aufgaben vorgelegt, die Sie bearbeiten sollen. Die erste und die zweite Aufgabe beziehen sich auf Ihre Fähigkeit, englische Texte (gesprochene und geschriebene) zu verstehen = **Rezeption**. Bei der dritten Aufgabe wird von Ihnen erwartet, dass Sie ein Schriftstück erstellen = **Produktion** eines englischen Textes. In der vierten Aufgabe sollen Sie Texte von der deutschen oder englischen in die jeweils andere Sprache übertragen = **Mediation**.

Die Prüfung beginnt mit der Hörverständnisaufgabe. Alle weiteren Aufgaben können in beliebiger Reihenfolge bearbeitet werden.

Rezeption I: Hörverstehen — 20 Punkte

Situation: Sie arbeiten in der Verkaufsabteilung der Firma GreatSpirits Ltd, einem Getränkegroßhändler in London, der sich auf Spirituosen, Weine und Biere spezialisiert hat. Die meisten Telefonanrufe, die Sie bekommen, erfordern Maßnahmen, daher machen Sie sich auch Notizen, während Sie telefonieren. Auf diese Art und Weise können Sie die Notizen an andere Kollegen und Kolleginnen oder Abteilungen, die Bestellungen durchführen oder sich um Probleme kümmern, weiterreichen.

54 **Aufgabe: Verwenden Sie die untenstehende Darstellung, um sich Notizen zu machen, während Sie sich das Telefongespräch anhören.**

Complaint form

Date:	
From:	
Company:	
Reason for call:	
Product(s) ordered:	
Problem(s):	
Reason for problem(s):	
Action taken / follow-up action:	
Call received by:	

Rezeption II: Leseverstehen — 20 Punkte

Situation: Als Auszubildende/r des CELUC Cash&Carry Markets sind Sie in der Marketingabteilung auch dafür zuständig, das jährliche Treffen der Verkaufsleiter/innen aus aller Welt zu planen. Das Treffen soll dieses Jahr in Dublin stattfinden.

Aufgabe: Informieren Sie sich im Internet und stellen Sie die wichtigsten Aspekte der möglichen Hotels für das Treffen tabellenartig auf Deutsch dar.

	The Duke's Head	Comfort Dublin Airport	The Jerome Hotel
Hotel allgemein			
Kategorie			
Zimmeranzahl			
Lage			
Besonderheit			
Konferenzräume			
Raumanzahl/Kapazitäten			
Ausstattung/Service			

FLIGHTS | HOTELS | CARS | PACKAGES | RESTAURANTS | DEALS | MORE

THE DUKE'S HEAD, DUBLIN

Our elegant three-star hotel is full of character and situated in the heart of Dublin, so it is ideally located for many visitor attractions. The Duke's Head offers 65 beautifully-decorated rooms in a collection of five charming Georgian townhouses. We are therefore one of the oldest hotels in the city, having been in operation since 1877. The Duke's Head has been a focal point in Dublin ever since.

We offer a wide-range of conference services to suit every need, whether it be a small intimate meeting or a larger international conference. The Beckett Suite accommodates up to 75 people, so is perfect for larger events. In addition, we have three smaller rooms: the Yeats Suite, which can accommodate up to 30 people, and the Sheridan and Joyce Suites which can each accommodate up to eight people. Furthermore, we offer two executive boardrooms which can seat up to 18 people and provide the use of a private lounge and air conditioning as well as covering all your technological needs. All our meeting rooms have free Wi-Fi and bottled water.

If you are interested in using our facilities, please contact our sales team who will be more than happy to help organize your successful event.

COMFORT DUBLIN AIRPORT

Our four-star hotel is located close to Dublin Airport and boasts a long-serving, very experienced team, some of whom have been with us for over 25 years. Our 24-hour shuttle service to and from the terminal building is much-appreciated and is completely free of charge. We have a large base of regular customers who enjoy our light and relaxed atmosphere, and who trust us to always make their event a success.

What better place could there be to hold a meeting than in one of our meeting or board rooms directly adjacent to the airport? Our four compact board rooms are ideal for small meetings of up to ten participants. We also have three larger spaces which can generously seat up to 30 guests. Our Executive Suite is our most flexible room: It can host up to 200 people or be divided into four sections to create a variety of rooms suitable for your special event. All our rooms offer natural daylight, complimentary Wi-Fi and an in-built presentation system with state-of-the-art projectors.

Participants can stay in one of our 280 comfort or executive rooms, and our experienced events team is on hand to deal with every aspect of planning your event so that you do not have to worry about a thing. Please contact us to discuss your requirements.

THE JEROME HOTEL, DUBLIN

The Jerome Hotel has long been one of the world's leading hotels, but it's recent renovation has completely updated all our facilities making your five-star experience even more luxurious.

There is no better location for a meeting in Dublin. The Jerome Hotel offers 350 stylish rooms in the very centre of the retail and cultural district, and is just a stone's throw from many historic sights. You just have to step out of the door to find great pubs and restaurants, and there is no shortage of nightlife and theatres nearby.

You can choose from seven elegant boardrooms suitable for 20 guests, or our deluxe suite which holds up to 250 guests. It goes without saying that all these luxurious, elegantly-decorated meeting rooms are fully equipped with the latest technology for your conference and are easily adapted to suit your individual needs.

We at The Jerome Hotel believe that we have a responsibility to our environment and work hard to make our hotel sustainable. Therefore, we only offer locally-sourced food and serve tap water instead of bottled water. Furthermore, all meeting rooms have waste baskets for recycling, lights are turned off once the room is not in use, and we only use recycled paper for photocopying and correspondence.

Produktion — 30 Punkte

Situation: Sie arbeiten für einen der drei in Deutschland führenden Büromaterialgroßhändler, der sich auf nachhaltige und umweltfreundliche Produkte spezialisiert hat. Auf der internationalen Importmesse (IIF) in Köln hat Ihre Firma unter anderem die Printprodukte einer interessanten niederländischen Firma kennengelernt und einige Muster zugesandt bekommen, die zu Ihrem Angebot an Büromaterialprodukten passen.

Aufgabe: Ihr Chef ist von der Qualität überzeugt und bittet Sie, eine Anfrage zu schreiben.

Einkauf:
- *Anfrage an Printqueen (info@printqueen.nl) schicken mit Bezug zum Messebesuch und Dankeschön für das Musterpaket.*
- *Produkte: 3000 Wandkalender DIN A3; 5000 Taschenkalender; 10.000 Buchkalender DIN A5*
- *Nachhaltige und umweltfreundliche Materialien wichtig! Zertifikate/Nachweise vorhanden?*
- *Erfragen Sie Liefer- und Zahlungsbedingungen und mögliche Preisnachlässe.*

Mediation

30 Punkte

Situation: Nach Ihrer Ausbildung arbeiten Sie für die Zweigstelle Ihrer Firma in England. Die Firma bietet Praktika für internationale Auszubildende, Studenten und Studentinnen an.

Aufgabe: Verwenden Sie die untenstehende Darstellung, um sich Notizen zu machen, während Sie sich das Telefongespräch anhören.

Infos über die Firma	
Ort des Praktikums	
Arbeitszeit	
Dauer des Praktikums	
Bezahlung	
Anforderungen an die Bewerber/Bewerberinnen	
Was bietet die Firma / Welche Inhalte lernt man?	
Verlangte Bewerbungsunterlagen und Art der Bewerbung	

PR INTERNSHIP

ECOWORLD is a different kind of furniture wholesaler. We sell beautiful furniture from sustainable wood production that is a living blueprint for our values: people and the planet are central to everything we do.

We are looking for an enthusiastic and motivated candidate full of creative ideas who can work two to four full days a week at our York office. A positive attitude is a must!

You will gain a deep insight into public relations. When the internship is completed, you will be ready to enter any PR department or firm.

Responsibilities:

- Monitoring the PR inbox for press enquiries
- Building relationships with the media
- Drafting press releases
- Updating the mailing list
- Posting on the *ECOWORLD* blog and social media
- Assisting with event management such as furniture fairs and press days
- Assisting with administrative duties
- Performing market research and analysis activities

This is an unpaid 3-month placement with the possibility to extend if required, but interns will receive *ECOWORLD* vouchers so that they can buy *ECOWORLD* products.

Further requirements:

- a solid understanding of the different social networks
- excellent verbal and written communication skills
- good knowledge of MS Office

Candidates must be currently studying at university or doing an apprenticeship.

To apply: Please submit a covering letter and CV by email with the subject line 'PR Internship' to hr@ecoworld.co.uk.

Mündliche Prüfung

Die mündliche Prüfung ist eine Tandem- oder Gruppenprüfung, bei der Sie Gespräche persönlichen und fachlichen Inhalts in der Fremdsprache führen sollen. Sie dauert pro Kandidat/in ca. 25 min. Zur Vorbereitung haben Sie 20 Minuten Zeit.

Phase I: Sie werden gebeten, sich zu persönlichen oder beruflichen Themen (z.B. Vorstellung des eigenen Werdegangs, der Firma und des Aufgabengebietes) zu äußern. Die Kandidaten/Kandidatinnen werden im Wechsel befragt.

Phase II: Im zweiten Teil sollen Sie zusammen mit einem/einer anderen Kandidaten/Kandidatin ein Rollenspiel durchführen. Dazu erhalten Sie vom Prüfer / von der Prüferin Rollenkarten, auf denen eine Situation beschrieben ist, die Sie vorspielen sollen.

Hilfsmittel: allgemeines zweisprachiges Wörterbuch

Interaktion

30 Punkte

Ihre Aufgaben für Phase I könnten wie folgt lauten:

Geben Sie Auskünfte über sich anhand folgender Stichworte:

Ihr beruflicher Werdegang:	– Ausbildung, Abschlüsse, Praktika usw. – Gründe für diese Berufswahl
Ihre Ausbildungsfirma:	– allgemeines Geschäftsfeld / Spezialisierungsbereiche – Anzahl der Beschäftigten, Arbeitsbedingungen usw.
Ihr Arbeitsalltag in der Firma:	– Verwaltungsaufgaben (Beispiele) – Vorlieben/Abneigungen
Ihre Pläne für die Zukunft:	– wo Sie beruflich gerne in fünf Jahren wären

Ihre Aufgaben für Phase II könnten wie folgt lauten:

Rollenkarte A

Sie besuchen eine europäische Berufsmesse in Belgien, da Sie sich für ein Praktikum in einem englischsprachigen Land interessieren. Ihre Ausbildung als Groß-und Außenhandelskauffrau/mann endet in einem halben Jahr. Sie sind noch nicht sicher, ob Sie in einer internationalen Firma arbeiten möchten oder ob Sie ein Studium der Logistik anschließen möchten. In jedem Fall erhoffen Sie sich aber eine Verbesserung Ihrer sprachlichen und beruflichen Kenntnisse.

Die Firma Globotrade aus England hat einen interessanten Stand. Sie nehmen Kontakt zu einem Repräsentanten auf, um Fragen bezüglich eines Praktikums zu klären.
Vorab haben Sie sich einen Notizzettel mit den für Sie wichtigsten Aspekten gemacht:

- Leistungsspektrum der Firma?
- Praktikum für sechs Monate möglich?
- Tätigkeit in verschiedenen Abteilungen möglich?
- Logistikabteilung vorhanden?
- Erfahrung mit Praktikanten/Praktikantinnen?
- Bezahlung?
- Unterbringung?

Rollenkarte B

Sie arbeiten für die Firma Globotrade aus Birmingham, England und vertreten diese heute auf einer europäischen Berufsmesse in Belgien.
Globotrade ist ein großes Handelsunternehmen, dass sich auf den Vertrieb von Autoreifen (*car tyres*) spezialisiert hat. Diese werden weltweit eingekauft und europaweit vertrieben per Bahn, per Schiff oder mit einer eigenen Lastwagenflotte. Im Unternehmen arbeiten zurzeit 145 Angestellte, verteilt auf mehrere Abteilungen.
Für Ihre Firma ist das Rekrutieren von Angestellten für die vielen verschiedenen Abteilungen wichtig, da dringend Leute mit Sprachkenntnissen gebraucht werden. Im letzten Jahr haben Sie erfolgreich Praktikanten und Praktikantinnen aus Frankreich und Polen anwerben können, die fest angestellt sind.
Ihre Firma tut einiges dafür passende Bewerber/innen zu finden, zwar gibt es keine Bezahlung bei einem Praktikum aber die Unterbringung in der Nähe der Firma und das Essen in der Kantine sind kostenlos. Darüber hinaus können Interessenten *evening courses* an der nahe gelegenen Berufsschule besuchen.
Ihnen ist es wichtig etwas über die Motivation, die Zukunftspläne und den bisherigen beruflichen/schulischen Werdegang eines Bewerbers / einer Bewerberin zu erfahren.

G Grammar

Simple present

1 I **work** in the Export department of a manufacturing company. I **arrange** for goods to be shipped abroad.
2 The company **produces** components for the automobile industry.
3 The company **doesn't ship** its goods to Asia.

- Das *simple present* wird für wiederholte, oft regelmäßige Handlungen in der Gegenwart verwendet.
- Signalwörter: *regularly, sometimes, often, always, normally* usw.
- Manche Verben, die keine Handlung, sondern einen Zustand ausdrücken (*need, like, want, hate, love, know, believe*), stehen (fast) ausschließlich im *simple present*.
- In der 3. Person (*he, she, it, Peter, the firm* usw.) wird ein -s angefügt (2).
- Verneinungen werden mit *doesn't/don't* gebildet (3).

Present progressive

1 Our department **is** currently **trying** to find a new supplier.
2 The managers **are negotiating** with a company from Poland right now.

- Das *present progressive* wird gebraucht, wenn man gerade ablaufende oder noch nicht abgeschlossene Handlungen beschreibt.
- Signalwörter: *at the moment, (right) now, just, currently* usw.

Questions and short answers

1 **Do** you **write** a lot of enquiries? – Yes, I **do**. / No, I **don't**.
2 **Did** you **reply** to her email? – Yes, I **did**. / No, I **didn't**.
3 **Can** you **book** the hotel online? – Yes, you **can**. / No, you **can't**.
4 **Is** it easy to use? – Yes, it **is**. / No, it **isn't**.
5 **When/Why/How did** you **find** a new supplier?

- Fragen im *simple present* werden mit *do/does* gebildet (1).
- Fragen im *simple past* werden mit *did* gebildet (2).
- In Sätzen mit Hilfsverben (*is/have/can/will/should/…*) bildet man Fragen, indem man das Hilfsverb des Aussagesatzes vor das Subjekt stellt (3, 4).
- Kurzantworten bestehen aus *yes/no* + Personalpronomen + Hilfsverb (+ *n't*) (1–4).
- Fragewörter stehen immer am Anfang des Fragesatzes (5).

Simple past

1 I **talked** to my line manager about the complaint last week.
2 I **ordered** the new office supplies we need yesterday.
3 What time **did** you **start** work?
4 My first day at work **was** a disaster.

Eine Liste der unregelmäßigen Verben befindet sich auf S. 255.

- Das *simple past* verwendet man, um zu sagen, wann etwas geschehen ist (1, 2), oder um über Vergangenes zu berichten (4).
- Signalwörter: *yesterday, last week, two days ago, in 1998, When …?* usw.
- Bei den regelmäßigen Verben wird im *simple past* in allen Personen meist *-ed* angehängt.
- Verneinungen und Fragen werden in allen Personen mit *did/didn't* gebildet.

Past progressive

1 I **was working** in the Marketing department last week.
2 I **was talking** to a customer when a colleague **bumped** into me and I **dropped** the phone.

- Mit dem *past progressive* drückt man aus, dass eine Handlung oder ein Vorgang zu einer bestimmten Zeit in der Vergangenheit gerade im Verlauf war (1).
- Es beschreibt oft eine Handlung, die gerade im Verlauf war, als eine zweite Handlung einsetzte. Die zweite Handlung steht im *simple past* (2).

Present perfect

1 We**'ve** just **updated** the organigram on our website.
2 We**'ve** recently **reviewed** our terms and conditions.
3 We **haven't found** out why the delivery was late yet.
4 **Have** you **been able** to decide which marketing strategy is best?

Eine Liste der unregelmäßigen Verben befindet sich auf S. 255.

- Mit dem *present perfect* sagt man, dass (nicht: wann!) etwas geschehen ist.
- Signalwörter (Zeitadverbien): *this week, already, just, recently, yet* usw.
- Mit *for* (z. B. *for two years*) and *since* (z. B. *since 2015*) drückt man auch aus, wie lange oder seit wann ein Zustand schon andauert.

Future with *will* and *going to*

1 I think the meeting **will take** about two hours.
2 We've run out of stationery. – OK. **I'll (will) contact** the supplier.
3 We **won't (will not) need** the order until next week.
4 We**'re going to refurnish** all the offices next year.
5 This old computer **is going to break down** soon.

- *Will* wird verwendet, um Vorhersagen zu machen oder Vermutungen über die Zukunft auszudrücken (1).
- *Will* wird für spontane Entscheidungen, Angebote und Versprechen verwendet (2).
- Im gesprochenen Englisch lautet die Verneinung *won't*, ansonsten *will not* (3).
- *Be going to* (+ Infinitiv des Verbs) wird verwendet, um über Pläne oder Absichten zu sprechen (4), oder wenn die Gewissheit (oder ein Anzeichen dafür) besteht, dass etwas geschehen wird (5).

Passive forms

1 The goods **are stored** in our new modern warehouse.
2 The order **was delivered** on Tuesday morning.
3 The shipment **has** already **been dispatched**.
4 The new materials **could be bought** from a local supplier.
5 The equipment **will be installed by** them as part of their customer service.

- Das Passiv wird oft verwendet, wenn man auf eher unpersönliche Art und Weise über Fakten, Vorgänge und Zahlen berichtet.
- Das Passiv wird mit der entsprechenden Form von *be* + Partizip Perfekt (3. Verbform) gebildet. Es können alle Zeiten gebildet werden.
- Passivsätze mit modalen Hilfsverben werden mit einem modalen Hilfsverb + *be* + Partizip Perfekt (3. Verbform) gebildet (4).
- „Von" und „durch" werden in Passivsätzen durch *by* ausgedrückt (5).

Conditional sentences

1 Type 1: **If** you **order** over 200 items, you**'ll receive** a 5% discount.
2 Type 2: If there **was** a delay, we **would inform** you immediately.
3 Type 2: I **wouldn't do** that if I **was/were** you.
4 Type 3: If we **had advertised** the product in the right places, we **would have sold** more.

- Ein *if*-Satz des Typs 1 drückt eine Bedingung aus, die der Sprecher für durchaus möglich oder wahrscheinlich hält. Der damit verbundene Hauptsatz drückt eine Vorhersage aus, die je nach Situation als Warnung, Versprechen o. ä. zu verstehen ist (1).
- Durch einen *if*-Satz des Typs 2 gibt der Sprecher seinem Gesprächspartner einen Ratschlag oder teilt ihm mit, dass er die Erfüllung der Bedingung für unmöglich, unwahrscheinlich (2) oder nicht wünschenswert (3) hält.
- Ein *if*-Satz des Typs 3 drückt eine nicht mehr erfüllbare Bedingung aus. Die Bedinging bezieht sich auf die Vergangenheit (4).
- Steht der *if*-Nebensatz an erster Stelle, wird er durch ein Komma vom Hauptsatz abgetrennt (1, 2, 4).

Relative clauses

1 Our customer service agents are the people **who/that deal with customer complaints**.
2 The supplier **(which/that) our company uses** is based in Berlin.
3 MegaKauf**, which is our biggest competitor,** offers a similar product for a lower price.

- Relativpronomen leiten Relativsätze ein.
- Es gibt den notwendigen und den nicht notwendigen Relativsatz. Notwendige Relativsätze sind für das Verständnis des Satzes unbedingt erforderlich (1, 2) und stehen ohne Komma. Nicht notwendige geben lediglich Zusatzinformationen und werden durch Kommata getrennt (3).
- In notwendigen Relativsätzen kann das Relativpronomen wegfallen, wenn es Objekt ist, d. h. wenn im Relativsatz ein Subjekt steht (2).

Verb + infinitive or *-ing* form

1 I enjoy **working** in a team.
2 I expect **to qualify** as an export assistant in June.
3 I began **working / to work** for the company last year.
4 I'd prefer **to work** from home more often.
5 I'm interested in **getting** some work experience abroad.

- Auf eine Gruppe von Verben folgt immer die *-ing*-Form (1). Zu diesen Verben gehören *dislike, enjoy, finish, give up, imagine, involve, keep, mind, miss, practise, recommend, risk, stop, suggest.*
- Auf eine zweite Gruppe von Verben folgt immer ein *to*-Infinitiv (2). Zu diesen Verben gehören *afford, agree, arrange, choose, decide, expect, hope, learn, manage, offer, plan, promise, want.*
- Auf eine dritte Gruppe von Verben kann sowohl die *-ing*-Form als auch ein *to*-Infinitiv folgen (3). Zu diesen Verben gehören *begin, continue, hate, like, love, prefer, start.*
- Nach *would hate, would like, would love* and *would prefer* (Kurzform *'d like* usw.) steht nur der *to*-Infinitiv (4).
- Nach einer Präposition kommt immer die *-ing*-Form (5).

Gerunds

1 **Travelling** from place to place means there is a lot of variety in my job.
2 Do you like **working** in the office?
3 My work consists of **dealing** with orders and shipment.

- Das Gerundium (= *-ing*-Form des Verbs) kann die Rolle eines Nomens übernehmen.
- Das Gerundium kann als Subjekt (1), Objekt (2) oder nach Präpositionen (3) verwendet werden.

Comparatives and superlatives

1 The new system is **harder/easier** to use.
2 It's **more expensive than** shipping the goods by rail.
3 It's the **simplest** and **cheapest** offer, but not the **best**.
4 This type of trade fair stand is the **most flexible** solution.
5 The company spent **less** money on advertising last year.
6 The new system is**n't as easy** to update **as** the old one.

- Einsilbige Adjektive und zweisilbige Adjektive, die auf *-y* enden, steigert man mit *-er/-est* (1).
- Zweisilbige Adjektive, die nicht auf *-y* enden, und alle Adjektive mit mehr als zwei Silben steigert man mit *more/most* (2).
- Unregelmäßig sind: *good – better – best, bad – worse – worst, little* (wenig) *– less – least, far – farther/further – farthest/furthest* (3, 5).
- Vergleiche bildet man mit *than* und *(not) as ... as* (2, 6).

Reported speech

1 The Sales Manager **said** that sales **had risen** since last year.
2 The intern **asked** if she **could take part** in the meeting.
3 My line manager **told** me that the trade fair **is** always **held** in Frankfurt.

- Man verwendet die indirekte Rede, um zu berichten, was jemand gesagt hat.
- Steht das einleitende Verb (*ask, say* usw.) in der Vergangenheit, verschieben sich die Verben im Satz entsprechend (1, 2).
- Wenn das Berichtete immer oder immer noch gültig ist, muss keine Zeitverschiebung erfolgen (3).

direkte Rede	**indirekte Rede**
simple present	simple past
present progressive	past progressive
simple past	past perfect
present perfect	past perfect
will	would
can	could

Adverbs of frequency

1 The trainees **sometimes** attend trade fairs during their training.
2 We have **often** attended sales meetings abroad.
3 The Sales Director is **frequently** away on business.
4 We deliver goods to China **weekly**.

- Häufigkeitsadverbien der unbestimmten Zeit stehen vor dem ersten Hauptverb (1), nach dem ersten Hilfsverb (2), und nach *to be* (3). Zu ihnen gehören: *already, always, ever, frequently, mostly, never, soon* usw.
- Häufigkeitsadverbien der bestimmten Zeit stehen meistens am Satzende, z. B. *annually, daily, monthly, once, twice, weekly, yearly* (4). Dies gilt auch für *a lot, before, very much, yet.*

Modals and their substitutes

1 I **can** work from home two days a week.
2 I **could** work longer hours if I lived closer to the office.
3 The manufacturing costs **must** be covered by the retail price.
4 You **will be able to** order the new product line from May onwards.
5 We **won't be allowed to** install the new software on our own.
6 We **should** compare the costs of the different methods of transport.
7 Some items in the consignment were broken and **had to** be replaced.
8 You **mustn't** accept an offer before talking to your line manager.
9 You **needn't** ring the supplier. I'll do it in a minute.
10 I **would** like to gain some work experience abroad.

- Modale Hilfsverben wie *can, could, may, would* usw. drücken eine Fähigkeit, eine Erlaubnis, eine Empfehlung, ein Verbot oder einen Wunsch aus.
- Modale Hilfsverben haben in allen Personen die gleiche Form; bei der Verneinung gibt es zusammengezogene Kurzformen.
- Modale Hilfsverben stehen normalerweise in der Gegenwartsform, manche auch in der Vergangenheit. Ersatzverben (*substitutes*) werden benutzt, um alle übrigen Zeiten zu bilden.

Hilfsverb	Ersatzverb
can	*be able to*
could	
may	*be allowed to*
might	
must	*have to*
need not	*don't have to*
shall	
should/ought to	
must not	*not be allowed to*

T Transcripts

Track 2: Unit 1, Foundation, exercise 1A

Hello. My name is Sophie, I'm 19 years old. I'm from Bremen. I left school last year with A levels in English, German and Mathematics. I work at Import/Export GmbH where I'm training to be a management assistant in wholesale and foreign trade. My apprenticeship lasts for three years. I'm doing a work-based apprenticeship. I work in the office from 9 to 5 and do block release at vocational school every three months. I get a small salary from the company. It's not much, but I still live with my parents, so I don't have expenses like rent or food. My colleagues are great and help me a lot. I'd like to work in one of the company's foreign branches one day.

Track 3: Unit 1, Foundation, exercise 1B

My name is Robert Köpke, I'm 18 years old and I come from Berlin. I left school with A levels in German and Computer Studies. I work at ABC Manufacturing where I'm training to be an industrial management assistant. My apprenticeship lasts for two and a half years. It's a work-based apprenticeship. I work in the office three days a week from eight a.m. till four p.m. and I have day-release at vocational college one and a half days a week. The company pays for my course and I also get a small salary. I hope I'll be offered a permanent position in the company when I've finished my training.

Track 4: Unit 1, Part A, exercise 2A

1 Lisa

Mirko Hi, I'm Mirko from Finland. Is it all right if I interview you?
Lisa Yes, go ahead. I'm Lisa from Germany.
Mirko Thanks. So, what size company do you work for?
Lisa I work for a large company. It's a consumer electronics retailer with branches all over Europe.
Mirko A consumer electronics retailer ... and which department are you in?
Lisa I'm in Procurement. We buy goods from suppliers, but I'll soon be in a different department.
Mirko And you're in Procurement ... OK, I've got that. How many other apprentices are there at your company?
Lisa I really can't say! It's so big. All I know is that Procurement has ten apprentices.
Mirko That's fine. Now I need to find out about the hours you work, your breaks and overtime.
Lisa I work seven hours a day, five days a week.
Mirko So that's 35 hours a week. And when do you start and finish each day?
Lisa I clock in just before 7 a.m. and clock out at 3 p.m.
Mirko And what about breaks?
Lisa I usually have an hour's lunch break in the canteen between 12 and 1 p.m.
Mirko Is that all? Don't you have a morning break?
Lisa Not officially. I just get a cup of coffee when I feel like it.
Mirko I see. And what about overtime?
Lisa There's no regular overtime, but if there's a big event like an open day, my boss expects everyone to stay late the night before and clear up when it's over. That usually means about 3 hours' overtime.
Mirko Ah yes, I see what you mean. Now what about a dress code? Do you have one at your company?
Lisa Oh, yes. We have it in writing and it's quite strict because we often visit our suppliers and customers all over Germany.
Mirko Ah yes, of course. You need to look smart for the customers. And your trips are all over Germany?
Lisa Yes, and next month I'm going to the Czech Republic to visit a supplier. I'm really looking forward to that.
Mirko So you also go on business trips abroad. We only have a few more questions now. The next one is: when can your boss contact you?
Lisa Only during working hours. We don't get phone calls or texts outside working hours.
Mirko Not even when you're on standby?
Lisa Well, apprentices don't have to be on standby in my department, so that never happens.
Mirko I see. Now I need to know about your office. How big is it?
Lisa I work in a large open-plan office with about 50 people in it, so it's never really quiet, but I like it. And we also hot-desk.
Mirko Hot-desk? What's that?
Lisa We don't have our own personal desks in the office. We just take a free desk anywhere and log in.
Mirko I see. And what facilities and benefits does your company give its employees?
Lisa Well, as I said, we have a canteen; there are free drinks from drinks machines on each floor; and we have a snack bar on the ground floor.
Mirko Any benefits?
Lisa Benefits ... just let me think. Ah yes, they pay for my travel ticket, and we all have a tablet that we can keep after the apprenticeship ... and we get discounts on some of the goods.
Mirko Well, that sounds like a very good employer, Lisa. My final questions are whether you want to stay on after your apprenticeship and what job offer you expect?
Lisa I very much want to stay on and I think I'll get at least a one-year contract when I finish.
Mirko That's it. Thanks for that, Lisa.
Lisa You're welcome.

2 Lukas

Fabienne Hi, I'm Fabienne from France. You're from Germany aren't you, Lukas?
Lukas Yes, that's right.
Fabienne Is it all right if I interview you?
Lukas No problem. What would you like to know?
Fabienne Well, first I want to know how big your company is?
Lukas It's a small company, a family business with about 20 employees. We make furniture and sell it all over the world.
Fabienne A small company ... and what department are you in?
Lukas I'm in the Logistics department at the moment.
Fabienne And how many apprentices are there at your company?
Lukas I'm the only apprentice.
Fabienne I see. Now what about your working hours?
Lukas Well, officially I work 8 hours a day from Monday to Friday.
Fabienne So that's 40 hours per week.

Lukas	Yes, we all start very early at 6.30 a.m. and we have a 30-minute break together at 9 o'clock. There's one hour for lunch at 1 o'clock and we all finish at 4 p.m.
Fabienne	And do you clock in and out?
Lukas	No, we don't have to. We all come and go at the same time.
Fabienne	And what about overtime?
Lukas	I do a lot of overtime! We have to meet our delivery deadlines, so I sometimes do up to 8 hours a week.
Fabienne	That's a lot. My next question is about a dress code. Is there one at your company?
Lukas	No, there's no dress code. We can wear what we want.
Fabienne	So you don't go on business trips?
Lukas	No, never. They need me in the office.
Fabienne	I see. And when can your boss contact you?
Lukas	Whenever he needs to, really. If there's a problem, he phones or texts me after work. I don't mind. That's what it's like in a small company.
Fabienne	So he can contact you at any time?
Lukas	Yes, that's right.
Fabienne	Now please describe your office, the facilities at your company and any benefits you may get.
Lukas	Office, facilities and benefits ... OK, I work in a small office with one other person. We have a hot and cold drinks machine and that's about it.
Fabienne	And do you have a company phone, tablet or laptop?
Lukas	No, nothing like that.
Fabienne	Any other benefits like discounts and so on?
Lukas	Well, come to think of it, I could buy the furniture we make at cost price if I wanted, so that's a big discount.
Fabienne	And now for my last two questions. Would you like to stay at the company after your apprenticeship and if so, what offer do you think your boss will make you?
Lukas	I'm not sure about staying on because it's a very small company. My boss has already said I could get a permanent contract if I wanted to, but I need to think about it.
Fabienne	And that completes the questionnaire. Thanks.
Lukas	That was quick!

Track 5: Unit 1, Part B, exercise 1B/C

Trainer	I'm so pleased to be working with an international group today and I think we'll all learn a lot from each other at this seminar. OK, now you've all had some time to guess the names of the countries and I think some of you will be surprised when you hear the answers. Now let's start with the only country in which employers don't have to pay their employees for national holidays and annual leave. Which one is it?
Apprentice 1	Japan?
Trainer	I'm afraid not. We hear a lot about the Japanese never taking time off work, but they are second to last in our diagram with ten days' paid annual leave and no paid national holidays.
Apprentice 2	The US?
Trainer	Exactly! That's why they call the US the "no vacation nation". OK, so we have Japan and the US. Now let's look at the country with most paid holiday and leave. Which one is it?
Apprentice 2	Germany?
Trainer	Almost! Germany has the second highest number of paid days off work with 30 days in all, but the winner is Austria! It has the highest number of paid days off work with 38 in all. OK, so now we have Japan, the US, Germany and Austria, so let's look at the two remaining countries – Greece and the UK. Which of these two has to pay its employees for 28 days' annual leave but not for national holidays?
Apprentice 1	The UK?
Trainer	Exactly! And by the way, that explains why shops in the US and the UK are open 365 days a year because the national holidays there are unpaid. Now I want to look at productivity in these countries. Which, would you say, has the highest productivity per working hour?
Apprentice 2	Germany?
Trainer	Almost! Once again it has the second highest. The highest is the US. Then comes Germany and then ...?
Apprentice 1	Austria?
Trainer	Very good! And after that?
Apprentice 2	Japan?
Trainer	Sorry, it's the UK in fourth place followed by ...?
Apprentice 1	Japan and Greece.
Trainer	That's right. So to sum up the US has the highest productivity, followed by Germany, Austria, the UK, Japan and Greece, which has the lowest productivity. Let's take a break now and ...

Track 6: Unit 1, Communication, exercise 1A

Martyna	Hello. I'm Martyna Nowak. I'm 42. I was born in Poland. I'm a human resources manager.
Halil	Good morning. My name is Halil Özdemir. I'm 29 years old. I was born in Germany. I'm a training supervisor.
Deema	Good afternoon. My name is Deema Mansour. I'm 19. I was born in Syria. I'm an apprentice office management assistant.
Robert	Hello. I'm Robert Klein. I'm 21. I was born in Austria. I'm an IT management assistant.
Canan	Hello. I'm Canan Tolon. I'm 25 years old. I was born in Turkey. I'm a management assistant for office communication.
Alexei	Good morning. My name is Alexei Melnyk. I'm 29 years old. I was born in Ukraine. I'm a management assistant in wholesale and foreign trade.

Track 7: Unit 2, Foundation, exercise 2A

Hello everybody. Thank you for being here. My name is Alisha Warner and I'm an office consultant. I plan offices in which people should be able to do their work efficiently and happily. For me, the main purpose of a good office environment is to support the people who work there. Whether it's writing, telephoning or computer work, every office should be a nice place to work in. So, today, I'd like to compare two very different types of offices: the small office and the open-plan office. Let's look first at the small office.

This is one of the oldest types of offices, a small room which is generally used by one or two people. We all know these offices from visits to public administration buildings. You walk down a long corridor and see one door after another. The doors are closed but you know that someone is in there, working. The benefit of this type of office is that it lets people focus on their work. Most employees who work in a small office say they enjoy being able to concentrate on their work without being interrupted.

In contrast – and it's a big contrast – we have the open-plan office where everyone works together in one big room. There are two ways to set up an open-plan office. First, there's the cubicle set-up. Each desk is hidden by a low partition, and the employees sit in their cubicles and get on with the work. Some employees like this set-up, others say that their open-plan office is noisy and they can't concentrate on what they're doing.

The second set-up is the open-plan office in which there are no partitions at all. You'll often see this kind of thing in start-ups. The desks and workplaces are completely open and everyone can move about easily. Sometimes the employees share one large table. Two big advantages of working at one table are that it supports a sense of community in the workplace and, if employees are working on a team project, they're able to complete it quickly because they can communicate better.

Another idea is hot-desking, the employees don't have their own desk, they just work at any desk that's free. There are pros and cons attached to hot-desking. At the end of the day, each space must be cleared and ready for whoever uses it next, so the office is always neat and tidy. The downside of this is that employees can't put their personal mark on their section of the office. This may result in an office lacking warmth or personality, and feeling uninviting.

So, what's the answer? A small office or an open-plan office? An open-plan office with partitions and cubicles, or a totally open, shared working space? A lot depends on the type of business you do, but whatever your business, employees should always feel happy and comfortable in their place of work. That way, they'll do a better job.

Track 8: Unit 2, Part A, exercise 2A/B

1 The people in my department are responsible for a whole contract. We sometimes get very big orders, so we always have a lot to do. Our responsibilities include supervising work at customers' sites, checking that everything is on schedule, and sometimes also training the customers' staff to operate our machines.

2 Finding new customers, making offers to old customers and keeping the price down – that's what I do most of the time. My job also means going to trade fairs, talking to potential customers at our stand and making them offers.

3 I'm in charge of planning and supervising the budget – which is not always so easy. This entails analysing sales figures and profit margins every month and reporting them to the board of directors.

4 I really enjoy doing my job and I learn something new every day. The field I work in is very large, but I would say that, to put it simply, my work involves understanding what materials need to be bought and then finding the best supplier at the lowest possible price.

Track 9: Unit 2, Part B, exercise 2A/B

1 We travel all over the world in our department and I often go to Scandinavia. Most of our work involves negotiating the best possible terms with suppliers and then making sure they deliver on time.

2 Well, I'm basically responsible for finding the best person for the job. My department also sometimes organizes in-house training courses to help people with personal problems.

3 I'm in charge of public relations, so I manage the company's Facebook page and sometimes organize events.

4 Working in my department means understanding customs regulations. We have to obtain the right shipping documents and we also track freight movements, so we know where the goods are all the time.

5 As the manager of my department it's my responsibility to make sure that we sell as many of our products as possible, so each employee has to hand in a report every month. We use this information to analyse our sales figures.

6 In my department we oversee the whole manufacturing and delivery process from beginning to end. We agree standards with our customers and always make sure that they are kept to.

Track 10: Unit 2, Communication, exercise 2

Hi, this is Roger Dalton from Esher Engineering. Thanks for your message. I'm afraid we'll have to change the date of the maintenance technicians' visit to check the lathes. We have a Chinese delegation here on Tuesday, 7 June, so we can offer you Wednesday, 8 June, any time in the afternoon after 1 o'clock. If that doesn't work for you, the technicians can come on Friday, 10 June, but only in the morning from 7 to 12. Please confirm one of these dates with my secretary, Sandy. Her number is 0044 1372 464022. Bye for now.

Track 11: Unit 2, Communication, exercise 3B

Receptionist Esher Engineering, good morning. This is Duncan speaking. How can I help?
Niklas Good morning, it's Niklas Hartmann from Hamm Engineering UK. Could I speak to Mr Dalton, please?
Receptionist Just a moment, sir. I'll see if he's in. Please hold the line.
Niklas Thanks.
Receptionist I'm afraid his line is engaged. Would you like to call back later?
Niklas Well, it's pretty important.
Receptionist In that case, would you like to speak to someone else?
Niklas How about his personal assistant, Simon Smith?
Receptionist Simon Smith … I'm trying to connect you …
Niklas Thanks.
Receptionist I'm sorry, but Mr Smith is unavailable at the moment.
Niklas Oh dear … looks like I'm out of luck today.
Receptionist I could put you through to Mr Dalton's secretary. Perhaps she can help you.
Niklas Yes, all right.
Receptionist I'll put you through.
Niklas Thanks.
Secretary Hello, Mr Dalton's office, Sandy speaking. How can I help?
Niklas Hello, I'm trying to get through to Mr Dalton. It's urgent and I hope you can help me. It's about our technicians' visit next week.
Secretary I see. Who's calling, please?
Niklas Oh, sorry. I forgot to introduce myself. It's Niklas Hartmann from Hamm Engineering.
Secretary Nicholas … er … Could you spell your name, please?

Niklas Yes, certainly. Niklas is my first name. That's N - i - k - l - a - s and my surname is Hartmann spelt H - a - r - t - m - a - n - n.

Secretary Thanks. I'm afraid Mr Dalton is out all day today. Would you like to leave a message?

Niklas Yes, all right. Please tell him that our maintenance technicians are coming to check the lathes on Friday, 10 June, at 2 p.m.

Secretary I'm sorry, I didn't catch that. Could you repeat that, please?

Niklas Yes, our maintenance technicians are coming to check the lathes on Friday, 10 June, at 2 p.m. ...

Track 12: KMK Exam practice 1, exercise 2, Hörverstehen

1

Machine Monday September 5, 8.30 p.m

Caller 1 Good evening, this is Carol Myers from Office Experts in Dublin. I'm returning a call from Michael Sullivan asking for more information about our new ergonomic swivel chairs. Can he please call me back tomorrow afternoon? I've already sent our brochure and price list by mail, but it makes much more sense to talk about it personally. My number is 003531- 564229. Thank you, goodbye.

2

Machine Wednesday February 13, 1.30 a.m.

Caller 2 Hello, my name is Carl Jefferson and I work for the website and blog "Worldwide Apprenticeships". I'm not sure whether I've reached the correct department, but we're looking for apprentices training to become a management assistant for wholesale and foreign trade. We'd like someone to write a personal report for our website. It would be great if the Human Resources Manager could return my call to talk about details. My number is 001-312-555421. I really appreciate it.

Track 13: Unit 3, Part A, exercise 2A/B

Tour 1

Geide Good morning, gentlemen. My name is Rolf Geide. I'm the Managing Director of Cantec, and this morning I'm also your guide. Please come this way. Welcome to Cantec and to Germany. We are delighted to welcome you to our company. You've had a very long trip here from China Tomato in Xinjiang and we very much hope you enjoy your stay here in Germany.

Interpreter Managing Director Wang Wei and his colleagues wish to thank you for your kind invitation to Cantec in Germany. He believes this is the beginning of a long friendship between our two companies. Cantec's canning technology will be an efficient way for Chinese farmers to keep their tomatoes fresh for over a year, so they can be sold all over China and abroad. At the moment, many rot in the fields because it takes too long to transport them to their destination. Canning technology will solve this problem.

Geide We are glad we can help, Mr Wang. We are also sure that this is the beginning of a long friendship and look forward to visiting you at your company in China next month.

Are there any questions before we begin? ... In that case, we'll start here in the conference room with a short presentation about Cantec, its products, services and history ... Well, that was a brief overview of the company. Are there any questions? No? In that case, I'll now take you down the corridor to the Design department.

Interpreter Excuse me, Mr Geide.

Geide Yes, Mr Chang?

Interpreter What is the name of the Head of the Design Department?

Geide His name is Dr Lentz.

Interpreter Thank you, Mr Geide.

Geide You're welcome, Mr Chang. ... Now this is the Design department. The gentleman to the left of the window is Dr Lentz. He and his team will design whatever components we need. Now, we take quality very seriously at Cantec, so our next stop is the Quality Management department, where you will meet our head of Quality Management, Mr Sieke. He and his colleagues check all our processes all of the time ... Well, now you've met the Quality Management team, it's time to go downstairs to see how our machines are built, so let's just take the lift over here ...

We're in the assembly hall now. Here you can see how our production lines are put together, which is what will happen at your canning plant in China next month. There's an END-O-MAT machine for the lids, and over there you can see a CAN-O-MAT for the bodies. Now please follow me to the showroom, which is the last stop of our tour ... Well, that concludes our tour. I hope you enjoyed it and if you have any questions, please feel free to ask them. After that we will take you on a tour of Essen, including the Gruga Exhibition Centre ...

Tour 2

Steinwender Good morning, ladies and gentlemen and welcome to Cantec. My name is Mareike Steinwender, I work in the Human Resources department, and we very much hope you will enjoy your time here. There are also other work experience students being shown round the company at the moment. They all speak English or German, and you'll meet them when we finish the tour. I'm your guide for the next hour, so please feel free to ask any questions.

We're starting our tour here in the showroom. You can see our two main products, the CAN-O-MAT and the END-O-MAT, and a very wide range of cans.

Student 1 May I ask a question?

Steinwender Yes, certainly.

Student 1 How many cans can these machines produce?

Steinwender The CAN-O-MAT produces up to 1,300 can bodies per minute and the END-O-MAT up to 4,000 can ends. Any more questions? ... In that case, let's spend a few more minutes here to look around and then I'll show you the production hall. ...

We're now in the production hall where we make the parts for our equipment. Some of you will be working alongside our specialists here, and they will show you how the machines work. Any questions? ... Yes?

Student 1 How long does it take to ...

Steinwender So let's now take the lift upstairs to the third floor ...

OK, now we're on the third floor and I'm going to take you to meet Mr Keller, the head of the Project Management department, and his team. ... Good morning, Mr Keller!

Keller Good morning!

Everyone Good morning.

Keller Welcome to the Project Management department. My name is Matthias Keller and here you will see how customers' orders are turned into projects. Each order has its own project manager who sees the project through from start to finish. Would you like to ask any questions?

Student 2 Yes, I would like to ask a question, please. Which countries do you export to?

Keller We export all over the world but a lot of our work is in Asia and Africa, and at the moment we're working on a big project for South Africa.

Student 2 Thank you.

Steinwender Thanks, Mr Keller. Let's now go on to the Purchasing department, which is just down the corridor ... This is where all the materials for our machines are ordered and also the tools needed to make them. I can see this department is very busy today, so let's now go to our last stop, which is Mr Geide's office. Mr Geide is our Managing Director, and he's going to tell you something about the history of the company. The Managing Director's office is just down here ...

Track 14: Unit 3, Part B, exercise 1C

Good morning, ladies and gentlemen and welcome to Cantec. We're delighted to have you here in Essen and we hope you will enjoy your visit. My name is Vanessa Koch and I work in the Sales department. The agenda for today's meeting is in the folder in front of you. Right, I'd like to begin by giving you a presentation about the company. I'll start with some background information and company statistics, and will then move on to our products and services. Then at the end, I'll be happy to answer any questions you may have.

Cantec in Germany is a high-tech company manufacturing high-end can-making machines. We have a workforce of 162 and last year our turnover was approximately 39 million euros. We export 98% of our products and have a global market share of about 40%.

As you can see from this slide, we belong to a group of companies. The parent company is Soudronic in Switzerland. The Soudronic Group has subsidiaries in Germany, France and Italy.

This next slide shows how our products are exported all over the world and in particular to Africa and Asia, where canning facilities are often used by farmers to overcome poor transport infrastructure.

Now, let's move on to our next point: the products and services that Cantec has to offer. Our speciality at Cantec is providing the customer with a whole production line. We transport all the components to our customers in containers and assemble them on site. Customers can design their cans themselves or choose one of our standard models. We also train the customers' employees to operate our machines.

The next thing I'd like to show you is our production hall. It has state-of-the-art machinery and ample space for a large number of orders to be handled at the same time.

That was a brief overview of Cantec, Germany. Many thanks for listening. Now if you'd like to ask any questions, I'd be delighted to answer them and then we can go to lunch ...

Track 15: Unit 4, Part A, exercise 2A/B

Dialogue 1

Salesperson 1 Good afternoon, sir. On behalf of TopLine Sanitär I would like to welcome you to our booth. My name is Torsten Meyer from the Sales department. I'm sure we have something to interest you, so please feel free to look around and, of course, don't hesitate to ask if you have any questions.

Customer 1 Thanks. Actually, I ...

Salesperson 1 And might I draw your attention to our special offer for mixer taps for the bath, shower and washbasin? Wholesalers can buy our *Free Flow* model at a discount of 20% this week. Do you think your customers would be interested, Mr ...?

Customer 1 Brown ... But look, what I've actually come about is fixtures and fittings for ...

Salesperson 1 Fixtures and fittings! Well, you've come to the right place, Mr Brown! We have more than 10,000 fixtures and fittings in stock with overnight delivery all over Europe. Where is your company located?

Customer 1 Just outside Canterbury but ...

Salesperson 1 Canterbury! That's a beautiful city with a cathedral and not far from the port of Dover. As you can see, I know a lot about England, but let's get back to business, shall we? Here's a brochure on our latest offers, including the *Free Flow* mixer taps you are so interested in. Each tap comes with a five-year guarantee, and remember, our special 20% offer is valid until the end of this week, so I would advise you to place your order while stocks last!

Customer 1 Thanks, but I have to go now. Bye.

Salesperson 1 But, Mr Brown! ...

Dialogue 2

Customer 2 Good morning. Is it all right if I look around for a few moments?

Salesperson 2 Suit yourself.

Customer 2 Thanks. Er ... is this shower enclosure suitable for a fitness studio?

Salesperson 2 Look at what it says on the box.

Customer 2 OK, thanks ... I'm sorry but there's no information on the box. Perhaps there's a leaflet inside. Do you know if there's a leaflet inside?

Salesperson 2 How should I know? You can see the box is sealed.

Customer 2 Ah yes, of course. Look, could I just open the box and look for a leaflet? I really would like to know if this shower enclosure is suitable for fitness studios and sports centres.

Salesperson 2 You'll have to buy it if you open the box.

Customer 2 Well, I'm afraid I really must look at the article more closely before I can decide. If I open the box very carefully, I'm sure it can easily be re-sealed.

Salesperson 2	I don't make the rules. If you open it, you'll have to buy it.
Customer 2	Look, I've seen a number of shower enclosures at this trade fair and this one seems to be what I'm looking for, but as my fitness centres are used around the clock, I need a heavy-duty version that will last for years. If this shower enclosure is suitable, I'll order 200 units for a start and perhaps another 200 later.
Salesperson 2	In that case, you'll have to wait for my boss to come back.
Customer 2	And when might that be?
Salesperson 2	No idea.
Customer 2	Well, I'll call by again tomorrow … perhaps …

Dialogue 3

Salesperson 3	Good afternoon, madam.
Customer 3	Good afternoon. Is it all right if I look around for a while?
Salesperson 3	No problem at all. Just let me know if you need any help.
Customer 3	Thanks.
…	
Customer 3	Excuse me. These mixer taps here, the *Free Flow* model. I like the look of them but as they're still in the box, is it all right if I take one out and take a closer look at it?
Salesperson 3	Let me do that for you, madam. Here we are.
Customer 3	Thanks … It's surprisingly light but feels very solid.
Salesperson 3	Yes, they're top quality and can be used everywhere. Is it for private or commercial use?
Customer 3	Commercial. It's for use in hotel rooms.
Salesperson 3	I see. So you'd probably need one mixer tap per room.
Customer 3	Two actually. Our 5-star hotels have double washbasins. Do you have a matching set for a bath and shower?
Salesperson 3	Yes, madam. And we also have thermostatically controlled mixer taps for showers, bathtubs, Jacuzzis and so on. We have all these items in stock and we have a special offer for the fair. We're offering wholesalers a 20% discount on the catalogue price if they order this week.
Customer 3	Sounds good. Could I look at the entire range? Do you have them all here?
Salesperson 3	We most certainly do, madam. Just let me get them out for you. They're very hard-wearing, delivery is from stock and we give a five-year guarantee.
…	
Customer 3	Well, I'm interested. How long did you say the special offer was valid for?
Salesperson 3	Until the end of this week. Any company that places an order by Friday will get a 20% discount.
Customer 3	Well, in that case could you let me have an offer for 100 sets? Here's my card.
Salesperson 3	Thanks. We'll email you an offer today …

Track 16: Unit 4, Part B, exercise 2A/B

Hannah	Good afternoon, ladies and gentlemen. My name is Hannah Klein. Welcome to BodyLine Fischer! We're delighted to see you all here today and we're sure that you'll go away with some exciting new ideas for your customers. All our latest products are here in the showroom, and you'll get a catalogue on our entire range at the end of the morning. We also have some samples of our latest energy drinks and snacks for you, so please help yourselves! Let's start with our new treadmill and for this I need a volunteer! … Is anybody willing to try it out? How about you, Mr Lee?
Mr Lee	Yes, no problem.
Hannah	Thanks, Mr Lee. Please step on the belt … that's right and look at the display. What's the first thing you see?
Mr Lee	"Slow start".
Hannah	Exactly! Now if a treadmill starts too fast, it can be dangerous, but ours has a special slow-start feature for extra safety, so please press the slow-start button, Mr Lee. Now, as you can see the belt starts very slowly. How does that feel, Mr Lee?
Mr Lee	Fine.
Hannah	And that's how it should feel – no risk at all for our customers. Right, now I need a volunteer for the rowing machine …
…	
Hannah	Now you've tried out the treadmill and the rowing machine I'd like to point out that our models require next to no maintenance. This is because they're made of the very best, extremely durable materials and come with a lifetime guarantee on parts and wear items and a 10-year guarantee on the frame. I'm now going to call on Mark to help us. He's a professional gym instructor and he's going to demonstrate some of our other new products. Mark, will you show us some exercises with the exercise ball and exercise mat? … Here you can see that Mark is using one of our thicker exercise mats together with an exercise ball. Our mats come in four thicknesses – thinnest for yoga, thin for Pilates and thicker for gymnastics and martial arts, and our new exercise balls are available in five different sizes and colours. Now Mark is going to demonstrate some exercises with our new folding trampoline. It's designed to be used flat or at a 45° angle, and here he's using it for easy press-ups. This model is suitable both for home use and in the gym. And finally, Mark will now show us the new multifunctional weight bench and all the extras that go with it. This is the heavy-duty model for up to 150 kg, but whether you're training for the Olympics or just want to tone up your muscles, this is the bench for you! ... Thanks, Mark. I'd now like to round off the morning with a video on our new user-friendly console. It has lots of new features, including media streaming and internet connectivity, so we've put together a video to explain them all. Please take a seat, relax, enjoy the show and don't forget the snacks and drinks!

Track 17: Unit 4, Communication, exercise 1B

Manager I'll just give you my email address. It's t m dot martin at technical underscore tools dot de.

Mary-Anne Sorry, could you repeat that, please?

Manager No problem. t m dot martin at technical underscore tools dot de. You can reach me directly with that address.

Mary-Anne Thank you. Well, my email address is mary hyphen anne hyphen brown at five plus five services dot net. The fives are written as numbers. Oh, and my first name, Mary-Anne – Anne is written with an e.

Manager OK. I'll just read that back to you. Mary hyphen Anne hyphen brown at five plus five services dot net. Mary-Anne with a hyphen, the fives written as numbers and Mary-Anne written with an e at the end of Anne.

Mary-Anne Yes. That's correct.

Track 18: KMK Exam practice 2, exercise 1, Hörverstehen

Chris CCA Clothing, Chris Mitchell, good morning.

Martina Hello, this is Martina Beyer of Fair Flowers and Promotional Gifts.

Chris Ah, Ms Beyer, I'm glad you called! Will you be able to attend the opening?

Martina Oh yes, we're looking forward to it. In your invitation you also mentioned that you had some business to discuss with our company.

Chris Yes, indeed. I hope we can work something out. We would like to decorate the new store and we thought it would be good to use flowers and plants. Is it possible to rent big plants for the entrance from you?

Martina Sure, that shouldn't be a problem. I just need to know the amount and the type and height of plant you would like.

Chris I think two plants about 2 metres high and ten about 1.5 metres. I'm not sure what types we should use though ...

Martina OK. We'll send you our PDF catalogue to look at, and then you can get back to me when you've chosen the ones you want.

Chris Great, that sounds like a good idea. I'll do that as soon as I get the catalogue. Then if you could send me an offer as soon as possible.

Martina Yes, of course.

Chris Ah, I almost forgot the most important thing. We would like to have white roses as a giveaway for all the guests. We need 500 white roses for the pre-opening on Thursday 3rd and another 2000 roses for the official opening two days later. I think you have a special offer on your website?

Martina Yes, we do. We'll order them immediately so that they arrive on time for the opening.

Chris Thank you very much, I appreciate that.

Martina Is there anything else I can do for you today?

Chris Well, yes, maybe there is. We would like to offer special discounts with additional promotional gifts at the official opening. Since your company seems to be an expert, we would be interested in the promotional gifts you have on offer.

Martina That shouldn't be a problem at all. We can send one of our sales reps with a choice of samples, and you can come to our showroom.

Chris Sounds perfect! Could you get a sales rep to call my assistant to arrange that? And could my colleague also visit your showroom next Thursday?

Martina Sure, I'll see to it. My assistant will be available on Thursday for a tour of the showroom, and if your colleague is interested, he can also have a look around our warehouse.

Chris Great, thanks. I look forward to seeing the sample gifts. Thank you for your help. I'll talk to you soon. Have a nice day.

Martina Thank you. Goodbye.

Track 19: Unit 5, Part A, exercise 2

Ben Good morning everyone and welcome to today's meeting to discuss how to market our new line. I'm Ben Kaiser, the Managing Director of Textil-Vertrieb Mahler, and I'm delighted to welcome Mary Garcia from P&Q Marketing. Mary's put a lot of thought into this project and today she's going to outline her strategy. Over to you, Mary!

Mary Thanks Ben, and good morning to you all. I think you have a great new line! Now some of you may already know about the approach I'm going to use to get the right marketing mix for this line. It's called the four Ps. It's a well-established marketing strategy, and I'm going to outline how to use it.
The first of the four Ps is the product itself: What is the exact nature of the product? We have taken a very close look at your line, and I can see that your products are all about sustainability because that's what socially-responsible consumers expect nowadays. In your case, the bottom line here is not just profits. Your product has a *triple* bottom line – people, planet *and* profits! The *people* – these are the consumers – need to know how they are helping the *planet* and understand that your company also needs to make a *profit*. No tricks. Everything must be out in the open from beginning to end, and that's why I have a very special name for this line. I want to call it the *Honesty* line. What do you think?

Ben The *Honesty* line! That's a great idea, Mary! I really like it and I'm sure we all agree that that's what this company is all about.

Voice 1 Yes, I agree!

Voice 2 Good idea!

Voice 3 Exactly!

Mary I'm glad you all like it. Now the second P stands for promotion. This means *how* we tell the consumer about the line, so what I'm basically talking about is branding and advertising. Advertising is changing fast, and we're less interested in the traditional mass media for these new products. They need to be promoted through social media and internet search engines like Google and YouTube, but this is such a big field that I want to deal with this separately. Is that all right, Ben?

Ben Fine by me, Mary.

Mary Great! So let's move on to the third of our four Ps – place. By place we mean where and how the line will be sold, so what we're talking about is distribution. The question is what does the consumer have to do to get an article of clothing from this new line? Let's all think for a moment. How do you all buy your clothes? Think of the last thing you bought and how you bought it. Who'd like to start? … Yes?

Markus My name's Markus Koch and I'm pretty lazy, so I get most of my clothes online.

Mary Online … How about the rest of you?

Ben Well, I'm old-fashioned because I get mine from a shop.

Mary Well, I have news for both of you. You're neither lazy nor old-fashioned because you represent today's two big sales channels – online sales and bricks and mortar outlets.

Markus I'm sorry but I'm not sure what bricks and mortar means.

Mary No problem, Markus. It means a real shop, not a virtual, online shop. We call this the stationary trade.

Markus Thanks.

Mary You're welcome, Markus. Now let's move on to the last of the four Ps. The price … and we're talking here about the recommended retail price. For this we need to look at the consumers. What sort of people are they and, above all, how much are they prepared to pay for this sort of product? Let's start with the *Honesty* jacket. We know it costs about 25 euros to make this jacket, but do we want the price to be as low as possible, let's say under 100 euros? Or can we go for a higher price? I'm thinking of 200 euros plus. Or is it somewhere in between – at about the 150 euro mark? I want you to talk to each other about the price now and then we can discuss it as a group …

Track 20: Unit 5, Part B, exercise 2A/B

Reporter Hi, this is Jenny Andrews reporting today from Germany on a very unusual event. … It's rush hour here at Dusseldorf Central Station, and I'm standing outside a pop-up shop with a long queue of people loaded up with plastic bottles. Let's talk to Ben Kaiser, the managing director of Textil-Vertrieb Mahler, to find out what's happening. What's going on, Ben?

Ben Well, there's a lot going on today because my company wants to do something about the huge problem of plastic water bottle pollution in the oceans. 20,000 bottles are bought all over the world every *second*, and last year billions of bottles were thrown away and ended up in the oceans. That's why each of our new *Honesty* jackets is made from 25 recycled plastic bottles.

Reporter A jacket made from recycled plastic bottles! That's a great idea, but why are the people all *carrying* empty plastic bottles themselves?

Ben That's because today is Day 1 of our *Save the Oceans* campaign and just for today, we're asking people to pay for the jacket not with cash but with plastic bottles, which we will recycle for them. The regular price is 150 euros but today it's 25 plastic bottles because that's how many are recycled in one jacket. We're not taking cash today, just bottles, so to all the people listening to this programme, come to the station with 25 plastic bottles, get an *Honesty* jacket and help save the oceans.

Reporter And if they can't make it to the station today?

Ben Our *Honesty* jackets will be on sale in sports shops and online via our mobile phone app and website as from next week, but for 150 euros not 25 bottles.

Reporter That's good to know, Ben, but let's just talk to one of the customers waiting in the queue. Excuse me, madam. I'm from the BBC. May I ask you a question?

Customer Sure, go ahead.

Reporter Would you have recycled those 25 plastic bottles if you hadn't heard about this event?

Customer Yes, I would have taken them to the recycling centre, but I know a lot of people who wouldn't.

Reporter Thanks … Just a moment, Ben. Something's happening outside the shop!

Ben Yes, Germany's no. 1 surfer, Timo von Struck, has just arrived. He's here with his new surfboard made entirely out of recycled plastic bottles and he's going to paddle down the Rhine and collect plastic litter all the way.

Reporter Wow! All the way down the Rhine on a surfboard! That's a long way!

Ben Yes, it's twelve hundred kilometres and he plans to do it in 28 days.

Reporter Can we get Timo over here, Ben? I'm sure our listeners would love to hear what he has to say about his trip.

Ben Yes, he's just finished his TV interview. Timo! Come over here for a moment, please! Here he comes …

Reporter Great to have you here today, Timo! Everybody knows you as Germany's top surfer, but today you're here for a very different reason.

Timo Yes, I'm here to help stop the destruction of our oceans and waterways. I hope my trip down the Rhine will make people think again before they throw away a plastic bottle, and I'd also like to say that my trip wouldn't have been possible if Textil-Vertrieb Mahler hadn't offered to sponsor me and my team. We also hope that other surfers will join me along the way and help clean up the Rhine. This is going to be a big event and we need all the help we can get!

Reporter So if you hadn't had a sponsor, you couldn't have done it.

Timo Exactly.

Reporter Sounds like a great idea. Is there anything else you'd like to say to our listeners, Ben?

Ben Yes, I want to thank Timo von Struck for his support. If he hadn't been prepared to help, we wouldn't have recycled so many bottles today. You'll soon be able to watch Timo's progress down the Rhine on his YouTube vlog, which we're also sponsoring. He'll be giving you a day-by-day update, so you won't miss a thing and remember: recycle your plastic, cheer Timo on when he paddles past, and wear an *Honesty* jacket!

Track 21: Unit 5, Communication, exercise 2A

I'd like to move on now to this table. As you can see, this company's sales in the UK were at 10.3 million euros in the first quarter of the financial year and, in the second quarter, sales rose rapidly to 11.4 million euros. However, when we look at the third quarter, we can see that sales dropped drastically to 8.2 million euros. By the end of the year, things had recovered and sales rose to 10.3 million euros, reaching the same volume of sales as in the first quarter. Now, you can see at a glance that sales figures for Germany over the same period were much lower. We start off with …

Track 22: Unit 6, Foundation, exercise 2

Penny I've made a list of all the things we have to do for the meeting next month. Shall we just go through it point by point to make sure I haven't forgotten anything?
Niklas Yes, that's a good idea. So what do we need to do before the meeting?
Penny My first point is to check the number of participants, so we know which room to reserve.
Niklas I checked with the CEO's PA and the number is still six, so we don't need a big room.
Penny In that case, they can use the small conference room. How about equipment in the room?
Niklas The CEO wants to give a presentation, so she'll need the data projector and perhaps a flipchart.
Penny OK, so the second point is to reserve the room and equipment.
Niklas And order refreshments. What do you think they'll want?
Penny I'm sure the Bolivians drink coffee, but I think we should also have tea and soft drinks.
Niklas So point three is to order refreshments. Can't we do that on the day?
Penny I think it's better to order them well in advance.
Niklas Yes, OK, that's safer. What's next on your list?
Penny Point four is to send out invitations to the participants by email.
Niklas Any attachments?
Penny Yes, they'll need the agenda and the documents they're going to discuss at the meeting.
Niklas So that's send invitations, agenda and documents. Anything else we should do before the day of the meeting?
Penny We'll need to make hard copies of the agenda, the minutes of the last meeting and the documents needed at the meeting a few days earlier.
Niklas Yes, we certainly can't leave that until the day of the meeting, even though it's at 9.30 a.m.
Penny So point five is to make hard copies of the agenda, minutes and documents.
Niklas Anything else before the meeting?
Penny Yes, name tags. We need to make a name tag for each participant well in advance.
Niklas So name tags are point six. How many points have you got, Penny?
Penny Twelve. We're halfway down my list.
Niklas I see. So let's have the next point.
Penny The next points are things to do on the day of the meeting. We have to check the room that day to make sure it's ready.
Niklas So what do we need to check?
Penny As it'll be January, we'll need to check the heating and also make sure that there are enough chairs. People sometimes take a chair and don't put it back.
Niklas Ah yes, of course. So point seven is to check the room, heating and chairs. How about directions to the room. Will they all be able to find it?
Penny I expect so, but if anyone arrives late or in a hurry we should remind reception to display the meeting on the info screen at the entrance to the building. They'll then see the name of the meeting, the time and the room.
Niklas Yes, good idea. So that was point eight, display the meeting on the info screen at the entrance. Point nine?
Penny Point nine is extremely important. We have to lay each place in the conference room with everything the participants need.
Niklas Meaning copies of the agenda and the documents to be discussed?
Penny Yes, but not only that. Each participant will also need writing materials and a cup and saucer for tea or coffee, and a glass for soft drinks.
Niklas So point nine is … agenda, documents, writing materials, cup, saucer, glass. Right. I've got that. So what are the last three points?
Penny There are two more on the day of the meeting. Provide refreshments in the conference room and put out the name tags on a table by the door for people to pick up as they come in.
Niklas So ten is refreshments and eleven is name tags. After the meeting?
Penny I only have one point, and that is to circulate the minutes of the meeting to all the participants and any absentees.
Niklas So circulate minutes to participants and absentees is point twelve. Great! Let's get started …

Track 23: Unit 6, Foundation, exercise 3

Mary … Now, I've drafted the agenda for the meeting with the two representatives from Grano de Cacao next month and I'd like you to send it out to everyone by email with some other documents when we've finished this discussion.
Niklas Yes, fine.
Mary We're starting the meeting at 9.30. The CEO will be chairing it, so she'll welcome everyone and then go over the minutes of the last meeting and answer any questions.
Niklas And how long will that take?
Mary I think half an hour should be enough, so ten o'clock should be a good time for opening negotiations. I've planned two hours for that, so that'll be from 10 to 12. Have you reserved the small conference room?
Niklas Yes, it's reserved and we've also ordered refreshments and a data projector for the CEO's presentation.
Mary Excellent. Then Helen Clark is going to take everyone on a tour of the warehouse. She's aiming to finish at 12.30 so I've planned lunch from 12.45 to a quarter to two.
Niklas In that case, I'll tell the canteen to reserve a table for six.
Mary Yes, good idea. Now people will want to freshen up after lunch, so the second part of the meeting is scheduled for 2 o'clock. The CEO aims to finalize negotiations and sign the contract at around half-past four, and then there will be the usual things – any other business and the date of the next meeting.
Niklas So the meeting should be over by 5 p.m., right?
Mary Yes, I would say five. Here are the documents I'd like you to send out with the agenda and also copy for each participant on the day.
Niklas Thanks.
Mary Anything we've forgotten?
Niklas No, I think we have everything now.
Mary Good. So you can get started, and please let me know if there's anything else you need.
Niklas We will, thanks …

Track 24: Unit 6, Part A, exercise 2

Sarah	Good morning everybody and welcome to today's meeting. I'm Sarah Bonrath, the Export Sales Director at B2B here in Germany, and since we don't all know each other, the first item on today's agenda is our new agent in Singapore. Would you like to introduce yourself, Wen Fang?
Wen Fang	Sure. I'm Wen Fang from Singapore Trading. I came on board six weeks ago, so I'm the new girl.
Sarah	Thanks for that, Wen Fang. Would the others like to introduce themselves to Wen Fang? Donald, would you go first, please?
Donald	Hi. I'm Donald Masters at UK Wholesale Trading in London. I've been acting as an agent for B2B for about three years.
Sarah	Thanks, Donald. Rajiv?
Rajiv	Good morning. My name is Rajiv Mittal. My company is called India Trading Services Private Limited and I have had the pleasure of acting on behalf of B2B for ten years now.
Sarah	Many thanks, Rajiv. Our next topic is Rajiv's presentation, so would you go ahead please, Rajiv?
Rajiv	Certainly, Sarah. My presentation is called "Beer in Mumbai" ...
...	
Rajiv	... To conclude, I would say the figures are very positive.
Sarah	Many thanks, Rajiv. Would anyone like to comment or ask a question?
Donald	I'd just like to say that Rajiv's done a great job!
Sarah	Yes, I agree. Well done, Rajiv! Let's move on to the next topic, which is our current order situation. Can you all give us a brief update? Donald?
Donald	As you can see from this graph, my orders are up 10% on last year.
Sarah	Wen Fang?
Wen Fang	It's too early to say much, but they're rising.
Sarah	Rajiv?
Rajiv	My orders are up 5% on last year.
Sarah	Thanks, Rajiv. Let's move on to the next topic, which is deliveries. How are things going here? Are there any issues?
Donald	Deliveries are now punctual 95% of the time, which is better than last year when only 85% of deliveries were punctual.
Sarah	That's good to hear! Anything else on deliveries? No? In that case, the next point is complaints. Are there any complaints?
Wen Fang	Well, it's only a small thing but could I just say that some of the equipment is arriving dirty.
Sarah	Dirty! Well, we can't have that. Any idea why, Wen Fang?
Wen Fang	I think it's poor packing, and I think it makes a bad impression when the equipment arrives dirty.
Donald	Can I come in on that, Sarah?
Sarah	Go ahead, Donald.
Donald	I thoroughly agree with Wen Fang. We can't deliver dirty equipment. It's bad for our image.
Sarah	Yes, I agree. I'll pass that on to our Logistics department. Any other complaints? No? All right, so we've covered point no. 4, delivery, and point no. 5, complaints, and we've decided to postpone the topic of installing and operating equipment, so we've covered all five items on today's agenda. Let's wrap up the meeting with AOB, shall we? I just have the one final point here from Rajiv – travel expenses. I've checked with Finance and they'll get back to you next week, Rajiv. Is that all right?
Rajiv	That's fine, Sarah.
Sarah	Well, that would seem to be it. You'll be getting the minutes by email tomorrow. Many thanks for coming to the meeting ...

Track 25: Unit 6, Part B, exercise 1B/C

Wenzel	Good morning, Mr Popescu. Please take a seat.
Popescu	Good morning, Ms Wenzel. I'm very pleased to be here. Munich is such a beautiful city and the weather is so good today!
Wenzel	Let's get down to business, shall we, Mr Popescu? I wrote in my email that we are reviewing all contracts because of the stiff competition in the denim market, so are you prepared to reduce your prices?
Popescu	Well, it's not so easy at the moment.
Wenzel	I need a straight answer, Mr Popescu.
Popescu	I think we can ... a little.
Wenzel	We need a 10% reduction. Can you reduce your prices by 10%?
Popescu	10%! That's a big reduction for a small company like mine. Can I think about it?
Wenzel	I have a lot of meetings today, Mr Popescu, and I also want to talk about quantity and delivery. The market for low-priced denim is expanding fast, so we need to increase our sales by 20%. Will your company be able to increase production by 20%?
Popescu	20% is a lot. We would need more machines and more workers ...
Wenzel	And we also need guaranteed delivery within 30 days. Too many shipments have been late. Will you give us a guaranteed delivery period of 30 days?
Popescu	The freight forwarder we are using has old lorries that break down a lot ...
Wenzel	Do you accept these terms, Mr Popescu? I need an answer now and the next supplier is waiting.
Popescu	This is very hard for me, Ms Wenzel, very hard ...

Track 26: Unit 6, Part B, exercise 2A

Wenzel	Good morning, Mr Popescu. How nice to see you again! I hope you're well.
Popescu	Good morning, Ms Wenzel. I'm very well thank you and I hope you are, too.
Wenzel	Yes, I'm fine thanks. Did you have a good trip?
Popescu	Yes, thank you. I flew straight here from Bucharest yesterday.
Wenzel	Excellent! Now, let's take a look at our business arrangements, shall we? We need to review a few points.
Popescu	Yes, fine.
Wenzel	As I said in my email, competition is very stiff and our competitors are 10% cheaper than us. Do you see what I mean?
Popescu	Yes, I understand. A 10% reduction ... just let me think for a moment ...

Wenzel	Please take your time, Mr Popescu, and I have something for you because we are thinking of ordering 20% more from your company.
Popescu	20% more! That's great, but I would need more workers and machines, and I can't afford new machines.
Wenzel	We can help you with that, Mr Popescu. We can provide you with more machines if you can find more workers.
Popescu	Well, I can certainly find the workers.
Wenzel	And we need to talk about the delivery period, as well.
Popescu	The delivery period? Is 30 days too long?
Wenzel	30 days is fine, but it's sometimes a week longer and that is a problem for us. We need a *maximum* delivery period of 30 days.
Popescu	I understand, but the problem is the freight forwarder. His lorries break down a lot.
Wenzel	And I have the name of another company for you, Mr Popescu. I suggest that you use Road Train GmbH. Here's their card.
Popescu	Thank you!
Wenzel	Would you like some time to think about the new terms? Shall we take a break for coffee?
Popescu	Yes, fine.
...	
Wenzel	Have you had enough time to think about the new terms?
Popescu	Yes, and we are happy to accept them. I've phoned my boss and we can reduce the price by 5% as from next month and 10% as soon as we get the new machines. I've also phoned Road Train and they can start working for us next month.
Wenzel	That's good news, Mr Popescu! Now let's ...

Track 27: Unit 6, Communication, exercise 2

Paul	Guten Morgen. Top Mode Großhandel, Paul Smith am Apparat
Mary	Good morning. This is Mary Doyle calling from Dublin. I'd like to speak to Paul Smith, please.
Paul	Good morning, Ms Doyle. Paul Smith speaking. How can I help you?
Mary	Oh, hello, Mr Smith. I'm sorry to call at such short notice, but I'm afraid I have to reschedule our meeting on Thursday morning. I'm sorry, but something has come up and, unfortunately, I can't get out of it.
Paul	Oh. That's a pity. Do you have another time in mind?
Mary	Well, could we postpone the meeting until Friday at the same time? Would that suit you?
Paul	Hmm. I'll just check my diary .... Yes. That would be fine.
Mary	Oh. Thank you so much. I'm sorry to have inconvenienced you.
Paul	Don't worry. These things happen. OK, then. I'm looking forward to meeting you on Friday the twenty-seventh at 9.30.
Mary	Thank you. I look forward to meeting you, too. Bye.

Track 28: KMK exam practice 3, exercise 2, Hörverstehen

Mr Warden	OK, thanks for coming along this morning. Erm ... as I said in my email of 4 September, the purpose of the meeting this morning is for us to brainstorm some ideas. We're looking for promotional activities, basically, that we can use to make sure that the launch of the "Food Business Solutions Limited website" is a success right from the start. I'm very open to any ideas ... and we've got no limitation in our budget ... at the moment, anyway ... so fire away!
Stephanie	Fantastic, no budget constraints!
Claudine	That's great! I'm thinking television ... and radio!
Stephanie	Well, that really sounds big and exciting.
Mr Warden	Go ahead, Claudine.
Claudine	Well, if we have no limitation on the budget, we could reach a wide audience with something like that, and we could focus on some of the big business network television channels. If we want to reach a global market, I mean, if that's what we're aiming at ...
Stephanie	Yeah, TV and radio have been quite successful for some of our other projects, haven't they?
Mr Warden	That's right, it is definitely a focused way of advertising. But is it too focused and therefore a bit limited?
Stephanie	Well, I've been working on some cheaper solutions, just in case there are budget problems. I thought we could do some effective online promotion, which is actually quite cheap. We should definitely do direct mailing, but we should also register the site effectively with the big search engines. That way, anybody who surfs the net looking for business solutions comes up with our website.
Mr Warden	Well, yes, we should definitely do some of that.
Claudine	What about press advertising? Traditional newspapers, business magazines, journals?
Mr Warden	Yes, good idea. We've done that effectively in the past. We've had some good response rates to the ads we've placed before.
Claudine	Yes, and that would be something we could do more often, not just once, but in a kind of campaign, over a period of time.
Stephanie	And then, going back to cheaper solutions, we could use the database we've got, you know, all the market research we've been doing for this website. We've got some very good contacts from that. I think we could send out glossy brochures, maybe a demonstration CD ...
Mr Warden	That sounds like a good idea. What do you think ...

Track 29: Unit 7, Foundation, exercise 2A

1: Row stands
Row stands open onto the aisle. They have two neighbouring stands, one on each side. The benefit of row stands is that visitors walk past each stand as they go along the aisle. These are the cheapest stands to rent.

2: Corner stands
Corner stands are located at the end of a row and open onto two aisles which meet at the corner. These two aisles lead more visitors to this type of stand. Rental fees for a corner stand are higher than for a row stand.

3: End of block stands
End of block stands open onto three aisles. This openness makes this stand appear more welcoming than a row stand or a corner stand. End of block stands are more expensive than corner stands.

4: Island stands
Island stands are surrounded by aisles on all sides. The fact that they stand alone makes them very welcoming to visitors. These are the most expensive type of stand.

5: Outdoor stands
These stands are outside the exhibition hall. They are best for showing very large products like construction equipment. The rent for outdoor stands varies, depending on the product being shown.

Track 30: Unit 7, Part A, exercise 2

Dermot Good morning and thank you for calling Booth-Tech. You're through to Dermot. How can I help?
Lena Good morning, it's Lena Richter from Ökobau Müller in Germany. I'm calling about a stand for the Architecture and Building Expo in Dublin next year.
Dermot And we'll be delighted to help you! Let me take down some details about what you need. First of all, what is the purpose of your stand? Is your company launching a new product, for example?
Lena Well, no actually. We make eco-friendly house-building materials and we want to show our products to architects from all over Europe at the exhibition.
Dermot So your purpose is brand awareness.
Lena Yes, brand awareness. That sounds right.
Dermot And what size should the stand be?
Lena We want to show samples of our products – building materials for walls, floors, roofs and so on.
Dermot Walls, floors and roofs … In that case, I would suggest having a larger stand, so you have enough room for all your products. I would say about ten by five metres,
Lena Yes, that sounds about right and it also needs to be high.
Dermot We can go up to four metres.
Lena Four metres should be enough.
Dermot So that's ten by five and four metres high. Now what features should it have?
Lena Well, we'd like a counter at the front and a big screen for video loops.
Dermot Counter and screen … And how about seating? Tables and chairs, or bar tables and stools?
Lena Just let me think … I think a table, or perhaps even two tables, with three or four chairs each would be best.
Dermot So let's say two tables and chairs … And I would also recommend having some literature racks for your sales literature.
Lena Yes, that's a good idea. I think we'll need two literature racks for brochures and so on.
Dermot OK, fine. Anything else on the stand?
Lena We'd like some storage space.
Dermot Shall we include a lockable cupboard? I would strongly recommend including one, so you can store your valuables.
Lena Ah yes, that's a good idea.
Dermot And how is the space on the stand to be divided up? How much space will you need for your building materials?
Lena … I'd say about twenty-five square metres.
Dermot So that means 50% of the space will be for building materials in the product demonstration area. Now what about the other 25 square metres? How do you want to divide it up?
Lena Well, we'll need some space for the tables and chairs and some in front of the screen, and then there's the counter …
Dermot OK, I suggest that you split the other 25 square metres 50/50, and say half for the tables and chairs and the other half for the rest, the rest being the counter, the screen and the lockable cupboard. All right?
Lena Sounds good.
Dermot And how often do you want to use the stand?
Lena Well, we're also going to exhibit in the UK and Scandinavia after the trade fair in Dublin ... so if we can re-use the stand, that would be great.
Dermot So it's for multiple use. And have you thought about whether you want the stand to be one of a row of stands with access from the front only or do you want it to stand alone with access from all sides?
Lena I think access from all sides would be better.
Dermot In that case I would recommend that you have an island stand because that gives you access from all sides.
Lena Yes, I think that would be best.
Dermot OK, I've got that. Now what type of stand would suit you best – modular, shell scheme or bespoke?
Lena Well, as our products are building materials, we like the idea of a shell scheme stand because it can be made to look like the framework of a house.
Dermot Yes, that makes good sense, Lena. We always recommend using a shell scheme stand if you're exhibiting at different locations. Can I just have your details, so I can send you an offer?
Lena Yes, it's Ökobau Müller … that's spelt …

Track 31: Unit 7, Part B, exercise 2A

Dialogue 1: Japanese businessman
Alina Good morning, Mr Nakashima, and welcome back to our booth. I hope you are enjoying your visit to London.
Visitor 1 Good morning, Ms Adler. Yes, I love the culture in London and there is a lot to do here.
Alina Yes, I agree. Everybody finds something interesting to do in London. Would you like something to drink? A cup of coffee or tea or a mineral water?
Visitor 1 Mineral water, please.
Alina Still or sparkling?
Visitor 1 Still, please.
Alina Here you are.
Visitor 1 Thank you.
Alina You were interested in seeing the technical drawings of the adjustable table you looked at yesterday. Would you like to look at them now?
Visitor 1 Yes, please.
Alina Here you are.
Visitor 1 Thank you.
…
Visitor 1 Are the legs made of metal or wood?
Alina They're made of wood.
Visitor 1 Thank you. Can the length of the table be adjusted?
Alina Yes, it can be between 120 and 220 centimetres and the height is adjustable, too, so it can be a coffee or dining-room table. Would you like me to send you an offer for this table, Mr Nakashima? It's one of our best-selling lines.
Visitor 1 Perhaps later, Ms Adler.

Alina No problem at all, Mr Nakashima. Would you like to call by again tomorrow? It's the last day of the fair, but we'll still have some time to talk and if you place your order before the end of the month, you'll get a 20% discount.
Visitor 1 Yes, we can think about that and perhaps talk again. I need to talk to my colleagues.
Alina Yes, of course, Mr Nakashima. Thank you for …

Dialogue 2: Italian businessman

Alina Good morning, Mr Lombardi. It's nice to see you again.
Visitor 2 Good morning, Ms Adler. I'm very pleased to be back, and the weather is very good for London at this time of year, don't you think?
Alina Yes, indeed. I was expecting rain but it's a beautiful sunny day again.
Visitor 2 And we both have a lot of work to do before we can go outside and enjoy London. Have you been to the new Botticelli exhibition at the Tate Gallery?
Alina Yes, I went last weekend and I really enjoyed it.
Visitor 2 So did I. Each time I see his work I discover something new.
Alina Exactly. Would you like something to drink? Tea, coffee or water perhaps?
Visitor 2 No, thanks. I'm fine.
Alina Would you like me to demonstrate the adjustable table for you now, Mr Lombardi?
Visitor 2 Well, as it's almost midday, I thought we could first have lunch somewhere quieter and talk about our two companies and also get to know each other a little better before we do business. Do you have a lunch appointment?
Alina No, not today.
Visitor 2 Good because there's a very nice little restaurant just a few minutes from here.
Alina That's a nice idea, Mr Lombardi. But I have to be back by …
Visitor 2 Excuse me, Ms Adler. Pronto! … Arrivederci. That was my boss on the phone. He wants me to report back about the trade fair this evening and he also wants to know about your company before he places an order, so shall we go for lunch now before the restaurant gets very full?
Alina Yes, let's do that.
Visitor 2 Benissimo!

Dialogue 3: American businesswoman

Alina Good afternoon, Ms Parker. It's nice to see you again.
Visitor 3 Yes, I'm glad I was able to make it back. I have so much to do at the moment.
Alina Yes, I understand. Would you like something to drink? Coffee, tea or water perhaps?
Visitor 3 Thanks, but I really don't have much time right now. Let's talk about that adjustable table, shall we? The one right here in front of us. You gave me a brochure about it.
Alina Yes, that's right. Shall I demonstrate it to you?
Visitor 3 No, thanks. I've seen what I need to know. Look, I want to make you an offer for that table right now.
Alina Well … yes, if you have all the information you need.
Visitor 3 I do and if you can supply it for … Excuse me while I switch off my cell. Sorry about that.
Alina No problem.
Visitor 3 Well, as I was saying, if you can supply these tables for €200 per unit, you have a deal. Now, as I was saying …

Track 32: Unit 7, Communication, exercise 1

Katy British Airways Booking Service. Katy Atkins speaking. How can I help you?
Maria Good morning, Katy. This is Maria Weber in Berlin.
Katy Hi, Maria. Lovely to hear you. I haven't heard from you for ages. How are things in Berlin?
Maria They're fine, Katy. And how are you?
Katy Everything's just great, Maria. Still working for British Airways ... So, what can I do for you today?
Maria Well, I'm going to a conference in London, so I need two return flights, please. I'd like direct flights from Berlin to London on Thursday, April 19th, returning to Berlin on Monday, April 23rd.
Katy OK. Just a minute … Berlin to London, Thursday, April 19th, returning to Berlin on Monday, April 23rd. Business class or economy?
Maria I'm travelling with my assistant, so economy class, please.
Katy Right. What time do you want to leave Berlin?
Maria Sometime around nine in the morning would be good.
Katy I have a departure from Berlin, Tegel at 8.55 a.m., arriving in London, Heathrow at 9.50 a.m. That's BA flight 995. There are a few seats available in economy class on that flight. Only aisle seats left, I'm afraid; but I have two aisle seats in the same row, so you can talk across the aisle, if you want.
Maria I suppose that's OK. What about the return flight? That should be sometime in the late afternoon.
Katy Monday, 23rd, late afternoon. That looks more difficult. All the direct flights are booked till the early evening. Hang on, though … Here's flight BA 320. It's a direct flight, departure from London Heathrow at 19.40, arrival in Berlin at 22.35. Would that be OK? I have two seats next to each other, one of them is a window seat.
Maria Hmm. Listen. Can you reserve those seats on both flights for me, please? I'd like to check with my assistant if the later flight is OK with her.
Katy Of course. Just a moment, please … There you go. They're reserved till tomorrow at this time.
Maria Thanks, Katy. I'll get my assistant to call and confirm. Listen. When are you coming over to Berlin again?

Track 33: Unit 7, Communication, exercise 3A

1

Receptionist Good morning. Welcome to the International Hotel.
Guest 1 Good morning. My name is Rossi – Giovanni Rossi. I have a reservation.
Receptionist Here we are. Giovanni Rossi.
Guest 1 Yes. From Rossi Technology, Rome.
Receptionist Thank you. You're in room 303, on the third floor.
Guest 1 What time is breakfast served?
Receptionist We serve a buffet breakfast in the dining room between 8 and 10 a.m.
Guest 1 Eight till 10? Can I have a swim before breakfast?
Receptionist Yes, of course. The swimming pool is open from 6 a.m. till 10 p.m.
Guest 1 That's great. Thank you.
Receptionist You're welcome. Enjoy your stay, Mr Rossi.

2

Receptionist Good morning. Welcome to the International Hotel.
Guest 2 Good morning. I have a reservation under McGregor, McGregorRobotics.

Receptionist	Mary McGregor, from Glasgow.
Guest 2	Yes. That's right. I booked a room on the ground floor, with wheelchair access.
Receptionist	Yes, that's correct. You're in room 15, on this floor.
Guest 2	Does the dining room have wheelchair access?
Receptionist	Yes, it does. All of our rooms and facilities have wheelchair access.
Guest 2	Good. Thank you.
Receptionist	Let me know if you need any extra towels or pillows.
Guest 2	That's very kind of you.
Receptionist	My pleasure. Have a good stay, Ms McGregor.

3

Receptionist	Good morning. Welcome to the International Hotel.
Guest 3	Thank you. I would like to check in.
Receptionist	Of course. What name is the reservation under?
Guest 3	My name is Yusuf Zuabi.
Receptionist	Could you spell your surname, please?
Guest 3	Yes. It's Z U A B I, "Zuabi", with a Z. The reservation may be under the name of my company, Tech Solutions.
Receptionist	Thank you. Ah, yes, here it is, Tech Solutions, Berlin, Mr Yusuf Zuabi. You're in room 201, on the second floor. Here's your key. The buffet breakfast is served in the dining room between 8 and 10 a.m.
Guest 3	Thank you. I have a question. Where can I park my car?
Receptionist	There's a secure car park at the back of the hotel. The man at the gate will let you in.
Guest 3	Good. Thank you.
Receptionist	No problem. Enjoy your stay.

Track 34: Unit 8, Foundation, exercise 2B

Hello everybody, and welcome to today's Business Matters podcast. Today, I'm going to talk about what to look for in a supplier. We're all looking for a good deal, but the lowest price is not always the best value for money. Don't jump at an offer just because the price is inviting. Remember the saying, "You get what you pay for". Keeping this in mind, you should always check the whole package before you make a decision about a supplier. Here are five important things to take into consideration.

Firstly, the quality of the goods you buy needs to be consistent. Your customers will associate poor quality with you, not your suppliers, so it's important to find out if a new supplier can consistently provide high-quality goods. One way to judge this is to ask them how long they have been working with their other clients. It's a good sign if they have long-standing relationships with other buyers. References from other clients might be useful. Ask friends and business acquaintances. You're more likely to get an honest assessment of the strengths and weaknesses of a prospective supplier from someone who has used its services. Be careful with anonymous recommendations on the internet.

You should also take warranties into account. The most common warranty deals with the product being free from defects when it leaves a supplier. Usually, these are limited warranties, and a buyer has to make a claim within a specific time. Look into warranties very carefully before you finally decide on a supplier and make sure that they suit you.

Next, you should look at terms and conditions. It's important that you know your Incoterms. How are the responsibilities and obligations for the transport of the goods shared? Make sure that you are happy with the conditions a supplier is offering before you decide to go into business with them. You should also consider the terms of payment carefully. The best option for you would be open account terms, but a new supplier might ask for payment in advance until your relationship is established.

Last but not least, it's especially important to find out about the solvency of the supplier you're considering. If you don't do this, you might put your business at risk. Financial stability is important, especially if you are entering into a long-term contract or if the vendor is the only source of a particular item you need for your business. Search the internet for a company that will do a credit check for you before you make your final choice.

Well, I hope these ideas will help you when you are choosing a new supplier. Our next topic on Business Matters is …

Track 35: Unit 8, Part A, exercise 3

Sauerwald	Cantec GmbH, Dirk Sauerwald am Apparat. Was kann ich für Sie tun?
Booysen	Good morning, Mr Sauerwald. It's Luke Booysen from AgriTrade on the line. How are things?
Sauerwald	I can't complain … and how about you?
Booysen	It's another sunny day here in South Africa, so we can't complain, either.
Sauerwald	That's good to hear, Mr Booysen. How can I help you?
Booysen	The reason I'm calling is to ask a few questions about your company's initial proposal. Do you have a few moments?
Sauerwald	I most certainly do. What would you like to know?
Booysen	There are only a few points, so it won't take long. Let's start with the delivery period. How soon can you deliver?
Sauerwald	Well, after you have accepted our offer it normally takes about seven months.
Booysen	I see. Is there any chance of earlier delivery? Could you do three months?
Sauerwald	Well, that would be very difficult for us, Mr Booysen. We already have a number of orders. We can probably deliver in six months instead of seven, but I'm afraid we can't do three months. Sorry.
Booysen	All right, I've made a note of that. The next point is training. According to your proposal, you'll train our staff to operate the production line. Would that be here in South Africa?
Sauerwald	No, it's here in Germany. Your staff will be invited to our factory here in Essen, where your CAN-O-MAT production line will be up and running. We will then train them how to operate and maintain it, and we'll also show them how to troubleshoot if there are any problems.
Booysen	Very good. Now I see that the whole production line costs eight hundred thousand euros, but does this price include delivery to the port of Cape Town? That would be ideal for us because we are only 60 kilometres away.
Sauerwald	Delivery from Germany to the port of Cape Town would be CIF or CFR Cape Town and that would be a lot more expensive for you. Our price is an FOB price, meaning in this case that we will deliver the goods to a European North Sea port. The nearest ports to us are Rotterdam or Hamburg.

Booysen	So that means that we're responsible for shipping from Europe to South Africa. I see ... Will you be able to assist us with finding a suitable shipping company?
Sauerwald	We most certainly will, Mr Booysen. And the good news is that our price includes seaworthy packing to make sure the goods arrive in Cape Town in perfect condition.
Booysen	Great! Now what about payment? How much do you need in advance, 30%?
Sauerwald	Well, 33% in fact, which is usual in this sector.
Booysen	I see. And when would you require us to pay the remainder?
Sauerwald	When the goods are shipped. We'll let you have all the details in our official offer. Anything else I can do for you?
Booysen	Yes, I'd like to know a little more about after-sales service, but that's my last point. What does your after-sales service include?
Sauerwald	Well, it includes spare parts, of course, but we also store details of all the machinery we supply on a database, so if there's a problem, we first try to diagnose it remotely. We then know what spare parts to send you or what to repair.
Booysen	That's an excellent service, but what if remote diagnosis doesn't find the fault? Do you have a local representative or agent in South Africa?
Sauerwald	No, not yet, but if remote diagnosis doesn't work, we send over a technician from Germany and any parts needed are delivered by express.
Booysen	Good. I think I have all the information I need now. When can I expect your offer?

Track 36: Unit 8, Part B, exercise 2

1: Electricity generators

Majlen	Hej, Energi AB, Majlen Lofquist.
Sven	Hej, Sven Maier. Forstar du engelska?
Majlen	Yes, I do. How can I help?
Sven	Well I'm glad you speak English, because that's all the Swedish I know!
Majlen	No problem at all, Mr Maier. How can I help you?
Sven	I'm a buyer at MegaKauf in Dusseldorf, Germany. I'm phoning to enquire about your electricity generators. We're interested in buying fifteen of your Full Power 500 model.
Majlen	Full Power 500 ... just a moment ... I have it here on the screen. It's a very popular generator.
Sven	Exactly. We know what the basic price is, so now we'd like to talk about your terms of delivery.
Majlen	I see. A lot of our German customers give us the name of a ship to load the goods onto at the port of Malmö and then pick them up at the port of Hamburg. Our factory is in Lund, which is close to the port of Malmö. Shall we do that for you?
Sven	Thanks, but we'd prefer to pick them up at Dusseldorf Central Station. Can you send them to us to arrive in Dusseldorf by rail?
Majlen	No problem. With or without insurance?
Sven	With insurance, please. Could you send me a quotation?
Majlen	Yes, certainly. By rail from our factory in Lund to Dusseldorf Central Station, with insurance ...

2: Garden furniture

Ken	Hello, Shenzhen Trading China. How can I help you?
Sven	Hello, It's Sven Maier from MegaKauf in Dusseldorf, Germany. Can I speak to Mr Woo, please?
Ken	Speaking, Mr Maier. How can I help you?
Sven	Hello, Mr Woo. My company is interested in your garden furniture.
Ken	We are very pleased to hear that you are interested in our products, Mr Maier. Would you like some more information?
Sven	Yes, can I ask you some questions about shipment of your furniture?
Ken	Certainly, Mr Maier. What would you like to know?
Sven	Well, we're interested in a full container load, which we would like to collect at the port of Rotterdam.
Ken	I see. Rotterdam in the Netherlands. Not Hamburg?
Sven	We are, in fact, nearer Rotterdam than Hamburg here. Can you ship the container to Rotterdam, with insurance?
Ken	With insurance to the port of Rotterdam ... That is possible, but the Chinese shipping line we use is booked up for eight weeks.
Sven	Eight weeks! Oh dear, that's a long time. Can *we* suggest a German shipping line to you? I'm thinking of the Hamburg Süd line.
Ken	Yes, Mr Maier but then your shipping line must collect the container at the port of Shenzhen. This means that we will load the container onto a German ship at the port of Shenzhen and you will organize transport from there.
Sven	That's fine, Mr Woo. I'll contact Hamburg Süd and get them to pick up the container at the port of Shenzhen ...

3: LED displays

Lorna	Dublin Electronics, you're through to Lorna. How can I help?
Sven	Hello, it's Sven Maier from MegaKauf in Dusseldorf, Germany. Can I speak to someone about ordering a thousand LED displays, type SA15?
Lorna	I can help you with that. Just let me check ... Yes, we have them in stock. And you need – how many did you say, a thousand?
Sven	Yes, that's right. How soon can you deliver?
Lorna	Well, we can add them to our container on board a ship leaving Dublin port and docking in Rotterdam next Friday. That's the cheapest option but it's without insurance, Sven.
Sven	From Dublin port to Rotterdam next Friday without insurance. Well, that's a bit too slow for us, Lorna. Is there a faster option?
Lorna	What if we send them by air? They're pretty light.
Sven	Yes, that's right and we're very near Dusseldorf airport. How soon would we get them?
Lorna	48 hours after receipt of order. Would that be soon enough?
Sven	Yes, that would be fine. Could you send me an offer today?
Lorna	Yes, no problem. With or without insurance to Dusseldorf airport?
Sven	Well, they're not breakable and the displays aren't expensive. I'd say without insurance.
Lorna	So that's delivery to Dusseldorf Airport without insurance ...

Track 37: Unit 9, Part A, exercise 3

Luke Good morning, Murphy's Homecare Ltd. You're through to Luke O'Connor. How can I help?

Leonie Good morning, Luke. It's Leonie Hartmann from MegaKauf in Germany.

Luke Hi, Leonie. Thanks for getting back to me so quickly. How are you?

Leonie I'm fine thanks, Luke. How are you?

Luke Busy as always, but that's the way I like it. Now I'm sure you're phoning me about the gas barbecues. Is that right?

Leonie Yes, that's right. I got your email asking for an offer and I think we have exactly what you're looking for.

Luke I'm all ears, Leonie.

Leonie Well, our best-selling model over here is the Greber Classic model. It has two burners, two side tables, electronic ignition, a built-in lid thermometer, a gas tank holder and wheels so you can move it around.

Luke A built-in lid thermometer?

Leonie Yes, that's right, so you can check the temperature without losing heat.

Luke Sounds good. Does it have two or four wheels?

Leonie Two. That makes it safer because it can't roll away.

Luke I see what you mean. What materials is it made of?

Leonie The cooking plates are cast iron. The lid and body are aluminium.

Luke I see. Can you send me some literature on it, so I can study the details more closely?

Leonie Yes, certainly. I'll email you a brochure.

Luke And what about the price?

Leonie Our basic price is €200 per unit FCA Dusseldorf and our terms of payment are 30 days net.

Luke FCA Dusseldorf ... so we would have to organize transport of the goods from Dusseldorf to our warehouse in Kildare.

Leonie Yes, that's right. Isn't Kildare near Dublin?

Luke Yes, it's about 60 kilometres from Dublin. Could you stretch to CIF Dublin Port for the same price?

Leonie Well, there's a big difference between FCA Dusseldorf and CIF Dublin. We'd have to charge you at least 10% more for that because CIF would include the main carriage and also insurance.

Luke I see ... Look, before we finalize the price let me tell you that we're thinking of ordering a hundred units. Would that qualify for a discount?

Leonie Yes, we could give you 5% on a hundred units.

Luke And would they all fit into a standard 20-foot container?

Leonie Easily. We supply them flat-packed to save space.

Luke Good, and ideally we'd like you to deliver the barbecues to our warehouse.

Leonie We can do a door-to-door delivery for you, Luke. And what about risks in transit. Do you want coverage for that?

Luke Yes, we'd need that.

Leonie In that case, delivery would be DAP your premises in Kildare, but it would make the price more expensive.

Luke Can you give me a quote?

Leonie Yes, certainly. DAP Kildare, Ireland ... That would come to €2,250.

Luke Oh, I see ... Is there a cheaper option?

Leonie How about CIF Dublin Port as you mentioned earlier? That includes insurance in transit and would cost you ... €1,250, but you would need to collect the goods at the port yourself.

Luke I think that sounds like the best option because we're close to Dublin here. How long would it take?

Leonie Three days from Dusseldorf to Dublin.

Luke And what about the final price for the barbecues if we order a hundred units?

Leonie Well, as I said, we can offer you a 5% discount on a hundred units, so that would bring the price down from €20,000 to €19,000.

Luke So I save €1,000 on the price and pay €1,250 for delivery.

Leonie Exactly. I think that the CIF price is pretty reasonable. Anything else you need to know?

Luke Yes, one more thing. What's your delivery period?

Leonie 14 days after receipt of order.

Luke Excellent! We have a deal, Leonie. Would you send me all this in writing?

Leonie I most certainly will ...

Track 38: Unit 9, Part B, exercise 3

Dialogue 1

Maria Pronto?

Emil Buongiorno. Sono Emil Partmann in Germania. Do you speak English?

Maria Yes, I do, Mr Partmann. How can I help you?

Emil I work for Megakauf in Germany. My boss saw your furniture at the Ambiente trade fair in Frankfurt, and now I'm calling about your Allaperto garden sets. We would like to know what your terms are.

Maria With pleasure, Mr Partmann. What would you like to know?

Emil My boss told me that the price was €700 DAP Dusseldorf. Is that right and is there a minimum order quantity?

Maria The price and Incoterm are correct. There is no minimum order quantity for an initial order, but after that it's five sets.

Emil I see. How long does it take to deliver them?

Maria Our delivery period is 13 days, door-to-door to you in Dusseldorf.

Emil Door-to-door ... thanks. Could you tell me what your terms of payment are?

Maria CWO or letter of credit. If you place regular orders, our terms are 30 days net.

Emil Good. What guarantee do you give?

Maria Five years on all structural parts.

Emil Do you grant a quantity discount?

Maria How many sets are you thinking of ordering?

Emil 20 sets.

Maria Well, we could grant you a quantity discount of 2% but on 100 sets.

Emil I see.

Maria Is there anything else you would like to know, Mr Partmann?

Emil That's it for the time being. I'll be in touch.

Maria Thanks for calling. Have a nice day.

Emil You too. Bye.

Maria Bye.

Dialogue 2

Amélie Bonjour, merci d'appeler Projardin. Je suis Amélie. Que puis-je faire pour vous?

Emil Bonjour. Ici Emil Partmann en Allemagne. Do you speak English?

Amélie Yes, I do, monsieur Partmann. How can I help you?

Emil I'm calling you from Megakauf in Germany. Our Purchasing Director saw your furniture at the *Ambiente* trade fair in Frankfurt, and we'd like to know what your terms are for your Saint-Tropez garden sets.

Amélie Of course, monsieur Partmann. We have a special offer for them at the moment.

Emil Excellent!

Amélie They cost €700 and we also deliver DAT to your local terminal. Where is that for you, monsieur Partmann?

Emil Dusseldorf Central Station. We're very near it, so we would only need to collect the load and take it to our premises. Is there a minimum order quantity?

Amélie: Yes, it's five sets.

Emil Thanks. How long would it take to deliver?

Amélie We have the garden sets in stock, so it would take one day from here to Dusseldorf.

Emil Yes, it isn't very far from Metz to Dusseldorf. Could you tell me what your terms of payment are?

Amélie They are CWO for an initial order, then 10 days 2%, 30 days net for regular orders.

Emil Thanks. How long is your guarantee?

Amélie Three years on all structural parts.

Emil What about discounts?

Amélie If 50 or more sets are ordered, we grant a 3% discount.

Emil 3% ... thanks.

Amélie Is there anything else you'd like to know, monsieur Partmann?

Emil That's all for the time being. I'll be in touch.

Amélie Thanks for calling Projardin. Bye.

Emil Thank you. Bye.

Track 39: Unit 9, Communication, exercise 1B/C

Mary Marx Kitchens, Sales Department. Mary Hamilton speaking. How can I help you?

John Ah. Good morning. This is John Jamieson speaking. I've just received an offer in reply to an enquiry I sent last week, but some of the details are missing.

Mary Oh. I'm sorry to hear that, Mr Jamieson. Just a moment, please. Is that J-A-M-I-E-S-O-N?

John Erm, yes.

Mary OK, I have a copy of the offer here. It appears to be complete. Shall we go through the details together?

John Yes. I think that would be the best idea. I need the goods urgently, so I really would like to have everything sorted out as soon as possible.

Mary Of course. If you could just tell me what you need to know.

John Well, first of all, I'd like to know your terms of delivery.

Mary We deliver within six weeks, cost, insurance, freight. I see you're in Liverpool, so that's CIF to Liverpool.

John CIF, Liverpool. Good. There's a note here about smaller numbers of items being delivered from stock. How many items would that be?

Mary Anything up to ten items.

John OK. Ten. And what about bulk orders? There's mention of a discount on bulk orders, but there's no mention of how many items that covers.

Mary We give a discount on orders of more than 50 items.

John And how much is the discount?

Mary The discount is three per cent.

John OK. Three per cent discount on bulk orders of more than 50 items. Erm. There's a note here about payment for first orders, but again, the most important information is missing.

Mary For new customers, we prefer cash with the first order.

John I understand that. That's no problem. Cash with first order. OK. So, the last thing is, the catalogue was enclosed with the offer, but I can't see any information on page 6 about the VAT. Do your prices include VAT or not?

Mary I'm afraid our prices do not include VAT.

John Ah. I thought that might be the case. Well, I think I have all the information I need now.

Mary Mr Jamieson, I really must apologize for the problems with the offer. I'm so sorry that you've had to go to all this trouble. Is there anything else I can help you with?

John No, I don't think so, Ms Hamilton. I'd like to discuss the offer with my partner before we go any further. Thank you. Goodbye.

Track 40: Unit 9, Communication, exercise 2A

John Jamieson and Walker, John Jamieson speaking.

Mary Good morning, Mr Jamieson. Mary Hamilton, Marx Kitchens here. Is this a good time to call?

John Yes, of course. Nice to hear from you. What can I do for you, Ms Hamilton?

Mary Well, it's about your order.

John Oh, dear. I hope there aren't any problems with the delivery.

Mary No. There aren't any problems with the delivery. It's just that there are a few mistakes in the order form which we should clear up.

John OK. Hang on a second. I'll just call it up on my screen. Here we are: "Microwave ovens and electric kettles".

Mary Yes. That's the first problem, I'm afraid. Do you have a copy of our catalogue handy?

John Yes. I do. Here we are.

Mary I need to know the item number of the ovens you'd like, and the item number of the kettles.

John Oh, sorry ... just a moment ... Here it is. The oven we'd like to order is MM 89 in white, and the number of the kettle is EK 39, blue.

Mary Aha. MM 89 white, and EK 39, the blue kettle.

John That's correct. The blue kettle.

Mary Now, the next thing is the final payment. If you remember, we discussed the discount on bulk orders. I'm afraid you have to buy 50 of each of the items before you get that discount.

John Oh dear. Sorry about that. I must have misunderstood.

Mary No problem. The last thing is the VAT. I'm afraid we need to recalculate the total price.

John Of course. Should I re-submit the order?

Mary No, don't worry, Mr Jamieson. I'll ask my assistant to make the corrections and I'll email you a new copy of the order. All right?

John Thank you, Ms Hamilton. I really appreciate that.

Track 41: Unit 10, Part A, exercise 2A

Nasir A.P. Leather International. Good morning, Nasir Mahmood speaking. How can I help you?
Sven Good morning, Mr Mahmood. It's Sven Maier from MegaKauf in Germany.
Nasir Good morning, Mr Maier! It's very nice to hear from you again. Are the leather garments selling well?
Sven Indeed they are, Mr Mahmood and I would like to order some more.
Nasir That is excellent news, Mr Maier. How many would you like?
Sven Well, before we talk about that, I'd like to discuss our terms and prices.
Nasir I see, Mr Maier. Our prices are already very competitive.
Sven Yes, but so far we have only placed orders for 400 items and now we would like to order much larger quantities.
Nasir This sounds very good, Mr Maier.
Sven And we require delivery CIF Bremen for the same price.
Nasir The same price! We will go bankrupt, Mr Maier! That is impossible. I'm very sorry but we cannot afford that. Our ex works price is already very competitive.
Sven Now we wish to order 6,000 items.
Nasir 6,000 items!
Sven On a regular basis. I mean every three months. And for that we want open account terms with quarterly settlement.
Nasir 6,000 items every three months! That's 24,000 a year. Let me think …
Sven Well, don't think for too long, Mr Mahmood because we have customers waiting over here.
Nasir Look, we can offer you FCA Lahore. That is much better for your driver when he comes to collect the goods here in Lahore, because we will load them onto his lorry for him.
Sven I'm afraid that isn't enough, Mr Mahmood. We have other suppliers who offer much more.
Nasir All right, Mr Maier. We will accept all risks and pay the transport costs of the goods from Lahore to the port of Karachi including loading and export clearance.
Sven So you're offering FOB Karachi … And your terms of payment?
Nasir Yes, FOB Karachi and please understand that to finance production of such large numbers of leather garments we will still need part of the payment in advance.
Sven We're already paying you 25% in advance, Mr Mahmood.
Nasir But for such big orders we need to make a much bigger investment here … Look, I can offer you one-third with order, one-third on delivery and one-third 30 days after delivery.
Sven All right, Mr Mahmood. To get you started, we'll accept FOB Karachi, but then the terms of payment must be one-third with order, one-third on delivery and one-third 90 days after delivery.
Nasir 90 days …
Sven Yes, and we'll accept those terms for one year only starting today. After that, we'll expect open account terms. And there's another thing, Mr Mahmood. So far, we've had groupage consignments, but that's a security risk.
Nasir But your orders have not filled a container, Mr Maier, so that's why they were LCL.
Sven Yes, but now we want FCL.
Nasir No problem, Mr Maier, because 6,000 items will be a full container load, so we can change the terms from LCL to FCL.
Sven But I want a guarantee in writing, Mr Mahmood. It must *always* be FCL and *never* LCL.
Nasir All right, it's a deal, Mr Maier.
Sven Good, but these new terms are only valid for one year, Mr Mahmood. After that we'll review everything again. Please send me an email confirming the new terms in writing, then I'll email you our order straight away.
Nasir You'll get my email in a few minutes, Mr Maier …

Track 42: Unit 10, Part B, exercise 3A

Louisa Guten Morgen, Brewery-2-Brewery, Sie sprechen mit Louisa Schneider. Was kann ich für Sie tun?
Kevin Good morning. This is Kevin King from Harpoon Brew Supply in Bedford, Massachusetts. I hope you speak English, ma'am.
Louisa No problem, Mr King. How can I help you?
Kevin Well, I'm phoning about the microbrewery that we ordered. It's order no. MB721A. Have you shipped it yet?
Louisa Just a moment, Mr King … MB721A … Ah yes, here it is. Yes, we shipped it yesterday. It's at the port of Hamburg now and will be loaded on MS Arcadia, which sails for the port of Boston tomorrow. The consignment is due to arrive in Boston at the end of next week.
Kevin Well, thank goodness I phoned you in time!
Louisa I don't understand, Mr King.
Kevin Well, I have bad news for you. We've had a big fire in our warehouse here in Bedford, Massachusetts. The whole building has burned down, so we won't be able to pay for the microbrewery until the insurance company has paid us. I thought it best to warn you as soon as possbible. The good news is that we've found another customer in Philadelphia who will buy the microwbrewery. The customer is Lopez Catering Incorporated. They have agreed to buy the equipment if we deliver it to their door, so we would like you to ship it to them instead.
Louisa Just a minute, Mr King. Let me check the terms of payment and delivery … I see that payment is by letter of credit with delivery CFR Boston, Massachusetts …
Kevin And we'd like you to change that to CFR Philadelphia for the new customer, Lopez Catering.
Louisa Well, I'm afraid we can't do that, Mr King. In fact we can't change anything at all because it's an irrevocable letter of credit.
Kevin Oh no! We have nowhere to put the microbrewery and we can't pay for it either!
Louisa But the good news is that as it's a *confirmed* letter of credit, we have already received payment from our bank. We presented the documents listed in the credit, they were in order and we received payment.
Kevin So where are the documents? We haven't heard anything from our bank yet.
Louisa They're somewhere in the banking system, Mr King. Our bank will send them to your bank and your bank will ask you to pay.
Kevin But we can't! That's the problem.
Louisa I understand that you're in a very difficult situation, Mr King, but as you already have a customer for the microbrewery, you now need to speak to your bank and ask them to release the documents to the new customer in Philadelphia instead of to you.
Kevin I see. So the consignment will arrive in Boston one way or another and then has to be shipped to Philadelphia.

Louisa Exactly. We can't change the destination now. I suggest you get onto your bank and transfer ownership of the consignment to Lopez Catering. Then you will have to arrange for shipment of the goods from Boston to Philadelphia. If you need help you can always contact Nancy Kline, our agent in New York. I'll send you her contact details.
Kevin OK, I'll give it a try. Thanks for your help.
Louisa You're welcome, Mr King. Is there anything else I can do for you?
Kevin No thanks, Ms Schneider. Have a nice day,
Louisa You too, Mr King. Bye for now.
Kevin Bye.

Track 43: Unit 10, Part B, exercise 4A/B

Kevin Harpoon Brew, this is Kevin King speaking. How may I help you?
Nancy Good morning, Mr King. It's Nancy Kline from Brewery-2-Brewery in New York. I'm calling about the microbrewery.
Kevin Good morning, Ms Kline. Thanks for getting back to me. Have you spoken to Lopez Catering?
Nancy Yes, I've been in touch with them and I think we have a solution now, Mr King.
Kevin You mean you can reroute it?
Nancy Not exactly, but as good as. As you know, the equipment is still on board a ship in the Atlantic and the documents are in the banking system. You now need to get onto your bank and transfer ownership to Lopez Catering in Philadelphia. I've spoken to Lopez Catering myself and they will pay your bank for the equipment after it has been unloaded in Boston. We'll organize the rest for you.
Kevin That sounds good. Can I now leave it all to you and the bank?
Nancy Well, not exactly, Mr King. Remember that it's a CFR delivery, which means that the buyer pays for unloading at the port of destination, in this case the port of Boston.
Kevin And at this moment I'm still the buyer, right?
Nancy Exactly, so you'll have to pay for that. And then the goods will have to be collected at the port of Boston and transported to Lopez Catering in Philadelphia.
Kevin So I'll have to pay for that too …
Nancy Yes, but remember that you're lucky to have found a buyer so quickly, Mr King!
Kevin Yes, I suppose you're right. OK, so tell me about transporting the goods to Philadelphia. Would it not be easiest just to send the consignment from Boston to Philadelphia by ship? It could be loaded onto another ship in Boston and finally unloaded in Philadelphia.
Nancy I see what you mean, but according to the terms of the documentary credit, the goods need to be unloaded in Boston first and transshipment is not allowed.
Kevin I see. So what do you suggest?
Nancy Well, we can either send the equipment to Philadelphia by rail or road.
Kevin I see. What about the price? I want to keep it as low as possible.
Nancy I understand, Mr King. Six wooden crates packed in three containers delivered CPT Philadelphia train station would cost $1,590, but that's without insurance and you would still need to have the containers picked up and taken to Lopez Catering.
Kevin And by road?
Nancy DAP delivery by road to Lopez Catering would cost $1,600.
Kevin And insurance?
Nancy DAP includes insurance.
Kevin Well, as Lopez Catering wants door-to-door delivery, that sounds like the best option but, just out of interest, how much would it cost to ship the consignment to the port of Philadelphia by sea?
Nancy It would cost $2,160 for delivery port-to-port. In this case it would be CFR Philadelphia and it would take at least seven days.
Kevin That's a big difference.
Nancy And it wouldn't be door-to-door.
Kevin Ah yes, of course. What's the delivery time overland?
Nancy One day.
Kevin Well, I think you've found the best option, Ms Kline. What do I do next?
Nancy You will be contacted by Pennsylvania Logistics. That's the freight forwarder I recommend because they've worked for us in the past. They will send you a contract of carriage for you to sign and they'll do the rest.
Kevin Well, thanks for your help, Ms Kline. That's a load off my shoulders!
Nancy You're welcome, Mr King, and we'll make sure the load gets to Lopez Catering for you …

Track 44: KMK Exam practice 5, exercise 3, Hörverstehen

Hi, there, Tom here, sorry I was very busy this morning, and now you're away. Well, I guess the old answering machine will do …
I haven't finished all my research yet, but here's what I've found out so far. There are two options in the region. The first warehouse is only about 400 metres away, so it's actually in the direct neighbourhood of our warehouse. It's rather big, 600 square metres, and in good condition. It was renovated recently and is completely equipped with thermal insulation. It will be available next spring. My contact was a Mr Miller, a very friendly person, and he showed me the whole place. I'm no expert but it looks good. By the way, Mr Miller is in the picture and you can call him directly for more information. That would be 0767 3294418.
The second warehouse I looked at was in Chester, about one mile away from the company. It consists of two parts that could be connected, so it would be either 200 square metres or 450 square metres. The good thing is that we could rent it straight away as there is no tenant at the moment. But frankly, the place looks rather shabby and it was dirty, perhaps we need to look somewhere else … Anyway, I don't have a contact person for that warehouse yet, apart from the estate agent who gave me the address. The facility manager of the place didn't call me back so I just went there on my own. That's why I'd suggest writing an official mail. You can find all the information on the website of Benson Warehousing, the email address is benson@spaceplace.com, that's B-E-N-S-O-N.
Oh, I nearly forgot: prices! Benson is £35 per square metre, per quarter. The agent had a list for me. The other one, you know, the one nearby, is £160 per square metre, per year.
OK, that's all for now. You said you needed the information quickly. If you have any questions, or if I've forgotten anything, just call me on my mobile. Have a nice day!

Track 45: Unit 11, Foundation, exercise 3

… We all know that mistakes happen every so often, and we have to complain to our suppliers too every now and then. In case you ever have to deal with a complaint, I'd just like to run through a few points with you. Let's start with telephone complaints. Before you make the call, have all the paperwork you need beside you. And have something you can make notes with.

At the start of the call, get the name of the person you're talking to. And, by the way, always be polite. The person you speak to on the phone is not responsible for the mistake. That person is simply an employee of a company, just like you are, so remember to stay calm and keep cool.

No matter what the problem is, follow up your telephone complaint with an email to the supplier so that everyone has a record of what has been agreed. Copy in your line manager so that everyone knows that the complaint is being dealt with.

When you make a complaint in writing, start with the details of the transaction, things like the order number and the date of delivery.

In the body of the letter, describe the problem clearly and point out the inconvenience this is causing the company.

Make a suggestion how to resolve the problem, for example, the company could send a replacement or give you a discount.

In conclusion, ask for immediate action. OK. That's it. Any questions? No? Good. It's not too difficult to deal with a complaint as long as you …

Track 46: Unit 11, Part A, exercise 3A/B

Tamara Guten Morgen, MegaKauf GmbH. Sie sprechen mit Tamara Beck. Was kann ich für Sie tun?

Gunner Good morning, it's Gunner Kristoffersen from Fixit DIY Stores in Copenhagen. I hope you speak English.

Tamara Yes, I do, Mr Kristoffersen. How can I help you?

Gunner The reason I'm calling is to tell you that we're extremely dissatisfied with the EW1 smoke alarms we received from you last week. Some of the alarms are faulty, meaning that they don't work when tested. Others are discoloured, and in some of the boxes the batteries and mounting screws are missing.

Tamara Oh dear, faulty, discoloured and also missing parts! I'm very sorry to hear that, Mr Kristoffersen. Could I have the order number, please?

Gunner Yes, it's order number SA450, dated the twelfth of last month.

Tamara Let me just check … Yes, I've got it here. An order for 500 EW1 smoke alarms.

Gunner Yes, and let me point out that the alarms are still under warranty and we sell them to our customers in Denmark with both the statutory 24-month warranty and an extra three years' guarantee on our part, meaning they must last at least five years. These alarms haven't lasted a week!

Tamara We're extremely sorry to hear that, Mr Kristoffersen. We take customers' complaints very seriously and I assure you we'll find a solution as soon as possible.

Gunner Well it had better be soon because our customers are complaining and we don't want to lose them. We have our company's good name to think of!

Tamara I fully understand, Mr Kristoffersen. I'll contact the manufacturer immediately and get back to you.

Gunner We expect you to replace the whole consignment free of charge. And we won't be paying for the alarms until we are perfectly satisfied.

Tamara I see … Well, the terms of payment are 10 days 2%, 30 days net, so we still have some time.

Gunner If we don't get replacements, we'll return the whole consignment carriage forward and cancel all future orders.

Tamara I'm sure that won't be necessary, Mr Kristoffersen.

Gunner We'll see. You have exactly one week to send us replacements and no longer.

Tamara Please let me apologize for the inconvenience this has caused you, Mr Kristoffersen. You'll be hearing from us again very soon, and I'm sure we'll find a solution.

Gunner I hope so. Goodbye.

Tamara Thanks for calling, Mr Kristoffersen. Goodbye.

Track 47: Unit 11, Part B, exercise 4A/C

Rita MegaKauf Großhandel GmbH, Ronstadt, guten Morgen. Was kann ich für Sie tun?

Rory Good morning, it's Rory Kelly from Sligo Potteries. Am I speaking to Rita Ronstadt?

Rita Yes, you are, Mr Kelly. Thanks for calling. Is it about the statement?

Rory Yes, that's right. I got your email yesterday. Sorry about the mix-up with the prices and so on, but I think I've got to the bottom of it now.

Rita Good. What went wrong? Did you just forget the credit note?

Rory Well, it's not as simple as that. Let me first explain why it wasn't included. The €498 was for goods returned to us last year, and we sent you a credit note in the form of a code. That meant we would deduct €498 from your next order.

Rita Well, I understand, but our next order on 9 January was only for €300 so we didn't include the code.

Rory That's no problem, but it should have been included at some time during the quarter and it wasn't, so that's why it was omitted from your statement.

Rita Oh, I see. Is it too late now?

Rory No, you can still include it, and then we'll update your account.

Rita Good. And what about the special offer for Shamrock crockery? What happened there?

Rory I've investigated that as well and I've found out what went wrong. You saw the offer on our website, didn't you?

Rita Yes, that's right. We were delighted because the Shamrock line sells well over here, so we ordered immediately.

Rory I'm glad to hear that, Ms Ronstadt, but you didn't order through the website … You didn't click the button on the website to place your order and get your special price discount.

Rita Well, that was our Purchasing department. It looks like they didn't order through the website, because they ordered some champagne flutes as well. They probably just ordered everything together in the usual way by email.

Rory Well, that explains why you didn't get the special offer because our software was programmed to grant the reduction on all orders placed via the button on the website.

Rita I see. So what's going to happen now? We're talking about a difference of more than €2,000.
Rory I have the solution, Ms Ronstadt. I'll send you an email with a special link to your account. If you then type in the details of your order for the Shamrock crockery again, and also include the code for the credit note we sent you for €498, our software will update your account with the right amounts and we'll send you a new statement. Is that all right?
Rita Yes, that's fine, Mr Kelly. When can I expect your email?
Rory I'll send it straight away. Is there anything else I can do for you?
Rita No, thanks very much.
Rory Well, I'm glad we were able to sort it all out. Please get in touch if you have any more queries.
Rita I'll do that, Mr Kelly. Thanks for calling. Bye.
Rory Bye.

Track 48: Unit 11, Communication, exercise 2A

Melissa Wolf.
Jerzy Oh. Hello. Erm. Do you speak English?
Melissa Yes.
Jerzy Oh. Good. This is Jerzy Adamczyk calling from the Anatol Kaminski Clinic in Warsaw. Is that MedEquip in Berlin ... the Sales department?
Melissa Yes.
Jerzy And, erm, who am I speaking to, please?
Melissa Wolf.
Jerzy Ah. Ms Wolf. Erm. Is, erm, are you the correct person to take a complaint about a delivery?
Melissa What's the problem?
Jerzy It's about my order for operating theatre monitors. Both of the monitors were damaged. One of them – the screen on one of the monitors is scratched, and the other monitor is dented. I mean, the metal casing is dented. I think that ...
Melissa What's the order number?
Jerzy 942761.
Melissa OK. I can't do anything at the moment. I'll get it sorted after lunch.
Jerzy So, will you phone me back? My phone number is ...
Melissa It's here on the display.
Jerzy 0048 129 577 042?
Melissa Yes.
Jerzy And my name is Adamczyk. You will be sure to look into this? Well, thank you very much.

Track 49: Unit 11, Communication, exercise 2B

Melissa Guten Morgen. MedEquip GmbH, Verkaufsabteilung. Melissa Wolf am Apparat.
Jerzy Oh. Hello. Erm. Do you speak English?
Melissa Yes, of course. How can I help you?
Jerzy Oh. Good. This is Jerzy Adamczyk calling from the Anatol Kaminski Clinic in Warsaw. Is that the Sales department?
Melissa Yes, this is the Sales department. My name's Melissa Wolf.
Jerzy Ah. Mrs, erm, Ms Wolf. Hmm. Is, erm, are you the correct person to take a complaint about a delivery?
Melissa It depends on what it's about. Could you give me some details?
Jerzy It's about my order for operating theatre monitors. Both of the monitors were damaged. One of them – the screen on one of the monitors is scratched and the other monitor is dented. I mean, the metal casing is dented. I think that there was a problem during transport.
Melissa Oh, I'm sorry to hear that. Could you give me the order number, please?
Jerzy It's 942761.
Melissa Just a moment, please. Right. 942761. I have it here. Two X-ray machines. And you say that both of them are damaged?
Jerzy That is correct. I am sorry, but I have to say that I am disappointed about this business. This is a trial order, but I had to complain last week because the equipment didn't arrive on the date we agreed. Now the monitors are here and I can't use them.
Melissa Oh, dear. I'm extremely sorry to hear that you've had so much trouble. I'm sure my superior would like to discuss this with you. Can I ask her to phone you when she comes in to work tomorrow?
Jerzy Yes. All right. I'll be at home all day tomorrow, so she should call me there. The number is 0048 129 546 993.
Melissa 0048 129 546 993. Yes. You'll get a call from my superior tomorrow, Mr Adamczyk.
Jerzy Could you tell me her name, please?
Melissa It's Mia Richter.
Jerzy Mia Richter. Good. Thank you very much, Ms Wolf.
Melissa You're welcome, Mr Adamczyk. Thank you for calling.
Jerzy Goodbye.

Track 50: Unit 11, Communication, exercise 3C

Jeanette Good morning. Sheffield Metal, Sales Department, Jeannette Hogg speaking.
Max Good morning. This is Max Jahn from MedEquip in Germany.
Jeanette Good morning, Mr Jahn. How can I help you?
Max I'm calling to enquire about my order for containers for medical equipment. The order was sent almost one month ago, on 18 April, and delivery was promised by 3 May but, so far, nothing has arrived.
Jeanette Oh. I'm sorry to hear that. Could you give me the order number?
Max Yes. It's DF54736.
Jeanette DF54736. Just a moment, please. I'll check. I'm sorry, Mr Jahn. I don't seem to have any record of your order. Can I just check that I've understood everything? The order number is DF54736 and you ordered the containers on 18 April. Could you give me the exact details of the order, please?
Max Yes, it's an order for your aluminium containers for medical equipment.
Jeanette Aluminium containers for medical equipment. Mr Jahn, I'll have to speak to my colleague to find out what the problem is. Can I get back to you later?
Max Well, yes. But I hope it won't take long. We can't fulfil our orders until we have your containers.
Jeanette Yes. I realize that, Mr Jahn. I'm very sorry about this and I will do my best to get back to you as soon as possible.
Max Many thanks for your help, Ms Hogg.

Track 51: Unit 12, Foundation, exercise 1

1: Maren

Presenter Hello, and welcome to this week's podcast. This week, we're talking to a group of people who have recently gained their business qualifications. Let's start with you, Maren. Would you like to introduce yourself?
Maren OK. I'm Maren, and I've just completed my apprenticeship as a customer services specialist in the wholesale trade.
Presenter What did you like best about your apprenticeship?
Maren I liked the mixture of going to vocational college and doing practical work.
Presenter What do you do at work?
Maren I respond to customers' enquiries and guide them through the purchasing process.
Presenter Right. Now, what about the future? What would you like to do in the future?
Maren I'd like to become a customer services manager.
Presenter Well, all the best Maren.

2: Garry

Garry My name's Garry and I'm a marketing assistant.
Presenter OK. What did you enjoy most about your apprenticeship, Garry?
Garry I enjoyed going to meetings.
Presenter Apart from going to meetings, what else do you do in your job?
Garry Well, I usually work on my own. I analyse data and write reports. I also help with marketing projects.
Presenter Sounds as if the work is quite varied. Now that you've finished your training, where do you go from here?
Garry Oh, that's easy. I'd like to get another qualification and become an office manager.
Presenter Oh. That's great!

3: Delon

Presenter Hello. Can you tell us your name and something about your apprenticeship?
Delon Yes. My name's Delon, and I've just qualified as an office management assistant.
Presenter What did you like best about your apprenticeship?
Delon I enjoyed learning from experienced people.
Presenter What does an office management assistant do at work?
Delon Basically, an office management assistant supports managers. It's general office work, really so it can be anything from writing emails to organizing a business trip.
Presenter Hmm. Now that you've qualified, what about the future? Where would you like to work?
Delon I'd like to find a job abroad where I can use my English.
Presenter That sounds good.

Track 52: Unit 12, Part B, exercise 1A

Interview 1: Tobias Klein

Tobias Hallo?
Jennifer Good evening. Am I speaking to Tobias Klein?
Tobias Wer ist das? Ich versteh' nichts. Bist du das Kati?
Jennifer This is Jennifer Winters. I'm the Recruitment Manager at Energy International plc. Am I speaking to Mr Tobias Klein?
Tobias Oh! Oh yes! Energy International plc. Yes, I understand. Yes, my name is Tobias Klein. Please wait a moment. I must go outside ...
Jennifer Is this a good time to call you, Mr Klein?
Tobias Yes! It's very good! No problem, Mrs Winter. We can talk in a moment. Just let me go outside with my mobile ...
Jennifer I can't hear you very ...
Tobias Thank you for calling me, Miss Winters! I am very happy to answer your questions!
Jennifer Could you tell me what job you're doing at the moment, Mr Klein?
Tobias Yes, I'm an Azubi – I mean a trainee, but I've finished now, so I'm not, but I was ... but I'm still at Atlas Machinery in Frankfurt!
Jennifer I see ... I think we ... problem ... signal strength.
Tobias Strength? Yes, I have strengths, Mrs Winter. I am very good at work and at school and at football because I am a team player.
Jennifer I see ... And what about your weaknesses?
Tobias Weaknesses? I sometimes forget important things ... but I now use the reminder function on my mobile. That helps.
Jennifer And why do you want a job at Energy International, Mr Klein?
Tobias I've always wanted to work in Manchester. It has a famous football team and very nice people.
Jennifer We are in London, Mr Klein, but that doesn't really matter now. Could you tell me something about your plans for the future?
Tobias Well, I want a well-paid job so I can be independent and free.
Jennifer I see. Are there any questions you would like to ask about the job, Mr Klein?
Tobias I'm sorry. I didn't hear what you said, Miss Winter. The signal is very bad and the battery of my mobile is almost ...

Interview 2: Bianca Tiemeyer

Bianca Tiemeyer?
Jennifer Good morning. Am I speaking to Bianca Tiemeyer?
Bianca Yes, that's right.
Jennifer This is Jennifer Winters. I'm the Recruitment Manager at Energy International plc. Is this a good time to talk to you for a few minutes about your application for the post of a German-speaking customer services specialist?
Bianca Yes, I'm at work but I have permission to use the office phone because it's my father's company – Tiemeyer Import/Export in Dortmund.
Jennifer Oh I see. Now I've studied your CV and would like to know a little more about you. Would you like to take me through your CV?
Bianca Well, I think the CV says everything, really. I haven't got a copy in front of me now, but it lists my skills and abilities. I went to the States for a year, so my English is very good.
Jennifer And what other strengths do you have?
Bianca Other strengths? That's a standard question isn't it? Anyway, I would say I have all the usual strengths – I'm punctual, so I'm reliable, honest, hard-working and so on.
Jennifer I see. And weaknesses?
Bianca That's a very good question. Weaknesses ... Well, perhaps I expect too much from other people. My own standards

are very high, and I suppose it's unfair to want everyone to be perfect.

Jennifer And why do you want this job in particular?

Bianca Why this job? Well, I think I'm probably best qualified for it. My grades at school were very good and I'd like to work abroad for a few years.

Jennifer I see. What are your future plans, Miss Tiemeyer? Where do you see yourself in five years' time?

Bianca I really can't say. It depends whether I like the job or not. If I like it, I'll stay on for a few years. It depends on the people, really.

Jennifer Do you have any questions you wish to ask?

Bianca That's another standard question, isn't it? Actually, I do have one question. Would you help me to find a good flat? I want something comfortable and not too far from the company.

Jennifer I'll pass the question on, Miss Tiemeyer. Is there anything else you'd like to know?

Bianca No, that's all, thanks. When will I hear from you?

Jennifer Within the next 48 hours. Thanks for answering my questions. Goodbye.

Bianca Bye.

Interview 3: Sebastian Hartmann

Sebastian Hartmann?

Jennifer Good evening. Am I speaking to Sebastian Hartmann?

Sebastian Yes, that's right.

Jennifer This is Jennifer Winters. I'm the Recruitment Manager at Energy International plc. Is this a good time to talk to you for a few minutes about your application for the post of a German-speaking customer services specialist?

Sebastian Yes, evenings are fine.

Jennifer Good. Um I've studied your CV and would like to know a little more about you. Would you like to take me through it?

Sebastian Yes, certainly. I would say one of my skills is the ability to work in a team and get the best out of myself with the help of others. That's one of the reasons why my team won the Team Project Management Competition. I also organized a programme for some Norwegian visitors to the company last year. It was great fun and they've invited me back to Norway next summer. And I learned a lot about living and working in the UK when I worked for Commercial Services in York. I saw very good customer services there and would like to offer the same standard myself.

Jennifer So, in a nutshell, what would you say your strengths are?

Sebastian Teamwork, taking the initiative, working independently and understanding what the customer wants.

Jennifer And what about your weaknesses?

Sebastian I'm sure I have many but I would say a lack of experience. That's why I want to start work now.

Jennifer What made you apply for this job?

Sebastian The skills listed are exactly what I have learned in my traineeship. There is also a link with Germany, so I feel I can make a special contribution. And I like working in the UK, so I see it as the perfect opportunity.

Jennifer What are your plans for the future?

Sebastian I hope to develop in the job. I want to gain experience and then perhaps study for higher qualifications in the evening. London is a good place for that.

Jennifer Would you like to ask any questions yourself?

Sebastian Yes, on your website it says you sometimes send employees to India or the Far East, for example. Would this be an option for me?

Jennifer Not in the first year, but if you stay longer, you can apply to be posted overseas. Many young people do this. Any other questions?

Sebastian That was the most important one, thanks.

Jennifer In that case we'll be in touch again within 48 hours and thank you for answering my questions.

Sebastian My pleasure. Goodbye.

Jennifer Goodbye, Mr Hartmann.

Track 53: Unit 12, Part B, exercise 3B

Presenter Thanks for coming along to talk to us today, Pat.

Pat My pleasure. It's nice to be here.

Presenter Good. Now, today you're going to give us advice about how to prepare for an interview.

Pat Correct. I'm going to go through each of the five stages of a job interview and talk about how candidates can prepare themselves. So, stage one, greetings and introductions. That's perhaps the easiest part of the interview but it still needs some preparation. First of all, you should find out where the interview location is and how to get there so that you arrive in good time. Try to give yourself enough time to relax and calm down. You should also make sure that you're wearing appropriate clothes.

Presenter First impressions count. Would you advise people to buy new clothes specially for the interview?

Pat No, not particularly. Your clothes need to be appropriate for the job, clean and smart, that's all. They don't have to be new.

Presenter Right. What about body language at the start of the interview?

Pat Body language is important. Walk into the room as confidently as possible, shake hands and make eye contact. Don't be shy. Look directly at the interviewer or interviewers. You'll be asked to take a seat, and there will be a bit of small talk.

Presenter Talking about the weather, your journey, that kind of thing?

Pat That's right. There might also be a question about where you live or your hobbies.

Presenter Some people find it difficult to make small talk, even in their own language. What advice can you give us there, Pat?

Pat I think the best thing to do is to simply get into the habit of making small talk in English with a colleague or a friend.

Presenter That's a good idea. Practise making small talk whenever you can.

Pat That's it. Now, let's move on to the main part of the interview. You'll be asked questions by one or more interviewers.

Presenter The interview might be conducted by more than one person?

Pat That's correct. Sometimes there's a panel of interviewers. Now, preparation for this part is extremely important. Think about the questions you might be asked and make a list. You'll definitely be asked to talk about yourself. Perhaps the interviewer will ask you about your strengths and weaknesses. Write down the questions – and think about how you're going to answer. And always remember to relate your answers to the job on offer.

Presenter Yes, that's important. Keep focused on the job. What should a candidate do if he or she doesn't understand a question?

Pat If you don't understand a question, ask the interviewer to clarify. You can say: "Could you explain what you mean by … ?" – whatever it is. A good interviewer will ask the question again in a slightly different way.

Presenter Hmm. I hope so. Now, earlier you mentioned questions from the candidate. I remember my very first interview. I had no idea what to ask.

Pat Oh, dear. Some preparation would have helped. It's important to do some background research into the company before you go for the interview. Find out about the company's most recent developments and the future prospects of the company you hope to work for. Go to the firm's home page on the internet, read the business section of your newspaper, or look through business magazines. As you're doing your research, note down any questions that occur to you concerning the company. You should also, of course, prepare some questions about the job itself. Then, when you're asked if you have any questions, this is your chance to show your interest in the company and the job.

Presenter Right. Be prepared with questions about the company and the job! And that's the end of the interview and you can say goodbye.

Pat Well, not quite. Before the interview comes to an end, the interviewer usually says when the candidate can expect to hear from the company or if there's to be a further interview or a test – hmm – say, in the form of an assessment centre evaluation. So, only after these arrangements have been made, is your last task as a candidate to say thank you and goodbye. Again, a good, firm handshake and a smile, and that's it.

Presenter Well, thank you, Pat, for these very helpful interviewing tips. I'm sure our listeners have learned a lot today and that they'll be able to put your tips to good use in their interviews. Now, next week's podcast is about …

Track 54: KMK Mock Exam, Rezeption I, Hörverstehen

Floyd GreatSpirits Ltd, Miranda Floyd speaking. How can I help you?

Graham Hello, Ms Floyd. This is Tim Graham from Richard Bond Ltd in York.

Floyd Oh, hello Mr Graham! Nice to hear from you again! How are you?

Graham I'm fine, thank you. How about you?

Floyd I'm OK. We have a lot of work right now, as we have lots of orders to deal with. Are you calling to place an order?

Graham No, that's not the reason for my call. Unfortunately, we have a few problems with your last delivery.

Floyd Oh, really? I'm sorry to hear that. What seems to be the problem?

Graham First of all, the sparkling wine didn't arrive on the date you promised. That's a big problem because we need it for our company anniversary party, which is the day after tomorrow.

Floyd Oh dear. I can see that that is a problem.

Graham That's right. But more to the point, when the delivery arrived this morning, it was not the correct brand and there were only 700 bottles instead of the 1000 bottles we ordered.

Floyd I'm very sorry about that, Mr Graham. One moment, please. Let me put my colleague Gavin Porter on the speakerphone as well. He's in charge of the North England sales area. Maybe he can explain what has happened and what we can do now.

Graham Thank you very much, I'd appreciate that.

Floyd Please hold the line for a second …

…

Porter Mr Graham? This is Gavin Porter.

Graham Yes, hello, Mr Porter.

Porter Ms Floyd has informed me about the reason for your call, and I think I know what has caused the problem. There was a mix-up at the transport company; they confused two deliveries and sent you the wrong container. Your sparkling wine was delivered to another customer's warehouse in Leeds this morning. They called 15 minutes ago to complain.

Graham Oh, no! What a mess! But what can you do about it? We really need the delivery as soon as possible. It's our anniversary party in two days' time!

Porter It's OK. I've already made arrangements to sort things out. SuperCarrier, a local transport company, will pick up the wrong containers and deliver them to the right company. They've promised to deliver your container this afternoon and pick up the wrong one.

Graham Oh, that would be great! I'll make sure that the container that was delivered to us is ready to be picked up. Thanks for your help!

Porter You're welcome! In addition, we would like to offer you a 20% discount on this order. We really appreciate our long-term business relationship, so I'll also send you a box of our best champagne for your company anniversary. Of course, we'll also make sure that wrong deliveries like this don't happen again.

Graham Yes, I hope so too. Anyway, thanks for your help … and the champagne! Goodbye!

Porter You're welcome. Goodbye.

Incoterms® 2010

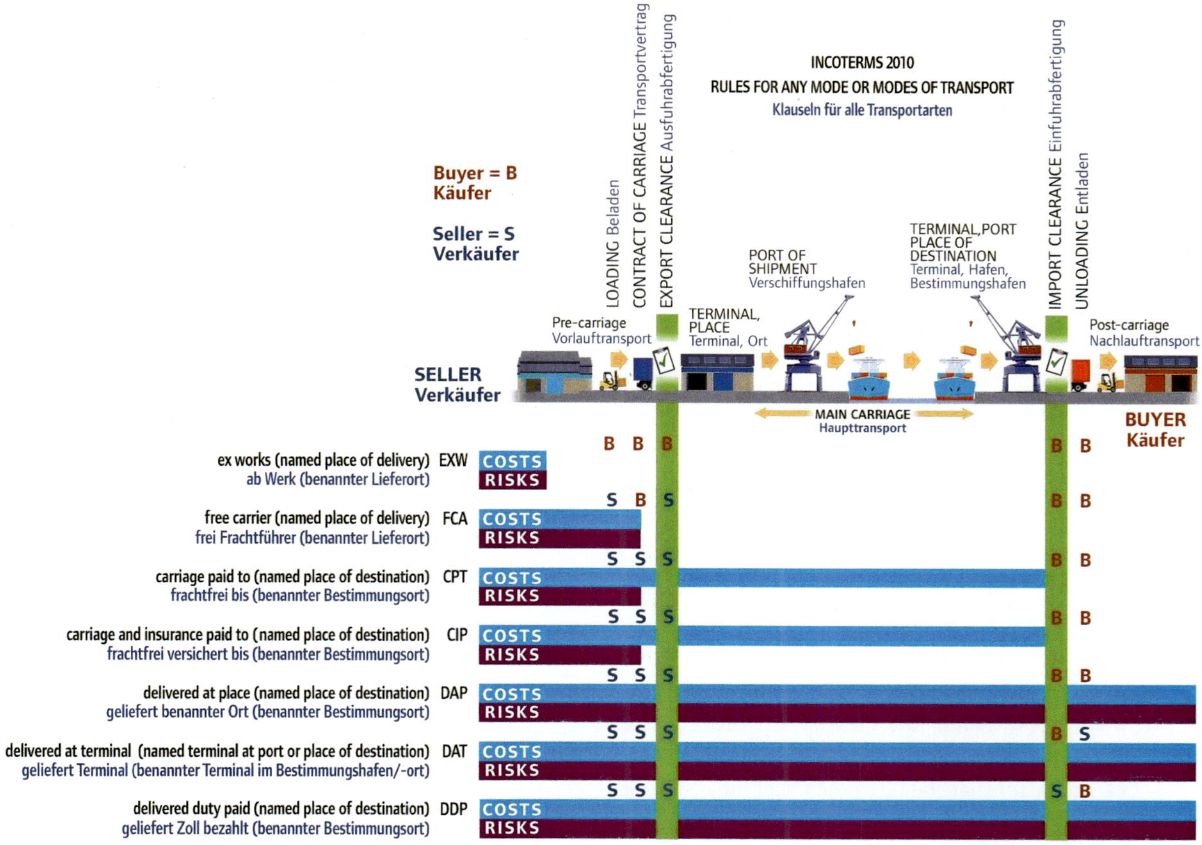

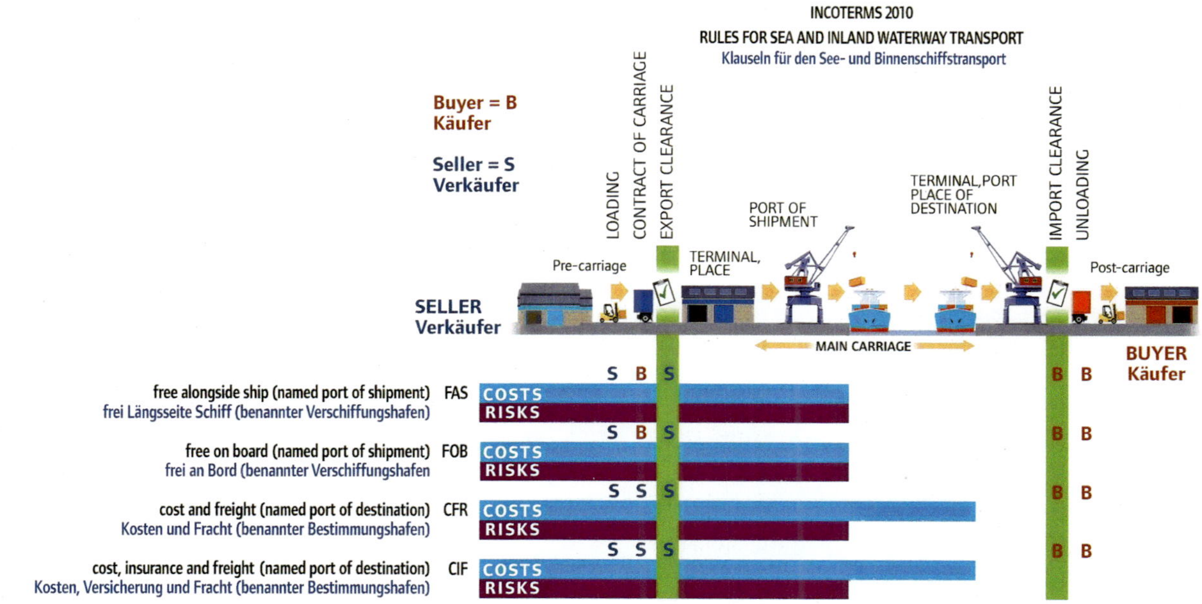

In international trade the eleven Incoterms® 2010 Rules (international commercial terms) are used in contracts of sale to define the rights and obligations of the buyer and seller as regards risk, transport, insurance, packing, customs duty and documentation. They are terms of delivery.

Rules for any mode or modes of transport

EXW – EX WORKS (... named place of delivery)
The seller makes the goods available at his premises in the customary packing. The seller assists the buyer in obtaining any documentation needed at the buyer's expense. The buyer is responsible for loading the goods, transporting them to their destination, customs clearance and insurance.

FCA – FREE CARRIER (... named place of delivery) Multimodal transport
The seller is not responsible for the main carriage of the goods. The seller delivers the goods at his own expense and risk, in the customary packing, cleared for export to the carrier nominated by the buyer. The seller provides the commercial invoice and, if requested, a certificate of origin at the buyer's expense. If the goods are collected at the seller's premises, the seller loads the goods. The seller bears the risks until the goods are in the custody of the first carrier. After that the buyer bears all the costs and risks of transporting the goods to their destination.

CPT – CARRIAGE PAID TO (... named place of destination) Multimodal transport
The seller pays for the main carriage of the goods. The seller delivers the goods, in the customary packing, cleared for export to the carrier which he nominates. The seller bears the risk until the goods have been delivered into the custody of the first carrier. The seller pays the transport costs for the goods, excluding transport insurance, up to the named destination. The buyer is responsible for insuring the goods for the main carriage and pays all import duties and taxes.

CIP – CARRIAGE AND INSURANCE PAID TO (... named place of destination) Multimodal transport
The seller pays for the main carriage of the goods. The seller delivers the goods in the customary packing, cleared for export to the carrier which he nominates. The seller bears the risk until the goods have been delivered into the custody of the first carrier. The seller pays the transport costs for the goods, including transport insurance, up to the named destination. The buyer pays all import duties and taxes.

DAP – DELIVERED AT PLACE (... named place of destination) Multimodal transport
The seller is responsible for the carriage of the goods in the customary packing, cleared for export to the named terminal at the destination by the carrier which he nominates. He bears the risk until the goods have been delivered to the named terminal. The buyer is responsible for unloading the goods at the place of destination and pays all import duties and taxes.

DAT – DELIVERED AT TERMINAL (... named terminal at port or place of destination) Multimodal transport
The seller is responsible for the carriage of the goods in the customary packing, cleared for export to the named terminal at the destination by the carrier which he nominates. He bears the risk until the goods have been delivered to the named terminal. The seller is responsible for unloading the goods at the place of destination. The buyer pays all import duties and taxes.

DDP – DELIVERED DUTY PAID (... named place of destination) Multimodal transport
The seller is responsible for the carriage of the goods in the customary packing, cleared for export to the named terminal at the destination by the carrier which he nominates. He bears the risk until the goods have been delivered to the named destination. The seller pays all import duties and taxes. The buyer is responsible for unloading the goods at the place of destination.

Rules for sea and inland waterway transport

FAS – FREE ALONGSIDE SHIP (... named port of shipment)
The seller is not responsible for the main carriage of the goods. The seller delivers the goods at his own expense and risk, in the customary packing, cleared for export, alongside the vessel selected by the buyer at the named port of shipment. Thereafter, the buyer bears all the costs and risks of transporting the goods to their destination.

FOB – FREE ON BOARD (... named port of shipment)
The seller is not responsible for the main carriage of the goods. The seller delivers the goods at his own expense and risk, in the customary packing, cleared for export, on board the vessel selected by the buyer unless otherwise agreed, at the named port of shipment. Thereafter, the buyer bears all the costs and risks of transporting the goods to their destination.

CFR – COST AND FREIGHT (... named port of destination)
The seller pays for the main carriage of the goods. The seller delivers the goods at his own expense and risk, in the customary packing, cleared for export, on board the vessel selected by the buyer, at the named port of shipment. The seller pays the transport costs for the goods, excluding transport insurance, up to the named port of destination. The buyer is responsible for insuring the goods for the main carriage and pays all import duties and taxes.

CIF – COST INSURANCE FREIGHT (... named port of destination)
The seller pays for the main carriage of the goods. The seller delivers the goods at his own expense and risk, in the customary packing, cleared for export, on board the vessel selected by the buyer, at the named port of shipment. The seller pays the transport costs for the goods, including transport insurance, up to the named port of destination. The buyer pays all import duties and taxes.

Terms of payment

payment in advance	Vorauszahlung/Vorkasse
cash with order (CWO)	Barzahlung bei Auftragserteilung
payment by irrevocable and confirmed documentary (letter of) credit	Zahlung durch unwiderrufliches und bestätigtes Dokumentenakkreditiv
documents against payment (D/P) / cash against documents (CAD)	Kasse gegen Dokumente
cash on delivery (COD)	gegen Nachnahme
1/3 with order, 1/3 on delivery, 1/3 within 30 days after delivery	1/3 bei Auftragserteilung, 1/3 bei Lieferung, 1/3 innerhalb von 30 Tagen nach Lieferung
payment within 60 days from date of invoice	Zahlung innerhalb von 60 Tagen nach Rechnungsdatum
10 days 2%, 30 days net	Zahlung innerhalb 10 Tagen abzüglich 2 % Skonto oder innerhalb 30 Tagen netto
payment on receipt of goods	Zahlung bei Erhalt der Waren
payment on receipt of invoice	Zahlung bei Rechnungserhalt
documents against (three months') acceptance (D/A)	Dokumente gegen (Dreimonats-)Akzept
open account terms with monthly/quarterly settlement	offenes Zahlungsziel mit monatlicher/vierteljährlicher Abrechnung

U Useful phrases

Describing apprenticeships	**Unit 1**
– I work for … (name of employer) in … (place).	– *Ich arbeite für … (Name des Arbeitgebers) in … (Ort).*
– I'm in the first/second/third/last year of my apprenticeship.	– *Ich befinde mich im ersten/zweiten/dritten/letzten Jahr meiner Ausbildung.*
– I go to vocational training college on day release every … (e.g. Monday and Tuesday).	– *Ich gehe jeden … (z. B. Montag und Dienstag) in die Berufsschule zum berufsbegleitenden Unterricht.*
– … on block release for six weeks / three months twice/three times a year.	– *… habe Blockunterricht für sechs Wochen / drei Montate zwei-/dreimal im Jahr.*
– I decided to train as a management assistant in wholesale and foreign trade because I like working in commerce / buying and selling.	– *Ich entschied mich, eine Ausbildung zum/zur Groß- und Außenhandelskaufmann/-frau / Kaufmann/-frau im Groß- und Außenhandel zu machen, weil ich gerne im Handel arbeite / kaufe und verkaufe.*
– My apprenticeship lasts/takes three years / is three years long.	– *Meine Ausbildung dauert drei Jahre / geht drei Jahre lang.*

Making introductions	**Unit 1**
Greeting people you do not know	
– Good morning/afternoon/evening. I'm …	– *Guten Morgen/Tag/Abend. Ich bin …*
– How do you do? My name is …	– *Freut mich. Mein Name ist …*
– Nice/Pleased to meet you.	– *Es freut mich, Sie kennen zu lernen.*
– Nice to meet you, too.	– *Ganz meinerseits.*
– Excuse me. Are you …?	– *Entschuldigung. Sind Sie …?*
– Yes, I am. / No, I'm not. I'm …	– *Ja, das bin ich / Nein, das bin ich nicht … Ich heiße …*
– Welcome to …	– *Herzlich willkommen bei/in …*
– Thank you. It's nice to be here.	– *Dankeschön. Es ist schön, hier zu sein.*
Introducing people	
– This is … . / These are my colleagues, John and Mary.	– *Das ist … . / Das sind meine Kollegen, John und Mary.*
– I'd like to introduce … from the … department.	– *Darf ich Ihnen … aus der …-Abteilung vorstellen?*
Making small talk	
– I hope you're well.	– *Ich hoffe, es geht dir/Ihnen gut.*
– … is such a beautiful city!	– *… ist so eine schöne Stadt.*
– The weather is so good today!	– *Das Wetter ist heute so schön.*
– Did you have a good trip/flight?	– *Hattest du / Hatten Sie eine gute Reise / einen guten Flug?*

Describing jobs and responsibilities	**Unit 2**
– I work in a team of management assistants.	– *Ich arbeite in einem Team von Managementassistenten/-assistentinnen.*
– I make sure that we sell as many products as possible.	– *Ich stelle sicher, dass wir so viele Produkte wie möglich verkaufen.*
– I report directly to the Export Sales Manager.	– *Ich bin dem/der Vertriebsleiter/in direkt unterstellt.*
– I arrange for goods to be shipped abroad.	– *Ich organisiere den Güterversand ins Ausland.*
– I make sure our products get to our customers.	– *Ich stelle sicher, dass unsere Produkte zu unseren Kunden/Kundinnen geliefert werden.*
– It's my responsibility to obtain the necessary shipping documents.	– *Ich bin dafür verantwortlich, die Lieferpapiere zu besorgen.*

– I'm in charge of public relations, so my work involves managing our Facebook page and sometimes organizing events.	– *Ich bin für die Öffentlichkeitsarbeit zuständig/verantwortlich. Unter anderem betreue ich unsere Facebook-Seite und organisiere ab und an Veranstaltungen.*
– I am responsible for maintaining our customer database.	– *Ich bin dafür verantwortlich, die Kundendatenbank zu pflegen.*
– Working in my department means understanding customs regulations.	– *Für die Arbeit in meiner Abteilung ist es wichtig, die Zollvorschriften zu kennen.*
– I work fixed hours / a 39-hour week.	– *Ich habe feste Arbeitszeiten / eine 39-Stunden-Woche.*
– I do a lot of overtime.	– *Ich mache viele Überstunden.*

Telephoning	**Unit 2**
Identifying yourself	
– Good morning. My name's …	– *Guten Morgen. Ich heiße …*
– Good afternoon. This is … from … (company).	– *Guten Tag. Hier spricht … von … (Firma).*
– Good evening. I work for …	– *Guten Abend. Ich arbeite bei …*
Explaining the reason for your call	
– I'm enquiring about …	– *Ich wollte mich nach … erkundigen.*
– I'd like some information on …	– *Ich hätte gern nähere Informationen zu …*
Asking for a person/department	
– I'd like to speak to Mr/Ms …	– *Ich würde gerne (mit) Herrn/Frau … sprechen.*
– Could you put me through to the … department, please?	– *Könnten Sie mich bitte zur …-Abteilung durchstellen/weiterleiten?*
Saying what you want to do	
– Can I leave a message?	– *Kann ich eine Nachricht hinterlassen?*
– I'll call again later.	– *Ich rufe später noch einmal an.*
– Could you ask Mr/Ms … to call me back?	– *Könnten Sie Herrn/Frau … bitten, mich zurückzurufen?*
Ending the call	
– Thank you for your help/assistance.	– *Vielen Dank für Ihre Hilfe/Unterstützung.*
– You're welcome.	– *Gern geschehen. / Bitte sehr.*
– Goodbye.	– *Auf Wiederhören.*
– Have a nice day/evening.	– *Einen schönen Tag/Abend noch.*

Taking telephone calls	Unit 2
– Who's calling, please?	– *Wie ist Ihr Name bitte?*
– Could you spell your name, please?	– *Könnten Sie bitte Ihren Namen buchstabieren?*
– I'm sorry, I didn't understand. Could you repeat that, please?	– *Es tut mir leid, ich habe das nicht verstanden. Könnten Sie das bitte wiederholen?*
– I'll put you through.	– *Ich stelle Sie durch.*
– I'm trying to connect you.	– *Ich versuche, Sie zu verbinden.*
– Please hold the line.	– *Bleiben Sie bitte dran.*
– I'm afraid the line is engaged.	– *Der Anschluss ist leider besetzt.*
– I'm sorry, … (name) is unavailable at the moment.	– *Es tut mir leid, aber … (Name) ist im Moment nicht da.*
– Would you like to speak to someone else?	– *Möchten Sie mit jemand anderem sprechen?*
– Would you like to leave a message?	– *Möchten Sie eine Nachricht hinterlassen?*

Showing visitors around the company	Unit 3
Giving a tour of the company	
– Let's start by visiting …	– *Lassen Sie uns zuerst mit dem Besuch der/des … beginnen.*
– Here we have the … department.	– *Hier ist die … -Abteilung.*
– On the left/right, you can see …	– *Zu Ihrer Linken/Rechten sehen Sie …*
– This is where we make/dispatch …	– *Hier stellen wir … her / versenden wir …*
Asking for and giving directions	
– Could you tell me the way to …, please?	– *Könnten Sie mir bitte sagen, wie ich nach/zur/zum … komme?*
– Yes, certainly.	– *Ja, selbstverständlich.*
– Go down the corridor until you get to …	– *Gehen Sie den Flur entlang, bis Sie zur/zum … kommen.*
– Take the first/second/last door on your right.	– *Nehmen Sie die erste/zweite/letzte Tür rechts.*
– Turn right at the end of the corridor.	– *Biegen Sie am Ende des Flures rechts ab.*
Offering help/refreshments	
– Can I take your coat?	– *Möchten Sie Ihren Mantel ablegen?*
– Would you like something to drink?	– *Darf ich Ihnen etwas zu trinken anbieten?*
– Would you like some tea/coffee/water?	– *Möchten Sie Tee/Kaffee/Wasser?*

Describing companies	Unit 3
Describing your company	
– We are based/located in … (country/city).	– *Wir sind in … (Land/Stadt) ansässig.*
– Our headquarters is in … (country/city).	– *Unsere Hauptfiliale befindet sich in … (Land/Stadt).*
– The company was founded in … (year).	– *Das Unternehmen wurde im Jahr … gegründet.*
– We are in the … industry.	– *Wir sind in der … -Branche (tätig).*
– We are a multinational/local/small company/ business.	– *Wir sind ein internationales/regionales/kleines Unternehmen / ein kleiner Betrieb.*
– We are a start-up.	– *Wir sind ein Start-Up(-Unternehmen).*
– We have branches/subsidiaries/offices in … (country) / all over the world.	– *Wir haben Filialen/Tochterfirmen/Büros in … (Land) / überall auf der Welt.*
– We have … (number) employees.	– *Wir haben … (Anzahl) Angestellte.*
– We are a privately-owned company / corporation.	– *Wir sind ein Privatunternehmen.*
Talking about the company's products/services	
– We make/produce/manufacture …	– *Wir produzieren/erzeugen … / stellen … her.*
– We sell/distribute …	– *Wir verkaufen/vertreiben …*
– We offer/provide …	– *Wir liefern … / bieten … an.*
– We make sure the goods get from A to B.	– *Wir stellen sicher, dass die Güter von A nach B geliefert werden.*

Giving presentations	Unit 3
Introduction	
– My name is … and this is my partner, …	– *Mein Name ist … und das ist meine/e Partner/in, …*
– We are apprentices at … in Germany.	– *Wir sind Auszubildende bei … in Deutschland.*
– This morning, I'm / we're going to talk about …	– *Heute spreche ich / sprechen wir über …*
– Our topic today is …	– *Das heutige Thema lautet …*
Structure	
– I've divided my presentation into three main parts, as follows: …	– *Ich habe meine Präsentation in drei (Haupt-)Teile gegliedert, und zwar …*
– First/Firstly, … ; Second/Secondly, … ; After that / Then …	– *Erstens, … ; Zweitens, … ; Anschließend/Dann …*

Signposts	
– To begin with, …; Next, …; Now …	– *Zuerst, …; Als Nächstes, …; Jetzt …*
– The next topic I'm going to talk about is …	– *Das nächste Thema, das ich behandeln möchte, lautet …*
– Now I'd like to move on to …	– *Jetzt möchte ich zum Thema … übergehen.*
Handouts	
– I've prepared a few things/handouts for you to take away.	– *Ich habe etwas/Handouts für Sie zum Mitnehmen vorbereitet.*
– I hope you'll find these copies of the graphics useful.	– *Ich hoffe, dass Sie diese Kopien der Grafiken nützlich finden.*
Conclusion	
– Before I finish my presentation, I'd just like to mention …	– *Bevor ich meinen Vortrag beende, möchte ich … kurz erwähnen.*
– I'd like to go over the main points again.	– *Ich möchte die Hauptpunkte/Hauptargumente nochmals kurz darlegen.*
– Finally, …; In conclusion, …; In summary, …	– *Zum Schluss …; Abschließend …; Zusammenfassend …*
Questions / Thanking the audience	
– Are there any questions?	– *Gibt es / Haben Sie noch Fragen?*
– We have time for a few questions / one last question.	– *Wir haben noch Zeit für ein paar Fragen / eine letzte Frage.*
– Well, that's the end of my presentation.	– *Damit bin ich am Ende meiner Präsentation angelangt.*
– Thank you for your attention / for listening.	– *Vielen Dank für Ihre Aufmerksamkeit / fürs Zuhören.*

Advising customers	**Unit 4**
Greeting a potential customer	
– Good morning/afternoon/evening, Mr/Ms … / sir/ madam.	– *Guten Morgen/Tag/Abend, Herr/Frau …*
– Is there anything (in particular) I can do for you, or would you like just to look around?	– *Kann ich etwas für Sie tun oder möchten Sie sich erstmal umschauen?*
– Just let me know if you need any help.	– *Lassen Sie mich wissen, wenn Sie Hilfe brauchen.*
Asking about the customer's needs	
– What sort of thing are you looking for?	– *Nach was / Wonach genau suchen Sie?*
– Is it for commercial/industrial or private use?	– *Ist es für den geschäftlichen/gewerblichen oder privaten Gebrauch gedacht?*
Suggesting suitable products/services	
– How about / What about … (product)?	– *Wie wäre es mit … (Produkt)?*
– Here's a(n) … . Is this the sort of thing you're looking for?	– *Hier ist ein/e … . Suchen Sie (nach) so etwas?*
Following up the discussion	
– Would you like me to send you an offer?	– *Soll/Darf ich Ihnen ein Angebot schicken / zukommen lassen?*
– You'll get our offer today/tomorrow / by the end of the week.	– *Sie erhalten unser Angebot heute/morgen / bis zum Ende der Woche.*

Writing emails	**Unit 4**
Salutation	
– Dear Sir or Madam (*formal*)	– *Sehr geehrte Damen und Herren,*
– Dear Mr/Ms Smith (*formal*)	– *Sehr geehrter Herr / Sehr geehrte Frau Schmidt,*
– Dear Paul (und Paula)	– *Lieber Paul (, Liebe Paula),*
– Good morning, Paul (*less formal*)	– *Guten Morgen, Paul,*
– Hi/Hello Paula (*less formal*)	– *Hallo Paula,*

Complimentary close	
– Yours faithfully (*formal*)	– *Mit freundlichen Grüßen*
– Regards / Best regards / Best wishes / Yours sincerely (*formal*)	– *Mit freundlichen Grüßen / Freundliche Grüße*
– Regards / Best regards / Best wishes	– *Viele Grüße / Mit freundlichen Grüßen*
– All the best (*less formal*)	– *Alles Gute / Herzliche Grüße*
Opening sentence	
– I'm just writing to … (*formal*)	– *Ich schreibe Ihnen, um zu / weil …*
– Just a quick note/message to … (*less formal*)	– *Nur eine kurze Mitteilung/Nachricht, um zu …*
Conclusion	
– I look forward to your reply / to hearing from you. (*formal*)	– *Ich freue mich auf Ihre Antwort.*
– Many thanks in advance. (*formal*)	– *Vielen Dank im Voraus.*
– I hope to hear from you soon. (*less formal*)	– *Ich freue mich, bald von Ihnen/dir zu hören.*

Describing graphs	**Unit 5**
– The graph/chart shows/presents …	– *Die Grafik / Das Diagramm zeigt … / stellt … dar.*
– The horizontal/vertical axis has a scale from … to …	– *Die waagerechte/senkrechte Achse hat eine Skala von … bis …*
– The x axis / The y axis is divided into … units/sections each representing …	– *Die X-Achse / Die Y-Achse ist unterteilt in … Einheiten/Abschnitte, die … darstellen.*
– The number of export sales decreased slightly last month.	– *Die Zahl der Exportverkäufe ging im letzten Monat leicht zurück.*
– The number of orders jumped sharply in June.	– *Die Zahl der Bestellungen nahmen im Juni stark zu.*
– They reached their peak in August, then levelled off towards the end of the year.	– *Sie erreichten ihren Höhepunkt im August und blieben dann bis zum Ende des Jahres gleich.*
– New customers accounted for about/roughly/ approximately one third of all orders.	– *Neukunden machten etwa/annähernd/ungefähr ein Drittel aller Bestellungen aus.*
– Sales to China made up just over/under one tenth of export sales.	– *Exporte nach China machten etwas über/unter ein Zehntel der Exportverkäufe aus.*

Taking part in meetings	**Unit 6**
Starting the meeting	
– Good morning everybody and welcome to …	– *Guten Tag alle zusammen und Willkommen zu …*
– The first item on today's agenda is …	– *Der erste Punkt der heutigen Tagesordnung lautet …*
Asking someone to speak	
– Would you go ahead, please?	– *Würden Sie / Würdest du bitte fortfahren?*
– Can you give us a brief update?	– *Könnten Sie / Könntest du uns einen kurzen Zwischenstand geben?*
Asking for reactions	
– Would anyone like to comment or ask a question?	– *Möchte jemand einen Kommentar abgeben oder eine Frage stellen?*
– Are there any issues?	– *Gibt es Probleme?*
Asking for opinions	
– What do you think about …?	– *Wie denken Sie / denkst du über …?*
– What's your opinion of / view on …?	– *Was ist Ihre/deine Meinung zu …?*
Expressing a point of view	
– It seems to me (that) …	– *Mir kommt es so vor, als ob …*
– In my opinion, …	– *Meiner Meinung nach …*
– From what I can see, …	– *Soweit ich sagen kann, …*

Asking to speak	
– Could I just say that ...?	– *Darf ich (kurz) anmerken, dass ...?*
– Can I come in on that?	– *Darf ich dazu etwas sagen?*
Agreeing	
– Yes, I agree.	– *Ja, ich stimme zu / ich bin (damit) einverstanden.*
– I thoroughly agree with ... (name).	– *Ich stimme ... (Name) völlig zu.*
Disagreeing politely	
– (I'm afraid) I don't agree with ... (name).	– *Leider stimme ich ... (Name) nicht zu. / Ich kann ... (Name) leider nicht zustimmen.*
– I agree up to a point, but ...	– *Ich stimme bis zu einem gewissen Punk zu, aber ...*
– Actually, / In fact, I think (that) ...	– *Eigentlich/Vielmehr denke ich, dass ...*
Starting a new topic	
– Let's move on to the next topic, which is ...	– *Lassen Sie uns / Lass uns mit dem nächsten Thema fortfahren, es handelt sich um ...*
– The next point is ...	– *Der nächste Punkt lautet ...*
Promising action	
– I'll pass that on to ...	– *Ich werde das an ... weiterleiten.*
– We'll get back to you.	– *Wir werden auf Sie/dich zurückkommen.*
Finishing the meeting	
– Let's wrap up the meeting with ...	– *Lassen Sie uns / Lass uns das Treffen damit zum Abschluss bringen.*
– Well, that would seem to be it.	– *Gut, das scheint alles zu sein.*

Negotiating	**Unit 6**
Direct approach	
– Are you prepared to ...?	– *Sind Sie bereit, ...?*
– Can you reduce the price by ... (e.g. €20)?	– *Können Sie den Preis um ... (z. B. € 20) reduzieren?*
– Will you increase ... (e.g. production) by ...?	– *Werden Sie ... (z. B. die Produktion) um ... steigern?*
– Are you able to guarantee ... (e.g. delivery)?	– *Können Sie ... (z. B. die Auslieferung) garantieren?*
– Do you accept these terms?	– *Akzeptieren Sie diese Bedingungen?*
Indirect approach	
– We need to talk about ...	– *Wir müssen über ... sprechen.*
– ... is a problem for us.	– *... ist ein Problem für uns.*
– ... (e.g. our competitors) are ...% cheaper.	– *... (z. B. unsere Konkurrenz) ist/sind ... % günstiger.*
– We're thinking of ordering more/less ...	– *Wir denken darüber nach, mehr/weniger ... zu bestellen.*
– We need a maximum/minimum of ...	– *Wir benötigen ein Maximum/Minimum von ...*
– How much more ... can you produce?	– *Wie viel mehr ... können Sie produzieren?*
Offering help	
– We can help you with ...	– *Wir können Ihnen helfen, indem wir ...*
– We can give you ... if you can ...	– *Wir können Ihnen ... geben, wenn Sie ... (können).*
– I suggest that you ...	– *Ich schlage vor, (dass) Sie ...*
Accommodating changes to the offer	
– I have some room to move.	– *Ich habe etwas Spielraum.*
– OK. I'm prepared to offer you that.	– *In Ordnung. Das kann ich Ihnen gern anbieten.*
– Yes, I think we can do that for you.	– *Ja, ich denke, dass wir das für Sie tun können.*
Refusing what the client asks for	
– I'm sorry, but the price that I quoted you is the best I can do.	– *Es tut mir leid, aber dies ist der äußerste Preis. Mehr kann ich Ihnen nicht anbieten.*
– No. I'm afraid I can't do that.	– *Nein, das kann ich leider nicht tun.*
– Well, I can't offer you .... But what I can do is ...	– *Ich kann Ihnen kein/e ... anbieten. Ich kann Ihnen jedoch ...*

Making arrangements — Unit 6

Inviting sb to a meeting	
– Ms Smith would like to invite you to a meeting on … (day) at … (time).	– *Frau Smith möchte Sie zu einem Treffen am … (Tag) um … (Zeit) Uhr einladen.*
– I would like to invite you to lunch/dinner.	– *Ich würde Sie gern zum Mittagessen/Abendessen einladen.*
– The meeting will take place at my office / our premises in … (place/city).	– *Das Treffen findet in meinem Büro / in unseren Räumlichkeiten in … (Ort/Stadt) statt.*
Accepting/Declining the invitation	
– Thank you for your invitation to meet you at … (place).	– *Vielen Dank für Ihre Einladung zum Treffen in … (Ort).*
– I am pleased / We are delighted to accept your invitation/offer.	– *Gern nehme(n) ich/wir Ihre Einladung / Ihr Angebot an.*
– I'm sorry, but I'm … (reason) on that date / at that time.	– *Es tut mir leid, aber ich kann an diesem Tag / zu dieser Zeit nicht, da … (Grund).*
Making an alternative suggestion	
– How about meeting on … (day) at … (time) instead?	– *Wie wäre es, wenn wir uns stattdessen am … (Tag) um … (Uhrzeit) treffen?*
Conclusion	
– I look forward to your reply. (*formal*)	– *Ich freue mich auf Ihre Antwort.*
– I hope to hear from you soon. Many thanks.	– *Ich hoffe, bald von Ihnen zu hören. Besten Dank.*

Writing enquiries — Unit 8

Source of address	
– I was most impressed by the … (product[s]) you showed me on your stand at the … (name of – trade fair / exhibition).	– *Ich war von den … (Produkten), die Sie mir an Ihrem Stand auf der … (Name der Handelsmesse/ Ausstellung) gezeigt haben, sehr beeindruckt.*
– We have seen your company's advertisement in the current edition of … (name of publication) and are most interested in your products.	– *Wir haben Ihre Anzeige in der aktuellen Ausgabe von … (Name der Veröffentlichung) gesehen und interessieren uns sehr für Ihre Produkte.*
– We note from your company's website that you sell a wide range of … (products).	– *Wir entnehmen der Homepage Ihres Unternehmens, dass Sie ein breites Sortiment an/von … (Produkten) anbieten.*
– You have been recommended to us by … (name of the person/company), who tells us that you have brought out … (product).	– *Sie wurden uns von … (Name der Person/Firma) empfohlen, der/die uns mitgeteilt hat, dass Sie … (Produkt) auf den Markt gebracht haben.*
Description of your company	
– We are a rapidly growing / leading producer/ importer/exporter/wholesaler of … with excellent business contacts all over … (region/country) and beyond.	– *Wir sind ein schnell wachsender / führender Produzent von … / Importeur/Exporteur/Großhändler für … mit hervorragenden Geschäftskontakten in ganz … (Region/Land) und darüber hinaus.*
– Our company is a major/well-established (German) wholesaler of … (goods) both at home and abroad.	– *Unser Unternehmen ist ein bedeutender / gut eingeführter (deutscher) Großhändler von (Waren/ Dienstleistungen) im In- und Ausland.*
– We have many long-standing customers all over Europe.	– *Wir haben viele langjährige Kunden in ganz Europa.*
Reason for your enquiry	
– At present we are particularly interested in … (goods/ services) at reasonable prices.	– *Gegenwärtig gilt unser besonderes Interesse … (Waren/Dienstleistungen) zu vernünftigen Preisen.*
– We are looking for a supplier of …	– *Wir suchen nach einem Lieferanten für …*
– … as goods of this nature are currently in great demand.	– *… da zurzeit eine große Nachfrage für Waren dieser Art besteht.*

Your requirements	
– Please send us a favourable quotation for these items / for … (products).	– *Bitte schicken Sie uns ein passendes (Preis)Angebot für diese Artikel / für … (Produkte).*
– We would welcome a quotation for …	– *Wir hätten gerne ein (Preis)Angebot für …*
– We would therefore/also be grateful if you would let us have details of your entire range.	– *Wir wären Ihnen deshalb/ebenso dankbar, wenn Sie uns Einzelheiten über Ihre gesamte Produktpalette schicken würden.*
– Please let us have your latest catalogue …	– *Bitte lassen Sie uns Ihren neuesten Katalog … zukommen.*
– … and export price list	– *… und Exportpreisliste*
– … including all discounts granted	– *… einschl. aller gewährten Rabatte*
– Please also let us know if you are able to provide samples.	– *Bitte teilen Sie uns auch mit, ob Sie Muster/Proben zur Verfügung stellen können.*
– … including details of your terms of delivery and payment.	– *… einschl. Einzelheiten über Ihre Liefer- und Zahlungsbedingungen.*
– Details of your terms of delivery and payment would also be appreciated.	– *Bitte lassen Sie uns Informationen zu Ihren Liefer- und Zahlungsbedingungen zukommen.*
– We would require delivery … (e.g. within 6 weeks / by the end of the month) at the latest.	– *Die Lieferung hätten wir gerne spätestens … (z. B. innerhalb 6 Wochen / bis Ende des Monats).*
– How soon can you deliver?	– *Wie schnell können Sie liefern?*
– We would be grateful if a representative could call on us.	– *Wir wären dankbar, wenn uns ein/e Außendienstmitarbeiter/in besuchen könnte.*
References	
– References are available on request.	– *Referenzen sind auf Wunsch erhältlich.*
Polite ending	
– If your products meet our requirements, we will place a substantial order.	– *Wenn Ihre Produkte unseren Anforderungen entsprechen, werden wir einen größeren Auftrag erteilen.*
– We look forward to hearing from you soon / in the near future.	– *Wir hoffen auf baldige Antwort. / Wir freuen uns auf Ihre Antwort.*
– We look forward to your early reply with interest.	– *Wir sehen Ihrer baldigen Antwort mit Interesse entgegen.*

Writing business letters	**Unit 9**
Salutation	
– Dear Sir or Madam (*to a firm*)	– *Sehr geehrte Damen und Herren,*
– Dear Mr/Ms Brown	– *Sehr geehrte/r Herr/Frau Brown,*
– Dear Sharon	– *Liebe Sharon,*
Complimentary close	
– Yours faithfully (*BE: to a firm*)	– *Mit freundlichen Grüßen*
– Yours very truly / Cordially yours (*AE: to a firm*)	– *Mit freundlichen Grüßen*
– Yours sincerely (*BE*)	– *Mit freundlichen Grüßen*
– Sincerely yours / Best personal regards (*AE*)	– *Mit freundlichen Grüßen / Beste Grüße*

Writing offers	Unit 9
Reference to enquiry	
– As agreed in our telephone conversation of this morning (of today) …	– *Wie heute (Morgen) telefonisch vereinbart …*
– We were delighted to receive your enquiry dated … about our … product(s).	– *Wir waren sehr erfreut, Ihre Anfrage vom … über unser(e) … Produkt(e) zu erhalten.*
– I am pleased to let you have details of our offer in writing.	– *Gerne lasse ich Ihnen ein schriftliches Angebot zukommen.*
– Many thanks for the above-mentioned enquiry / your enquiry dated …	– *Wir danken für die oben genannte Anfrage / Ihre Anfrage vom …*
Description of your company/goods/services	
– We are a major distributor of … (product/s) …	– *Wir sind ein bedeutender Großhändler für … (Produkt/e) …*
– … with an excellent reputation throughout Europe.	– *… mit einem hervorragenden Ruf in ganz Europa.*
– Our company manufactures a wide range of high-quality (engineering) products …	– *Unser Unternehmen stellt eine breite Palette von hochwertigen (Maschinenbau)Produkten her …*
– … and already has many satisfied customers throughout Western Europe and North America.	– *… und hat bereits viele zufriedene Kunden überall in Westeuropa und Nordamerika.*
Sales material	
– A brochure on … / Our current catalogue and price list is/are attached/enclosed for your information.	– *Zu Ihrer Information ist/sind ein Prospekt über … / unser aktueller Katalog und eine aktuelle Preisliste angehängt/beigefügt.*
– To download details of our entire range together with our export price list, please visit our website at www.cantec.com.	– *Um Einzelheiten über unsere gesamte Produktpalette sowie unsere Exportpreisliste herunterzuladen, besuchen Sie bitte Sie unsere Homepage unter www.cantec.com.*
– Samples are available on request.	– *Muster sind auf Wunsch erhältlich.*
Price	
– As regards the goods requested, we are pleased to submit the following quotation:	– *Was die gewünschten Waren betrifft, freuen wir uns, Ihnen folgendes Angebot zu unterbreiten:*
– … and will be pleased to supply you with … (product/s) at … (price) each.	– *… und liefern Ihnen gerne … (Produkt/e) zu je … (Preis).*
– at … (price, e.g. €10) per unit	– *zu … (Preis, z. B. € 10) pro Stück*
Terms and discounts	
– Our prices are quoted FOB Hamburg.	– *Unsere Preise verstehen sich FOB Hamburg.*
– Delivery will be made CIP Frankfurt Airport / DDP your premises.	– *Die Lieferung erfolgt CIP Flughafen Frankfurt / DDP Ihren Geschäftsräumen.*
– Wholesalers are granted a trade discount of …%.	– *Großhändlern wird ein Handelsrabatt von … % eingeräumt.*
– A quantity discount of …% is granted on orders for 10 or more … (e.g. machines, items).	– *Bei Abnahme von 10 oder mehr … (z. B. Geräten, Artikeln) wird ein Mengenrabatt von … % gewährt.*
– Our terms of payment for an initial order are CWO.	– *Bei Erstauftrag kann lediglich bar bei Auftragserteilung gezahlt werden.*
– Our usual terms of payment are 1/3 with order and 2/3 by irrevocable and confirmed documentary letter of credit.	– *Unsere üblichen Zahlungsbedingungen sind 1/3 bei Auftragserteilung und 2/3 per unwiderrufliches und bestätigtes Doumentenakkreditiv.*
– … or, with favourable references, 10 days 3%, 30 days net.	– *… oder bei günstigen Referenzen, 3 % Skonto bei Zahlung innerhalb von 10 Tagen, netto bei Zahlung innerhalb von 30 Tagen.*
– Regular customers may be granted preferential terms.	– *Stammkunden können wir ein Angebot zu günstigen (Zahlungs-)Konditionen machen.*
– If regular orders are placed with our company, open account terms may be granted.	– *Wenn unserer Firma regelmäßige Aufträge erteilt werden, kann ein offenes Zahlungziel gewährt werden.*

Delivery	
– within … days after receipt of order	– *innerhalb von … Tagen nach Auftragseingang*
– Delivery is made within approx. 30 days after receipt of order.	– *Die Lieferung erfolgt innerhalb von ca. 30 Tagen nach Auftragseingang.*
– while stocks last	– *solange der Vorrat reicht*
Polite ending	
– We look forward to receiving your order.	– *Wir freuen uns über Ihren Auftrag.*
– We feel sure that a trial order will convince you of the quality of our products.	– *Wir sind sicher, dass ein Probeauftrag Sie von der Qualität unserer Produkte überzeugen wird.*
– We hope our offer is to your liking …	– *Wir hoffen, dass unser Angebot Ihnen zusagt …*
– … and look forward to doing business with you.	– *… und freuen uns auf die Zusammenarbeit.*
– Please do not hesitate to contact us if you require further details.	– *Bitte zögern Sie nicht, mit uns Kontakt aufzunehmen, wenn Sie weitere Einzelheiten benötigen.*

Clarifying details on the phone	Unit 9
Repeating what somebody says	
A: We can deliver everything by Thursday.	*A: Wir können alles am Donnerstag liefern.*
B: Thursday. Right.	*B: Donnerstag, in Ordnung.*
Asking for clarification	
A: My address is 23 Fairfield Gardens.	*A: Meine Adresse lautet 23 Fairfield Gardens.*
B: Sorry. Did you say 23 or 33?	*B: Entschuldigung, sagten Sie 23 oder 33?*
Reading something back	
A: My number is 0171 452869.	*A: Meine Nummer lautet 0171452869.*
B: I'll just read that back to you. 0171 452869.	*B: Ich wiederhole: 0171 452869.*
– Can you just read that back to me?	– *Könnten Sie das bitte wiederholen?*
– Can I just check that? It's …	– *Kann ich das kurz kontrollieren/überprüfen? Es ist die …*

Writing orders	Unit 10
Reference to offer	
– Many thanks for your offer dated …	– *Vielen Dank für Ihr Angebot vom …*
– Having seen your offer on the internet and spoken to you on the telephone …	– *Nachdem wir Ihr Angebot im Internet gesehen und mit Ihnen gesprochen haben …*
– We have seen your offer for … on the internet.	– *Wir sind im Internet auf Ihr Angebot von … aufmerksam geworden.*
Details of goods/services ordered	
– We now wish to place an order / a trial order for the following goods:	– *Wir möchten einen Auftrag/Probeauftrag über folgende Waren erteilen:*
– [*Headings*] Quantity / Description / Size / Article no.	– *[Überschriften] Menge / Beschreibung / Größe / Artikel-Nr.*
Price(s) and discount(s)	
– [*Headings*] Unit price / List price / Catalogue price / Total	– *[Überschriften] Stückpreis / Listenpreis / Katalogpreis / Gesamt*
– Subtotal / Total price	– *Zwischensumme / Gesamtpreis*
– 19% VAT (value added tax)	– *19 % USt/MwSt (Umsatzsteuer/Mehrwertsteuer)*
Delivery	
– delivery date/period	– Liefertermin/-zeit
– within 10 days after receipt of order	– innerhalb 10 Tagen nach Auftragserhalt
– by 30 June 20..	– bis zum 30. Juni 20..
Transport/Insurance	
– Transport and insurance of the goods from … to … via …	– *Versand und Versicherung der Ware von … nach … über …*
– …will be arranged by us/you.	– *… wird von uns/Ihnen übernommen.*

Payment	
– 30% in advance, 70% after completion	– *30 % im Voraus, 70 % bei Fertigstellung*
– by transfer to our a/c at ... (bank)	– *per Überweisung auf unser Konto bei ... (Geldinstitut)*
Acknowledgement/Advice of dispatch	
– We look forward to receiving your advice of dispatch.	– *Wir freuen uns auf den Erhalt Ihrer Versandanzeige.*
– Please send us your confirmation of order and advice of dispatch in the near future.	– *Bitte schicken Sie uns Ihre Auftragsbestätigung und Versandanzeige in den nächsten Tagen zu.*
Polite ending	
– We trust the goods will arrive punctually and in good condition ...	– *Wir vertrauen darauf, dass die Ware pünktlich und in gutem Zustand ankommt ...*
– ... and will place further/regular orders if they sell well.	– *... und werden weitere/regelmäßige Aufträge erteilen, wenn sie sich gut verkauft.*

Making complaints	**Unit 11**
Reference to goods	
– The above-mentioned goods were delivered on ... and forwarded to our customers all over Germany/ Europe.	– *Die obengenannten Waren wurden am ... geliefert und unseren Kunden überall in Deutschland/Europa zugestellt.*
– We regret to inform you that they/we are dissatisfied with them.	– *Leider müssen wir Ihnen mitteilen, dass sie/wir damit unzufrieden sind.*
Description of problem	
– On examining the goods / When they opened the boxes ...	– *Bei Prüfung der Ware / Beim Öffnen der Kartons ...*
– ... we / our customers discovered that ...	– *... stellten wir / unsere Kunden fest, dass ...*
– ... some/all of the articles/appliances were dirty/ discoloured / (badly) damaged.	– *... einige/alle Artikel/Geräte verschmutzt/verfärbt / (stark) beschädigt waren.*
– The appliances have proved to be unreliable and (often) produce ... (e.g. poor results / half-cooked food).	– *Die Geräte haben sich als unzuverlässig* – *erwiesen und liefern (oft) ... (z. B. schlechte Ergebnisse / halbgare Lebensmittel).*
– We enclose/attach photographs of these items for your information.	– *Wir fügen Fotos dieser Artikel zu Ihrer Information bei.*
Request for explanation	
– Please explain why our order was so poorly executed / how this could happen.	– *Bitte erklären Sie, warum unser Auftrag so schlecht ausgeführt wurde / wie dies geschehen konnte.*
– We would welcome your explanation of the damage.	– *Wir würden eine Erklärung (von Ihnen) für den Schaden begrüßen.*
Consequences for the buyer and seller	
– Whatever the case may be, ...	– *Wie dem auch sei, ...*
– ... we are returning the damaged/faulty/defective goods to you carriage forward.	– *... wir schicken die beschädigten/fehlerhaften/ defekten Güter unfrei an Sie zurück.*
– You will appreciate that ...	– *Bitte haben Sie Verständnis, dass ...*
– ... we cannot sell these articles (at the normal price).	– *... wir diese Artikel nicht (zum normalen Preis) verkaufen können.*
Request for action	
– We must therefore insist that you ...	– *Wir müssen daher darauf bestehen, dass Sie ...*
– We must therefore ask you to ...	– *Wir müssen Sie deshalb bitten, ...*
– ... supply us with replacements free of charge by return.	– *... uns umgehend kostenlosen Ersatz liefern.*
– ... replace the entire consignment.	– *... die ganze Lieferung (zu) ersetzen.*
– ... as these goods are needed urgently / are still under warranty.	– *... da die Waren dringend benötigt werden / da es sich um einen Garantiefall handelt.*
– We must therefore ask you to reduce the price by ...%.	– *Wir bitten Sie daher, den Preis um ... % zu reduzieren.*

Polite ending	
– We feel sure you will appreciate that …	– *Sie werden sicherlich dafür Verständnis haben, dass …*
– … our future business relationship will depend on how this matter is dealt with.	– *… die Fortsetzung unserer Geschäftsbeziehung von der Regelung dieser Angelegenheit abhängig ist.*
– We trust you will deal with this matter without delay.	– *Wir vertrauen darauf, dass Sie sich unverzüglich mit dieser Angelegenheit befassen werden.*
– We expect to hear from you in the very near future.	– *Wir erwarten, von Ihnen recht bald zu hören.*
– We look forward to receiving your comments on this matter without delay.	– *Wir erwarten Ihre unverzügliche Stellungnahme zu dieser Angelegenheit.*

Responding to complaints	Unit 11
Acknowledgement of complaint	
– We have (just) received your email/letter regarding the above-mentioned consignment of …	– *Wir haben (soeben) Ihre E-Mail / Ihren Brief bezüglich der oben erwähnten Lieferung … erhalten.*
– Your complaint is now being investigated.	– *Ihre Beschwerde wird jetzt geprüft.*
First expression of regret	
– We are sorry to hear the consignment was delayed and that some of the good are below standard.	– *Es tut uns leid zu hören, dass die Sendung verzögert eintraf und dass einige der Waren nicht der Qualität entsprachen.*
– … and are dismayed to hear that the consignment is unsatisfactory.	– *… und es tut uns (sehr) leid zu hören, dass die Lieferung unzufriedenstellend ist.*
Action taken	
– Since hearing from you, / receiving your email, …	– *Nach Erhalt Ihrer Nachricht/E-Mail …*
– … we have investigated the matter and discovered / found out that …	– *… haben wir die Angelegenheit untersucht und herausgefunden, dass …*
– … the wrong component was used in (some of the) … (e.g. the machines / appliances).	– *… das falsche Bauteil in (einigen) … (z. B. Maschinen / Geräten) benutzt wurde .*
– … there was an error in our dispatch section / quality control department.	– *… es einen Fehler in unserer Versand- / Qualitätssicherungsabteilung gab.*
Solution	
– In the meantime, we are sending you replacements at no extra charge by return.	– *In der Zwischenzeit schicken wir Ihnen umgehend kostenlosen Ersatz.*
– The missing… (articles) / Replacements will be delivered to you carriage paid within 24/48 hours.	– *Die fehlenden … (Artikel) / Ersatzgeräte werden Ihnen innerhalb 24/48 Stunden frachtfrei geliefert.*
– If you are prepared to keep the … (goods), we will grant you a reduction in price of …%.	– *Wenn Sie bereit sind, die … (Waren) zu behalten, gewähren wir Ihnen einen Rabatt von … %.*
– Under the circumstances, we are willing to offer you a replacement consignment or a reduction in price of …% on the unsatisfactory items.	– *Unter diesen Umständen sind wir bereit, Ihnen eine Ersatzsendung oder eine Preisreduzierung von … % auf die nicht zufriedenstellenden Artikel anzubieten.*
Second apology	
– Please accept our apologies for this.	– *Wir entschuldigen uns vielmals.*
– In the meantime, please accept our apologies for the inconvenience caused (which was due to circumstances beyond our control).	– *Bitte entschuldigen Sie die Unannehmlichkeiten. Leider entzogen sich die Umstände in diesem Fall unserer Kontrolle.*
– We assure you it will not happen again.	– *Wir versichern Ihnen, dass es nicht wieder vorkommen wird.*
Polite ending	
– We hope this suggestion/solution will find your approval.	– *Wir hoffen, dass dieser Vorschlag / diese Lösung Ihre Zustimmung finden wird.*
– We look forward to doing further business with you.	– *Wir freuen uns darauf, weitere Geschäfte mit Ihnen zu tätigen.*

Querying invoices — Unit 11

Reference to invoice/statement	
– Thank you for the above-mentioned invoice/ statement for … (details, e.g. skiing boots / goods received last quarter).	– *Danke für die obengenannte (Ab)Rechnung für … (Einzelheiten, z. B. Skischuhe / die im letzten Quartal erhaltenen Waren).*
– We refer to your/our statement / invoice no. … dated … for … (amount).	– *Wir beziehen uns auf Ihre/unsere (Ab)Rechnung Nr. … vom … über … (Betrag).*
Reference to payment of statement/invoice	
– Our statement/invoice no. … is enclosed/attached for settlement.	– *Unsere (Ab)Rechnung Nr. … ist zwecks Zahlung beigefügt.*
– On receipt of your remittance for €1,000 the goods will be shipped.	– *Nach Erhalt Ihrer Überweisung von € 1.000 werden die Waren versandt.*
– Please note that payment was due on … (date).	– *Bitte nehmen Sie zur Kenntnis, dass die Zahlung am … (Datum) fällig war.*
– We would appreciate settlement of the total amount due in the next few days.	– *Wir bitten Sie, den fälligen Gesamtbetrag in den nächsten Tagen zu begleichen.*
Reference to discrepancies/errors/amendments	
– Having checked your statement/invoice against our (own) records, …	– *Nachdem wir Ihre (Ab)Rechnung mit unseren (eigenen) Aufzeichnungen verglichen haben, …*
– … we must point out that …	– *… müssen wir darauf hinweisen, dass …*
– … it is incorrect in the following points:	– *… sie in folgenden Punkten nicht korrekt ist:*
– … you have not included our credit note no. XYZ123 for €200 dated 10 August.	– *… Sie unsere Gutschrift Nr. XYZ123 über € 200 vom 10. August … nicht berücksichtigt haben.*
– … items 1 and 2 of your statement have been incorrectly charged.	– *… die Posten 1 und 2 Ihres Kontoauszugs nicht richtig belastet worden sind.*
– … you have omitted to include the quantity/special discount of …% granted on orders for 100 units or more.	– *… Sie haben versäumt, den Mengen-/Sonderrabatt von … %, der für Aufträge über 100 Stück oder mehr gewährt wird, einzubeziehen.*
– … the (special) discount granted on items 1 and 2 for … (e.g. skiing boots) is only 15% instead of 50%, as promised.	– *… der auf den Posten … / die Posten … und … gewährte (Sonder)Rabatt für … (z. B. Skischuhe) nur 15 % beträgt statt wie versprochen 50 %.*
– … you have overcharged/undercharged us by (a total of) €200.	– *… Sie uns (insgesamt) € 200 zu viel / zu wenig berechnet haben.*
– We can confirm that the …% discount promised on … (goods) was not granted.	– *Wir können bestätigen, dass der versprochene Rabatt von … % auf … (Ware) nicht gewährt wurde.*
– We are returning your statement/invoice and would request you …	– *Wir schicken Ihnen Ihre (Ab)Rechnung zurück und bitten Sie, …*
– … to amend it.	– *… diese abzuändern.*
– … to send us an amended statement/invoice, which we will pay by transfer to your account.	– *… uns eine berichtigte (Ab)Rechnung zu schicken, die wir per Überweisung auf Ihr Konto begleichen werden.*
– As soon as we have received your amended statement/invoice we will remit the sum owing.	– *Sobald wir Ihre berichtigte (Ab)Rechnung erhalten haben, werden wir Ihnen den geschuldeten Betrag überweisen.*
– An amended statement/invoice for … (amount) is enclosed/attached.	– *Wir fügen eine berichtigte (Ab)Rechnung über … (Betrag) bei.*
Polite ending	
– Please do not hesitate to contact us should you have any queries.	– *Bitte zögern Sie nicht, mit uns Kontakt aufzunehmen, wenn Sie irgendwelche Fragen haben.*
– We apologize for the inaccuracy/inaccuracies in our statement/invoice and assure you there will be no recurrence of this in the future.	– *Wir entschuldigen uns für die Unstimmigkeit(en) in unserer (Ab)Rechnung und versichern Ihnen, dass sich dies in Zukunft nicht wiederholen wird.*
– We apologize for the inconvenience and look forward to doing further business with you.	– *Wir entschuldigen uns für die Unannehmlichkeiten und freuen uns darauf, weitere Geschäfte mit Ihnen zu tätigen.*

– We look forward to receiving your corrected statement/invoice.	– *Bitte schicken Sie uns die berichtigte (Ab)Rechnung zu.*
– We trust you will be remitting the amount in question in the next few days.	– *Wir vertrauen darauf, dass Sie den ausstehenden Betrag in den nächsten Tagen überweisen werden.*
– If payment has already been made please disregard this letter/email.	– *Wenn die Zahlung bereits erfolgt ist, betrachten Sie diesen Brief / diese E-Mail bitte als gegenstandslos.*

Writing reminders

– I am writing in connection with the attached unpaid invoice for …	– *Ich schreibe in Zusammenhang mit der angefügten unbezahlten Rechnung für …*
– I would like to draw your attention to invoice no. …	– *Bitte sehen Sie sich Rechnung Nr. … noch einmal an.*
– We are sure this must be an oversight and have included a copy of the invoice for your convenience.	– *Wir sind uns sicher, dass es sich hierbei um einen Irrtum handelt, und fügen zu Ihrer Information eine Kopie der Rechnung bei.*
– Would you please settle your account by the end of the month at the latest.	– *Bitte begleichen Sie die Rechnung bis spätestens zu Ende des Monats.*
– If your payment of our invoice has crossed with this letter, we kindly ask you to ignore this reminder.	– *Falls Sie die Rechnung schon beglichen haben sollten, betrachten Sie dieses Schreiben bitte als gegenstandslos.*
– Payment is now … (length of time) overdue.	– *Ihre Zahlung is nun … (Zeitspanne) überfällig.*
– If we have not received your payment within the next seven days, we will have to instruct our solicitors to take legal action.	– *Wenn wir Ihre Zahlung nicht innerhalb der nächsten sieben Tage erhalten, werden wir unseren Anwalt hinzuziehen, um rechtliche Schritte einzuleiten.*

Writing covering letters **Unit 12**

Opening phrases	
– With reference to your advertisement in … (newspaper) of … (date), …	– *Bezugnehmend auf Ihre Ausschreibung in … (Zeitung) vom … (Datum), …*
– I would like / wish to apply for the above-mentioned position/post of … (job).	– *Hiermit möchte ich mich für die oben genannte Stelle als … (Berufsbezeichnung) bewerben.*
Education, training, present employment	
– I attended … (school/college) for … (length of time).	– *Von … bis … (Jahr) besuchte ich … (Schule/ Hochschule).*
– I studied … (subjects) at vocational school in … (place) from … (date) to … (date).	– *An der Berufs(fach)schule in … (Ort) lernte/belegte ich … (Fächer) von … (Datum) bis … (Datum).*
– At present I am working for a/an … (type of company) as a/an … (job).	– *Zurzeit arbeite ich bei einem/einer … (Firmenbezeichnung) als … (Berufsbezeichnung).*
– I will complete my period of training on … (date).	– *Am … (Datum) werde ich meine Ausbildung abschließen.*
Closing paragraph	
– I enclose / Enclosed is my CV (*BE*) / résumé (*AE*) / a list of my qualifications and experience.	– *Anbei finden Sie meinen Lebenslauf / eine Übersicht meiner Qualifikationen und Erfahrungen.*
– I am available for interview at your earliest convenience.	– *Für ein Vorstellungsgespräch stehe ich Ihnen jederzeit gern zur Verfügung.*
– I hope you will consider my application favourably and …	– *Über eine positive Antwort freue ich mich sehr und …*
– … (I) look forward to hearing from you in the near future.	– *… (ich) freue mich darauf, bald von Ihnen zu hören.*

Thematic vocabulary

Training and apprenticeships — Unit 1

A levels *pl*	Abitur, Abiturfächer
apprentice	Auszubildende/r, Lehrling
apprenticeship	Lehre, Ausbildung
block release	Blockunterricht (an der Berufsschule)
certificate	Zeugnis, Diplom
course	Studiengang
coursework	schriftliche Arbeit(en)
day release	tagweise Freistellung zur beruflichen Weiterbildung
degree	Abschluss
diploma	Abschlusszeugnis
final grade	Abschlussnote
grade	Note
internship	Praktikum
job experience	Berufserfahrung, praktische Erfahrung
living expenses *pl*	Lebenshaltungskosten
part-time	Teilzeit
to qualify	einen/den Abschluss machen
qualification	Qualifikation, Abschluss
salary	Gehalt
school leaving certificate	Schulabschluss
school qualification	Schulabschluss
theoretical	theoretisch
to train (to be a ...)	eine Aubildung (zum/zur ...) machen
trainee	Auszubildende/r
training company	Ausbildungsbetrieb
training course	Ausbildung
training supervisor	Ausbildungsleiter/in
vocational college/school	Berufsschule, Berufsfachschule
vocational training	Berufsausbildung
work experience	Praktikum
workplace	Arbeitsplatz

Job titles — Unit 2

accountant	Buchhalter/in
accounting manager	Buchhaltungsleiter/in
chief executive officer (CEO)	Vorstandsvorsitzende/r, Geschäftsführer/in
colleague	Kollege, Kollegin
commercial director	kaufmännische/r Leiter/in
employee	Arbeitnehmer/in, Beschäftigte/r
employer	Arbeitgeber/in, Unternehmer/in
factory manager	Betriebsleiter/in, Werksleiter/in
head of department	Abteilungsleiter/in
industrial management assistant	Industriekaufmann/-frau
IT management assistant	Informatikkaufmann/-frau
legal adviser	Justiziar/in
line manager	(direkte/r) Vorgesetzte/r
management assistant in wholesale and foreign trade	Kaufmann/-frau im Groß- und Außenhandel
manager	Manager/in
managing director	Geschäftsführer/in
office management assistant	Kaufmann/-frau für Büromanagement
personal assistant (PA)	Persönliche/r Assistent/in
production manager	Produktionsleiter/in
project manager	Projektleiter/in
purchasing director/manager	Einkaufsleiter/in
receptionist	Empfangsmitarbeiter/in
sales director	Vertriebsleiter/in
(sales) representative	(Handels-)Vertreter/in
secretary	Sekretär/in
specialist	Fachmann/-frau
staff	Personal
technician	Techniker/in
warehouse manager	Lagerleiter/in

Working conditions — Unit 1

availability	Verfügbarkeit
benefits *pl*	Zusatzleistungen, Sozialleistungen
business trip	Geschäftsreise
company car	Firmenwagen
condition	Bedingung
contract	Vertrag
dress code	Kleiderordnung
facilities *pl*	Einrichtungen, Anlagen
flexitime	Gleitzeit
hot-desking	Hotdesking
job prospects *pl*	berufliche Perspektiven
lunch break	Mittagspause
open-plan office	Großraumbüro
overtime	Überstunden
permanent	unbefristet
salary	Gehalt
shared desk	gemeinsamer Arbeits-/Schreibtisch
shift work	Schichtarbeit
working conditions *pl*	Arbeitsbedingungen
working hours *pl*	Arbeitszeit(en)

Company departments — Unit 2

Accounting / Accounts (department)	Buchhaltung
Administration	Verwaltung
board (of directors)	Geschäftsführung, Vorstand
department	Abteilung
Distribution (department)	Vertrieb
Finance (department)	Rechnungswesen
Financial Controlling (department)	Controlling
head office/headquarters	Zentrale
Human Resources (HR) (department)	Personal(abteilung)
labelling	Bezeichnung, Etikettierung
Legal department	Rechtswesen
management	Geschäftsleitung, Geschäftsführung
manufacturing	Fertigung, Herstellung
Market Research (department)	Marktforschung(sabteilung)
material delivery	Materialanlieferung

press	Presse
Pricing (department)	Kalkulation
project management	Projektleitung
Purchasing (department)	Einkauf(sabteilung)
Quality Assurance/ Management (department)	Qualitätssicherung
reception	Rezeption, Empfang
Research and Development (R&D) (department)	Forschung(s-) und Entwicklung(sabteilung)
Sales (department)	Verkauf(sabteilung), Vertrieb
warehouse	Lager(halle)

Company organization — Unit 3

(general) partnership	Personengesellschaft, offene Handelsgesellschaft (OHG)
limited company (Ltd) *BE* / **closed corporation** *AE*	Gesellschaft mit beschränkter Haftung (GmbH)
limited partnership	Kommanditgesellschaft (KG)
public limited company (plc) *BE* / **open corporation** *AE*	Aktiengesellschaft (AG)
share	Aktie
shareholder	Aktionär/in, Teilhaber/in
sole proprietor/trader	Einzelunternehmer/in

Business partners and traders — Unit 4

buyer	Käufer/in
carrier	Spediteur, Spedition
client	Klient/in
competition	Konkurrenz
competitor	Konkurrent/in, Konkurrenz
customer, client	Kunde, Kundin
exporter	Exporteur
forwarding agent	Spediteur, Spedition
freight forwarder	Spediteur, Spedition
importer	Importeur
retailer	Einzelhändler/in
seller	Verkäufer/in
supplier	Lieferant
wholesaler	Großhändler

Sales and marketing — Unit 5

to analyse	analysieren
cashier	Kassierer/in
check-out	Kasse
customer loyalty	Kundenbindung, Kundentreue
customer satisfaction	Kundenzufriedenheit
to customize sth	etw individuell anpassen
field research	Feldforschung
to gather data	Daten erfassen
to launch sth	etw auf den Markt bringen, etw starten
to market sth	etw vermarkten
market research	Marktforschung
marketing strategy	Vermarktungsstrategie
pricing strategy	Preisstrategie
primary research	Primärforschung
product brief	Produktbeschreibung
product launch	Produkteinführung
product line	Produktlinie
product range	Sortiment
to promote sth	für etw werben, etw promoten
to publish	veröffentlichen
purchasing history	Kaufhistorie, Einkaufsverhalten
questionnaire	Fragebogen
recommendation	Empfehlung
recommended retail price (RRP)	unverbindliche Preisempfehlung (UVP)
retail outlet	Einzelhandelsgeschäft
sales channel	Absatzweg, Vertriebskanal
secondary research	Sekundärforschung
specific	bestimmte/r/s
statistics	Statistik(en)
study	Untersuchung, Studie
survey	Umfrage
target group	Zielgruppe
to target sb	jdn ins Visier nehmen
unique selling proposition (USP)	Alleinstellungsmerkmal

Advertising strategies — Unit 5

to advertise sth	etw bewerben, für etw Werbung machen
advertising	Reklame, Werbung
brand	Marke
branding	Markenbildung
bricks and mortar outlet	stationäres Geschäft
campaign	(Werbe-)Kampagne
catalogue	Katalog
catchphrase	Schlagwort, Slogan
celebrity endorsement	Werbung mit Prominenten
consultant	Berater/in
customer discount	Kundenrabatt
discount	Rabatt, Skonto
giveaway	Werbegeschenk
to have sth on offer	etw im Angebot haben, etw anbieten
mass media *pl*	Massenmedien
niche	Nische
promotion	Werbung, Promotion
promotional	Werbe-
social media *pl*	soziale Medien
special deal	Sonderangebot
stealth advertising	heimliche Werbung, Schleichwerbung
targeted advertising	gezielte/zielgruppengenaue Werbung
testimonial	Erfahrungsbericht
traditional	traditionell, hergebracht
virtual	virtuell

Describing graphs — Unit 5

bar chart	Säulendiagramm
chart	Diagramm
decrease	Abnahme, Rückgang
to decrease	abnehmen, zurückgehen
drastic(ally)	drastisch
drop	Fall, Rückgang
to drop	fallen, zurückgehen
figures *pl*	Zahlen
financial year	Geschäftsjahr
to flatten out	auf gleichem Stand bleiben
graph	Diagramm, Kurve
to hit a maximum	einen Höchstwert/-stand erreichen
increase	Zunahme, Anstieg
to increase	zunehmen, ansteigen
to level off	sich einpendeln
line graph	Liniendiagramm
minimum	Tiefstwert, Tiefstand
output	Produktion
pie chart	Tortendiagramm
quarter	Quartal
quarterly	vierteljährlich, Quartals-
to recover	sich erholen
to remain constant	gleich bleiben
to rise	steigen, ansteien
sales figures *pl*	Umsatzzahlen, Verkaufszahlen
unit	Einheit, Stück
volume of sales	Umsatzvolumen
x-axis	X-Achse
y-axis	Y-Achse

Meetings and presentations — Unit 6

absence	Abwesenheit
absentee	Abwesende/r
agenda	Tagesordnung
any other business (AOB)	Verschiedenes
audience	Publikum
body language	Körpersprache
to call a meeting	eine Sitzung einberufen
to circulate sth	etw (an alle) verteilen
conference	Tagung, Konferenz
conference room	Besprechungsraum, Sitzungssaal
contact details *pl*	Kontaktdaten
to cover	(Thema) behandeln
date	Termin
eye contact	Blickkontakt
to face sb	sich jdm zuwenden, jdn anschauen
feedback	Reaktion(en), Rückmeldung(en)
gesture	Geste
to get a message across	eine Botschaft vermitteln
graphic	Grafik
handout	Arbeitsblatt, Broschüre
to highlight	hervorheben
index card	Karteikarte
invitation	Einladung
item on the agenda	Tagesordnungspunkt
minutes *pl*	Protokoll
to participate	teilnehmen
participant	Teilnehmer/in
to point to sth	auf etw deuten, auf etw zeigen
presenter	Redner/in, Vortragende/r, Moderator/in
prompt card	Moderationskarte
report	Bericht
to reserve	reservieren
screen	Leinwand, Bildschirm
slide	*(Präsentation:)* Folie
to take place	stattfinden
to take the chair / to be in the chair	die Sitzung leiten
talk/lecture	Vortrag
transparency	(Overhead-)Folie, Dia
to turn one's back on sb	jdm den Rücken zuwenden
visual aids *pl*	visuelle Hilfsmittel

Trade fairs — Unit 7

booth	(Messe-)Stand
brochure	Broschüre, Prospekt
corner stand	Eckstand
end of block stand	Kopfstand
event	Veranstaltung
exhibition hall	Messehalle, Ausstellungshalle
fair	Messe
flyer	Faltblatt
giveaway	Werbegeschenk
to hand sth out	etw austeilen, etw ausgeben
island stand	Inselstand
loyalty card	Kundenkarte
rental fee	Miete
sales literature	Verkaufsprospekte, Informationsmaterial
stand	(Messe-)Stand
trade fair	Fachmesse, Branchenmesse
venue	Veranstaltungsort

Business trips — Unit 7

accommodation	Unterkunft, Unterbringung
air-conditioned	klimatisiert
air conditioning	Klimaanlage, Klimatisierung
appointment	Termin
arrival	Ankunft
to attend sth	etw besuchen, an etw teilnehmen
to cancel	absagen, stornieren
to check in	sich anmelden, einchecken
to check out	sich abmelden, auschecken
conference centre	Tagungszentrum, Kongresszentrum
connecting flight	Anschlussflug
departure	Abreise, Abflug
dining room	*(Hotel:)* Speisesaal
excess *BE*	*(Versicherung:)* Selbstbehalt
front desk	Rezeption
insurance cover	Versicherungsschutz
meeting room	Sitzungszimmer, Konferenzraum
mileage	*(Mietwagen:)* (enthaltene) Kilometer

one-way flight	einfacher Flug
passenger	Passagier/in
to postpone	verschieben
reception	Empfang, Rezeption
receptionist	Empfangsmitarbeiter/in
request	Bitte, Anfrage
requirement	Anforderung
reservation	Reservierung, Buchung
return flight	Hin- und Rückflug
shuttle	Zubringer
smoke-free	rauchfrei
trade fair	Messe
travel expenses *pl*	Reisekosten, Reisespesen

Commercial correspondence Units 8–10

address	Adresse
addressee	Empfänger/in
to attach sth	anhängen *(E-Mail)*
attachment	Anhang
attention (attn)	zu Händen
attention line	Zeile „zu Händen"
(Best) Regards	Viele Grüße, Mit freundlichen Grüßen
Best wishes	Mit freundlichen Grüßen
body	Haupttext
complimentary close	Schlussformel
date	Datum
Dear Sir or Madam	Sehr geehrte Damen und Herren,
to enclose	beifügen *(Brief)*
enclosure (enc)	Anlage
inside address	Innenadresse
letterhead	Briefkopf
paragraph	Absatz
reference (ref)	Zeichen
registered mail/post	Einschreiben
salutation	Anrede
sender	Absender
signature block	Signatur
signature	Unterschrift
subject (line)	Betreff(zeile)
Yours faithfully	Mit freundlichen Grüßen
Yours sincerely	Mit freundlichen Grüßen

Business transactions Units 8–10

acknowledgement/ confirmation (of an order)	Auftragsbestätigung
to acknowledge an order	einen Auftrag bestätigen
to adjust a complaint	eine Reklamation bearbeiten/ regulieren
advice of dispatch	Versandanzeige, Versandmitteilung
advice of payment	Zahlungsanzeige
complaint	Reklamation, Beschwerde
consignment	Sendung
contract	Vertrag
to deliver	liefern
delivery	Lieferung
to dispatch	versenden, absenden
enquiry	Anfrage
to fill an order	einen Auftrag erledigen
to place an order	einen Auftrag erteilen
order	Auftrag, Bestellung
order form	Bestellformular
order number	Bestellnummer
quotation	Angebot, Kostenvoranschlag
receipt (of goods)	Erhalt, (Waren-)Eingang
repeat order	Folgeauftrag
sales *pl*	Verkäufe, Umsatz
sample	Muster
to ship	versenden
shipping documents *pl*	Versandpapiere
stock	Ware(n), (Lager-)Bestand
terms of delivery *pl*	Lieferbedingungen
terms of payment *pl*	Zahlungsbedingungen
trial order	Probeauftrag
turnover	Umsatz

Shipping documents Units 8–10

advice of dispatch	Versandanzeige
airfreight	Luftfracht
air waybill (AWB)	Luftfrachtbrief
approval: on approval	zur Ansicht, auf Probe
bill of lading (B/L)	Seefrachtbrief, Konnossement
bonded warehouse	Zollverschlusslager
cargo	Ladung, Fracht
cargo liner	Frachtschiff
cargo space	Frachtraum
certificate of origin (C/O)	Ursprungszeugnis
chamber of (industry and) commerce	(Industrie- und) Handelskammer
combined transport waybill	kombinierter Warenbegleitschein
commercial invoice	Handelsrechnung
consignment note [road or rail]	Frachtbrief [Straßen- oder Bahn-]
consignee	Empfänger/in
consignor	Absender/in, Versender/in
consular invoice	Konsularrechnung, Konsultatsfaktura
contract of carriage	Beförderungsvertrag
customs clearance	Zollabfertigung
customs declaration	Zollinhaltserklärung
customs invoice	Zollrechnung, Zollfaktura
dangerous goods certificate	Gefahrgutbescheinigung
delivery note	Lieferschein
destination; port of destination	Bestimmungsort; Bestimmungshafen
export licence	Exportlizenz
forwarder's certificate of receipt (FCR)	Spediteurübernahmebescheinigung
freight	Fracht
freight rates	Frachttarife
import licence	Einfuhrgenehmigung
to take out insurance	eine Versicherung abschließen
insurance certificate (IC)	Versicherungsschein, -police

to insure goods against a risk	Ware gegen ein Risiko versichern
to issue	ausstellen, ausfertigen
loss; total or partial loss	Verlust; Gesamt- oder Teilverlust
packing list	Packliste
pro forma invoice (P/I)	Proforma-Rechnung
rail consignment note	Bahnfrachtbrief
receipt	Erhalt; Empfangsbescheinigung
ro-ro (roll on-roll off) ferry/vessel	von Straßenfahrzeugen befahrbare/s Fähre/Schiff
shipping note (S/N)	Schiffszettel, Warenbegleitschein
single administrative document	Einheitspapier
waybill (WB)	Frachtbrief

Packaging

bag	Tasche (groß); Beutel (klein)
bale	Ballen
barrel	Fass, Tonne
basket	Korb
bottle	Flasche
box	Kasten, Kiste, Schachtel
can, tin	Dose
carton	Karton
crate	Kiste
drum	Tonne
packet	Paket
pallet	Laderost, Pallette
pouch (small)	Tasche
roll	Rolle
sack	Sack
sea container	Seecontainer
tube	Tube

Complaints — Unit 11

apology	Entschuldigung
broken	zerbrochen
to cancel sth	etw stornieren
compensation	Entschädigung
credit note	Gutschrift
damaged	beschädigt
dented	verbeult
dirty	verschmutzt
discoloured	verfärbt
discrepancy	Unstimmigkeit, Diskrepanz
dissatisfied	unzufrieden
delayed	verspätet
faulty	mangelhaft, defekt
free of charge	unentgeltlich, kostenlos
inconvenience	Unannehmlichkeiten
late	verspätet
mix-up	Durcheinander, Verwechslung
to overcharge sb	jdm zu viel berechnen
to query sth	etw infrage stellen, etw anzweifeln
to rectify defects	Mängel beheben
to reimburse sb	jdm Geld zurückzahlen, jdn entschädigen
reimbursement	Rückerstattung
to remit	*(Geld:)* überweisen
to replace sth	etw ersetzen
replacement	Ersatz
to resolve sth	etw lösen
scratched	verkratzt
soiled	beschmutzt
statutory	gesetzlich vorgeschrieben
unsatisfactory	unzulänglich, unbefriedigend
warranty period	Gewährleistungszeit

Conversion tables

Distance

1 inch (in)	= 2.54 centimetres
1 foot (ft)	= 30.48 centimetres
1 yard (yd)	= 0.9144 metres
1 mile (mi)	= 1.609 kilometres
1 centimetre	= 0.3937 inches (⅜ inch)
1 metre	= 39.37 inches (3 feet, 3 ⅜ inches)
1 kilometre	= 0.62137 miles

Area

1 square inch (in^2)	= 6.452 square centimetres
1 square foot (ft^2)	= 0.0929 square metres
1 square mile (m^2)	= 2.59 square kilometres
1 square centimetre	= 0.155 square inches
1 square metre	= 10.764 square feet
1 square kilometre	= 0.3861 square miles

Mass/Weight

1 ounce (oz)	= 28.35 grams
1 pound (lb)	= 0.453 kilograms
1 UK ton ('long ton')	= 1,016 kilograms
1 US ton ('short ton')	= 907 kilograms
1 gram	= 0.035 ounces
1 kilogram	= 2 pounds, 3.3 ounces

Volume

1 UK pint (pt)	= 0.568 litres
1 UK quart (qt)	= 1.137 litres
1 UK gallon (gal)	= 4.546 litres
1 US pint	= 0.473 litres
1 US quart	= 0.946 litres
1 US gallon	= 3.785 litres
1 cubic inch (in^3)	= 16 cubic centimetres
1 cubic foot (ft^3)	= 0.03 cubic metres

1–12 Unit word list

Dieses Wörterverzeichnis enthält alle neuen Wörter aus *Trade Matters – 4th Edition* in der Reihenfolge ihres Erscheinens (Seitenzahlen sind angegeben). Nicht angeführt sind die Wörter aus dem Grundwortschatz (vgl. **Handreichungen für den Unterricht**). Wörter aus den Hörverständnisübungen sind mit einem T (Transkript) und Wörter aus den *Partner files* mit einem P gekennzeichnet. Die Zahl am linken Rand gibt die Seitenzahl an.

Abkürzungen			
	AE = amerikanisches Englisch	*jdm* = jemandem	*pl* = plural noun
	BE = britisches Englisch	*jdn* = jemanden	*sb* = somebody
	etw = etwas	*jds* = jemandes	*sth* = something

UNIT 1

6	**condition** [kən'dɪʃn]	Bedingung
	working conditions *pl* [ˌwɜːkɪŋ kən'dɪʃnz]	Arbeitsbedingungen
	apprenticeship [ə'prentɪʃɪp]	Lehre, Ausbildung
	apprentice [ə'prentɪs]	Auszubildende/r, Lehrling
	consumer electronics [kənˌsjuːmər ˌɪlek'trɒnɪks]	Unterhaltungselektronik
	wholesaler ['həʊlseɪlə]	Großhändler
	trainee [treɪ'niː]	Auszubildende/r, Lehrling
	section ['sekʃn]	Bereich, Abschnitt
	line manager [laɪn 'mænɪdʒə]	(direkte/r) Vorgesetzte/r
	A levels *pl* ['eɪ levlz]	Abitur, Abiturfächer
	to **train to be a …** ['treɪn tə bi]	eine Ausbildung zum/zur … machen
	wholesale ['həʊlseɪl]	Großhandel
	foreign trade [ˌfɒrən 'treɪd]	Außenhandel
	management assistant in wholesale and foreign trade [mænɪdʒmənt əˌsɪstənt ɪn ˌhəʊlseɪl ənd ˌfɒrən 'treɪd]	Kaufmann/-frau im Groß- und Außenhandel
	block release [ˌblɒk rɪ'liːs]	Blockunterricht *(an der Berufsschule)*
	vocational school [vəʊˌkeɪʃənl 'skuːl]	Berufsschule
	salary ['sæləri]	Gehalt
	expenses *pl* [ɪk'spensɪz]	Kosten, Auslagen
	rent [rent]	Miete
	branch [brɑːntʃ]	Niederlassung, Filiale
	school qualification [ˌskuːl kwɒlɪfɪ'keɪʃn]	Schulabschluss
	training company ['treɪnɪŋ kʌmpəni]	Ausbildungsbetrieb
	living expenses *pl* ['lɪvɪŋ ɪkspensɪz]	Lebenshaltungskosten
	to **qualify** ['kwɒlɪfaɪ]	einen/den Abschluss machen
	training course ['treɪnɪŋ kɔːs]	Ausbildung
	to **divide sth** [dɪ'vaɪd]	etw aufteilen
T	**computer studies** *pl* [kəm'pjuːtə stʌdiz]	Informatik
	industrial management assistant [ɪnˌdʌstriəl ˌmænɪdʒmənt ə'sɪstənt]	Industriekaufmann/-frau
	day release ['deɪ rɪliːs]	*tagweise Freistellung zur beruflichen Weiterbildung*
	permanent ['pɜːmənənt]	unbefristet
7	to **structure** ['strʌktʃə]	aufbauen, strukturieren
	vocational training [vəʊˌkeɪʃənl 'treɪnɪŋ]	Berufsausbildung
	degree [dɪ'griː]	Abschluss
	to **enter a scheme** [ˌentər ə 'skiːm]	an einem Programm teilnehmen
	job experience [ˌdʒɒb ɪk'spɪəriəns]	Berufserfahrung, praktische Erfahrung
	theoretical [ˌθɪə'retɪkl]	theoretisch, Theorie-
	vocational college [vəʊˌkeɪʃənl 'kɒlɪdʒ]	Berufsschule, Berufsfachschule
	profession [prə'feʃn]	Beruf
	depending on … [dɪ'pendɪŋ ɒn]	je nach
	contract ['kɒntrækt]	Vertrag
	to **fire sb** ['faɪə]	jdn entlassen
	to **gain sth** [geɪn]	etw erlangen, etw erwerben, etw gewinnen
	standard ['stændəd]	Maßstab, Norm
	throughout … [θruː'aʊt]	in ganz …
	recognized ['rekəgnaɪzd]	anerkannt
	even though ['iːvn ðəʊ]	auch wenn
	to **train** [treɪn]	eine Ausbildung machen
	commerce ['kɒmɜːs]	Handel, Wirtschaft
	to **split sth** [splɪt]	etw aufteilen
	in-company ['ɪn kʌmpəni]	betriebsintern
	explanation [ˌeksplə'neɪʃn]	Erläuterung
8	to **encourage sb** [ɪn'kʌrɪdʒ]	jdn ermutigen, jdn ermuntern
	trainer ['treɪnə]	Ausbilder/in
	to **brainstorm** ['breɪnstɔːm]	Ideen sammeln

	medium-sized [ˈmiːdiəm saɪzd]	mittelgroß, mittelständisch
	to **subsidize** [ˈsʌbsɪdaɪz]	subventionieren, bezuschussen
	smart [smɑːt]	*(Kleidung:)* schick
	open-plan office [ˌəʊpənplæn ˈɒfɪs]	Großraumbüro
	flexitime [ˈfleksitaɪm]	Gleitzeit
	shift work [ˈʃɪft wɜːk]	Schichtarbeit
	company car [ˈkʌmpəni kɑː]	Firmenwagen
	dress code [ˈdres kəʊd]	Kleiderordnung
	to **give reasons for sth** [ˌɡɪv ˈriːznz fə]	etw begründen
	to **conduct sth** [kənˈdʌkt]	etw durchführen
	survey [ˈsɜːveɪ]	Umfrage
	in my opinion [ɪn maɪ əˈpɪniən]	meiner Meinung nach
	participant [pɑːˈtɪsɪpənt]	Teilnehmer/in
	department [dɪˈpɑːtmənt]	Abteilung
	working hours *pl* [ˌwɜːkɪŋ ˈaʊəz]	Arbeitszeit(en)
	overtime [ˈəʊvətaɪm]	Überstunden
	business trip [ˈbɪznəs trɪp]	Geschäftsreise
	availability [əˌveɪləˈbɪləti]	Verfügbarkeit
	facilities *pl* [fəˈsɪlətiz]	Einrichtungen, Anlage(n)
	benefits *pl* [ˈbenɪfɪts]	Zusatzleistungen, Sozialleistungen
	job prospects *pl* [ˈdʒɒb prɒspekts]	berufliche Perspektiven
T	**Go ahead.** [ˌɡəʊ əˈhed]	Nur zu! Na los!
	retailer [ˈriːteɪlə]	Einzelhändler/in
	procurement [prəˈkjʊəmənt]	Beschaffung
	goods *pl* [ɡʊdz]	Ware(n), Güter
	supplier [səˈplaɪə]	Zulieferer, Lieferant/in, Anbieter
	to **clock in/out** [ˌklɒk ˈɪn/ˈaʊt]	ein-/ausstempeln
	morning break [ˈmɔːnɪŋ breɪk]	Frühstückspause
	official(ly) [əˈfɪʃl]	offiziell
	to **feel like sth** [ˈfiːl laɪk]	Lust auf etw haben
	event [ɪˈvent]	Veranstaltung
	open day [ˈəʊpən deɪ]	Tag der offenen Tür
	to **clear up** [ˌklɪər ˈʌp]	aufräumen
	in writing [ɪn ˈraɪtɪŋ]	schriftlich, in Schriftform
	strict [strɪkt]	streng
	text (message) [tekst]	SMS
	standby [ˈstændbaɪ]	Bereitschaft
	to **log in** [ˌlɒɡ ˈɪn]	sich einloggen
	drinks machine [ˌdrɪŋks məˈʃiːn]	Getränkeautomat
	ground floor [ˌɡraʊnd ˈflɔː]	Erdgeschoss
	discount [ˈdɪskaʊnt]	Rabatt, Skonto
	to **stay on** [ˌsteɪ ˈɒn]	bleiben, dableiben
	job offer [ˈdʒɒb ɒfə]	Stellenangebot
	That's it. [ðætsˈ ɪt]	Das war's.
	You're welcome. [jɔː ˈwelkəm]	Bitte (sehr). Gern geschehen.
	family business [ˈfæməli bɪznəs]	Familienunternehmen
	furniture [ˈfɜːnɪtʃə]	Möbel
	logistics [ləˈdʒɪstɪks]	Logistik
	deadline [ˈdedlaɪn]	Frist, Fertigstellungstermin
	to **meet a deadline** [ˌmiːt ə ˈdedlaɪn]	eine Frist einhalten
	to **text sb** [tekst]	jdm eine SMS schicken
	I don't mind. [aɪ dəʊnt ˈmaɪnd]	Ich habe nichts dagegen.
	Come to think of it … [kʌm tə ˈθɪŋk əv ɪt]	Wenn ich es mir recht/genau überlege …
	at cost price [ət ˌkɒst ˈpraɪs]	zum Selbstkostenpreis
	questionnaire [ˌkwestʃəˈneə]	Fragebogen
9	to **look the part** [ˌlʊk ðə ˈpɑːt]	entsprechend (rollengerecht) aussehen
	appearance [əˈpɪərəns]	Erscheinungsbild, Auftreten
	acceptable [əkˈseptəbl]	zulässig, akzeptabel
	allowed [əˈlaʊd]	zulässig
	suit [suːt]	Anzug; Kostüm
	tie [taɪ]	Krawatte
	trouser suit [ˈtraʊzə suːt]	Hosenanzug
	skirt [skɜːt]	Rock
	blouse [blaʊz]	Bluse
	dress [dres]	Kleid
	loud [laʊd]	*(Farbe:)* grell, knallig, bunt
	low-cut [ˌləʊ ˈkʌt]	tief ausgeschnitten
	top [tɒp]	Oberteil
	flat [flæt]	flach
	heel [hiːl]	*(Schuh:)* Absatz
	trainers *pl* [ˈtreɪnəz]	Turnschuhe, Sportschuhe
	jewellery [ˈdʒuːəlri]	Schmuck
	earring [ˈɪərɪŋ]	Ohrring
	visible [ˈvɪzəbl]	sichtbar
	excessive [ɪkˈsesɪv]	übermäßig, übertrieben
	to **react** [riˈækt]	reagieren
	to **dress** [dres]	sich kleiden
	importance [ɪmˈpɔːtns]	Bedeutung, Wichtigkeit
	workplace [ˈwɜːkpleɪs]	Arbeitsplatz
10	**productivity** [ˌprɒdʌkˈtɪvəti]	Produktivität
T	**surprised** [səˈpraɪzd]	überrascht, erstaunt
	off (work) [ɒf]	frei
	to **take time off (work)** [teɪk ˌtaɪm ˈɒf]	sich frei nehmen
	winner [ˈwɪnə]	Sieger/in
	by the way [baɪ ðə ˈweɪ]	übrigens
	remaining [rɪˈmeɪnɪŋ]	übrige/r/s
	unpaid [ˌʌnˈpeɪd]	unbezahlt
	to sum up [tə ˌsʌm ˈʌp]	zusammenfassend (gesagt)
	to **take a break** [ˌteɪk ə ˈbreɪk]	eine Pause machen
	obligation [ˌɒblɪˈɡeɪʃn]	Pflicht, Verpflichtung
11	**career** [kəˈrɪə]	(berufliche) Laufbahn, Karriere
	diploma [dɪˈpləʊmə]	Abschlusszeugnis
	course [kɔːs]	Studiengang

	business administration [ˈbɪznəs ədmɪnɪstreɪʃn]	Betriebswirtschaft
	grade [greɪd]	Note
	final grade [ˌfaɪnl ˈgreɪd]	Abschlussnote
	coursework [ˈkɔːswɜːk]	schriftliche Arbeit(en)
	internship [ˈɪntɜːnʃɪp]	Praktikum
	for free [fə ˈfriː]	umsonst
	folks [fəʊks]	Leute
	tuition fees *pl* [tjuˈɪʃn fiːz]	Studiengebühren
	part-time [ˌpɑːtˈtaɪm]	Teilzeit
	convenience store *AE* [kənˈviːniəns stɔː]	*lang geöffneter Laden (oft mit Tankstelle)*
	to **be in debt** [bi ɪn ˈdet]	Schulden haben, verschuldet sein
	goal [gəʊl]	Ziel
	buyer [ˈbaɪə]	Einkäufer/in
	clothing industry [ˌkləʊðɪŋ ˈɪndəstri]	Kleidungsbranche
	to **get into debt** [ˌget ɪntə ˈdet]	sich verschulden
	to **earn sth** [ɜːn]	etw verdienen
	intermediate [ˌɪntəˈmiːdiət]	mittlere/r/s
	assessor [əˈsesə]	Betreuer/in, Gutachter/in
	to **upload** [ˌʌpˈləʊd]	hochladen
	portfolio [pɔːtˈfəʊliəʊ]	Arbeitsmappe
	fees *pl* [fiːz]	Gebühren
	limit [ˈlɪmɪt]	Beschränkung, Begrenzung
	final examination [ˌfaɪnl ɪgzæmɪˈneɪʃn]	Abschlussprüfung
	advanced [ədˈvɑːnst]	fortgeschritten, weiterführend
	long-term [ˌlɒŋˈtɜːm]	langfristig
	introductions *pl* [ˌɪntrəˈdʌkʃnz]	Bekanntmachen, Vorstellen
	academic [ˌækəˈdemɪk]	akademisch, Universitäts-, universitär
	qualification [ˌkwɒlɪfɪˈkeɪʃn]	Abschluss, Qualifikation
	finance [ˈfaɪnæns]	Finanz(en)
	assessment [əˈsesmənt]	Beurteilung, Bewertung, Einschätzung, Urteil
	industrialized country [ɪnˌdʌstriəlaɪzd ˈkʌntri]	Industrieland, -staat
	to **vary** [ˈveəri]	variieren, sich unterscheiden
	pros and cons *pl* [ˌprəʊz ənd ˈkɒnz]	Argumente dafür und dagegen, Vor- und Nachteile
	practical [ˈpræktɪkl]	praktisch, Praxis-
12	**Human Resources (HR)** [ˌhjuːmən rɪˈsɔːsɪz]	Personal(abteilung)
	computerized [kəmˈpjuːtəraɪzd]	Computer-
	personnel [ˌpɜːsəˈnel]	Personal, Mitarbeiter/innen
	personnel file [ˌpɜːsəˈnel faɪl]	Personalakte
	place of birth [ˌpleɪs əv ˈbɜːθ]	Geburtsort
	job description [ˈdʒɒb dɪskrɪpʃn]	Stellenbeschreibung

	training supervisor [ˌtreɪnɪŋ ˈsuːpəvaɪzə]	Ausbildungsleiter/in
	office management assistant [ˌɒfɪs mænɪdʒmənt əˈsɪstənt]	Bürokaufmann/-frau, Kaufmann/-frau für Büromanagement
	IT management assistant [aɪ ˌtiː mænɪdʒmənt əˈsɪstənt]	Informatikkaufmann/-frau
13	**formal(ly)** [ˈfɔːml]	formell, förmlich
	suitable [ˈsuːtəbl]	geeignet, passend
	to **avoid** [əˈvɔɪd]	vermeiden
	illness [ˈɪlnəs]	Krankheit
	politics [ˈpɒlətɪks]	Politik
	journey [ˈdʒɜːni]	Fahrt, Anreise
	meeting place [ˈmiːtɪŋ pleɪs]	Treffpunkt
	pay [peɪ]	Bezahlung, Gehalt
	response [rɪˈspɒns]	Antwort, Reaktion
	to **be based in …** [bi ˈbeɪst ɪn]	seinen Sitz in … haben, in … sein
	fantastic [fænˈtæstɪk]	phantastisch, toll
	view [vjuː]	Aussicht, Blick
	in fact [ɪn ˈfækt]	genau genommen, tatsächlich, eigentlich
	Excuse me. [ɪkˈskjuːz miː]	Verzeihung. Entschuldigung.
	to **hold up sb** [ˌhəʊld ˈʌp]	jdn aufhalten
	coat [kəʊt]	Jacke, Mantel
T	to **keep sb waiting** [kiːp ˈweɪtɪŋ]	jdn warten lassen
	refreshment [rɪˈfreʃmənt]	Erfrischung

UNIT 2

14	**administration** [ədˌmɪnɪˈstreɪʃn]	Verwaltung
	inventory [ˈɪnvəntri]	Bestandsliste, -aufnahme, Inventar
	equipment [ɪˈkwɪpmənt]	Geräte, Ausstattung, Ausrüstung
	to **key sth in** [ˌkiː ˈɪn]	etw *(am Computer)* eingeben
	data [ˈdeɪtə]	Daten
	likes and dislikes *pl* [ˌlaɪks ən ˈdɪslaɪks]	Vorlieben und Abneigungen
	photocopy [ˈfəʊtəʊkɒpi]	Fotokopie
15	**consultant** [kənˈsʌltənt]	Berater/in
T	**efficient(ly)** [ɪˈfɪʃnt]	effizient
	purpose [ˈpɜːpəs]	Zweck
	to **support** [səˈpɔːt]	unterstützen
	benefit [ˈbenɪfɪt]	Vorteil, Nutzen
	to **focus on sth** [ˈfəʊkəs ɒn]	sich auf etw konzentrieren
	to **concentrate on sth** [ˈkɒnsntreɪt ɒn]	sich auf etw konzentrieren
	to **interrupt** [ˌɪntəˈrʌpt]	unterbrechen, stören
	in contrast [ɪn ˈkɒntrɑːst]	im Gegensatz (dazu)
	to **set sth up** [ˌset ˈʌp]	etw einrichten, etw aufbauen
	cubicle [ˈkjuːbɪkl]	Arbeitsplatz *(im Großraumbüro)*

	set-up ['setʌp]	Anordnung, Einrichtung, System
	to **hide sth** [haɪd]	etw verbergen
	partition [pɑː'tɪʃn]	Trennwand
	to **get on with one's work** [get ˌɒn wɪð wʌnz 'wɜːk]	seine Arbeit machen
	noisy ['nɔɪzi]	laut
	sense of community [ˌsens əf kə'mjuːnəti]	Gemeinschaftssinn
	to **communicate** [kə'mjuːnɪkeɪt]	kommunizieren
	to **be attached to sth** [bi ə'tætʃt tə]	mit etw verbunden sein
	to **clear a space** [klɪər ə 'speɪs]	einen Platz räumen
	neat and tidy [niːt ən 'taɪdi]	sauber und ordentlich
	downside ['daʊnsaɪd]	Nachteil, Schattenseite
	to **put your personal mark on sth** [pʊt jɔː ˌpɜːsnl 'mɑːk ɒn]	einer Sache seinen persönlichen Stempel aufdrücken
	to **result in sth** [rɪ'zʌlt ɪn]	zu etw führen, etw ergeben
	to **lack sth** [læk]	etw nicht haben
	warmth [wɔːmθ]	Wärme
	personality [ˌpɜːsə'næləti]	Persönlichkeit
	uninviting [ˌʌnɪn'vaɪtɪŋ]	wenig einladend
	to **depend on sth** [dɪ'pend ɒn]	von etw abhängen
	according to [ə'kɔːdɪŋ tə]	gemäß, entsprechend, zufolge
	airy ['eəri]	luftig
	spacious ['speɪʃəs]	geräumig
	to **identify** [aɪ'dentɪfaɪ]	identifizieren, bestimmen
	to **handle sth with care** [ˌhændl wɪð 'keə]	etw mit Vorsicht behandeln
	move [muːv]	Umzug
	to **be in order** [bi ɪn 'ɔːdə]	in Ordnung sein
	premises *pl* ['premɪsɪz]	Räumlichkeiten, Firmengelände
	title ['taɪtl]	Titel, Überschrift
	tally list ['tæli lɪst]	Abhakliste, Strichliste
16	**organization chart** [ˌɔːgənaɪ'zeɪʃn tʃɑːt]	Organigramm
	canning ['kænɪŋ]	Konservenherstellung
	machinery [mə'ʃiːnəri]	Maschinen, Geräte
	manufacturer [ˌmænju'fæktʃərə]	Hersteller/in
	management ['mænɪdʒmənt]	Geschäftsleitung, Geschäftsführung
	head of department [ˌhed əv dɪ'pɑːtmənt]	Abteilungsleiter/in
	commercial director [kəˌmɜːʃl də'rektə]	kaufmännische/r Leiter/in
	managing director [ˌmænɪdʒɪŋ də'rektə]	Geschäftsführer/in
	quality management ['kwɒləti mænɪdʒmənt]	Qualitätssicherung
	press [pres]	Presse
	manufacturing [ˌmænju'fæktʃərɪŋ]	Fertigung, Herstellung
	pricing ['praɪsɪŋ]	Kalkulation
	Research & Development (R & D) [rɪˌsɜːtʃ ən dɪ'veləpmənt]	Forschung und Entwicklung
	purchasing ['pɜːtʃəsɪŋ]	Einkauf
	financial controlling [faɪˌnænʃl kən'trəʊlɪŋ]	Controlling
	project management [ˌprɒdʒekt 'mænɪdʒmənt]	Projektleitung
	assembly [ə'sembli]	Montage
	accounts [ə'kaʊnts]	Buchhaltung
	to **work sth out** [ˌwɜːk 'aʊt]	etw berechnen, etw ausrechnen
	to **monitor** ['mɒnɪtə]	überwachen
	component [kəm'pəʊnənt]	Bestandteil, Bauteil
	existing [ɪg'zɪstɪŋ]	bestehend, existierend
17	to **be in charge of sth** [bi ɪn 'tʃɑːdʒ əv]	für etw zuständig/verantwortlich sein
	to **coordinate** [kəʊ'ɔːdɪneɪt]	miteinander abstimmen, koordinieren
	material [mə'tɪəriəl]	Baustoff, Rohmaterial, Material
	to **deal with sth** ['diːl wɪð]	sich um etw kümmern, sich mit etw befassen
	invoice ['ɪnvɔɪs]	Rechnung
	potential [pə'tenʃl]	möglich, potenziell
	to **report to sb** [rɪ'pɔːt tə]	jdm unterstehen
T	**responsibility** [rɪˌspɒnsə'bɪləti]	Aufgabe, Zuständigkeit, Verantwortlichkeit
	to **supervise sth** ['suːpəvaɪz]	etw beaufsichtigen, etw betreuen, etw überwachen
	site [saɪt]	Standort, Gelände
	schedule ['ʃedjuːl]	Zeitplan
	on schedule [ɒn 'ʃedjuːl]	planmäßig, termingerecht
	to **operate sth** ['ɒpəreɪt]	etw bedienen
	trade fair ['treɪd feə]	Fachmesse, Branchenmesse
	budget ['bʌdʒɪt]	Etat, Budget
	to **entail sth** [ɪn'teɪl]	etw mit sich bringen
	to **analyze** ['ænəlaɪz]	analysieren
	sales figures *pl* ['seɪlz fɪgəz]	Umsatzzahlen, Verkaufszahlen
	profit margin ['prɒfɪt mɑːdʒɪn]	Gewinnspanne
	to **report sth to sb** [rɪ'pɔːt tə]	jdm etw melden
	board of directors [ˌbɔːd əv də'rektəz]	Vorstand
	field [fiːld]	Gebiet, Bereich, Feld
	to **put** [pʊt]	formulieren, sagen
	to put it simply [tə ˌpʊt ɪt 'sɪmpli]	vereinfacht gesagt
	to **involve sth** [ɪn'vɒlv]	etw beinhalten, etw umfassen
	to **run sth** [rʌn]	etw leiten
	shipment ['ʃɪpmənt]	Sendung
18	**job profile** ['dʒɒb prəʊfaɪl]	Stellenprofil
	work experience ['wɜːk ɪkspɪəriəns]	Praktikum

	assignment	[ə'saɪnmənt]	Auftrag, Aufgabe
	accounting	[ə'kaʊntɪŋ]	Buchhaltung
	quality assurance	['kwɒləti əʃʊərəns]	Qualitätssicherung
	to **determine sth**	[dɪ'tɜːmɪn]	etw festlegen, etw bestimmen
	to **handle sth**	['hændl]	etw bearbeiten
	payment	['peɪmənt]	Zahlung
	receipt	[rɪ'siːt]	Beleg, Quittung
	norm	[nɔːm]	Norm
	to **maintain sth**	[meɪn'teɪn]	etw warten, etw instand halten
	performance	[pə'fɔːməns]	Leistung
	manpower	['mænpaʊə]	Arbeitskräfte
	financial report	[faɪˌnænʃl rɪ'pɔːt]	Finanzbericht
	to **obtain sth**	[əb'teɪn]	etw erhalten, sich etw verschaffen
	shipping documents *pl*	['ʃɪpɪŋ dɒkjumənts]	Transportpapiere, Versanddokumente
	to **recruit**	[rɪ'kruːt]	*(Personal)* einstellen
	to **promote sb**	[prə'məʊt]	jdn befördern
	to **ship**	[ʃɪp]	versenden, verschicken
	plant	[plɑːnt]	Werk, Fabrik
19	**recording**	[rɪ'kɔːdɪŋ]	Aufzeichnung, Aufnahme
	to **negotiate**	[nɪ'gəʊʃieɪt]	verhandeln, (etw) aushandeln
	terms *pl*	[tɜːmz]	(Vertrags-)Bedingungen
	customs regulations *pl*	['kʌstəmz regjuleɪʃnz]	Zollvorschriften
	process	['prəʊses]	Verfahren, Prozess
T	**on time**	[ɒn 'taɪm]	pünktlich
	in-house	[ˌɪn 'haʊs]	betriebsintern
	to **track**	[træk]	verfolgen
	freight	[freɪt]	Fracht
	to **hand sth in**	[ˌhænd 'ɪn]	etw einreichen, etw abgeben
	to **oversee sth**	[ˌəʊvə'siː]	etw überwachen, etw beaufsichtigen
	to **agree sth**	[ə'griː]	etw vereinbaren
	to **keep to sth**	['kiːp tə]	sich nach etw richten, sich an etw halten
	to **expand sth**	[ɪk'spænd]	etw ausweiten, etw erweitern
	to **miss sth**	[mɪs]	etw übersehen
	project manager	[ˌprɒdʒekt 'mænɪdʒə]	Projektleiter/in
	to **take responsibility**	[teɪk rɪˌspɒnsə'bɪləti]	Verantwortung übernehmen
	chain	[tʃeɪn]	Kette
	to **supply sth**	[sə'plaɪ]	etw liefern, etw bereitstellen
	specifications *pl*	[ˌspesɪfɪ'keɪʃnz]	technische Daten, Spezifikationen
	production manager	[prə'dʌkʃn mænɪdʒə]	Produktionsleiter/in
	accounting manager	[ə'kaʊntɪŋ mænɪdʒə]	Buchhaltungsleiter/in
	daily operations *pl*	[ˌdeɪli ɒpə'reɪʃnz]	Tagesgeschäft
	overall	[ˌəʊvər'ɔːl]	Gesamt-
	in good time	[ɪn ˌgʊd 'taɪm]	rechtzeitig

	to **be one's turn**	[bi wʌnz 'tɜːn]	an der Reihe sein
	flow chart	['fləʊ tʃɑːt]	Flussdiagramm
	blackboard	['blækbɔːd]	Wandtafel
20	**work placement** *BE*	['wɜːk pleɪsmənt]	Praktikum
	subsidiary	[səb'sɪdiəri]	Niederlassung
	to **leave a message**	[ˌliːv ə 'mesɪdʒ]	eine Nachricht hinterlassen
	voicemail	['vɔɪsmeɪl]	Mailbox
	engineering	[ˌendʒɪ'nɪərɪŋ]	Technik, Maschinenbau
	to **call back**	[ˌkɔːl 'bæk]	zurückrufen
	on behalf of sb	[ɒn bɪ'hɑːf əv]	für jdn, in jds Namen
	as follows	[əz 'fɒləʊz]	wie folgt
	to **confirm**	[kən'fɜːm]	bestätigen
	lathe	[leɪð]	Drehbank, Drehmaschine
	factory manager	['fæktəri mænɪdʒə]	Betriebsleiter/in, Werksleiter/in
	maintenance	['meɪntənəns]	Wartung, Instandhaltung, Pflege
	technician	[tek'nɪʃn]	Techniker/in
	at the latest	[ət ðə 'leɪtɪst]	spätestens
	to **pass sth on**	[ˌpɑːs 'ɒn]	etw weiterleiten
	to **take a (phone) call**	[ˌteɪk ə 'kɔːl]	ein Gespräch entgegennehmen
	frequent(ly)	['friːkwənt]	häufig
	expression	[ɪk'spreʃn]	Ausdruck
T	**Speaking.**	['spiːkɪŋ]	*(Telefon:)* Am Apparat.
	to **hold the line**	[ˌhəʊld ðə 'laɪn]	*(Telefon:)* am Apparat bleiben
	engaged	[ɪn'geɪdʒd]	*(Telefon:)* besetzt
	in that case	[ɪn 'ðæt keɪs]	in diesem Fall
	to **connect (to/with sth)**	[kə'nekt]	(mit etw) verbinden, (an etw) anschließen
	to **be unavailable**	[bi ˌʌnə'veɪləbl]	*(Telefon:)* nicht zu sprechen sein
	to **put sb through**	[ˌpʊt 'θruː]	*(Telefon:)* jdn durchstellen
	urgent(ly)	['ɜːdʒənt]	dringend
	to **catch sth**	[kætʃ]	etw verstehen, etw mitbekommen
	to **be missing**	[bi 'mɪsɪŋ]	fehlen
21	**digit**	['dɪdʒɪt]	Ziffer
	separate(ly)	['seprət]	einzeln
	except for	[ɪk'sept fə]	außer
	instruction	[ɪn'strʌkʃn]	Anweisung
	to **improvise**	['ɪmprəvaɪz]	improvisieren

KMK Exam practice 1

22 T	to **return a call**	[rɪˌtɜːn ə 'kɔːl]	zurückrufen
	ergonomic	[ˌɜːgə'nɒmɪk]	ergonomisch
	swivel chair	['swɪvl tʃeə]	Drehstuhl
	brochure	['brəʊʃə]	Broschüre, Prospekt
	to **make sense**	[meɪk 'sens]	sinnvoll sein

	to **appreciate sth** [əˈpriːʃieɪt]	etw zu schätzen wissen
	including sth [ɪnˈkluːdɪŋ]	mit etw, einschließlich einer Sache
	contact details *pl* [ˈkɒntækt diːteɪlz]	Kontaktdaten
23	**CEO (Chief Executive Officer)** [ˌtʃiːf ɪɡˈzekjətɪv ɒfɪsə]	Vorstandsvorsitzende/r, Geschäftsführer/in
	internal [ɪnˈtɜːnl]	intern
	external [ɪkˈstɜːnl]	extern
	cooperation [kəʊˌɒpəˈreɪʃn]	Zusammenarbeit
	to **establish sth** [ɪˈstæblɪʃ]	etw schaffen, etw festlegen
	framework [ˈfreɪmwɜːk]	Rahmen
	director [dəˈrektə]	Vorstandsmitglied
	regional director [ˌriːdʒənl dəˈrektə]	Regionalleiter/in
	agent [ˈeɪdʒənt]	zuständige/r Mitarbeiter/in
	to **achieve** [əˈtʃiːv]	*(Ziel)* erreichen
	objective [əbˈdʒektɪv]	Ziel
	to **meet responsibilities** [ˌmiːt rɪˌspɒnsəˈbɪlətiz]	Aufgaben erfüllen
	development manager [dɪˌveləpmənt ˈmænɪdʒə]	Entwicklungsleiter/in
	strategy goals *pl* [ˈstrætədʒi ɡəʊlz]	strategische Ziele, Geschäftsziele
	to **ensure sth** [ɪnˈʃʊə]	für etw sorgen
	to **be compliant with sth** [bi kəmˈplaɪənt wɪð]	etw *(Norm usw.)* erfüllen, etw *(Vorschrift usw.)* einhalten
	to **lay sth down** [ˌleɪ ˈdaʊn]	etw festlegen
	guidelines *pl* [ˈɡaɪdlaɪnz]	Richtlinien
	financial director [faɪˌnænʃl dəˈrektə]	Finanzvorstand
	to **be licensed to do sth** [bi ˈlaɪsnst tə]	etw (mit offizieller Genehmigung) tun
	transaction [trænˈzækʃn]	Geschäft, Vorgang, Transaktion
	overseas transactions *pl* [əʊvəˌsiːz trænˈzækʃnz]	Auslandsgeschäft
	tax [tæks]	Steuer(n)
	revenue [ˈrevənjuː]	Einkünfte, Einnahmen
	section [ˈsekʃn]	Abteilung
	to **evaluate sth** [ɪˈvæljueɪt]	etw auswerten, etw einschätzen, etw beurteilen
	written correspondence [ˌrɪtn ˌkɒrɪˈspɒndəns]	Schriftverkehr
	concerning sth [kənˈsɜːnɪŋ]	etw betreffend
	to **deal with sb** [ˈdiːl wɪð]	mit jdm umgehen
	recruitment [rɪˈkruːtmənt]	Einstellung, Anwerbung *(von Personal)*
	redundancy [rɪˈdʌndənsi]	(betriebsbedingte) Kündigung
	pension scheme [ˈpenʃn skiːm]	Altersversorgung
	to **initiate sth** [ɪˈnɪʃieɪt]	etw veranlassen
	annual [ˈænjuəl]	jährlich
	evaluation [ɪˌvæljuˈeɪʃn]	Beurteilung, Evaluierung
	obligatory [əˈblɪɡətri]	obligatorisch, zwingend vorgeschrieben
	member of staff [ˌmembər əf ˈstɑːf]	Mitarbeiter/in

UNIT 3

24	**business partner** [ˈbɪznəs pɑːtnə]	Geschäftspartner/in
	timeline [ˈtaɪmlaɪn]	Zeitachse, Zeitschiene
	to **surf the internet** [ˌsɜːf ði ˈɪntənet]	im Internet surfen
	businessman [ˈbɪznəsmən]	Geschäftsmann
	inventor [ɪnˈventə]	Erfinder/in
	brand [brænd]	Marke
	worth [wɜːθ]	wert
	billion [ˈbɪliən]	Milliarde
	empire [ˈempaɪə]	Reich, Imperium
	business venture [ˈbɪznəs ventʃə]	Unternehmen, Geschäftsvorhaben
	to **plant sth** [plɑːnt]	etw pflanzen
	profit [ˈprɒfɪt]	Gewinn, Profit
	technically speaking [ˈteknɪkli spiːkɪŋ]	genaugenommen
	sole trader [ˌsəʊl ˈtreɪdə]	Einzelunternehmer/in
	to **intend to do sth** [ɪnˈtend tə duː]	beabsichtigen, etw zu tun
	unlimited [ʌnˈlɪmɪtɪd]	unbeschränkt, unbegrenzt
	liability [ˌlaɪəˈbɪləti]	Haftung
	rabbit [ˈræbɪt]	Kaninchen
	record [ˈrekɔːd]	Schallplatte
	mail order [ˌmeɪl ˈɔːdə]	Versandhandel
	brand name [ˈbrænd neɪm]	Markenname
	to **take business away from sb** [teɪk ˌbɪznəs əˈweɪ frəm]	jdm das Wasser abgraben
	conventional [kənˈvenʃənl]	herkömmlich, konventionell
	to **set up** [ˌset ˈʌp]	*(Unternehmen usw.)* gründen
	unknown [ˌʌnˈnəʊn]	unbekannt
	artist [ˈɑːtɪst]	Künstler/in
	private limited company (Ltd) [ˌpraɪvət ˌlɪmɪtɪd ˈkʌmpəni]	Gesellschaft mit beschränkter Haftung (GmbH)
	member [ˈmembə]	Mitglied
	liable [ˈlaɪəbl]	haftbar
	to the extent of sth [tə ði ɪkˈstent əv]	bis zu etw
	investment [ɪnˈvestmənt]	Beteiligung, Einlage
	personal wealth [ˌpɜːsnl ˈwelθ]	Privatvermögen
	to **break out** [ˌbreɪk ˈaʊt]	ausbrechen
	to **found sth** [faʊnd]	etw gründen
	airline [ˈeəlaɪn]	Fluggesellschaft
	to **finance** [ˈfaɪnæns]	finanzieren
	public limited company (plc) [ˌpʌblɪk ˌlɪmɪtɪd ˈkʌmpəni]	Aktiengesellschaft (AG)
	share [ʃeə]	Aktie

	stock exchange ['stɒk ɪkstʃeɪndʒ]	Börse
	chairman ['tʃeəmən]	Vorstandsvorsitzende/r
	shareholder ['ʃeəhəʊldə]	Aktionär/in
	short-term [ˌʃɔ:t'tɜ:m]	kurzfristig
	to **enter the railway business** [ˌentə ðə 'reɪlweɪ bɪznəs]	ins Bahngeschäft einsteigen
	franchise ['fræntʃaɪz]	Konzession, Lizenz
	route [ru:t]	Strecke
	to **undercut sb** [ˌʌndə'kʌt]	jdn unterbieten
	financial services *pl* [faɪˌnænʃl 'sɜ:vɪsɪz]	Finanzdienstleistungen
	to **launch sth** [lɔ:ntʃ]	etw starten, etw *(Unternehmen usw.)* gründen
	to **operate** ['ɒpəreɪt]	geschäftlich tätig sein
	spectacular [spek'tækjələ]	spektakulär
	adventure [əd'ventʃə]	Abenteuer
	space travel ['speɪs trævl]	Raumfahrt
	voyage ['vɔɪɪdʒ]	Reise, Fahrt
	barrier ['bæriə]	Hindernis
	to **overcome sth** [ˌəʊvə'kʌm]	etw bewältigen, etw überwinden
	spacecraft ['speɪskrɑ:ft]	Raumschiff
	to **crash** [kræʃ]	abstürzen
	test flight ['test flaɪt]	Testflug
	to **kill sb** [kɪl]	jdn töten
	healthcare clinic ['helθkeə klɪnɪk]	Klinik
	to **hit the headlines** [hɪt ðə 'hedlaɪnz]	Schlagzeilen machen
	gas balloon [gæs bə'lu:n]	Gasballon
	drone [drəʊn]	Drohne
	robotics [rəʊ'bɒtɪks]	Robotertechnik
25	**recording studio** [rɪ'kɔ:dɪŋ stju:diəʊ]	Tonstudio
	train service ['treɪn sɜ:vɪs]	Zugbetrieb
	healthcare ['helθkeə]	Gesundheitswesen
	to **research sth** [rɪ'sɜ:tʃ]	etw recherchieren
	to **take a decision** [ˌteɪk ə dɪ'sɪʒn]	eine Entscheidung treffen
	closed [kləʊzd]	geschlossen
	circle ['sɜ:kl]	Kreis
	to **invest** [ɪn'vest]	investieren
	public ['pʌblɪk]	Öffentlichkeit
	bankruptcy ['bæŋkrʌpsi]	Konkurs
	to **sketch sth out** [ˌsketʃ 'aʊt]	etw (vor)zeichnen
	graphic ['græfɪk]	Grafik
	visual(ly) ['vɪʒuəl]	visuell
	appealing [ə'pi:lɪŋ]	ansprechend
	gallery walk ['gæləri wɔ:k]	Galerierundgang
	clarity ['klærəti]	Klarheit, Deutlichkeit
	to **get a message across** [get ə ˌmesɪdʒ ə'krɒs]	eine Botschaft vermitteln
26	to **export** [ɪk'spɔ:t]	exportieren, ausführen
	guided tour [ˌgaɪdɪd 'tʊə]	Führung
	layout ['leɪaʊt]	Grundriss, Anordnung, Plan
	labelling ['leɪblɪŋ]	Bezeichnung, Etikettierung

	material delivery [mə'tɪəriəl dɪlɪvəri]	Materialanlieferung
	showroom ['ʃəʊru:m]	Ausstellungsraum, Verkaufsraum
	spare part [ˌspeə 'pɑ:t]	Ersatzteil
	entrance ['entrəns]	Eingang
	works council [ˌwɜ:ks 'kaʊnsl]	Betriebsrat
	stairs *pl* [steəz]	Treppe, Treppenhaus
	starting point ['stɑ:tɪŋ pɔɪnt]	Ausgangspunkt
	finishing point ['fɪnɪʃɪŋ pɔɪnt]	Endpunkt
T	**guide** [gaɪd]	Führer/in
	this way ['ðɪs weɪ]	hier entlang
	friendship ['frendʃɪp]	Freundschaft
	fresh [freʃ]	frisch
	to **rot** [rɒt]	verfaulen, verrotten
	destination [ˌdestɪ'neɪʃn]	(Reise-, Fahrt-)Ziel, Zielort
	to **solve** [sɒlv]	lösen
	conference room ['kɒnfərəns ru:m]	Besprechungsraum, Sitzungssaal
	brief [bri:f]	kurz, knapp
	overview ['əʊvəvju:]	Überblick
	corridor ['kɒrɪdɔ:]	Flur, Gang
	gentleman ['dʒentlmən]	Herr
	to **take sth seriously** [teɪk 'sɪəriəsli]	etw ernst nehmen
	stop [stɒp]	Station, Halt
	downstairs [ˌdaʊn'steəz]	(nach) unten
	lift *BE* [lɪft]	Aufzug, Fahrstuhl
	assembly hall [ə'sembli hɔ:l]	Montagehalle
	lid [lɪd]	Deckel
	body (of a can) ['bɒdi]	Dosenrumpf, Dosenkörper
	to **conclude sth** [kən'klu:d]	etw beschließen, etw beenden
	exhibition centre [ˌeksɪ'bɪʃn sentə]	Messezentrum
	lady ['leɪdi]	Dame
	to **feel free to do sth** [fi:l 'fri: tə]	etw ruhig tun, gern etw tun können
	wide range [waɪd 'reɪndʒ]	großes Angebot, breite Palette
	can [kæn]	(Konserven-)Dose
	can end ['kæn end]	Dosendeckel
	production hall [prə'dʌkʃn hɔ:l]	Fertigungshalle, Produktionshalle
	to **work alongside sb** [ˌwɜ:k ə'lɒŋsaɪd]	mit jdm arbeiten
	specialist ['speʃəlɪst]	Fachmann/-frau
	to **turn sth into sth** ['tɜ:n ɪntə]	etw zu etw machen, etw in etw umwandeln
	to **see sth through** [ˌsi: 'θru:]	etw *(Projekt)* durchgehend betreuen
	tool [tu:l]	Werkzeug, Instrument
27	to **give directions** [ˌgɪv də'rekʃnz]	den Weg beschreiben
	opposite ['ɒpəzɪt]	gegenüber

upstairs [ˌʌpˈsteəz] (nach) oben
elevator *AE* [ˈelɪveɪtə] Aufzug, Fahrstuhl
polite(ly) [pəˈlaɪt] höflich
article [ˈɑːtɪkl] Artikel
including sth [ɪnˈkluːdɪŋ] mit etw, einschließlich einer Sache

representative [ˌreprɪˈzentətɪv] Vertreter/in
first of all [ˌfɜːst əv ˈɔːl] zuerst, zunächst
tour [tʊə] Rundgang
to **be delighted** [bi dɪˈlaɪtɪd] (hoch)erfreut sein, sich sehr freuen
to **label** [ˈleɪbl] bezeichnen, etikettieren
to **cover** [ˈkʌvə] *(Thema)* behandeln

28 **slide** [slaɪd] *(Präsentation:)* Folie
heading [ˈhedɪŋ] Überschrift, Rubrik
interior [ɪnˈtɪəriə] Innenbereich, das Innere
parent company [ˌpeərənt ˈkʌmpəni] Muttergesellschaft
turnover [ˈtɜːnəʊvə] Umsatz
approximately [əˈprɒksɪmətli] ungefähr, zirka
percentage [pəˈsentɪdʒ] Anteil, Prozentsatz
market share [ˌmɑːkɪt ˈʃeə] Marktanteil
production line [prəˈdʌkʃn laɪn] Fertigungslinie
slitter [ˈslɪtə] Schneidemaschine, Schlitzer
welding machine [ˈweldɪŋ məʃiːn] Schweißmaschine
seam covering [ˈsiːm kʌverɪŋ] Falzabdeckung, Bördeln
curing oven [ˈkjʊərɪŋ ʌvn] Einbrennofen

T **agenda** [əˈdʒendə] Programm, Tagesordnung
folder [ˈfəʊldə] Mappe, Ordner
background [ˈbækgraʊnd] Hintergrund
statistics [stəˈtɪstɪks] Statistik(en)
to **be happy to do sth** [bi ˈhæpi tə duː] etw gern tun
to **manufacture** [ˌmænjuˈfæktʃə] fertigen, herstellen
workforce [ˈwɜːkfɔːs] Belegschaft, Arbeitskräfte
global market share [ˌgləʊbl ˈmɑːkɪt ʃeə] Weltmarktanteil
in particular [ɪn pəˈtɪkjələ] insbesondere
transport infrastructure [ˌtrænspɔːt ˈɪnfrəstrʌktʃə] Verkehrsnetz
speciality [ˌspeʃiˈæləti] Spezialität
to **assemble** [əˈsembl] montieren, zusammenbauen
on site [ɒn ˈsaɪt] vor Ort
state-of-the-art [ˌsteɪt əv ði ˈɑːt] auf dem neuesten Stand der Technik, hochmodern
ample space [ˌæmpl ˈspeɪs] genügend Platz

29 **handout** [ˈhændaʊt] Arbeitsblatt, Broschüre
to **guide** [gaɪd] leiten, führen
audience [ˈɔːdiəns] Publikum
visuals *pl* [ˈvɪʒuəlz] visuelles Hilfsmittel
to **deal with sth** [ˈdiːl wɪð] mit etw umgehen, sich mit etw befassen

conclusion [kənˈkluːʒn] Schluss
aid [eɪd] Hilfsmittel
colourful [ˈkʌləfl] bunt, farbenfroh
illustrated [ˈɪləstreɪtɪd] bebildert, illustriert
transparency [trænsˈpærənsi] (Overhead-)Folie, Dia

30 **structure** [ˈstrʌktʃə] Aufbau, Struktur
signpost [ˈsaɪnpəʊst] Wegweiser
to **invite sth** [ɪnˈvaɪt] zu etw auffordern, um etw bitten

correctness [kəˈrektnəs] Richtigkeit
spelling [ˈspelɪŋ] Rechtschreibung
prompt card [ˈprɒmt kɑːd] Moderationskarte
to **come across** [ˌkʌm əˈkrɒs] wirken
presenter [prɪˈzentə] Redner/in, Vortragende/r, Moderator/in

either [ˈaɪðə] jedes *(von zweien)*
to **highlight** [ˈhaɪlaɪt] hervorheben
index card [ˈɪndeks kɑːd] Karteikarte
workshop [ˈwɜːkʃɒp] Werkstatt

31 to **face sb** [feɪs] sich jdm zuwenden, jdn anschauen

visual aids *pl* [ˈvɪʒuəl eɪdz] visuelle Hilfsmittel
to **overload** [ˌəʊvəˈləʊd] überladen
to **hand over to sb** [ˌhænd ˈəʊvə tə] an jdn übergeben
attire [əˈtaɪə] Kleidung
gesture [ˈdʒestʃə] Geste
body language [ˈbɒdi læŋgwɪdʒ] Körpersprache
contact details *pl* [ˈkɒntækt diːteɪlz] Kontaktdaten
business card [ˈbɪznəs kɑːd] Visitenkarte
appropriate [əˈprəʊpriət] angemessen, passend
eye contact [ˈaɪ kɒntækt] Blickkontakt
to **turn one's back on sb** [ˌtɜːn wʌnz ˈbæk ɒn] jdm den Rücken zuwenden
to **point to sth** [ˈpɔɪnt tə] auf etw deuten, auf etw zeigen

screen [skriːn] Leinwand, Bildschirm
key word [ˈkiː wɜːd] Stichwort
feedback [ˈfiːdbæk] Reaktion(en), Rückmeldung(en)

improvement [ɪmˈpruːvmənt] Verbesserung
to **support** [səˈpɔːt] *(Argumentation)* untermauern

manner [ˈmænə] Art (und Weise)
overall score [əʊvərˌɔːl ˈskɔː] Gesamtpunktzahl

UNIT 4

32 **fact sheet** [ˈfækt ʃiːt] Informationsblatt
end consumer [end kənˈsjuːmə] Endverbraucher/in
involved (in sth) [ɪnˈvɒlvd] (an etw) beteiligt

	to update sth [ˌʌpˈdeɪt]	etw aktualisieren
	booth [ˈbuːð]	(Messe-)Stand
33	**indirect** [ˌɪndəˈrekt]	indirekt
	distribution channel [ˌdɪstrɪˈbjuːʃn tʃænl]	Vertriebsweg, Vertriebskanal
	to change hands [ˌtʃeɪndʒ ˈhændz]	den Besitzer wechseln
	high street [ˈhaɪ striːt]	Einkaufsstraße
	everyday [ˈevrideɪ]	Alltags-
	consumer goods *pl* [kənˈsjuːmə gʊdz]	Konsumgüter
	neighbourhood [ˈneɪbəhʊd]	Nachbarschaft, Viertel
	drive [draɪv]	Fahrt *(mit dem Auto)*
	in bulk [ɪn ˈbʌlk]	en gros, in großen Mengen
	to sell sth on [ˌsel ˈɒn]	etw weiterverkaufen
	quantity [ˈkwɒntəti]	Menge, Anzahl
	warehouse [ˈweəhaʊs]	Lager
	middleman [ˈmɪdlmæn]	Mittelsmann, Zwischenhändler/in
	agent [ˈeɪdʒənt]	Vermittler/in, Zwischenhändler/in
	negotiation [nɪˌgəʊʃiˈeɪʃn]	Verhandlung
	seller [ˈselə]	Verkäufer/in
	network [ˈnetwɜːk]	Netz, Netzwerk
	market [ˈmɑːkɪt]	Markt
	direct mail [dəˌrekt ˈmeɪl]	Direktwerbung *(per Post)*
	catalogue [ˈkætəlɒg]	Katalog
	channel [ˈtʃænl]	Kanal
	to cut sb out of sth [ˌkʌt ˈaʊt əv]	jdn aus etw heraushalten
	to benefit sb [ˈbenɪfɪt]	jdm nützen
	to distribute sth [dɪˈstrɪbjuːt]	etw vertreiben
	to make sb aware of sth [ˌmeɪk əˈweər əv]	jdn auf etw aufmerksam machen
34	**sales talk** [ˈseɪlz tɔːk]	Verkaufsgespräch, Anpreisung(en) *(von Waren)*
	fixtures and fittings *pl* [ˌfɪkstʃəz ənd ˈfɪtɪŋz]	Armaturen, Zubehör
	technique [tekˈniːk]	Technik, Methode
	salesperson [ˈseɪlzpɜːsn]	Verkäufer/in
	scale [skeɪl]	Skala
	score [skɔː]	Punkte
	to be the life and soul of the party [bi ðə ˌlaɪf ənd ˈsəʊl əv ðə pɑːti]	eine Stimmungskanone sein
	suitability [ˌsuːtəˈbɪləti]	Eignung
	extrovert [ˈekstrəvɜːt]	extrovertierte Person
	to achieve [əˈtʃiːv]	*(Ziel)* erreichen
	to put sb off [ˌpʊt ˈɒf]	jdn abschrecken
	overconfident [ˌəʊvəˈkɒnfɪdənt]	zu selbstsicher, übertrieben selbstbewusst
	overexcited [ˌəʊvərɪkˈsaɪtɪd]	überdreht, übertrieben begeistert
	introvert [ˈɪntrəvɜːt]	introvertierte Person
	part … part [pɑːt pɑːt]	teils … teils
	enthusiastic [ɪnˌθjuːziˈæstɪk]	begeistert
	below-average [bɪˌləʊ ˈævərɪdʒ]	unterdurchschnittlich
	enthusiasm [ɪnˈθjuːziæzəm]	Begeisterung
	on display [ɒn dɪˈspleɪ]	ausgestellt, angeboten
	particular [pəˈtɪkjələ]	bestimmt, speziell
	item [ˈaɪtəm]	Artikel
	wrapped [ræpt]	verpackt
	to unwrap sth [ʌnˈræp]	etw auspacken
	feature [ˈfiːtʃə]	Merkmal, Eigenschaft
	sales material [ˈseɪlz mətɪəriəl]	Werbematerial, Verkaufsunterlagen
	hurry [ˈhʌri]	Eile
	to put sth aside [ˌpʊt əˈsaɪd]	etw zurücklegen
35	**to try sth out** [ˌtraɪ ˈaʊt]	etw ausprobieren
	stand [stænd]	(Messe-)Stand
T	**to hesitate** [ˈhezɪteɪt]	zögern
	to draw sb's attention to sth [ˌdrɔː əˈtenʃn tə]	jds Aufmerksamkeit auf etw lenken
	mixer tap [ˈmɪksə tæp]	Mischbatterie
	bath [bɑːθ]	Badewanne
	shower [ˈʃaʊə]	Dusche
	washbasin [ˈwɒʃbeɪsn]	Waschbecken, Waschtisch
	in stock [ɪn ˈstɒk]	vorrätig, auf Lager, lieferbar
	overnight [ˌəʊvəˈnaɪt]	über Nacht
	cathedral [kəˈθiːdrəl]	Dom, Kathedrale
	brochure [ˈbrəʊʃə]	Broschüre, Prospekt
	tap [tæp]	Wasserhahn
	guarantee [ˌgærənˈtiː]	Garantie
	valid [ˈvælɪd]	gültig
	to advise [ədˈvaɪz]	(jdm etw) raten
	while stocks last [waɪl ˌstɒks ˈlɑːst]	solange der Vorrat reicht
	Suit yourself. [ˌsuːt jəˈself]	Wie Sie wollen. / Wie du willst.
	shower enclosure [ˈʃaʊə ɪnˌkləʊʒə]	Duschkabine
	leaflet [ˈliːflət]	Merkblatt
	sealed [siːld]	verschlossen, versiegelt, eingeschweißt
	to look closely at sth [ˌlʊk ˈkləʊsli ət]	sich etw genau ansehen
	to re-seal [rɪˈsiːl]	wiederverschließen
	heavy-duty [ˌheviˈdjuːti]	strapazierfähig, für hohe Beanspruchung
	No idea. [nəʊ aɪˈdɪə]	Keine Ahnung.
	surprising(ly) [səˈpraɪzɪŋ]	erstaunlich
	solid [ˈsɒlɪd]	massiv, solide
	commercial use [kəˌmɜːʃl ˈjuːs]	gewerbliche Nutzung, gewerblicher Gebrauch
	matching [ˈmætʃɪŋ]	passend
	thermostatically controlled [θɜːməˌstætɪkli kənˈtrəʊld]	per Thermostat geregelt
	bathtub [ˈbɑːθtʌb]	Badewanne
	special offer [ˌspeʃl ˈɒfə]	Sonderangebot
	catalogue price [ˈkætəlɒg praɪs]	Listenpreis, Katalogpreis
	hard-wearing [ˌhɑːd ˈweərɪŋ]	strapazierfähig

to **place an order** [ˌpleɪs ən ˈɔːdə]	einen Auftrag erteilen, eine Bestellung aufgeben

	for the time being [fə ðə ˌtaɪm ˈbiːɪŋ]	einstweilen, fürs Erste
	currently [ˈkʌrəntli]	momentan
	to **modernize** [ˈmɒdənaɪz]	modernisieren
	flat *BE* [flæt]	Wohnung
	timeless [ˈtaɪmləs]	zeitlos
	anything particular [ˌeniθɪŋ pəˈtɪkjələ]	etwas Spezielles
	thermostatic mixer [θɜːməˌstætɪk ˈmɪksə]	Thermostat
36	to **enquire about sth** [ɪnˈkwaɪər əbaʊt]	sich nach etw erkundigen
	to **role-play** [ˈrəʊl pleɪ]	mit verteilten Rollen spielen
	prompt [prɒmpt]	Stichwort
37	**sports equipment** [ˈspɔːts ɪkwɪpmənt]	Sportartikel
	trade customer [treɪd ˈkʌstəmə]	Gewerbekunde/-in, Großhandelskunde/-in
	to **have sth on offer** [həv ˌɒn ˈɒfə]	etw im Angebot haben, etw anbieten
	speech bubble [ˈspiːtʃ bʌbl]	Sprechblase
	console [ˈkɒnsəʊl]	Konsole
	exercise ball [ˈeksəsaɪz bɔːl]	Gymnastikball
	exercise mat [ˈeksəsaɪz mæt]	Fitnessmatte, Yogamatte
	rowing machine [ˈrəʊɪŋ məʃiːn]	Rudergerät
	trampoline [ˈtræmpəliːn]	Trampolin
	treadmill [ˈtredmɪl]	Laufband
	weight bench [ˈweɪt bentʃ]	Hantelbank
	to **help oneself** [ˈhelp wʌnself]	sich bedienen
	angle [ˈæŋgl]	Winkel
	to **come** [kʌm]	*(Ware:)* erhältlich sein
	thickness [ˈθɪknəs]	Stärke, Dicke
	available [əˈveɪləbl]	erhältlich, verfügbar
	safety [ˈseɪfti]	Sicherheit
	connectivity [ˌkɒnekˈtɪvəti]	Anschluss, Anschlüsse, Verbindung

38	**range** [reɪndʒ]	Sortiment
T	**sample** [ˈsɑːmpl]	Probe, Muster, Probepackung
	volunteer [ˌvɒlənˈtɪə]	Freiwillige/r
	belt [belt]	Band
	to **point sth out** [ˌpɔɪnt ˈaʊt]	auf etw hinweisen, auf etw aufmerksam machen
	next to nothing [ˌnekst tə ˈnʌθɪŋ]	so gut wie nichts
	durable [ˈdjʊərəbl]	haltbar, strapazierfähig
	lifetime guarantee [ˌlaɪftaɪm gærənˈtiː]	lebenslange Garantie
	wear items *pl* [ˈweər aɪtəmz]	Verschleißartikel
	frame [freɪm]	Rahmen
	professional [prəˈfeʃənl]	professionell

gym instructor [ˈdʒɪm ɪnstrʌktə]	Fitnesstrainer/in
to **demonstrate sth** [ˈdemənstreɪt]	etw vorführen
gymnastics [dʒɪmˈnæstɪks]	Turnen, Gymnastik
martial arts *pl* [ˌmɑːʃl ˈɑːts]	Kampfsport
folding [ˈfəʊldɪŋ]	Falt-, faltbar
press-up *BE* [ˈpresʌp]	Liegestütz
Olympics *pl* [əˈlɪmpɪks]	Olympiade
to **tone up** [ˌtəʊn ˈʌp]	*(Muskeln:)* in Form bringen, kräftigen
muscle [ˈmʌsl]	Muskel
to **round sth off** [ˌraʊnd ˈɒf]	etw abrunden, etw abschließen
user-friendly [ˌjuːzəˈfrendli]	benutzerfreundlich
to **take a seat** [ˌteɪk ə ˈsiːt]	Platz nehmen

	exercise machine [ˈeksəsaɪz məʃiːn]	Trainingsgerät
	Regards [rɪˈgɑːdz]	*(Brief:)* Mit freundlichen Grüßen
	to **advise sb** [ədˈvaɪz]	jdn beraten
	to **advise sb to do sth** [ədˈvaɪz]	jdm raten, etw zu tun
	to **equip sth with sth** [ɪˈkwɪp wɪð]	etw mit etw ausstatten
	mirror [ˈmɪrə]	Spiegel
39	**programme** [ˈprəʊgræm]	Programm
	chat [tʃæt]	Plauderei, (informelles) Gespräch
	demo(nstration) [ˈdeməʊ, ˌdemənˈstreɪʃn]	Vorführung
	bouncy castle [ˌbaʊnsi ˈkɑːsl]	Hüpfburg
	magician [məˈdʒɪʃn]	Zauberer/Zauberin
	lucky draw [ˌlʌki ˈdrɔː]	Verlosung
	to **look sth up** [ˌlʊk ˈʌp]	etw nachschlagen, etw nachlesen
	technical term [ˌteknɪkl ˈtɜːm]	Fachbegriff
	buyer [ˈbaɪə]	Käufer/in
	delivery period [dɪˈlɪvəri pɪəriəd]	Lieferzeit
	after-sales service [ˈɑːftəseɪlz sɜːvɪs]	Kundendienst
	order form [ˈɔːdə fɔːm]	Bestellformular
	sales representative [ˈseɪlz reprɪzentətɪv]	(Handels-)Vertreter/in
	competitor [kəmˈpetɪtə]	Wettbewerber/in, Konkurrent/in
	to **perform sth** [pəˈfɔːm]	etw aufführen
	to **swap** [swɒp]	tauschen
40	**trade** [treɪd]	Gewerbe, Branche
	to **take care of sth** [ˌteɪk ˈkeər əv]	sich um etw kümmern, etw bearbeiten, etw erledigen
	enquiry [ɪnˈkwaɪəri]	Anfrage
	to **appear** [əˈpɪə]	vorkommen, auftauchen
	dot [dɒt]	Punkt
	hyphen [ˈhaɪfn]	Bindestrich, Minus

	underscore ['ʌndəskɔː]	Unterstrich
	to **dictate** [dɪk'teɪt]	diktieren
	to **spell** [spel]	buchstabieren
	subject line ['sʌbdʒɪkt laɪn]	Betreffzeile
	indication [ˌɪndɪ'keɪʃn]	Hinweis, Anzeichen
	to **state** [steɪt]	angeben, erklären, sagen, darlegen
	request (for sth) [rɪ'kwest]	Bitte (um etw)
	assistance [ə'sɪstəns]	Hilfe, Unterstützung
	to **announce** [ə'naʊns]	ankündigen
	change of plan [ˌtʃeɪndʒ əf 'plæn]	Planänderung
	covering letter ['kʌvərɪŋ letə]	Anschreiben, Begleitschreiben
	venue ['venjuː]	Veranstaltungsort
	flyer ['flaɪə]	Faltblatt
	to **attach** [ə'tætʃ]	*(E-Mail:)* anhängen
	update (on sth) ['ʌpdeɪt]	aktuelle Informationen (zu etw), aktueller Überblick (über etw)
	inclusive [ɪn'kluːsɪv]	einschließlich
	application [ˌæplɪ'keɪʃn]	Antrag, Bewerbung
	fair [feə]	Messe
	to **let sb know sth** [ˌlet 'nəʊ]	jdm etw mitteilen, jdm Bescheid sagen
	to **interview sb** ['ɪntəvjuː]	mit jdm ein Vorstellungsgespräch führen
	export clerk ['ekspɔːt klɑːk]	Außenhandelskaufmann/-frau
41	**reply (to sth)** [rɪ'plaɪ]	Antwort (auf etw)
	to **reply (to sth)** [rɪ'plaɪ]	(auf etw) antworten, (etw) beantworten
	screwdriver ['skruːdraɪvə]	Schraubenzieher, -dreher
	Phillips screwdriver [ˌfɪlɪps 'skruːdraɪvə]	Kreuzschlitzschraubenzieher
	screw [skruː]	Schraube
	Phillips screw ['fɪlɪps skruː]	Kreuzschlitzschraube
	slotted screwdriver [ˌslɒtɪd 'skruːdraɪvə]	Schlitzschraubenzieher
	slotted screw ['slɒtɪd skruː]	Schlitzschraube
	Yours faithfully [ˌjɔːz 'feɪθfəli]	*(Brief:)* Mit freundlichen Grüßen
	to **dispatch** [dɪ'spætʃ]	versenden
	complimentary close [ˌkɒmplɪˌmentri 'kləʊz]	*(Brief:)* Schlussformel
	salutation [ˌsælju'teɪʃn]	*(Brief:)* Anrede
	Dear Sir or Madam [ˌdɪə sɜː ɔː 'mædəm]	*(Brief:)* Sehr geehrte Damen und Herren,
	(Best) Regards/Regards [rɪ'gɑːdz]	*(Brief:)* Viele Grüße, Mit freundlichen Grüßen
	Best wishes [best 'wɪʃɪz]	*(Brief:)* Mit freundlichen Grüßen
	Yours sincerely [ˌjɔːz sɪn'sɪəli]	*(Brief:)* Mit freundlichen Grüßen
	All the best [ɔːl ðə 'best]	*(Brief:)* Viele Grüße

KMK Exam practice 2

42	**clothing** ['kləʊðɪŋ]	Kleidung
T	**promotional gift** [prə'məʊʃənl gɪft]	Werbegeschenk
	opening ['əʊpnɪŋ]	Eröffnung
	to **mention sth** ['menʃn]	etw erwähnen
	to **work sth out** [ˌwɜːk 'aʊt]	eine Lösung für etw finden, etw erarbeiten
	to **decorate sth** ['dekəreɪt]	etw *(Innenraum)* gestalten
	flower ['flaʊə]	Blume, Blüte
	plant [plɑːnt]	Pflanze
	to **rent** [rent]	mieten
	to **get back to sb** [ˌget 'bæk tə]	jdn zurückrufen, sich (wieder) bei jdm melden
	giveaway ['gɪvəweɪ]	Werbegeschenk
	immediately [ɪ'miːdiətli]	sofort, unverzüglich
	to **appreciate sth** [ə'priːʃieɪt]	etw zu schätzen wissen
	special discount [ˌspeʃl 'dɪskaʊnt]	Sonderrabatt
	additional [ə'dɪʃənl]	zusätzlich
	to **see to sth** ['siː tə]	sich um etw kümmern

	privately-owned ['praɪvətli əʊnd]	in Privatbesitz
	distribution [ˌdɪstrɪ'bjuːʃn]	Vertrieb
	trading company ['treɪdɪŋ kʌmpəni]	Handelsunternehmen
	trade [treɪd]	Handel
	to **source sth** [sɔːs]	etw *(Waren usw.)* beschaffen
	overseas [ˌəʊvə'siːz]	im Ausland, in Übersee
	core business ['kɔː bɪznəs]	Kerngeschäft
	head office [ˌhed 'ɒfɪs]	Zentrale, Hauptsitz
	to **be situated** [bi 'sɪtʃueɪtɪd]	sich befinden
	accessible [ək'sesəbl]	zugänglich, erreichbar
	motorway *BE* ['məʊtəweɪ]	Autobahn
	nearby ['nɪəbaɪ]	in der Nähe, nahegelegen
	established [ɪ'stæblɪʃt]	etabliert
	operation [ˌɒpə'reɪʃn]	Betrieb
	consequently ['kɒnsɪkwəntli]	dementsprechend, folgerichtig
	retail ['riːteɪl]	Einzelhandel
	to **range from … to …** ['reɪndʒ frəm tə]	von … bis … reichen
	department store [dɪ'pɑːtmənt stɔː]	Kaufhaus
	to **be due to do sth** [bi 'djuː tə]	etw (in der Zukunft) tun sollen
	milestone ['maɪlstəʊn]	Meilenstein
	purchase ['pɜːtʃəs]	Kauf
	freight forwarding company ['freɪt fɔːwədɪŋ kʌmpəni]	Spedition
	impressive [ɪm'presɪv]	beeindruckend
	fleet [fliːt]	Fuhrpark, Flotte
	capital ['kæpɪtl]	Kapital
	to **ensure sth** [ɪn'ʃʊə]	etw sicherstellen
43	**trader** ['treɪdə]	Händler/in

marketing channel [ˈmɑːkɪtɪŋ tʃænl]	Absatzweg, Vertriebskanal
durable goods *pl* [ˌdjʊərəbl ˈgʊdz]	Gebrauchsgüter
supply chain [səˈplaɪ tʃeɪn]	Lieferkette
to **feature sth** [ˈfiːtʃə]	etw *(Merkmal usw.)* aufweisen
link [lɪŋk]	Glied *(in einer Kette)*
distributor [dɪˈstrɪbjətə]	Vertragshändler
to **represent** [ˌreprɪˈzent]	vertreten, repräsentieren
to **maintain sth** [meɪnˈteɪn]	etw unterhalten
exclusive agreement [ɪkˌskluːsɪv əˈgriːmənt]	Exklusivvertrag
to **limit** [ˈlɪmɪt]	begrenzen, beschränken
to **enable sb to do sth** [ɪˈneɪbl]	jdm ermöglichen, etw zu tun
to **cover sth** [ˈkʌvə]	etw abdecken
territory [ˈterətri]	Gebiet, Territorium
point of contact [ˌpɔɪnt əf ˈkɒntækt]	Ansprechpartner/in, Anlaufstelle
prospective [prəˈspektɪv]	potenziell
rarely [ˈreəli]	selten
due to [ˈdjuː tə]	aufgrund von, wegen
to **have sth on hand** [həv ˌɒn ˈhænd]	etw zur Verfügung haben
to **acquire sth** [əˈkwaɪə]	etw erwerben, etw kaufen
to **tend to do sth** [ˈtend tə]	dazu neigen, etw zu tun
support [səˈpɔːt]	Unterstützung
high-volume [haɪˈvɒljuːm]	großvolumig, Groß-
purchase order [ˈpɜːtʃəs ɔːdə]	Auftrag, Bestellung
typically [ˈtɪpɪkli]	normalerweise
to **improve** [ɪmˈpruːv]	verbessern
buying power [ˈbaɪɪŋ paʊə]	Kaufkraft
to **purchase** [ˈpɜːtʃəs]	kaufen
merchandise [ˈmɜːtʃəndaɪs]	Ware
ranging from … to … [ˈreɪndʒɪŋ frəm tə]	von … bis …
storage space [ˈstɔːrɪdʒ speɪs]	Lagerfläche
costly [ˈkɒstli]	kostspielig, teuer
to **consist of sth** [kənˈsɪst əv]	aus etw bestehen
to **realize a profit** [ˌrɪəlaɪz ə ˈprɒfɪt]	einen Gewinn erzielen
to **coincide with sth** [ˌkəʊɪnˈsaɪd wɪð]	mit etw übereinstimmen, mit etw zusammenfallen
business objective [ˈbɪznəs əbdʒektɪv]	Unternehmensziel
competitive [kəmˈpetətɪv]	*(Preis:)* günstig
pricing [ˈpraɪsɪŋ]	Preise, Preisgestaltung
store rental [ˈstɔː rentl]	Ladenmiete
obviously [ˈɒbviəsli]	natürlich
to **be affected by sth** [bi əˈfektɪd baɪ]	von etw betroffen sein

UNIT 5

44 **marketing strategy** [ˈmɑːkɪtɪŋ strætədʒi]	Vermarktungsstrategie
market research [ˌmɑːkɪt rɪˈsɜːtʃ]	Marktforschung
sportswear [ˈspɔːtsweə]	Sportbekleidung
to **specialize in sth** [ˈspeʃəlaɪz ɪn]	sich auf etw spezialisieren
exercise equipment [ˈeksəsaɪz ɪkwɪpmənt]	Trainingsgeräte
option [ˈɒpʃn]	Möglichkeit
loyalty card [ˈlɔɪəlti kɑːd]	Kundenkarte
clothing [ˈkləʊðɪŋ]	Kleidung
specialist [ˈspeʃəlɪst]	Fachgeschäft
department store [dɪˈpɑːtmənt stɔː]	Kaufhaus
prize draw [ˈpraɪz drɔː]	Verlosung
stamp [stæmp]	Briefmarke
to **report back** [rɪˌpɔːt ˈbæk]	Bericht erstatten
to **disclose sth** [dɪsˈkləʊz]	etw preisgeben
privilege [ˈprɪvəlɪdʒ]	Vergünstigung
45 **recommendation** [ˌrekəmenˈdeɪʃn]	Empfehlung
customer satisfaction [ˌkʌstəmə ˌsætɪsˈfækʃn]	Kundenzufriedenheit
to **predict** [prɪˈdɪkt]	vorhersagen
field research [ˈfiːld rɪsɜːtʃ]	Feldforschung
primary research [ˈpraɪməri rɪsɜːtʃ]	Primärforschung
to **gather data** [ˌgæðə ˈdeɪtə]	Daten erfassen
to **publish** [ˈpʌblɪʃ]	veröffentlichen
study [ˈstʌdi]	Untersuchung, Studie
cashier [kæˈʃɪə]	Kassierer/in
to **swipe a card** [ˌswaɪp ə ˈkɑːd]	eine Karte durchziehen
check-out [ˈtʃekaʊt]	Kasse
purchasing history [ˈpɜːtʃəsɪŋ hɪstri]	Kaufhistorie, Einkaufsverhalten
strategy [ˈstrætədʒi]	Strategie
relationship [rɪˈleɪʃnʃɪp]	Beziehung
to **manage sth** [ˈmænɪdʒ]	etw verwalten
interaction [ˌɪntərˈækʃn]	Austausch, Kommunikation
database [ˈdeɪtəbeɪs]	Datenbank
to **access sth** [ˈækses]	auf etw zugreifen
instantly [ˈɪnstəntli]	sofort
to **boost sth** [buːst]	etw ankurbeln, etw erhöhen
to **improve** [ɪmˈpruːv]	verbessern
customer loyalty [ˌkʌstəmə ˈlɔɪəlti]	Kundenbindung, Kundentreue
to **target sb** [ˈtɑːgɪt]	jdn ins Visier nehmen
specific [spəˈsɪfɪk]	bestimmte/r/s
to **customize sth** [ˈkʌstəmaɪz]	etw individuell anpassen

	advertising [ˈædvətaɪzɪŋ]	Werbung
	to **waste** [weɪst]	verschwenden, vergeuden
	one-size-fits-all [wʌn ˌsaɪz fɪtsˈ ɔ:l]	Einheits-, Standard-, 08/15-
	advertising campaign [ˈædvətaɪzɪŋ kæmpeɪn]	Werbekampagne
	to **break sth down** [ˌbreɪk ˈdaʊn]	etw aufschlüsseln, etw aufgliedern
	social media *pl* [ˌsəʊʃl ˈmi:diə]	soziale Medien
	digital signage [ˌdɪdʒɪtl ˈsaɪnɪdʒ]	digitale Außenwerbung
	memo [ˈmeməʊ]	Notiz
	method [ˈmeθəd]	Verfahren, Methode
	firm [fɜ:m]	Firma
	target group [ˈtɑ:gɪt gru:p]	Zielgruppe
46	**product line** [ˈprɒdʌkt laɪn]	Produktlinie
	environmentally-friendly [ɪnˌvaɪrənˌmentəli ˈfrendli]	umweltfreundlich
	product range [ˈprɒdʌkt reɪndʒ]	Sortiment
	product brief [ˈprɒdʌkt bri:f]	Produktbeschreibung
	unique selling proposition (USP) [juˌni:k ˈselɪŋ prɒpəzɪʃn]	Alleinstellungsmerkmal
	organic cotton [ɔ:ˌgænɪk ˈkɒtn]	Bio-Baumwolle
	socially-responsible [ˌsəʊʃəli rɪˈspɒnsəbl]	sozial verantwortlich
	and beyond [ənd bɪˈjɒnd]	und darüber hinaus
	distribution [ˌdɪstrɪˈbju:ʃn]	Vertrieb
	stationary [ˈsteɪʃənri]	ortsgebunden, ortsfest, stationär
	trade [treɪd]	Handel
	to **attract sb** [əˈtrækt]	jdn anlocken, jdn ansprechen, jdn anziehen
	factor [ˈfæktə]	Faktor
	to **consider sth** [kənˈsɪdə]	etw in Betracht ziehen, über etw nachdenken, etw berücksichtigen
	to **launch sth** [lɔ:ntʃ]	etw auf den Markt bringen
T	to **market sth** [ˈmɑ:kɪt]	etw vermarkten
	thought [θɔ:t]	Gedanke(n)
	to **put a lot of thought into sth** [pʊt ə ˌlɒt əf ˈθɔ:t ɪntə]	intensiv über etw nachdenken
	to **outline** [ˈaʊtlaɪn]	skizzieren, darstellen
	approach [əˈprəʊtʃ]	Ansatz, Herangehensweise, Vorgehen
	well-established [ˌwel ɪˈstæblɪʃt]	bewährt, fest etabliert
	nature (of sth) [ˈneɪtʃə]	Wesen (einer Sache)
	sustainability [səˌsteɪnəˈbɪləti]	Nachhaltigkeit
	bottom line [ˌbɒtəm ˈlaɪn]	das, worauf es ankommt
	triple [ˈtrɪpl]	dreifach
	honesty [ˈɒnəsti]	Ehrlichkeit, Aufrichtigkeit
	promotion [prəˈməʊʃn]	Werbung, Promotion
	branding [ˈbrændɪŋ]	Markenbildung
	traditional [trəˈdɪʃənl]	traditionell, hergebracht
	mass media *pl* [ˌmæs ˈmi:diə]	Massenmedien
	to **promote sth** [prəˈməʊt]	für etw werben, etw promoten
	search engine [ˈsɜ:tʃ endʒɪn]	Suchmaschine
	to **deal with sth** [ˈdi:l wɪð]	etw *(Thema usw.)* behandeln
	separately [ˈseprətli]	separat, eigens
	Fine by me. [ˌfaɪn baɪ ˈmi:]	Von mir aus gern.
	lazy [ˈleɪzi]	faul, träge
	old-fashioned [ˌəʊldˈfæʃənd]	altmodisch
	to **represent** [ˌreprɪˈzent]	repräsentieren, vertreten, darstellen
	sales channel [ˈseɪlz tʃænl]	Absatzweg, Vertriebskanal
	bricks and mortar outlet [ˌbrɪks ən ˈmɔ:tər aʊtlet]	stationäres Geschäft
	virtual [ˈvɜ:tʃuəl]	virtuell
	recommended retail price (RRP) [rekəˌmend ˈri:teɪl praɪs]	unverbindliche Preisempfehlung (UVP)
	to **be prepared to do sth** [bi prɪˈpeəd tə du:]	bereit sein, etw zu tun
	mark [mɑ:k]	Marke
47	to **mention sth** [ˈmenʃn]	etw erwähnen
	optimization [ˌɒptɪmaɪˈzeɪʃn]	Optimierung
	keyword [ˈki:wɜ:d]	Schlagwort
	traffic [ˈtræfɪk]	Verkehr
	to **increase sth** [ɪnˈkri:s]	etw steigern, etw erhöhen
	viewer [ˈvju:ə]	Zuschauer/in, Betrachter/in
	conversion rate [kənˈvɜ:ʃn reɪt]	Umwandlungsquote, Konversionsrate
	wooden furniture [ˌwʊdn ˈfɜ:nɪtʃə]	Holzmöbel
	generic [dʒəˈnerɪk]	allgemein
	specific [spəˈsɪfɪk]	genau, bestimmt, spezifisch
	fitted kitchen [ˌfɪtɪd ˈkɪtʃɪn]	Einbauküche
	pine [paɪn]	Kiefer
	search result [ˈsɜ:tʃ rɪzʌlt]	Suchergebnis
	relevant (to sth) [ˈreləvənt]	wichtig (für etw), relevant (für etw)
	character [ˈkærəktə]	Zeichen
	to **direct** [dəˈrekt]	leiten, lenken
	to **rank higher** [ˌræŋk ˈhaɪə]	eine höhere Position einnehmen
	linked to sth [ˈlɪŋkt tə]	in direktem Zusammenhang mit etw
	compound [ˈkɒmpaʊnd]	zusammengesetzt
	custom-made [ˈkʌstəm meɪd]	individuell gefertigt
	category [ˈkætəgəri]	Kategorie, Klasse
	rowing [ˈrəʊɪŋ]	Rudern
	steel [sti:l]	Stahl
	item [ˈaɪtəm]	Punkt, Gegenstand

48	**product launch** [ˈprɒdʌkt lɔːntʃ]	Produkteinführung
	limit [ˈlɪmɪt]	(Ober-/Unter-)Grenze
	to **last** [lɑːst]	halten
	slave labour [ˈsleɪv leɪbə]	Sklavenarbeit
	You must be kidding! [juː ˌmʌst bi ˈkɪdɪŋ]	Das ist doch nicht dein/euer Ernst?
	reasonable [ˈriːznəbl]	vernünftig, angemessen
	to **afford sth** [əˈfɔːd]	sich etw leisten (können)
	consequence [ˈkɒnsɪkwəns]	Folge, Konsequenz
	pricing strategy [ˈpraɪsɪŋ strætədʒi]	Preisstrategie
	to **review sth** [rɪˈvjuː]	etw überprüfen, etw überdenken
49	**eco-friendly** [ˈiːkəʊ frendli]	umweltfreundlich
	to **devise sth** [dɪˈvaɪz]	etw entwickeln, etw ausarbeiten
	celebrity endorsement [səˌlebrəti ɪnˈdɔːsmnt]	Werbung mit Prominenten
	niche [nɪtʃ]	Nische
	stealth advertising [ˈstelθ ædvətaɪzɪŋ]	heimliche Werbung, Schleichwerbung
	testimonial [ˌtestɪˈməʊnɪəl]	Erfahrungsbericht
	unique [juˈniːk]	einzigartig
	satisfied [ˈsætɪsfaɪd]	zufrieden
	targeted advertising [ˌtɑːgɪtɪd ˈædvətaɪzɪŋ]	gezielte/zielgruppengenaue Werbung
	good cause [gʊd ˈkɔːz]	gute Sache, guter Zweck
	support [səˈpɔːt]	Unterstützung
	temporary [ˈtemprəri]	vorübergehend, vorläufig
	retail outlet [ˈriːteɪl aʊtlet]	Einzelhandelsgeschäft
	unconventional [ˌʌnkənˈvenʃənl]	unkonventionell
	to **advertise sth** [ˈædvətaɪz]	etw bewerben, für etw Werbung machen
50	**campaign** [kæmˈpeɪn]	(Werbe-)Kampagne
	to **agree sth** [əˈgriː]	sich auf etw einigen, etw beschließen
	to **cover sth** [ˈkʌvə]	*(Medien:)* über etw berichten
	broadcast [ˈbrɔːdkɑːst]	(Radio-)Sendung
T	**unusual** [ʌnˈjuːʒʊəl]	ungewöhnlich
	central station [ˈsentrəl steɪʃn]	Hauptbahnhof
	queue [kjuː]	Warteschlange
	loaded up with sth [ˌləʊdɪd ˈʌp wɪð]	mit etw beladen, voll mit etw
	pollution [pəˈluːʃn]	Verschmutzung
	ocean [ˈəʊʃn]	Ozean, Weltmeer
	to **throw sth away** [ˌθrəʊ əˈweɪ]	etw wegwerfen
	to **end up** [ˌend ˈʌp]	(irgendwo) landen
	cash [kæʃ]	Bargeld
	programme [ˈprəʊgræm]	(TV-, Radio-)Sendung
	station [ˈsteɪʃn]	Bahnhof
	recycling centre [ˌriːˈsaɪklɪŋ sentə]	Wertstoffhof

	surfboard [ˈsɜːfbɔːd]	Surfbrett
	entirely [ɪnˈtaɪəli]	völlig, ganz
	to **paddle** [ˈpædl]	paddeln
	Rhine [raɪn]	Rhein
	litter [ˈlɪtə]	Müll, Abfall
	listener [ˈlɪsnə]	Hörer/in
	destruction [dɪˈstrʌkʃn]	Zerstörung
	to **sponsor sb** [ˈspɒnsə]	jdn sponsern
	to **clean sth up** [ˌkliːn ˈʌp]	etw säubern
	progress [ˈprəʊgres]	Fortkommen, Fahrt
	day-to-day update [deɪ tə ˌdeɪ ˈʌpdeɪt]	täglicher aktueller Bericht
	to **cheer sb on** [ˌtʃɪər ˈɒn]	jdn anfeuern, jdm zujubeln
	to **maximize sth** [ˈmæksɪmaɪz]	etw maximieren
	attention [əˈtenʃn]	Aufmerksamkeit
	special deal [ˌspeʃl ˈdiːl]	Sonderangebot
	celebrity [səˈlebrəti]	Prominente/r
	to **video sth** [ˈvɪdiəʊ]	etw (auf Video) filmen
	to **go viral** [ˌgəʊ ˈvaɪrəl]	sich (im Internet) rasend schnell verbreiten
	past [pɑːst]	vergangen, in der Vergangenheit
	to **realize sth** [ˈrɪəlaɪz]	sich über etw im Klaren sein, etw wissen
	to **form** [fɔːm]	(sich) bilden
	waterway [ˈwɔːtəweɪ]	Wasserstraße
51	to **underline** [ˌʌndəˈlaɪn]	unterstreichen
	to **correspond** [ˌkɒrɪˈspɒnd]	entsprechen, korrespondieren
	catchphrase [ˈkætʃfreɪz]	Schlagwort, Slogan
	to **suit sb/sth** [suːt]	(zu) jdm/etw passen
	to **come up with sth / an idea** [ˌkʌm ˈʌp wɪð]	sich etw einfallen lassen
	handshake [ˈhændʃeɪk]	Handschlag
	pale [peɪl]	blass, hell
	tone [təʊn]	Farbton
	caption [ˈkæpʃn]	Bildunterschrift
	conscience [ˈkɒnʃəns]	Gewissen
	priority [praɪˈɒrəti]	Anliegen, Priorität
	clientele [kliːɒnˈtel]	Kundschaft, Klientel
	sense [sens]	Sinn
	responsibility [rɪˌspɒnsəˈbɪləti]	Verantwortung
	environmentally conscious [ɪnvaɪrənˌmentəli ˈkɒnʃəs]	umweltbewusst
52	**graph** [grɑːf]	Diagramm, Kurve
	chart [tʃɑːt]	Diagramm
	union [ˈjuːniən]	Gewerkschaft
	conference [ˈkɒnfərəns]	Tagung, Konferenz
	to **refresh** [rɪˈfreʃ]	auffrischen
	bar chart [ˈbɑː tʃɑːt]	Säulendiagramm
	line graph [ˈlaɪn grɑːf]	Liniendiagramm
	pie chart [ˈpaɪ tʃɑːt]	Tortendiagramm
	to **remain constant** [rɪˌmeɪn ˈkɒnstənt]	gleich bleiben
	to **increase** [ɪnˈkriːs]	zunehmen, ansteigen
	increase [ˈɪŋkriːs]	Zunahme, Anstieg
	to **hit a maximum** [ˌhɪt ə ˈmæksɪməm]	einen Höchstwert/-stand erreichen

	minimum [ˈmɪnɪməm]	Tiefstwert, Tiefstand
	to **flatten out** [ˌflætn ˈaʊt]	sich abflachen
	to **level off** [ˌlevl ˈɒf]	sich einpendeln
	to **decrease** [dɪˈkriːs]	abnehmen, zurückgehen
	decrease [ˈdiːkriːs]	Abnahme, Rückgang
	to **drop** [drɒp]	fallen, zurückgehen
	drop [drɒp]	Fall, Rückgang
	to **rise** [raɪz]	steigen, ansteigen, zunehmen
	rise [raɪz]	Anstieg
	to **fluctuate** [ˈflʌktʃueɪt]	schwanken
	fluctuation [ˌflʌktʃuˈeɪʃn]	Schwankung(en)
	to **climb** [klaɪm]	ansteigen
	climb [klaɪm]	Anstieg
	to **peak** [piːk]	einen Höchstwert/-stand erreichen
	peak [piːk]	Höchstwert, Höchststand
	traveller [ˈtrævələ]	Passagier, Fahrgast
	time of day [taɪm əv ˈdeɪ]	Tageszeit
P	**unit** [ˈjuːnɪt]	Einheit, Stück
	output [ˈaʊtpʊt]	Produktion
53	**figures** *pl* [ˈfɪgəz]	Zahlen
	quarterly [ˈkwɔːtəli]	vierteljährlich, Quartals-
T	**financial year** [faɪˌnænʃl ˈjɪə]	Geschäftsjahr
	drastic(ally) [ˈdræstɪk]	drastisch
	to **recover** [rɪˈkʌvə]	sich erholen
	volume of sales [ˌvɒljuːm əf ˈseɪlz]	Umsatzvolumen
	quarter [ˈkwɔːtə]	Quartal
	at a glance [ət ə ˈglɑːns]	auf einen Blick
	to **contrast sth** [kənˈtrɑːst]	etw (einander) gegenüberstellen, etw (miteinander) vergleichen
	lunch break [ˈlʌntʃ breɪk]	Mittagspause
	blue-collar workers *pl* [ˌbluːˈkɒlə wɜːkəz]	Arbeiter
	white-collar workers *pl* [ˌwaɪt kɒlə ˈwɜːkəz]	Angestellte

UNIT 6

54	**cocoa bean** [ˈkəʊkəʊ biːn]	Kakaobohne
	co-operative [kəʊˈɒpərətɪv]	Genossenschaft, Kooperative
	to **come up** [ˌkʌm ˈʌp]	bevorstehen
	minutes *pl* [ˈmɪnɪts]	Protokoll
	CEO (Chief Executive Officer) [ˌtʃiːf ɪgˈzekjətɪv ɒfɪsə]	Vorstandsvorsitzende/r, Geschäftsführer/in
	ref. [ref]	Unser Zeichen
	to **make arrangements** [meɪk əˈreɪndʒmənts]	Vorbereitungen treffen
55	to **reserve** [rɪˈzɜːv]	reservieren
T	**data projector** [ˌdeɪtə prəˈdʒektə]	Beamer
	in advance [ɪn ədˈvɑːns]	im Voraus
	invitation [ˌɪnvɪˈteɪʃn]	Einladung
	attachment [əˈtætʃmənt]	*(E-Mail:)* Anhang
	hard copy [ˌhɑːd ˈkɒpi]	Papierexemplar, Ausdruck
	name tag [ˈneɪm tæg]	Namensschild
	heating [ˈhiːtɪŋ]	Heizung
	directions *pl* [dəˈrekʃnz]	Wegbeschreibung
	to **remind sb (of sth)** [rɪˈmaɪnd]	jdn (an etw) erinnern
	reception [rɪˈsepʃn]	Empfang, Rezeption
	to **display sth** [dɪˈspleɪ]	etw *(auf einem Bildschirm)* anzeigen
	to **lay sth** [leɪ]	etw herrichten, etw *(Tisch)* decken, etw *(Gedeck)* auflegen
	saucer [ˈsɔːsə]	Untertasse
	to **circulate sth** [ˈsɜːkjəleɪt]	etw (an alle) verteilen
	absentee [æbsnˈtiː]	Abwesende/r
	to **draft** [drɑːft]	*(Text)* entwerfen, verfassen
	to **chair a meeting** [ˌtʃeər ə ˈmiːtɪŋ]	eine Sitzung leiten
	to **aim to do sth** [ˈeɪm tə duː]	beabsichtigen, etw zu tun; etw tun wollen
	to **freshen up** [ˌfreʃn ˈʌp]	sich frisch machen
	to **finalize sth** [ˈfaɪnəlaɪz]	etw abschließen
	to **sign** [saɪn]	unterzeichnen
	any other business (AOB) [eni ˌʌðə ˈbɪznəs]	*(Tagesordnung:)* Verschiedenes
	warehouse manager [ˌweəhaʊs ˈmænɪdʒə]	Lagerleiter/in
	purchasing manager [ˈpɜːtʃəsɪŋ mænɪdʒə]	Einkaufsleiter/in
	legal adviser [ˌliːgl ədˈvaɪzə]	Justiziar/in
56	**brewery** [ˈbruːəri]	Brauerei
	brewing equipment [ˈbruːɪŋ ɪkwɪpmənt]	Brauanlage(n)
	to **postpone** [pəˈspəʊn]	(nach hinten) verschieben
	to **be unable to do sth** [bi ʌnˈeɪbl tə]	etw nicht tun können
	to **schedule** [ˈʃedjuːl]	*(Termin)* ansetzen
	item [ˈaɪtəm]	Tagesordnungspunkt
	order situation [ˈɔːdə sɪtʒueɪʃn]	Auftragslage
T	**agent** [ˈeɪdʒənt]	Vertreter/in
	to **come on board** [ˌkʌm ɒn ˈbɔːd]	an Bord kommen
	to **act as sth** [ˈækt əz]	als etw fungieren
	pleasure [ˈpleʒə]	Vergnügen
	to conclude [tə kənˈkluːd]	abschließend
	to **comment** [ˈkɒment]	kommentieren, einen Kommentar abgeben
	issue [ˈɪʃuː]	Problem
	punctual [ˈpʌŋktʃuəl]	pünktlich
	complaint [kəmˈpleɪnt]	Reklamation, Beschwerde
	packing [ˈpækɪŋ]	Verpackung
	impression [ɪmˈpreʃn]	Eindruck
	to **agree thoroughly with sb** [əˌgriː ˈθʌrəli wɪð]	voll und ganz einer Meinung mit jdm sein
	to **wrap sth up** [ˌræp ˈʌp]	etw abschließen, etw zum Abschluss bringen

	travel expenses *pl* [ˈtrævl ɪkspensɪz]	Reisekosten, Reisespesen
	to **get back to sb** [ˌget ˈbæk tə]	jdn zurückrufen, sich (wieder) bei jdm melden
57	to **check sth against sth** [ˈtʃek əgenst]	etw mit etw abgleichen
	to **notice** [ˈnəʊtɪs]	bemerken
	attendee [əˌtenˈdiː]	Teilnehmer/in
	to **complain** [kəmˈpleɪn]	sich beklagen, sich beschweren
	due to [ˈdjuː tə]	aufgrund von, wegen
58	to **be in favour of sth** [bi ɪn ˈfeɪvər əv]	für etw sein, etw befürworten
	to **consult with sb** [kənˈsʌlt wɪð]	mit jdm Rücksprache halten, sich mit jdm besprechen
	to **load** [ləʊd]	beladen, verladen
	to **unload** [ˌʌnˈləʊd]	entladen
	lorry *BE* [ˈlɒri]	Lastwagen
	to **guarantee** [ˌgærənˈtiː]	garantieren
	paperwork [ˈpeɪpəwɜːk]	Unterlagen
P	**core time** [ˈkɔː taɪm]	Kernzeit
	to **invent sth** [ɪnˈvent]	etw erfinden
	married [ˈmærid]	verheiratet
	early shift [ˈɜːli ʃɪft]	Frühschicht
	in a row [ɪn ə ˈrəʊ]	nacheinander
59	to **host sb** [həʊst]	jdn *(als Gast)* empfangen
	trader [ˈtreɪdə]	Händler/in
	annual [ˈænjuəl]	jährlich
	to **take place** [ˌteɪk ˈpleɪs]	stattfinden
	terms *pl* **of business** [ˌtɜːmz əv ˈbɪznəs]	Konditionen
	outcome [ˈaʊtkʌm]	Ergebnis, Resultat, Auswirkung(en)
	in view of sth [ɪn ˈvjuː əv]	angesichts von etw
	because of sth [bɪˈkɒz əv]	wegen etw
	stiff competition [ˌstɪf kɒmpəˈtɪʃn]	harter Wettbewerb
	supplier's contract [səˌplaɪəz ˈkɒntrækt]	Liefervertrag, Lieferantenvertrag
	competitive [kəmˈpetətɪv]	konkurrenzfähig
	therefore [ˈðeəfɔː]	daher, folglich
	significant(ly) [sɪgˈnɪfɪkənt]	deutlich
	low-priced [ˌləʊˈpraɪst]	preisgünstig
	to **expand rapidly** [ɪkˌspænd ˈræpɪdli]	schnell wachsen
	to **keep up with sth** [ˌkiːp ˈʌp wɪð]	mit etw Schritt halten
	to **be expected to do sth** [bi ɪkˈspektɪd tə]	etw tun sollen
	worst-case scenario [wɜːst ˌkeɪs səˈnɑːriəʊ]	schlimmster anzunehmender Fall
T	**straight** [streɪt]	direkt
	reduction [rɪˈdʌkʃn]	Nachlass, Preissenkung, Reduzierung
	to **expand** [ɪkˈspænd]	expandieren
	freight forwarder [ˈfreɪt fɔːwədə]	Spediteur, Spedition
	to **break down** [ˌbreɪk ˈdaʊn]	*(Auto:)* eine Panne haben, liegen bleiben
	wording [ˈwɜːdɪŋ]	Formulierung
60 T	**business arrangements** *pl* [ˈbɪznəs əreɪndʒmənts]	Modalitäten
	range [reɪndʒ]	Bereich, Spielraum
	packing charge [ˈpækɪŋ tʃɑːdʒ]	Verpackungskosten
	quantity discount [ˈkwɒntəti dɪskaʊnt]	Mengenrabatt
	return [rɪˈtɜːn]	Retoure
61	**competition** [ˌkɒmpəˈtɪʃn]	Wettbewerb
	negotiator [nɪˈgəʊʃieɪtə]	Verhandler/in
	initial order [ɪˌnɪʃl ˈɔːdə]	Erstauftrag
	electric drill [ɪˈlektrɪk drɪl]	Bohrmaschine
	introductory discount [ɪntrəˌdʌktəri ˈdɪskaʊnt]	Einführungsrabatt
	terms *pl* **of payment** [ˌtɜːmz əf ˈpeɪmənt]	Zahlungsbedingungen
	score sheet [ˈskɔː ʃiːt]	Punktzettel
	to **adapt sth** [əˈdæpt]	etw anpassen, etw abändern
	rice bowl [ˈraɪs bəʊl]	Reisschale
	saleswoman/-man [ˈseɪlzwʊmən, ˈseɪlzmən]	Verkäufer/in
	competitive [kəmˈpetətɪv]	*(Preis:)* günstig
	cash with order (CWO) [ˌkæʃ wɪð ˈɔːdə]	Vorkasse
	demand [dɪˈmɑːnd]	Nachfrage
	to **be in great demand** [bi ɪn ˌgreɪt dɪˈmɑːnd]	stark nachgefragt sein
	priority [praɪˈɒrəti]	Vorrang
62	to **exhibit** [ɪgˈzɪbɪt]	ausstellen
	to **rearrange sth** [ˌriːəˈreɪndʒ]	etw *(Termin usw.)* verschieben
	to **set sth up** [ˌset ˈʌp]	etw *(Termin usw.)* vereinbaren
	to **get in touch with sb** [get ɪn ˈtʌtʃ wɪð]	sich bei jdm melden, sich mit jdm in Verbindung setzen
	either [ˈaɪðə]	eines *(von mehreren)*
63 T	**at short notice** [ət ˌʃɔːt ˈnəʊtɪs]	kurzfristig
	to **reschedule sth** [ˌriːˈʃedjuːl]	etw *(Termin usw.)* verschieben
	Something has come up. [sʌmθɪŋ həz ˌkʌm ˈʌp]	Es/Mir/Uns ist etwas dazwischen gekommen.
	to **get out of sth** [get ˈaʊt əv]	um etw herumkommen
	That's a pity. [ðæts ə ˈpɪti]	Das ist schade.
	to **have sth in mind** [həv ɪn ˈmaɪnd]	etw im Sinn haben, an etw denken
	to **suit sb** [suːt]	jdm passen
	to **inconvenience sb** [ˌɪnkənˈviːniəns]	jdm Umstände bereiten
	to **worry** [ˈwʌri]	sich Sorgen machen
	Don't worry. [dəʊnt ˈwʌri]	Keine Sorge.
	to **cancel** [ˈkænsl]	*(Termin)* absagen
	to **apologize** [əˈpɒlədʒaɪz]	sich entschuldigen

	to **trouble sb** [ˈtrʌbl]	jdm Umstände bereiten
	business associate [ˈbɪznəs əsəʊʃiət]	Geschäftspartner/in
	itinerary [aɪˈtɪnərəri]	Reiseplan
P	**buffet** [ˈbʊfeɪ]	Büfett
	association [əˌsəʊsiˈeɪʃn]	Verband

KMK Exam practice 3

64	**transformation** [ˌtrænzfəˈmeɪʃn]	(grundlegende) Veränderung, Wandel
	conference centre [ˈkɒnfərəns sentə]	Tagungszentrum, Kongresszentrum
	headquarters *pl* [ˌhedˈkwɔːtəz]	Zentrale, Hauptsitz
	convention centre [kənˈvenʃn sentə]	Tagungszentrum, Kongresszentrum
	accommodation [əˌkɒməˈdeɪʃn]	Unterkunft
	in addition [ɪn əˈdɪʃn]	außerdem
	to **request sth** [rɪˈkwest]	etw anfordern, um etw bitten
	evaluation [ɪˌvæljuˈeɪʃn]	Beurteilung, Evaluierung
	independent [ˌɪndɪˈpendənt]	unabhängig
	review [rɪˈvjuː]	Rezension, Kritik
	script [skrɪpt]	Manuskript, Drehbuch
	surroundings *pl* [səˈraʊndɪŋz]	Umgebung
	ranging from … to … [ˈreɪndʒɪŋ frəm tə]	von … bis …
	square foot [ˌskweə ˈfʊt]	Quadratfuß *(ca. 0,09 qm)*
	specialty [ˈspeʃəlti]	Besonderheit
	spa [spɑː]	Wellnessbereich
	gym [dʒɪm]	Fitness-Studio
	rating [ˈreɪtɪŋ]	Bewertung
	to **award sb sth** [əˈwɔːd]	jdm etw *(Preis usw.)* verleihen
	fair [feə]	mittelmäßig
	exceptional [ɪkˈsepʃənl]	außergewöhnlich
	registration [ˌredʒɪˈstreɪʃn]	Anmeldung
	beverage [ˈbevərɪdʒ]	Getränk
65	**promotional** [prəˈməʊʃənl]	Werbe-
T	**launch** [lɔːntʃ]	Start
	limitation [ˌlɪmɪˈteɪʃn]	Begrenzung, Beschränkung
	to **fire away** [ˌfaɪər əˈweɪ]	losschießen
	constraint [kənˈstreɪnt]	Beschränkung
	television channel [ˈtelɪvɪʒn tʃænl]	Fernsehsender
	to **aim at sth** [ˈeɪm ət]	etw zum Ziel haben
	focused [ˈfəʊkəst]	gebündelt, konzentriert
	limited [ˈlɪmɪtɪd]	beschränkt, begrenzt
	solution [səˈluːʃn]	Lösung
	to **register sth with sth** [ˈredʒɪstə wɪð]	etw bei etw anmelden
	response rate [rɪˈspɒns reɪt]	Rücklaufquote
	to **place an ad** [pleɪs ən ˈæd]	eine Anzeige schalten
	glossy brochure [ˌglɒsi ˈbrəʊʃə]	Hochglanzbroschüre

UNIT 7

66	to **call a meeting** [ˌkɔːl ə ˈmiːtɪŋ]	eine Sitzung einberufen
	up-to-date [ˌʌp tə ˈdeɪt]	aktuell, auf dem neuesten Stand
	exhibition hall [ˌeksɪˈbɪʃn hɔːl]	Messehalle, Ausstellungshalle
T	**row stand** [ˈrəʊ stænd]	Reihenstand
	aisle [aɪl]	(Mittel-)Gang
	neighbouring [ˈneɪbərɪŋ]	benachbart
	past sth [pɑːst]	an etw vorbei
	corner stand [ˈkɔːnə stænd]	Eckstand
	rental fee [ˈrentl fiː]	Miete
	end of block stand [ˌend əv ˈblɒk stænd]	Kopfstand
	openness [ˈəʊpənnəs]	Offenheit
	to **appear** [əˈpɪə]	wirken, scheinen
	welcoming [ˈwelkəmɪŋ]	einladend
	island stand [ˈaɪlənd stænd]	Blockstand, Inselstand
	to **surround sth** [səˈraʊnd]	etw umgeben
	construction equipment [kənˈstrʌkʃn ɪkwɪpmənt]	Baumaschinen
	to **rent** [rent]	mieten
67	**giveaway** [ˈgɪvəweɪ]	Werbegeschenk
	aspect [ˈæspekt]	Gesichtspunkt, Seite, Aspekt
	sales literature [ˈseɪlz ˌlɪtrətʃə]	Verkaufsprospekte, Informationsmaterial
	promotional [prəˈməʊʃənl]	Werbe-
	to **attract sb to sth** [əˈtrækt]	jdn zu etw locken
	corporate [ˈkɔːprət]	Unternehmens-
	to **hand sth out** [ˌhænd ˈaʊt]	etw austeilen, etw ausgeben
	immediately [ɪˈmiːdiətli]	sofort, unverzüglich
	tote bag [ˌtəʊt bæg]	Tragetasche
	hand sanitizer [ˈhænd sænɪtaɪzə]	Handdesinfektionsmittel
	reusable [ˌriːˈjuːzəbl]	wiederverwendbar
	beaker [ˈbiːkə]	Becher
	trade show [ˈtreɪd ʃəʊ]	Fachmesse
	keychain [ˈkiːtʃeɪn]	Schlüsselbund
	flashlight [ˈflæʃlaɪt]	Taschenlampe
	charger [ˈtʃɑːdʒə]	Ladegerät
	sticky notes *pl* [ˈstɪki nəʊts]	Haftnotizen
	to **link sth to sth** [ˈlɪŋk tə]	etw mit etw verknüpfen, etw mit etw verbinden
	memory stick [ˈmeməri stɪk]	Speicherstick
68	to **commission sth** [kəˈmɪʃn]	etw in Auftrag geben

	architecture [ˈɑːkɪtektʃə]	Architektur
	expo [ˈekspəʊ]	Messe, Ausstellung
	catering [ˈkeɪtərɪŋ]	Verpflegung
	to **raise sth** [reɪz]	etw steigern
	brand awareness [ˈbrænd əweənəs]	Bekanntheitsgrad einer Marke
	solution [səˈluːʃn]	Lösung
	shell scheme stand [ˈʃel skiːm stænd]	Systemstand
	box-shaped [ˈbɒks ʃeɪpt]	kastenförmig
	framework [ˈfreɪmwɜːk]	Rahmen
	post [pəʊst]	Säule, Pfosten
	multiple [ˈmʌltɪpl]	mehrfach
	to **fit** [fɪt]	passen
	vehicle [ˈviːəkl]	Fahrzeug
	modular [ˈmɒdjələ]	modular, in Modulbauweise
	wall panel [ˈwɔːl pænl]	Wandplatte
	bespoke [bɪˈspəʊk]	maßgeschneidert
	shape [ʃeɪp]	Form, Gestalt
	specifications *pl* [ˌspesɪfɪˈkeɪʃnz]	Vorgaben
	visualization [ˌvɪʒuəlaɪˈzeɪʃn]	Visualisierung
	requirements *pl* [rɪˈkwaɪəmənts]	Anforderungen, Bedürfnisse, Wünsche
	division of space [dɪˌvɪʒn əf ˈspeɪs]	Raumaufteilung
T	**architect** [ˈɑːkɪtekt]	Architekt/in
	roof [ruːf]	Dach
	counter [ˈkaʊntə]	Theke, Tresen
	seating [ˈsiːtɪŋ]	Sitzgelegenheiten
	bar table [ˈbɑː teɪbl]	Stehtisch
	stool [stuːl]	Hocker
	literature rack [ˈlɪtrətʃə ræk]	Prospektständer
	storage space [ˈstɔːrɪdʒ speɪs]	Lagerfläche, Stauraum
	to **include sth** [ɪnˈkluːd]	etw einplanen
	lockable [ˈlɒkəbl]	abschließbar, verschließbar
	valuables *pl* [ˈvæljuəblz]	Wertsachen
	to **divide sth up** [dɪˈvaɪd ʌp]	etw aufteilen
	square metre [ˈskweə miːtə]	Quadratmeter
	row [rəʊ]	Reihe
	access [ˈækses]	Zugang, Zutritt
	to **make sense** [meɪk ˈsens]	einleuchten
69	**with reference to** [wɪð ˈrefrəns tə]	mit Bezug auf, bezugnehmend auf
	pleasant [ˈpleznt]	angenehm, nett
	regarding [rɪˈgɑːdɪŋ]	betreffend
	display stand [dɪˈspleɪ stænd]	Präsentationsstand
	semi-closed [ˈsemɪ kləʊzd]	halbgeschlossen
	infill panel [ˈɪnfɪl pænl]	Ausfachung, Füllung
	backdrop [ˈbækdrɒp]	Messewand
	accessible [əkˈsesəbl]	zugänglich, erreichbar
	dimensions *pl* [dɪˈmenʃnz]	Abmessungen
	depth [depθ]	Tiefe
	sketch [sketʃ]	Skizze
	firm offer [ˌfɜːm ˈɒfə]	verbindliches Angebot
	panel [ˈpænl]	Platte, Tafel
70	**menu** [ˈmenjuː]	Menü
	to **cater for sth** [ˈkeɪtə fə]	für etw *(Veranstaltung usw.)* Speisen und Getränke liefern
	to **sit back** [ˌsɪt ˈbæk]	sich zurücklehnen
	selection [sɪˈlekʃn]	Auswahl
	hospitality [ˌhɒspɪˈtæləti]	Bewirtung
	pack [pæk]	Paket
	on request [ɒn rɪˈkwest]	auf Anfrage
	Please note: [ˌpliːz ˈnəʊt]	Bitte beachten Sie:
	cover [ˈkʌvə]	Gedeck
	waiting staff [ˈweɪtɪŋ stɑːf]	Servierkräfte
	in addition to sth [ɪn əˈdɪʃn tə]	zusätzlich zu etw
	sth is chargeable at £20 [ɪz ˈtʃɑːdʒəbl ət]	für etwas werden 20£ berechnet
	beverage [ˈbevərɪdʒ]	Getränk
	to **brew** [bruː]	*(Tee, Kaffee:)* kochen
	herbal tea [ˌhɜːbl ˈtiː]	Kräutertee
	decaffeinated [ˌdiːˈkæfɪneɪtɪd]	koffeinfrei
	sparkling water [ˌspɑːklɪŋ ˈwɔːtə]	Sprudelwasser
	ale [eɪl]	*brit. Biersorte*
	wine list [ˈwaɪn lɪst]	Weinkarte
	savoury [ˈseɪvəri]	herzhaft
	bites *pl* [baɪts]	Häppchen
	fork [fɔːk]	Gabel
P	**charge** [tʃɑːdʒ]	Gebühr
	labour price [ˈleɪbə praɪs]	Lohnkosten
71	**space-saving** [ˈspeɪs seɪvɪŋ]	raumsparend
	cultural [ˈkʌltʃərəl]	kulturell
	background [ˈbækgraʊnd]	Herkunft
	to **do research into sth** [du rɪˈsɜːtʃ ɪntə]	etw recherchieren, Recherchen über etw anstellen
	etiquette [ˈetɪket]	Umgangsformen
	awareness [əˈweənəs]	Bewusstsein, Sensibilität
	humour [ˈhjuːmə]	Humor
	rude [ruːd]	unhöflich
	anger [ˈæŋgə]	Verärgerung
	to **stress sth** [stres]	etw betonen
	to **respect** [rɪˈspekt]	respektieren, achten
	modesty [ˈmɒdəsti]	Bescheidenheit
	patience [ˈpeɪʃns]	Geduld
	intelligence [ɪnˈtelɪdʒəns]	Intelligenz
	plate [pleɪt]	Teller
	shoulder [ˈʃəʊldə]	Schulter
	silence [ˈsaɪləns]	Schweigen, Stille
72	**punctuality** [ˌpʌŋktʃuˈæləti]	Pünktlichkeit
	superior [suːˈpɪəriə]	Vorgesetzte/r
	view (of sb/sth) [vjuː]	Auffassung, Bild (von jdm/einer Sache)

	to approach sth [əˈprəʊtʃ]	an etw herangehen, etw angehen
	contrast [ˈkɒntrɑːst]	Gegensatz
	behaviour [bɪˈheɪvjə]	Verhalten, Benehmen
	to observe [əbˈzɜːv]	beobachten
	trading partner [ˈtreɪdɪŋ pɑːtnə]	Handelspartner/in
	to adapt to sb/sth [əˈdæpt tə]	sich an jdn/etw anpassen, sich an jdn/etw gewöhnen
	appointment [əˈpɔɪntmənt]	Termin
	focus [ˈfəʊkəs]	(inhaltlicher) Schwerpunkt
	interruption [ˌɪntəˈrʌpʃn]	Störung, Unterbrechung
	to reject sth [rɪˈdʒekt]	etw ablehnen, etw abweisen
T	**adjustable** [əˈdʒʌstəbl]	verstellbar
	best-selling [ˌbestˈselɪŋ]	meistverkauft
	indeed [ɪnˈdiːd]	in der Tat, allerdings
	midday [ˌmɪdˈdeɪ]	Mittag
	to switch sth off [ˌswɪtʃ ˈɒf]	etw ausschalten, etw abschalten
	cell (phone) *AE* [sel]	Handy
	deal [diːl]	Geschäft, Abschluss
74	**jar** [dʒɑː]	(Marmeladen-)Glas
	food industry [ˈfuːd ɪndəstri]	Nahrungsmittelbranche
	to hire sth [ˈhaɪə]	etw mieten
T	**for ages** [fər ˈeɪdʒɪz]	eine Ewigkeit
	departure [dɪˈpɑːtʃə]	Abreise, Abflug
	to suppose [səˈpəʊz]	vermuten, annehmen, glauben
	Hang on. [ˌhæŋ ˈɒn]	Einen Moment. Warte mal.
	arrival [əˈraɪvl]	Ankunft
	accommodation [əˌkɒməˈdeɪʃn]	Unterkunft, Unterbringung
	conference centre [ˈkɒnfərəns sentə]	Tagungszentrum, Kongresszentrum
	air-conditioned [ˈeəkəndɪʃənd]	klimatisiert
	to feature sth [ˈfiːtʃə]	etw *(Merkmal usw.)* aufweisen
	fitted with [ˈfɪtɪd wɪð]	ausgestattet mit
	gym [dʒɪm]	Fitness-Studio
	indoor pool [ˌɪndoː ˈpuːl]	Hallenbad
	range [reɪndʒ]	Auswahl, Angebot
	stylish [ˈstaɪlɪʃ]	elegant, stilvoll
	daily [ˈdeɪli]	täglich
	well-stocked [ˌwel ˈstɒkt]	gut sortiert
	lounge [laʊndʒ]	Gesellschaftsraum, Lounge
	to serve [sɜːv]	servieren
	snack [snæk]	Imbiss
	front desk [ˌfrʌnt ˈdesk]	Rezeption
	smoke-free [ˈsməʊk friː]	rauchfrei
	shuttle [ˈʃʌtl]	Zubringer
	nature reserve [ˈneɪtʃə rɪzɜːv]	Naturschutzgebiet
75	**receptionist** [rɪˈsepʃənɪst]	Empfangsmitarbeiter/in
	to check in [ˌtʃek ˈɪn]	sich anmelden, einchecken
T	**reservation** [ˌrezəˈveɪʃn]	Reservierung
	buffet breakfast [ˈbʌfeɪ brekfəst]	Frühstücksbüfett
	dining room [ˈdaɪnɪŋ ruːm]	*(Hotel:)* Speisesaal
	wheelchair [ˈwiːltʃeə]	Rollstuhl
	towel [ˈtaʊəl]	Handtuch
	pillow [ˈpɪləʊ]	Kopfkissen
	secure [sɪˈkjʊə]	sicher, bewacht
	gate [geɪt]	Tor, Einfahrt
	to check out [ˌtʃek ˈaʊt]	sich abmelden, auschecken
	air conditioning [ˈeə kəndɪʃnɪŋ]	Klimaanlage, Klimatisierung
	meeting room [ˈmiːtɪŋ ruːm]	Sitzungszimmer, Konferenzraum
	countryside [ˈkʌntrisaɪd]	Landschaft, ländliche Gegend
	mileage [ˈmaɪlɪdʒ]	*(Mietwagen:)* (enthaltene) Kilometer
	insurance cover [ɪnˈʃʊərəns kʌvə]	Versicherungsschutz
	excess *BE* [ˈekses]	*(Versicherung:)* Selbstbehalt
	accident [ˈæksɪdənt]	Unfall
	to pick sth up [ˌpɪk ˈʌp]	etw abholen
76	**terms** *pl* **of delivery** [ˌtɜːmz əv dɪˈlɪvəri]	Lieferbedingungen
	prospective [prəˈspektɪv]	potenziell
	to exchange sth [ɪksˈtʃeɪndʒ]	etw austauschen
	findings *pl* [ˈfaɪndɪŋz]	(Untersuchungs-)Ergebnisse

UNIT 8

77 T	**value for money** [ˌvæljuː fə ˈmʌni]	(preis)günstig
	to jump at sth [ˈdʒʌmp ət]	sich auf etw stürzen
	inviting [ɪnˈvaɪtɪŋ]	verlockend
	saying [ˈseɪɪŋ]	Sprichwort
	to keep sth in mind [ˌkiːp ɪn ˈmaɪnd]	etw nicht vergessen
	package [ˈpækɪdʒ]	Paket
	to take sth into consideration [ˌteɪk ɪntə kənˌsɪdəˈreɪʃn]	etw in Betracht ziehen, etw berücksichtigen
	consistent(ly) [kənˈsɪstənt]	gleichbleibend, beständig, durchgehend
	to associate sth with sth [əˈsəʊʃieɪt wɪð]	etw mit etw in Verbindung bringen
	to judge sth [dʒʌdʒ]	etw beurteilen
	client [ˈklaɪənt]	Kunde/Kundin
	long-standing [ˌlɒŋ ˈstændɪŋ]	langjährig
	reference [ˈrefərəns]	Referenz
	business acquaintance [ˈbɪznəs əkweɪntəns]	Geschäftsfreund/in
	strength [streŋθ]	Stärke
	weakness [ˈwiːknəs]	Schwäche
	anonymous [əˈnɒnɪməs]	anonym
	warranty [ˈwɒrənti]	Gewährleistung
	defect [ˈdiːfekt]	Mangel
	limited [ˈlɪmɪtɪd]	beschränkt, begrenzt

	English	Deutsch
	to **make a claim** [meɪk ə ˈkleɪm]	einen Anspruch / eine Forderung geltend machen
	to **look into sth** [ˌlʊk ˈɪntə]	etw prüfen
	terms and conditions *pl* [ˌtɜːmz ənd kənˈdɪʃnz]	Allgemeine Geschäftsbedingungen
	open account [ˌəʊpən əˈkaʊnt]	offenes Zahlungsziel
	to **establish** [ɪˈstæblɪʃ]	festigen
	last but not least [ˌlɑːst bʌt nɒt ˈliːst]	zu guter Letzt
	solvency [ˈsɒlvənsi]	Zahlungsfähigkeit
	to **put sth at risk** [ˌpʊt ət ˈrɪsk]	etw gefährden
	financial stability [faɪˌnænʃl stəˈbɪləti]	Finanzstabilität
	to **enter into a contract** [ˌentər ɪntu ə ˈkɒntrækt]	einen Vertrag (ab)schließen, in einen Vertrag eintreten
	vendor [ˈvendə]	Anbieter, Verkäufer
	source [sɔːs]	Quelle
	credit check [ˈkredɪt tʃek]	Bonitätsprüfung
	reliability [rɪˌlaɪəˈbɪləti]	Zuverlässigkeit
	to **rank** [ræŋk]	einstufen, (in einer Rangliste) bewerten
	ranking [ˈræŋkɪŋ]	Einstufung, Bewertung
	ethical [ˈeθɪkl]	ethisch, moralisch vertretbar
	to **treat sb** [triːt]	jdn behandeln
	attitude (to sth) [ˈætɪtjuːd]	Einstellung (zu etw)
	physical [ˈfɪzɪkl]	physisch
	health and safety [ˌhelθ ənd ˈseɪfti]	Arbeitsschutz
	regulations *pl* [ˌregjuˈleɪʃnz]	Vorschriften
	to **meet sth** [miːt]	etw *(Vorschriften usw.)* einhalten
	to **be free to do sth** [bi ˈfriː tə duː]	etw tun dürfen
	trade union [ˌtreɪd ˈjuːniən]	Gewerkschaft
	collective wage bargaining [kəˌlektɪv ˈweɪdʒ bɑːgɪnɪŋ]	Tarifverhandlungen
	reputation [ˌrepjuˈteɪʃn]	Ruf
	country of origin [ˌkʌntri əv ˈɒrɪdʒɪn]	Ursprungsland
	human rights *pl* [ˌhjuːmən ˈraɪts]	Menschenrechte
	sexual [ˈsekʃuəl]	sexuell
	discrimination [dɪˌskrɪmɪˈneɪʃn]	Diskriminierung
	suspicion [səˈspɪʃn]	Verdacht
	forced labour [ˌfɔːst ˈleɪbə]	Zwangsarbeit
	child labour [ˈtʃaɪld leɪbə]	Kinderarbeit
	issue [ˈɪʃuː]	Frage, Problem
	sustainable [səˈsteɪnəbl]	nachhaltig
	to **comply with sth** [kəmˈplaɪ wɪð]	etw *(Norm usw.)* erfüllen, etw *(Vorschrift usw.)* einhalten
	to **do one's bit** [du wʌnz ˈbɪt]	seinen Beitrag leisten
	domestic [dəˈmestɪk]	im Inland
	shipping [ˈʃɪpɪŋ]	Versand
	distance [ˈdɪstəns]	Entfernung
	carbon footprint [ˌkɑːbən ˈfʊtprɪnt]	CO_2-Fußabdruck
78	**sweetcorn** [ˈswiːtkɔːn]	Zuckermais, Süßmais
	to **go rotten** [gəʊ ˈrɒtn]	verfaulen
	to **note sth** [nəʊt]	etw zur Kenntnis nehmen
	fully-integrated [ˌfʊli ˈɪntɪgreɪtɪd]	vollintegriert
	three-piece [ˈθriː piːs]	dreiteilig
	producer [prəˈdjuːsə]	Produzent/in, Hersteller/in
	exporter [ɪkˈspɔːtə]	Exporteur, Ausführer
	to **cut costs** [kʌt ˈkɒsts]	Kosten senken
	transportation [ˌtrænspɔːˈteɪʃn]	Transport
	storage [ˈstɔːrɪdʒ]	Lagerung
	can-making [ˈkæn meɪkɪŋ]	Dosenherstellung
	initially [ɪˈnɪʃəli]	zu Anfang, zunächst
	diameter [daɪˈæmɪtə]	Durchmesser
	favourable [ˈfeɪvərəbl]	günstig
	quotation [kwəʊˈteɪʃn]	Preisangebot, Angebot, Offerte
79	**grateful** [ˈgreɪtfl]	dankbar
	to **call on sb** [ˈkɔːl ɒn]	jdn besuchen, bei jdm vorbeischauen
	to **meet requirements** [miːt rɪˈkwaɪəmənts]	Anforderungen erfüllen
	substantial [səbˈstænʃl]	erheblich, beträchtlich
	to **grant sth** [grɑːnt]	etw gewähren, etw einräumen
	proposal [prəˈpəʊzl]	Vorschlag
	initial proposal [ɪˌnɪʃl prəˈpəʊzl]	Erstvorschlag
T	to **be up and running** [bi ˌʌp ən ˈrʌnɪŋ]	in (laufendem) Betrieb sein
	to **troubleshoot** [ˈtrʌblʃuːt]	Fehler suchen, Fehler beheben
	to **assist sb** [əˈsɪst]	jdm helfen, jdn unterstützen
	shipping company [ˈʃɪpɪŋ kʌmpəni]	Reederei
	seaworthy [ˈsiːwɜːði]	seetüchtig
	condition [kənˈdɪʃn]	Zustand
	sector [ˈsektə]	Branche
	to **require sb to do sth** [rɪˈkwaɪə]	von jdm verlangen, etw zu tun
	remainder [rɪˈmeɪndə]	Rest
	official offer [əˌfɪʃl ˈɒfə]	offizielles Angebot
	to **diagnose** [ˈdaɪəgnəʊz]	diagnostizieren
	remotely [rɪˈməʊtli]	aus der Ferne
	remote diagnosis [rɪˌməʊt daɪəgˈnəʊsɪs]	Ferndiagnose
80	to **wholesale** [ˈhəʊlseɪl]	en gros handeln
	terms *pl* **of insurance** [ˌtɜːmz əv ɪnˈʃʊərəns]	Versicherungsbedingungen
	equivalent [ɪˈkwɪvələnt]	Entsprechung, Übersetzung
	insurance in transit [ɪnˌʃʊərəns ɪn ˈtrænzɪt]	Transportversicherung

	mode of transport [ˌməʊd əv ˈtrænspɔːt]	Beförderungsart, Verkehrsmittel
	loading [ˈləʊdɪŋ]	Verladen, Verladung
	unloading [ˌʌnˈləʊdɪŋ]	Entladung, Löschen
	port of shipment [ˌpɔːt əf ˈʃɪpmənt]	Verschiffungshafen
	carriage [ˈkærɪdʒ]	Transport, Beförderung, Fracht
	main carriage [ˈmeɪn kærɪdʒ]	Hauptlauf
	pre-carriage [ˈpriː kærɪdʒ]	Vorlauf
	post-carriage [ˈpəʊst kærɪdʒ]	Nachlauf
	contract of carriage [ˌkɒntrækt əv ˈkærɪdʒ]	Beförderungsvertrag, Frachtvertrag
	terminal [ˈtɜːmɪnl]	Terminal
	export clearance [ˈekspɔːt klɪərəns]	Ausfuhrabfertigung
	import clearance [ˈɪmpɔːt klɪərəns]	Einfuhrabfertigung
	place of destination [ˌpleɪs əv destɪˈneɪʃn]	Bestimmungsort
	insurance [ɪnˈʃʊərəns]	Versicherung
	duty [ˈdjuːti]	Zoll
	consignment [kənˈsaɪnmənt]	Sendung, Warensendung
	importer [ɪmˈpɔːtə]	Importeur, Einführer
81	**floor tiles** *pl* [ˈflɔː taɪlz]	Bodenfliesen
	seafood [ˈsiːfuːd]	Meeresfrüchte
	convenient [kənˈviːniənt]	geeignet, zweckmäßig
	to **cover** [ˈkʌvə]	*(Kosten)* decken
	to **bear sth** [beə]	etw *(Risiko, Kosten)* tragen
	to **hand sth over** [ˌhænd ˈəʊvə]	etw übergeben
	carrier [ˈkæriə]	Spediteur, Reederei, Transportunternehmen
	to **pass to sb** [ˈpɑːs tə]	auf jdn übergehen
	to **collect sth** [kəˈlekt]	etw abholen
	to **insure** [ɪnˈʃʊə]	versichern
	export licence [ˈekspɔːt laɪsns]	Ausführgenehmigung
	documentation [ˌdɒkjumenˈteɪʃn]	Papiere
	exception [ɪkˈsepʃn]	Ausnahme
	customs duty [ˌkʌstəmz ˈdjuːti]	Zollgebühr(en)
	to **refer to sth** [rɪˈfɜː tə]	auf etw zurückgreifen, etw zu Hilfe nehmen
	electricity generator [ɪˌlekˈtrɪsəti ˈdʒenəreɪtə]	Generator
T	**by rail** [baɪ ˈreɪl]	mit der Bahn
	booked up [ˌbʊkt ˈʌp]	ausgebucht
	to **dock** [dɒk]	festmachen
	receipt of order [rɪˌsiːt əv ˈɔːdə]	Auftragseingang
	breakable [ˈbreɪkəbl]	zerbrechlich
82	**transaction** [trænˈzækʃn]	Geschäft, Vorgang, Transaktion

	irrevocable and confirmed documentary letter of credit [ɪˌrevəkəbl ən kənˌfɜːmd dɒkjuˌmentri letər əf ˈkredɪt]	unwiderrufliches und bestätigtes Dokumentenakkreditiv
	simplified [ˈsɪmplɪfaɪd]	vereinfacht
	principle [ˈprɪnsəpl]	Grundsatz, Prinzip
	holder [ˈhəʊldə]	Inhaber/in
	to **take possession of sth** [teɪk pəˈzeʃn əv]	etw in Besitz nehmen
	commercial invoice [kəˌmɜːʃl ˈɪnvɔɪs]	Handelsrechnung
	insurance certificate [ɪnˌʃʊərəns səˈtɪfɪkət]	Versicherungsschein
	bill of lading (B/L) [ˌbɪl əv ˈleɪdɪŋ]	Konnossement
	air waybill [ˌeə ˈweɪbɪl]	Luftfrachtbrief
	consignment note [kənˈsaɪnmənt nəʊt]	Frachtbrief
	letter of credit (L/C) [ˌletər əf ˈkredɪt]	Akkreditiv
83	**document of title** [ˌdɒkjumənt əv ˈtaɪtl]	Dispositionspapier, Traditionspapier
	ownership [ˈəʊnəʃɪp]	Eigentum, Eigentumsrecht
	title to the goods [ˌtaɪtl tə ðə ˈgʊdz]	Eigentum(srecht) an den Waren
	to **inspect sth** [ɪnˈspekt]	etw prüfen
	to **charge a fee** [ˌtʃɑːdʒ ə ˈfiː]	eine Gebühr verlangen
	case study [ˈkeɪs stʌdi]	Fallstudie
	road construction [ˈrəʊd kənstrʌkʃn]	Straßenbau
	heavy machinery [ˌhevi məˈʃiːnəri]	Schwermaschinen
	reliable [rɪˈlaɪəbl]	zuverlässig
84	**layout** [ˈleɪaʊt]	Gestaltung, Aufbau, Layout
	medical supplies *pl* [ˌmedɪkl səˈplaɪz]	Sanitätsartikel
	clinic [ˈklɪnɪk]	Klinik
	body [ˈbɒdi]	*(Brief:)* Haupttext
	enclosure [ɪnˈkləʊʒə]	*(Brief:)* Anlage
	inside address [ˌɪnsaɪd əˈdres]	Innenadresse
	reference initials *pl* [ˈrefərəns ɪnɪʃlz]	*(Brief:)* Zeichen
	signature [ˈsɪgnətʃə]	Unterschrift
	signature block [ˈsɪgnətʃə blɒk]	Signatur
	attention line [əˈtenʃn laɪn]	Zeile „zu Händen"
	confirmation [ˌkɒnfəˈmeɪʃn]	Bestätigung
	to **enclose** [ɪnˈkləʊz]	*(Brief:)* beifügen
	to **pack** [pæk]	verpacken
	to **be pleased to do sth** [bi ˈpliːzd tə]	etw gern tun; sich freuen, etw zu tun
85	**for the attention of** [fə ði əˈtenʃn əv]	zu Händen
	operating theatre [ˈɒpəreɪtɪŋ θɪətə]	Operationssaal

	edition [ɪˈdɪʃn]	Ausgabe
	trade magazine [ˈtreɪd mæɡəziːn]	Fachzeitschrift
	hardware [ˈhɑːdweə]	Geräte
	outpatient clinic [ˈaʊtpeɪʃnt klɪnɪk]	Ambulanz
	high-definition [ˌhaɪ ˌdefɪˈnɪʃn]	hochauflösend
	trial order [ˌtraɪəl ˈɔːdə]	Probebestellung
	packaging [ˈpækɪdʒɪŋ]	Verpackung
	attention [əˈtenʃn]	Beachtung, Aufmerksamkeit

KMK Exam practice 4

86	**from the beginning** [frəm ðə bɪˈɡɪnɪŋ]	von Anfang an
	stationery [ˈsteɪʃənri]	Schreibwaren
	office supplies *pl* [ˈɒfɪs səplaɪz]	Bürobedarf
	launch [lɔːntʃ]	Eröffnung
	to **deal in sth** [ˈdiːl ɪn]	mit etw handeln
	to **stimulate sth** [ˈstɪmjuleɪt]	etw beleben, etw ankurbeln
	opportunity [ˌɒpəˈtjuːnəti]	Gelegenheit, Möglichkeit
	exhibitor [ɪɡˈzɪbɪtə]	Aussteller
	array of products [əˌreɪ əf ˈprɒdʌkts]	Produktangebot
	ranging from … to … [ˈreɪndʒɪŋ frəm tə]	von … bis …
	arts and crafts *pl* [ˌɑːts ənd ˈkrɑːfts]	Kunsthandwerk
	writing implement [ˈraɪtɪŋ ɪmplɪmənt]	Schreibgerät
	toy [tɔɪ]	Spielzeug
	gift [ɡɪft]	Geschenk
	to **prove sth** [pruːv]	sich als etw erweisen
	increasingly [ɪnˈkriːsɪŋli]	zunehmend
	achievement [əˈtʃiːvmənt]	Leistung
	to **attribute sth to sb** [əˈtrɪbjuːt tə]	jdm etw zuschreiben
	to **be well received** [bi ˌwel rɪˈsiːvd]	(großen) Zuspruch finden
	to **access sth** [ˈækses]	etw erreichen
	emerging markets *pl* [ɪˌmɜːdʒɪŋ ˈmɑːkɪts]	Wachstumsmärkte, Schwellenmärkte
	nearby [ˈnɪəbaɪ]	in der Nähe, nahegelegen
	continued [kənˈtɪnjuːd]	anhaltend, kontinuierlich
	support [səˈpɔːt]	Unterstützung
	to **go a long way in sth** [ɡəʊ ə ˌlɒŋ ˈweɪ ɪn]	viel zu etw beitragen, viel für etw tun
	high-quality [ˌhaɪ ˈkwɒləti]	hochwertig
	stamp [stæmp]	Marke, Stempel
	customer base [ˈkʌstəmə beɪs]	Kundenstamm
	to **display sth** [dɪˈspleɪ]	etw ausstellen, etw zeigen
87	to **entertain sb** [ˌentəˈteɪn]	jdn bewirten
	to **occur** [əˈkɜː]	*(Problem usw.:)* auftreten
	imagination [ɪˌmædʒɪˈneɪʃn]	Phantasie
	to **make sth up** [ˌmeɪk ˈʌp]	sich etw ausdenken, sich etw einfallen lassen
	to **reassure sb** [ˌriːəˈʃʊə]	jdn beruhigen
	to **get annoyed about sth** [ˌɡet əˈnɔɪd əbaʊt]	sich über etw ärgern
	voucher [ˈvaʊtʃə]	Gutschein

UNIT 9

88	to **submit sth** [səbˈmɪt]	etw einreichen, etw abgeben
	hiking [ˈhaɪkɪŋ]	Wandern
	template [ˈtempleɪt]	Vorlage
	to **quote a price** [ˌkwəʊt ə ˈpraɪs]	einen Preis angeben/nennen
	without obligation [wɪˌðaʊt ɒblɪˈɡeɪʃn]	unverbindlich, freibleibend
	agreement [əˈɡriːmənt]	Vereinbarung
	party [ˈpɑːti]	Partei
	to **respond to sth** [rɪˈspɒnd tə]	auf etw reagieren
	non-binding [ˌnɒn ˈbaɪndɪŋ]	unverbindlich, freibleibend
	subject to confirmation [ˌsʌbdʒɪkt tə kɒnfəˈmeɪʃn]	vorbehaltlich einer Bestätigung, freibleibend
	special conditions *pl* [ˌspeʃl kənˈdɪʃnz]	Sonderkonditionen
	in response to sth [ɪn rɪˈspɒns tə]	als Antwort auf etw
89	**backpack** [ˈbækpæk]	Rucksack
	as requested [əz rɪˈkwestɪd]	wie gewünscht
	addition (to sth) [əˈdɪʃn]	Neuheit
	litre [ˈliːtə]	Liter
	to **weigh** [weɪ]	wiegen
	to **convince sb of sth** [kənˈvɪns]	jdn von etw überzeugen
	windproof [ˈwɪndpruːf]	winddicht
	mountaineering [ˌmaʊntəˈnɪərɪŋ]	Bergsteigen
	reference to sth [ˈrefərəns tə]	Verweis auf etw, Bezug auf etw
	immediate [ɪˈmiːdiət]	direkt, sofortig
90	**DIY store** [ˌdiː aɪ ˈwaɪ stɔː]	Baumarkt, Heimwerkermarkt
	purchasing director [ˈpɜːtʃəsɪŋ dərektə]	Einkaufsleiter/in
	sales director [ˈseɪlz dərektə]	Vertriebsleiter/in
	dated [ˈdeɪtɪd]	(mit Datum) vom
	charcoal [ˈtʃɑːkəʊl]	Holzkohle
	barbecue [ˈbɑːbɪkjuː]	Grill
	above-mentioned [əˌbʌv ˈmenʃnd]	obengenannt
	distributor [dɪˈstrɪbjətə]	Vertragshändler
	to **supply sb with sth** [səˈplaɪ wɪð]	jdm etw liefern
	favourable [ˈfeɪvərəbl]	positiv
	to **require sth** [rɪˈkwaɪə]	etw benötigen, etw wünschen
91	**I'm all ears.** [aɪm ˌɔːl ˈɪəz]	Ich bin ganz Ohr.

T	**burner** [ˈbɜːnə]	Brenner, Flamme
	ignition [ɪɡˈnɪʃn]	Zündung
	built-in [ˌbɪltˈɪn]	eingebaut
	lid [lɪd]	Deckel, Haube
	holder [ˈhəʊldə]	Halter
	heat [hiːt]	Hitze
	cooking plate [ˈkʊkɪŋ pleɪt]	Kochplatte
	cast iron [ˌkɑːst ˈaɪən]	Gusseisen
	body [ˈbɒdi]	Gehäuse, Gestell
	literature [ˈlɪtrətʃə]	Informationsmaterial
	basic price [ˌbeɪsɪk ˈpreɪs]	Grundpreis
	per unit [ˌpɜː ˈjuːnɪt]	pro Stück
	net [net]	netto
	to **stretch to sth** [ˈstretʃ tə]	sich auf etw einlassen, jdm bis auf etw entgegenkommen
	to **charge sb sth** [tʃɑːdʒ]	etw *(Preis usw.)* von jdm verlangen
	to **finalize sth** [ˈfaɪnəlaɪz]	etw endgültig festlegen
	to **qualify for sth** [ˈkwɒlɪfaɪ fə]	zu etw berechtigen, für etw infrage kommen
	easily [ˈiːzəli]	locker
	flat-packed [ˈflæt pækt]	zur Selbstmontage
	door-to-door delivery [dɔː tə ˌdɔː dɪˈlɪvəri]	Haus-zu-Haus-Lieferung
	in transit [ɪn ˈtrænzɪt]	beim Transport
	coverage [ˈkʌvərɪdʒ]	Versicherungsschutz
	quote [kwəʊt]	(Preis-)Angebot
	We have a deal. [wiː ˌhæv ə ˈdiːl]	Abgemacht!
	stainless steel [ˌsteɪnləs ˈstiːl]	Edelstahl
	to **evaluate sth** [ɪˈvæljueɪt]	etw auswerten, etw einschätzen, etw beurteilen
	vessel [ˈvesl]	Schiff
	to **be/get in touch** [bi/get ɪn ˈtʌtʃ]	sich melden
92	**via** [ˈvaɪə]	per, mittels, über
	(furniture) set [set]	(Möbel-)Garnitur
	minimum order quantity [ˌmɪnɪməm ˈɔːdə kwɒntəti]	Mindestbestellmenge
	transit time [ˈtrænzɪt taɪm]	Laufzeit
	charge [tʃɑːdʒ]	Kosten
	shipping agent [ˈʃɪpɪŋ eɪdʒənt]	Spediteur
93	**import tax** [ˈɪmpɔːt tæks]	Einfuhrzoll
	shipping rate [ˈʃɪpɪŋ reɪt]	Frachtsatz, Versandkosten
	sea transport [ˈsiː trænspɔːt]	Seetransport
	to **handle sth** [ˈhændl]	etw erledigen
	on sb's behalf [ɒn bɪˈhɑːf]	für jdn
	request [rɪˈkwest]	Anfrage
94	**unit price** [ˌjuːnɪt ˈpraɪs]	Stückpreis
	closed wagon [ˌkləʊzd ˈwæɡən]	geschlossener Waggon
	in shared container [ɪn ˌʃeəd kənˈteɪnə]	in Sammelcontainer, als Beiladung
	applicable charges *pl* [əˌplɪkəbl ˈtʃɑːdʒɪz]	anfallende Gebühren
	My pleasure. [maɪ ˈpleʒə]	Ganz meinerseits! Gern geschehen!
95	**sub-total** [ˈsʌbtəʊtl]	Zwischensumme
T	**With pleasure.** [wɪð ˈpleʒə]	Aber gerne!
	structural parts *pl* [ˌstrʌktʃərəl ˈpɑːts]	tragende Bauteile
	fleet [fliːt]	Fuhrpark, Flotte
	to **transfer sth** [trænsˈfɜː]	etw übertragen
96	to **clarify** [ˈklærəfaɪ]	klären, abklären
	to **sort sth out** [ˌsɔːt ˈaʊt]	etw klären, etw regeln
	misunderstanding [ˌmɪsʌndəˈstændɪŋ]	Missverständnis
	error [ˈerə]	Fehler, Irrtum
T	**from stock** [frəm ˈstɒk]	ab Lager
	bulk order [ˌbʌlk ˈɔːdə]	Großauftrag, Großbestellung
	to **cover sth** [ˈkʌvə]	etw abdecken
	VAT (value added tax) [ˌvæljuː ˈædɪd tæks]	MwSt. (Mehrwertsteuer)
	to **omit sth** [əˈmɪt]	etw weglassen
	calculation [ˌkælkjuˈleɪʃn]	Berechnung, Kalkulation
T	**microwave oven** [ˌmaɪkrəweɪv ˈʌvn]	Mikrowellenherd
	kettle [ˈketl]	Wasserkocher
	to **misunderstand sth** [ˌmɪsʌndəˈstænd]	etw missverstehen, etw falsch verstehen
	to **recalculate** [rɪˈkælkjuleɪt]	neu berechnen
	total price [ˌtəʊtl ˈpraɪs]	Gesamtpreis
	to **re-submit sth** [ˌrɪ səbˈmɪt]	etw *(Bestellung)* erneut aufgeben
	correction [kəˈrekʃn]	Korrektur
	to **appreciate sth** [əˈpriːʃieɪt]	etw zu schätzen wissen
97	to **re-write sth** [rɪˈraɪt]	etw neu schreiben
	customer discount [ˌkʌstəmə ˈdɪskaʊnt]	Kundenrabatt

UNIT 10

98	**contract of sale** [ˌkɒntrækt əv ˈseɪl]	Kaufvertrag
	duty [ˈdjuːti]	Aufgabe, Pflicht
	authority [ɔːˈθɒrəti]	Befugnis, Vollmacht
	to **perform an obligation** [pəˌfɔːm ən ɒblɪˈɡeɪʃn]	eine Verpflichtung erfüllen
	prior to sth [ˈpraɪə tə]	vor etw
	work and costs [ˌwɜːk ən ˈkɒsts]	Arbeit und Kosten
	to **incur** [ɪnˈkɜː]	*(Kosten:)* anfallen
	purchase price [ˈpɜːtʃəs praɪs]	Kaufpreis
	sb can be assumed to do sth [kən bi əˈsjuːmd tə]	es kann davon ausgegangen werden, dass jd etw tut
	unconditional(ly) [ˌʌnkənˈdɪʃənl]	vorbehaltlos, uneingeschränkt

	defective [dɪˈfektɪv]	mangelhaft
	date of delivery [ˌdeɪt əv dɪˈlɪvəri]	Lieferdatum
99	**performance (of a contract)** [pəˈfɔːməns]	Erfüllung, Durchführung (eines Vertrags)
	circumstances *pl* [ˈsɜːkəmstənsɪz]	Umstände
	means [miːnz]	Mittel, Maßnahme
	promptly [ˈprɒmptli]	umgehend, unverzüglich, sofort
	to **assume responsibility** [əˌsjuːm rɪspɒnsəˈbɪləti]	die Verantwortung übernehmen
	loss [lɒs]	Verlust
	unless otherwise stated [ənles ˌʌðəwaɪz ˈsteɪtɪd]	sofern nicht anders angegeben
	due [djuː]	fällig
	to **cancel** [ˈkænsl]	*(Vertrag)* auflösen, annullieren
	cancellation [ˌkænsəˈleɪʃn]	*(Vertrag:)* Auflösung, Annullierung
	written [ˈrɪtn]	schriftlich
	statement [ˈsteɪtmənt]	Erklärung
	to **reject sth** [rɪˈdʒekt]	etw zurückweisen, etw beanstanden
100	to **acknowledge an order** [əkˌnɒlɪdʒ ən ˈɔːdə]	einen Auftrag bestätigen
	leather [ˈleðə]	Leder
	garment [ˈgɑːmənt]	Kleidungsstück
	fashion [ˈfæʃn]	Mode
	a/c (= account) [əˈkaʊnt]	Konto
	palletized [ˈpælətaɪzd]	auf Paletten, palettiert
	confirmation of order [kɒnfəˌmeɪʃn əv ˈɔːdə]	Auftragsbestätigung
	advice of dispatch [ədˌvaɪs əv dɪˈspætʃ]	Versandanzeige
	to **trust** [trʌst]	hoffen(, dass)
	punctually [ˈpʌŋktʃuəli]	pünktlich
101	**general purpose** [ˌdʒenrəl ˈpɜːpəs]	Allzweck-
	capacity [kəˈpæsəti]	Fassungsvermögen
	payload [ˈpeɪləʊd]	Zuladung, Nutzlast
	lb = pound [paʊnd]	Pfund *(ca. 454 g)*
	groupage consignment [ˈgruːpɪdʒ kənsaɪnmənt]	Sammelladung
	abbreviation [əˌbriːviˈeɪʃn]	Abkürzung
	inch [ɪntʃ]	Zoll *(ca. 2,54 cm)*
	validity [vəˈlɪdəti]	Gültigkeit
T	to **go bankrupt** [gəʊ ˈbæŋkrʌpt]	Pleite gehen
	quarterly settlement [ˌkwɔːtəli ˈsetlmənt]	vierteljährliche Abrechnung
	driver [ˈdraɪvə]	Fahrer/in
	investment [ɪnˈvestmənt]	Investition
	straight away [ˌstreɪt əˈweɪ]	sofort
102	**cash discount** [ˈkæʃ dɪskaʊnt]	Skonto
	trade discount [ˈtreɪd dɪskaʊnt]	Händlerrabatt
	sturdy [ˈstɜːdi]	stabil, robust
	carton [ˈkɑːtn]	Karton
	receipt of invoice [rɪˌsiːt əv ˈɪnvɔɪs]	Rechnungseingang
	currency sign [ˈkʌrənsi saɪn]	Währungssymbol
	tile [taɪl]	Fliese
103	**microbrewing equipment** [ˈmaɪkrəʊbruːɪŋ ɪkwɪpmənt]	Geräte für Klein(st)-brauereien
	application [ˌæplɪˈkeɪʃn]	*(Akkreditiv:)* Eröffnungsauftrag, Akkreditivauftrag
	documentary letter of credit (L/C) [dɒkjuˌmentri ˌletər əf ˈkredɪt]	Dokumentenakkreditiv
	negotiable [nɪˈgəʊʃiəbl]	begebbar
	transferable [trɑːnsˈfɜːrəbl]	übertragbar
	clean bill of lading [ˌkliːn ˌbɪl əv ˈleɪdɪŋ]	reines Konnossement
	foul bill of lading [ˌfaʊl ˌbɪl əv ˈleɪdɪŋ]	unreines Konnossement
	apparent [əˈpærənt]	anscheinend
	in good order and condition [ɪn gʊd ˌɔːdər ənd kənˈdɪʃn]	in einwandfreiem Zustand
	non-negotiable [ˌnɒn nɪˈgəʊʃiəbl]	nicht begebbar
	CMR document [ˌsiː em ˈɑː dɒkjumənt]	CMR-Frachtbrief
	truck waybill [ˈtrʌk weɪbɪl]	Lastwagenfrachtbrief
	multi-modal [ˌmʌlti ˈməʊdl]	multimodal
	to **prove sth** [pruːv]	etw nachweisen
	documentary credit transaction [dɒkjuˌmentri ˈkredɪt trænzækʃn]	Akkreditivgeschäft
	certificate of origin [səˌtɪfɪkət əv ˈɒrɪdʒɪn]	Ursprungszeugnis
	to **issue** [ˈɪʃuː]	*(Dokument)* ausstellen
	chamber of commerce [ˌtʃeɪmbər əv ˈkɒmɜːs]	Handelskammer
	to **assess sth** [əˈses]	*(Zollgebühren usw.)* ansetzen, berechnen
	packing list [ˈpækɪŋ lɪst]	Packliste
	bill of exchange [ˌbɪl əv ɪksˈtʃeɪndʒ]	Wechsel
	draft [drɑːft]	Tratte
104	**sign (of sth)** [saɪn]	Anzeichen (von etw)
	to **have sth in common** [həv ɪn ˈkɒmən]	etw gemeinsam haben
	to **calculate sth** [ˈkælkjuleɪt]	etw berechnen
	value [ˈvæljuː]	Wert
	to **present sb sth** [prɪˈzent]	jdm etw *(Dokument usw.)* vorlegen
	payable [ˈpeɪəbl]	zahlbar
	presentation [ˌpreznˈteɪʃn]	Vorlage *(eines Dokuments)*

	currency [ˈkʌrənsi]	Währung
	load [ləʊd]	Ladung
	to **split** [splɪt]	teilen
105	**file number** [ˈfaɪl nʌmbə]	Aktenzeichen
	applicant [ˈæplɪkənt]	*(Akkreditiv:)* Auftraggeber/in
	guarantor [ˌɡærənˈtɔː]	Bürge/Bürgin
	advising bank [ədˌvaɪzɪŋ ˈbæŋk]	avisierende Bank
	blank [blæŋk]	leer
	for account of sb [fər əˈkaʊnt əv]	auf jds Rechnung
	in favor of sb *AE* [ɪn ˈfeɪvər əv]	zu jds Gunsten, zugunsten von jdm
	beneficiary [ˌbenɪˈfɪʃəri]	Begünstigte/r
	expiration date [ˌekspəˈreɪʃn deɪt]	Verfallsdatum
	to **draw a draft** [ˌdrɔː ə ˈdrɑːft]	eine Tratte/einen Wechsel ziehen
	figure [ˈfɪɡə]	Ziffer
	covering [ˈkʌvərɪŋ]	Deckung
	to **specify sth** [ˈspesɪfaɪ]	etw (genau) angeben
	(at) sight [saɪt]	(bei) Vorlage
	partial shipment [ˌpɑːʃl ˈʃɪpmənt]	Teillieferung
	permitted [pəˈmɪtɪd]	erlaubt, gestattet
	transshipment [trænsˈʃɪpmənt]	Umladung
	taking in charge [ˌteɪkɪŋ ɪn ˈtʃɑːdʒ]	Übernahme
	merchandise [ˈmɜːtʃəndaɪs]	Ware
	microbrewery [ˈmaɪkrəʊbruːəri]	Klein(st)brauerei
	two-vessel brewhouse [tuː ˌvesl ˈbruːhaʊs]	Zweigerätesudhaus
	applicable [əˈplɪkəbl]	zutreffend
	insurance policy [ɪnˈʃʊərəns pɒləsi]	Versicherungspolice
	invoice value [ˈɪnvɔɪs væljuː]	Rechnungswert
	in duplicate [ɪn ˈdjuːplɪkət]	in zweifacher Ausfertigung
	to **effect sth** [ɪˈfekt]	etw ausführen, etw tätigen, etw erwirken
	war [wɔː]	Krieg
	full set [ˌfʊl ˈset]	vollständiger Satz *(von Dokumenten)*
	to **consign sth** [kənˈsaɪn]	etw übergeben
	to **notify sb** [ˈnəʊtɪfaɪ]	jdn in Kenntnis setzen, jdn benachrichtigen
	prepaid [priːˈpeɪd]	im Voraus bezahlt
	cover [ˈkʌvə]	Umschlag
	negotiating bank [nɪˌɡəʊʃieɪtɪŋ ˈbæŋk]	negoziierende Bank
	paying bank [ˌpeɪɪŋ ˈbæŋk]	ausführende Bank
	validation [ˌvælɪˈdeɪʃn]	Bestätigung
	to **authorize sb** [ˈɔːθəraɪz]	jdn ermächtigen, jdn bevollmächtigen
	by means of [baɪ ˈmiːnz əv]	mittels, durch
	to **debit** [ˈdebɪt]	*(Konto)* belasten, *(Geld)* abbuchen
	to **set forth** [ˌset ˈfɔːθ]	darlegen
	to **affect sth** [əˈfekt]	etw beeinflussen
	authorization [ˌɔːθəraɪˈzeɪʃn]	Ermächtigung, Vollmacht
	insufficient funds *pl* [ɪnsəˌfɪʃnt ˈfʌndz]	mangelnde Deckung, unzureichende Mittel
	setoff rights *pl* [ˈsetɒf raɪts]	Aufrechnungsrechte
	equity [ˈekwəti]	Billigkeit(srecht)
106	to **sail for …** [ˈseɪl fə]	nach … fahren
T	**Thank goodness!** [ˌθæŋk ˈɡʊdnəs]	Gott sei Dank!
	in time [ɪn ˈtaɪm]	rechtzeitig
	fire [ˈfaɪə]	Brand
	to **burn down** [ˌbɜːn ˈdaʊn]	niederbrennen
	to **warn sb** [wɔːn]	jdm (etw) sagen, jdn vorwarnen
	Incorporated (Inc.) [ɪnˈkɔːpəreɪtɪd]	GmbH
	instead [ɪnˈsted]	stattdessen
	to **release sth** [rɪˈliːs]	etw freigeben
	one way or another [ˌwʌn weɪ ɔːr əˈnʌðə]	so oder so
	to **give it a try** [ˌɡɪv ɪt ə ˈtraɪ]	es versuchen
	arrangements *pl* [əˈreɪndʒmənts]	Vereinbarungen, Abmachungen, Modalitäten
	formalities *pl* [fɔːˈmælətiz]	Formalitäten
	to **deal with sth** [ˈdiːl wɪð]	etw erledigen
	to **reroute sth** [riːˈruːt]	etw umleiten
	wooden crate [ˌwʊdn ˈkreɪt]	Holzkiste
	out of interest [aʊt əv ˈɪntrəst]	interessehalber
107	to **apply for sth** [əˈplaɪ fə]	etw beantragen
108	**dustproof** [ˈdʌstpruːf]	staubdicht
	waterproof [ˈwɔːtəpruːf]	wasserdicht
109	**battery-powered** [ˈbætəri paʊəd]	Akku-, batteriebetrieben

KMK Exam practice 5

110	**no matter what …** [nəʊ ˌmætə ˈwɒt]	ganz gleich, was …; egal, was …
	expertise [ˌekspəˈtiːz]	Fachwissen, Fachkenntnisse
	competitive advantage [kəmˌpetətɪv ədˈvɑːntɪdʒ]	Wettbewerbsvorteil
	challenging [ˈtʃælɪndʒɪŋ]	anspruchsvoll, fordernd
	to **evaluate sth** [ɪˈvæljueɪt]	etw einstufen
	thus [ðʌs]	auf diese Weise, so
	introductory level [ɪntrəˌdʌktəri ˈlevl]	Einstiegsniveau
	operational [ˌɒpəˈreɪʃənl]	Betriebs-, Arbeits-

	one-to-one [ˌwʌn tə ˈwʌn]	Einzel-
	quality-assured experts *pl* [ˌkwɒləti əʃʊəd ˈekspɜːts]	qualifiziertes Fachpersonal
	subject matter [ˈsʌbdʒɪkt mætə]	Materie, Unterrichtsstoff
	work pace [ˈwɜːk peɪs]	Arbeitstempo
	session [ˈseʃn]	Unterrichtseinheit
	to **return costs** [rɪˈtɜːn kɒsts]	Kosten erstatten
	partial(ly) [ˈpɑːʃl]	teilweise
	tax declaration [ˌtæks ˌdekləˈreɪʃn]	Steuererklärung
	increasingly [ɪnˈkriːsɪŋli]	zunehmend
	to **seek sth** [siːk]	etw suchen
	flexibility [ˌfleksəˈbɪləti]	Anpassungsfähigkeit, Flexibilität
	convenience [kənˈviːniəns]	Komfort
	cost-effectiveness [ˌkɒstɪˈfektɪvnəs]	Wirtschaftlichkeit
	provider [prəˈvaɪdə]	Anbieter
	return on investment [rɪˌtɜːn ɒn ɪnˈvestmənt]	Rendite, Ertrag
	to **time sth** [taɪm]	etw zeitlich abstimmen
	disruption (to sth) [dɪsˈrʌpʃn]	Störung (von etw)
	work schedule [ˈwɜːk ʃedjuːl]	Arbeitsablauf
	adaptable (to sth) [əˈdæptəbl]	anpassbar (an etw)
	shift [ʃɪft]	Schicht
	tailor-made (to sth) [ˌteɪləˈmeɪd]	individuell (auf etw) zugeschnitten
	tax-refundable [ˌtæks rɪˈfʌndəbl]	steuerlich absetzbar
	qualification offer [ˌkwɒlɪfɪˈkeɪʃn ɒfə]	Fortbildungsmaßnahme
	heterogeneous [ˌhetərəˈdʒiːniəs]	heterogen
	charges *pl* [ˈtʃɑːdʒɪz]	Gebühren, Kosten
	time savings *pl* [ˈtaɪm seɪvɪŋz]	Zeitersparnis
	comfort and relaxation [ˌkʌmfət ənd riːlækˈseɪʃn]	angenehme Atmosphäre
	to **strengthen** [ˈstreŋθn]	stärken
111 T	**answering machine** [ˈɑːnsərɪŋ məʃiːn]	Anrufbeantworter
	thermal insulation [ˌθɜːml ɪnsjuˈleɪʃn]	Wärmedämmung
	contact (person) [ˈkɒntækt]	Ansprechpartner/in
	to **consist of sth** [kənˈsɪst əv]	aus etw bestehen
	tenant [ˈtenənt]	Mieter
	frankly [ˈfræŋkli]	offen gesagt
	shabby [ˈʃæbi]	heruntergekommen, schäbig
	estate agent [ɪˈsteɪt eɪdʒənt]	Immobilienmakler/in
	facility manager [fəˈsɪləti mænɪdʒə]	Objektleiter/in, Gebäudeverwalter/in

UNIT 11

112	**appliance** [əˈplaɪəns]	(Elektro-)Gerät
	on arrival [ɒn əˈraɪvl]	bei Ankunft, bei Eintreffen
	majority [məˈdʒɒrəti]	Mehrheit, Großteil
	to **relate to sth** [rɪˈleɪt tə]	sich auf etw beziehen
113 T	**every so often** [ˌevri səʊ ˈɒfn]	hin und wieder
	every now and then [evri ˌnaʊ ən ˈðen]	ab und an
	in case [ɪn ˈkeɪs]	für den Fall, dass; falls
	no matter what … [nəʊ ˌmætə ˈwɒt]	ganz gleich, was …; egal, was …
	to **follow sth up** [ˌfɒləʊ ˈʌp]	etw nachbereiten, in einer Sache nachfassen
	record [ˈrekɔːd]	Aufzeichnung, Protokoll
	to **copy sb in** [ˌkɒpi ˈɪn]	*(E-Mail:)* jdn CC setzen
	order number [ˈɔːdə nʌmbə]	Bestellnummer, Auftragsnummer
	to **resolve sth** [rɪˈzɒlv]	etw lösen
	replacement [rɪˈpleɪsmənt]	Ersatz
	action [ˈækʃn]	Maßnahme(n)
	policy (on sth) [ˈpɒləsi]	Richtlinien (für etw)
	to **carry sth out** [ˌkæri ˈaʊt]	etw durchführen
	expectation [ˌekspekˈteɪʃn]	Erwartung
	interviewee [ˌɪntəvjuːˈiː]	Befragte/r
	acknowledgement [əkˈnɒlɪdʒmənt]	Eingeständnis, Würdigung
	as far as sth is concerned [əz fɑːr əz ɪz kənˈsɜːnd]	was etw betrifft
	apology [əˈpɒlədʒi]	Entschuldigung
	to **bring sth to the attention of sb** [brɪŋ tə ði əˈtenʃn əv]	jdn auf etw aufmerksam machen
	reimbursement [ˌriːɪmˈbɜːsmənt]	Rückerstattung
	compensation [ˌkɒmpənˈseɪʃn]	Entschädigung
	to **register sth** [ˈredʒɪstə]	etw melden, etw zum Ausdruck bringen
	satisfactory [ˌsætɪsˈfæktəri]	zufriedenstellend, befriedigend
	to **acknowledge sb** [əkˈnɒlɪdʒ]	jdn würdigen
	complainant [kəmˈpleɪnənt]	Beschwerdeführer/in
	to **reimburse sb** [ˌriːɪmˈbɜːs]	jdm Geld zurückzahlen, jdn entschädigen
	to **disappoint sb** [ˌdɪsəˈpɔɪnt]	jdn enttäuschen
	to **drive sb away** [ˌdraɪv əˈweɪ]	jdn vergraulen
114	**faulty** [ˈfɔːlti]	mangelhaft, defekt

smoke alarm ['sməʊk əlɑ:m] — Rauchmelder
since [sɪns] — seitdem
to **forward sth** ['fɔ:wəd] — etw weitersenden, etw verschicken
various ['veəriəs] — mehrere
to **discover sth** [dɪ'skʌvə] — etw feststellen
battery ['bætəri] — Batterie
mounting screw ['maʊntɪŋ skru:] — Befestigungsschraube
discoloured [dɪs'kʌləd] — verfärbt
to **execute** ['eksɪkju:t] — ausführen
whatever the case may be [wɒtevə ðə ˌkeɪs meɪ 'bi:] — wie dem auch sei
to **appreciate sth** [ə'pri:ʃieɪt] — etw verstehen, etw einsehen
to **replace sth** [rɪ'pleɪs] — etw ersetzen
entire [ɪn'taɪə] — gesamte/r/s, ganze/r/s
matter ['mætə] — Angelegenheit

115 **dissatisfied** [dɪs'sætɪsfaɪd] — unzufrieden
T to **point out** [ˌpɔɪnt 'aʊt] — darauf hinweisen(, dass …)
statutory ['stætʃətri] — gesetzlich vorgeschrieben
on our part [ɒn 'aʊə pɑ:t] — auf/von unserer Seite
meaning … ['mi:nɪŋ] — das heißt …
I assure you … [aɪ ə'ʃʊə ju:] — ich versichere Ihnen, …
free of charge [ˌfri: əf 'tʃɑ:dʒ] — unentgeltlich, kostenlos
carriage forward [ˌkærɪdʒ 'fɔ:wəd] — unfrei
to **cancel sth** ['kænsl] — etw stornieren
inconvenience [ˌɪnkən'vi:niəns] — Unannehmlichkeiten

to **distinguish** [dɪ'stɪŋgwɪʃ] — unterscheiden
warranty period ['wɒrənti pɪəriəd] — Gewährleistungszeit
to **rectify defects** [ˌrektɪfaɪ 'di:fekts] — Mängel beheben
it is assumed that … [ɪt ɪz ə'sju:md ðət] — es ist davon auszugehen, dass …
purchase ['pɜ:tʃəs] — Kauf
to **prove the opposite** [ˌpru:v ði 'ɒpəzɪt] — das Gegenteil beweisen
voluntary ['vɒləntri] — freiwillig
116 to **arrange sth** [ə'reɪndʒ] — etw anordnen, etw sortieren
carriage paid [ˌkærɪdʒ 'peɪd] — frachtfrei, franko
approval [ə'pru:vl] — Zustimmung
dismayed [dɪs'meɪd] — bestürzt
unsatisfactory [ˌʌnˌsætɪs'fæktəri] — unzulänglich
117 **quarterly statement** [ˌkwɔ:təli 'steɪtmənt] — Quartalsabrechnung
pottery ['pɒtəri] — Keramik
tableware ['teɪblweə] — Geschirr
discrepancy [dɪs'krepənsi] — Unstimmigkeit, Diskrepanz
crockery ['krɒkəri] — Geschirr
dinner service ['dɪnə sɜ:vɪs] — Tafelservice
teapot ['ti:pɒt] — Teekanne
clearance sale ['klɪərəns seɪl] — Ausverkauf
cutlery (set) ['kʌtləri] — Besteck
champagne [ʃæm'peɪn] — Champagner
flute [flu:t] — Flöte
to **overcharge sb** [ˌəʊvə'tʃɑ:dʒ] — jdm zu viel berechnen
statement ['steɪtmənt] — Abrechnung
amendment [ə'mendmənt] — Änderung, Berichtigung
as appropriate [əz ə'prəʊpriət] — je nachdem
118 to **query sth** ['kwɪəri] — etw infrage stellen, etw anzweifeln
records *pl* ['rekɔ:dz] — Unterlagen, Aufzeichnungen
credit note ['kredɪt nəʊt] — Gutschrift
in addition [ɪn ə'dɪʃn] — außerdem
tea service ['ti: sɜ:vɪs] — Teeservice
to **charge** [tʃɑ:dʒ] — *(Preis:)* berechnen
to **omit to do sth** [ə'mɪt] — es versäumen, etw zu tun
to **amend sth** [ə'mend] — etw ändern, etw berichtigen
to **remit** [rɪ'mɪt] — *(Geld)* überweisen
sum owing [ˌsʌm 'əʊɪŋ] — Forderung
query ['kwɪəri] — Frage, Rückfrage
term [tɜ:m] — Begriff
to **owe sb sth** [əʊ] — jdm etw schulden
procedure [prə'si:dʒə] — Vorgehen, Verfahren

T **mix-up** ['mɪks ʌp] — Durcheinander, Verwechslung
to **get to the bottom of sth** [get tu ðə 'bɒtəm əv] — etw herausfinden
to **deduct** [dɪ'dʌkt] — abziehen
to **type in sth** [ˌtaɪp 'ɪn] — etw eingeben, etw eintippen

120 **X-ray machine** ['eks reɪ məʃi:n] — Röntgengerät

T **dental clinic** [ˌdentl 'klɪnɪk] — Zahnklinik
scratched [skrætʃt] — verkratzt
dented ['dentɪd] — verbeult
casing ['keɪsɪŋ] — Gehäuse
to **get sth sorted** [ˌget 'sɔ:tɪd] — etw klären, sich um etw kümmern
disappointed [ˌdɪsə'pɔɪntɪd] — enttäuscht
business ['bɪznəs] — Angelegenheit, Sache

spelling ['spelɪŋ] — Schreibweise
container [kən'teɪnə] — Behälter
to **fulfil an order** [fʊlˌfɪl ən 'ɔ:də] — einen Auftrag abwickeln, eine Bestellung ausführen
121 **transcript** ['trænskrɪpt] — Mitschrift
record ['rekɔ:d] — Datensatz
I realize that. [aɪ 'rɪəlaɪz ðæt] — Das ist mir bewusst.

UNIT 12

122 **(job) application** [ˌæplɪ'keɪʃn] — Bewerbung

	to **apply for a job** [əˌplaɪ fər ə ˈdʒɒb]	sich um eine Stelle bewerben
	job agency [ˈdʒɒb eɪdʒənsi]	Arbeitsagentur, Arbeitsvermittlung
	experienced [ɪkˈspɪəriənst]	erfahren
T	**mixture** [ˈmɪkstʃə]	Mischung
	on one's own [ɒn wʌnz ˈəʊn]	alleine
	varied [ˈveərid]	vielfältig
123	to **develop** [dɪˈveləp]	(sich) entwickeln
	spreadsheet [ˈspredʃiːt]	Tabellenkalkulation, Tabelle
	job opportunities *pl* [dʒɒb ˌɒpəˈtjuːnətiz]	Arbeitsmöglichkeiten
	career prospects *pl* [kəˈrɪə prɒspekts]	berufliche Perspektiven
	sector [ˈsektə]	Bereich, Sektor
	to **pin sth to sth** [pɪn]	etw an etw heften
	CV (curriculum vitae) [ˌsiː ˈviː, kəˌrɪkjələm ˈviːtaɪ]	Lebenslauf
	standardized [ˈstændədaɪzd]	genormt
	self-assessment [ˌself əˈsesmənt]	Selbsteinstufung
	mobility [məʊˈbɪləti]	Freizügigkeit
	to **acquire sth** [əˈkwaɪə]	etw erlangen, etw erwerben
	certificate [səˈtɪfɪkət]	Zeugnis, Diplom
	supplement [ˈsʌplɪmənt]	Zusatz, Ergänzung
	agent [ˈeɪdʒənt]	zuständige/r Mitarbeiter/in
124	**job advert(isement)** [ˈdʒɒb ædvɜːt, ədvɜːtɪsmənt]	Stellenanzeige
	recruitment agency [rɪˈkruːtmənt eɪdʒənsi]	Personalvermittlung
125	**job title** [ˈdʒɒb taɪtl]	Stellenbezeichnung
	freight forwarding company [ˈfreɪt fɔːwədɪŋ kʌmpəni]	Spediteur, Spedition
	export customs entry [ˈekspɔːt kʌstəmz entri]	Ausfuhranmeldung
	to **classify** [ˈklæsɪfaɪ]	klassifizieren
	administrative work [ədˌmɪnɪstrətɪv ˈwɜːk]	Verwaltungstätigkeiten
	invoicing [ˈɪnvɔɪsɪŋ]	Fakturierung, Rechnungsstellung
	correspondence [ˌkɒrɪˈspɒndəns]	Schriftverkehr, Korrespondenz
	school leaving certificate [ˌskuːl liːvɪŋ səˈtɪfɪkət]	Schulabschluss
	fluent [ˈfluːənt]	*(Sprache:)* fließend
	to **take sb on** [ˌteɪk ˈɒn]	jdn einstellen, jdn übernehmen
	reference number [ˈrefərəns nʌmbə]	Aktenzeichen, Kennziffer
	exhibition [ˌeksɪˈbɪʃn]	Messe, Ausstellung
	accurate(ly) [ˈækjərət]	exakt, genau
	supervision [ˌsuːpəˈvɪʒn]	Aufsicht, Kontrolle
	continuous [kənˈtɪnjuəs]	ständig, kontinuierlich

	support [səˈpɔːt]	Betreuung
	opportunity [ˌɒpəˈtjuːnəti]	Gelegenheit, Möglichkeit
	follow-up education [ˌfɒləʊ ʌp edʒuˈkeɪʃn]	Weiterbildung
	promotion [prəˈməʊʃn]	Beförderung, Aufstieg
	candidate [ˈkændɪdət]	Bewerber/in
126	**(job) interview** [ˈɪntəvjuː]	Vorstellungsgespräch
	to **be shortlisted** [bi ˈʃɔːtlɪstɪd]	in die engere Auswahl kommen
	face-to-face [ˌfeɪs tə ˈfeɪs]	persönlich
T	**recruitment** [rɪˈkruːtmənt]	Einstellung, Anwerbung *(von Personal)*
	signal strength [ˈsɪgnəl streŋθ]	Signalstärke
	reminder function [rɪˈmaɪndə fʌŋkʃn]	Erinnerungsfunktion
	independent(ly) [ˌɪndɪˈpendənt]	unabhängig
	battery [ˈbætəri]	Akku
	post [pəʊst]	Posten, Stelle
	permission [pəˈmɪʃn]	Erlaubnis
	hard-working [ˌhɑːd ˈwɜːkɪŋ]	fleißig
	in particular [ɪn pəˈtɪkjələ]	ausgerechnet, gerade
	to **depend on sth** [dɪˈpend ɒn]	auf etw ankommen
	in a nutshell [ɪn ə ˈnʌtʃel]	kurz gesagt, mit einem Wort
	to **take the initiative** [ˌteɪk ði ɪˈnɪʃətɪv]	die Initiative ergreifen
	lack (of sth) [læk]	Mangel (an etw)
	traineeship [treɪˈniːʃɪp]	Ausbildung, Lehre
	link [lɪŋk]	Zusammenhang, Verbindung
	to **make a contribution** [ˌmeɪk ə ˌkɒntrɪˈbjuːʃn]	einen Beitrag leisten
	to **post sb to …** [ˈpəʊst tə]	jdn nach … versetzen
	role model [ˈrəʊl mɒdl]	Vorbild
	to **gather sth** [ˈgæðə]	etw zusammenstellen
	to **flick through sth** [ˈflɪk θruː]	etw durchblättern
	pile [paɪl]	Stapel, Haufen
	landline [ˈlændlaɪn]	Festnetz(telefon)
	to **charge** [tʃɑːdʒ]	*(Akku)* aufladen
	to **concentrate** [ˈkɒnsntreɪt]	sich konzentrieren
	appropriately [əˈprəʊpriətli]	angemessen
	to **meet sb's needs** [ˌmiːt ˈniːdz]	jds Bedürfnissen entsprechen, jds Anforderungen erfüllen
127	**clarification** [ˌklærɪfɪˈkeɪʃn]	Klärung, Erläuterung
P	**(job) vacancy** [ˈveɪkənsi]	offene Stelle
	applicant [ˈæplɪkənt]	Bewerber/in
	point of view [ˌpɔɪnt əv ˈvjuː]	Sicht, Perspektive
	to **justify** [ˈdʒʌstɪfaɪ]	rechtfertigen, begründen
T	**stage** [steɪdʒ]	Phase, Abschnitt

	to calm down [ˌkɑːm ˈdaʊn]	sich beruhigen
	Not particularly. [ˌnɒt pəˈtɪkjələli]	Eigentlich nicht.
	confident(ly) [ˈkɒnfɪdənt]	selbstbewusst
	to shake hands with sb [ˌʃeɪk ˈhændz wɪð]	jdm die Hand geben
	shy [ʃaɪ]	schüchtern
	habit [ˈhæbɪt]	Gewohnheit
	to get into the habit of doing sth [ˌget ɪntə ðə ˈhæbɪt əv]	sich daran gewöhnen, etw zu tun
	panel [ˈpænl]	Gremium
	to relate sth to sth [rɪˈleɪt tə]	etw auf etw beziehen
	to clarify sth [ˈklærəfaɪ]	etw erläutern
	slight(ly) [slaɪt]	geringfügig, etwas
	future prospects *pl* [ˌfjuːtʃə ˈprɒspekts]	Zukunftsperspektiven
	to occur to sb [əˈkɜː tə]	jdm einfallen
	concerning sth [kənˈsɜːnɪŋ]	etw betreffend
	firm handshake [ˌfɜːm ˈhændʃeɪk]	fester Händedruck
	to put sth to good use [pʊt tə ˌgʊd ˈjuːs]	etw sinnvoll nutzen
P	**to progress** [prəˈgres]	vorankommen
128	**mixed up** [ˌmɪkst ˈʌp]	durcheinander
	ability [əˈbɪləti]	Fähigkeit
	set [set]	vorgegeben, starr, fest
	to grab sb's attention [ˌgræb əˈtenʃn]	jds Aufmerksamkeit fesseln
	motivated [ˈməʊtɪveɪtɪd]	motiviert
	trade industry [ˈtreɪd ɪndəstri]	Handelsbranche
	reverse order [rɪˌvɜːs ˈɔːdə]	umgekehrte Reihenfolge
	chronological [ˌkrɒnəˈlɒdʒɪkl]	chronologisch
	employment [ɪmˈplɔɪmənt]	Beschäftigung, Anstellung
	achievement [əˈtʃiːvmənt]	Leistung
	driving licence [ˈdraɪvɪŋ laɪsns]	Führerschein
	socializing [ˈsəʊʃəlaɪzɪŋ]	Ausgehen
	data protection [ˈdeɪtə prətekʃn]	Datenschutz
	referee [ˌrefəˈriː]	Referenz(geber/in)
129	**to seek sth** [siːk]	etw suchen
	accountancy [əˈkaʊntənsi]	Buchführung
	economics [ˌiːkəˈnɒmɪks]	Wirtschaft
	native speaker [ˌneɪtɪv ˈspiːkə]	Muttersprachler/in
	tourist board [ˈtʊərɪst bɔːd]	Fremdenverkehrsamt
	to interact with sb [ˌɪntərˈækt wɪð]	mit jdm kommunizieren
	first aid [ˌfɜːst ˈeɪd]	Erste Hilfe
	athletics [æθˈletɪks]	Leichtathletik
130	**dispatch** [dɪˈspætʃ]	Versand
	confident [ˈkɒnfɪdənt]	selbstbewusst
	personable [ˈpɜːsnəbl]	umgänglich, sympathisch
	flexible [ˈfleksəbl]	flexibel
	atmosphere [ˈætməsfɪə]	Atmosphäre
131	**particularly** [pəˈtɪkjələli]	insbesondere
	to be keen to do sth [bɪ ˈkiːn tə]	jdm liegt sehr daran, etw zu tun
	to apply sth [əˈplaɪ]	etw anwenden
	on a daily basis [ɒn ə ˌdeɪli ˈbeɪsɪs]	täglich, jeden Tag

KMK Exam practice 6

132	**to be up to standard** [bi ˌʌp tə ˈstændəd]	den Anforderungen entsprechen
	workwear [ˈwɜːkweə]	Arbeitskleidung
	see below [ˌsiː bɪˈləʊ]	siehe unten
	crushed [krʌʃt]	eingedrückt
	stained [steɪnd]	fleckig
	forwarding agent [ˈfɔːwədɪŋ eɪdʒənt]	Spediteur, Spedition
	parcel [ˈpɑːsl]	Paket
	accidentally [ˌæksɪˈdentəli]	versehentlich
133	**visual inspection** [ˌvɪʒuəl ɪnˈspekʃn]	Sichtprüfung
	rough handling [ˌrʌf ˈhændlɪŋ]	unsanfte Behandlung
	surplus [ˈsɜːpləs]	überschüssig
	dial [ˈdaɪəl]	*(Uhr:)* Zifferblatt
	alarm clock [əˈlɑːm klɒk]	Wecker

A–Z word list

Dieses Wörterverzeichnis enthält alle neuen Wörter aus *Trade Matters – 4th Edition* in alphabetischer Reihenfolge. Nicht angeführt sind Wörter, die zum Grundwortschatz (*Basic word list*) gehören. Die Zahl nach dem Stichwort bezieht sich auf die Seite, auf der das Wort zum ersten Mal erscheint. Wörter aus den Hörverständnisübungen sind zusätzlich mit einem **T** (Transkript) und Wörter aus den *Partner files* mit einem **P** gekennzeichnet.

A

A levels *pl* *6* Abitur, Abiturfächer
abbreviation *101* Abkürzung
ability *128* Fähigkeit
above-mentioned *90* obengenannt
absentee *55T* Abwesende/r
academic *11* akademisch, Universitäts-, universitär
acceptable *9* zulässig, akzeptabel
access *68T* Zugang, Zutritt
to **access sth** *45* auf etw zugreifen; *86* etw erreichen
accessible *69* zugänglich, erreichbar
accident *75* Unfall
accidentally *132* versehentlich
accommodation *74* Unterkunft, Unterbringung
according to *15* gemäß, entsprechend, zufolge
account *100* Konto; **for ~ of sb** *105* auf jds Rechnung; **open ~** *77T* offenes Zahlungsziel
accountancy *129* Buchführung
accounting *18* Buchhaltung; **~ manager** *19* Buchhaltungsleiter/in
accounts *16* Buchhaltung
accurate(ly) *125* exakt, genau
to **achieve** *34* *(Ziel)* erreichen
achievement *128* Leistung
to **acknowledge: ~ sb** *113* jdn würdigen; **~ an order** *100* einen Auftrag bestätigen
acknowledgement *113* Eingeständnis, Würdigung
acquaintance, business ~ *77T* Geschäftsfreund/in
to **acquire sth** *123* etw erlangen, etw erwerben; *43* etw kaufen
to **act as sth** *56T* als etw fungieren
action *113T* Maßnahme(n)
to **adapt: ~ sth** *61P* etw anpassen, etw abändern; **~ to sb/sth** *72* sich an jdn/etw anpassen, sich an jdn/etw gewöhnen
adaptable (to sth) *110* anpassbar (an etw)
addition: ~ (to sth) *89* Neuheit; **in ~** *118* außerdem; **in ~ to sth** *70* zusätzlich zu etw
additional *42T* zusätzlich
adjustable *72T* verstellbar
administration *14* Verwaltung; **business ~** *11* Betriebswirtschaft
administrative work *125* Verwaltungstätigkeiten
advance, in ~ *55T* im Voraus
advanced *11* fortgeschritten, weiterführend
advantage, competitive ~ *110* Wettbewerbsvorteil
adventure *24* Abenteuer
to **advertise sth** *49* etw bewerben, für etw Werbung machen
advertising *45* Werbung; **stealth ~** *49* heimliche Werbung, Schleichwerbung; **targeted ~** *49* gezielte/zielgruppengenaue Werbung; **~ campaign** *45* Werbekampagne
advertisement, job ~ *124* Stellenanzeige
advice of dispatch *100* Versandanzeige
to **advise** *35T* (jdm etw) raten
to **advise: ~ sb** *38* jdn beraten; **~ sb to do sth** *38* jdm raten, etw zu tun
advising bank *105* avisierende Bank
to **affect sth** etw beeinflussen
affected, to **be ~ by sth** *43* von etw betroffen sein
to **afford sth** *48* sich etw leisten (können)
after-sales service *39* Kundendienst
age, for ~s *74T* eine Ewigkeit
agency, job ~ *122* Arbeitsagentur, Arbeitsvermittlung; **recruitment ~** *124* Personalvermittlung
agenda *28T* Programm, Tagesordnung
agent *33* Vermittler/in, Zwischenhändler/in; *56T* Vertreter/in; *123* zuständige/r Mitarbeiter/in; **estate ~** *111T* Immobilienmakler/in; **forwarding ~** *132* Spedition; **shipping ~** *92* Spediteur
to **agree: ~ sth** *19T* etw vereinbaren; *50* sich auf etw einigen, etw beschließen; **~ thoroughly with sb** *56T* voll und ganz einer Meinung mit jdm sein
agreement *88* Vereinbarung; **exclusive ~** *43* Exklusivvertrag
aid *29* Hilfsmittel; **visual ~s** *pl* *31* visuelle Hilfsmittel; **first ~** *129* Erste Hilfe
to **aim: ~ to do sth** *55T* beabsichtigen, etw zu tun; etw tun wollen; **~ at sth** *65T* etw zum Ziel haben
air-conditioned *74* klimatisiert
air conditioning *75* Klimaanlage, Klimatisierung
airline *24* Fluggesellschaft
air waybill *82* Luftfrachtbrief
airy *15* luftig
aisle *66T* (Mittel-)Gang
alarm clock *133* Wecker
ale *70* *brit. Biersorte*
allowed *9* zulässig
all the best *41* *(Brief:)* Viele Grüße
alongside, to **work ~ sb** *26T* mit jdm arbeiten
to **amend sth** *118* etw ändern, etw berichtigen
amendment *117* Änderung, Berichtigung
ample space *28T* genügend Platz
to **analyze** *17T* analysieren
anger *71* Verärgerung
angle *37* Winkel
to **announce** *40* ankündigen
annoyed, to **get ~ about sth** *87* sich über etw ärgern
annual *59* jährlich
anonymous *77T* anonym
answering machine *111T* Anrufbeantworter
any other business (AOB) *55T* *(Tagesordnung:)* Verschiedenes
to **apologize** *63* sich entschuldigen
apology *113* Entschuldigung
apparent *103* anscheinend
appealing *25* ansprechend
to **appear** *40* vorkommen, auftauchen; *66T* wirken, scheinen
appearance *9* Erscheinungsbild, Auftreten
appliance *112* (Elektro-)Gerät
applicable *105* zutreffend; **~ charges** *pl* *94* anfallende Gebühren
applicant *127P* Bewerber/in; *105* *(Akkreditiv:)* Auftraggeber/in
application *40* Antrag, Bewerbung; *103* *(Akkreditiv:)* Eröffnungsauftrag, Akkreditivauftrag
to **apply: ~ sth** *131* etw anwenden; **~ for sth** *107* etw beantragen; **~ for a job** *122* sich um eine Stelle bewerben
appointment *72* Termin

to **appreciate sth** *96T* etw zu schätzen wissen; *114* etw verstehen, etw einsehen
apprentice *6* Auszubildende/r, Lehrling
apprenticeship *6* Lehre, Ausbildung
approach *46T* Ansatz, Herangehensweise, Vorgehen
to **approach sth** *72* an etw herangehen, etw angehen
appropriate *31* angemessen, passend; **as ~** *117* je nachdem
approval *116* Zustimmung
approximately *28* ungefähr, zirka
architect *68T* Architekt/in
architecture *68* Architektur
to **arrange sth** *116* etw anordnen, etw sortieren
arrangements *pl* *106* Vereinbarungen, Abmachungen, Modalitäten; **business ~** *60T* Modalitäten; to **make ~** *54* Vorbereitungen treffen
array of products *86* Produktangebot
arrival *74T* Ankunft; **on ~** *112* bei Ankunft, bei Eintreffen
article *27* Artikel
artist *24* Künstler/in
arts *pl*: **martial ~** *38T* Kampfsport; **~ and crafts** *pl* *86* Kunsthandwerk
aspect *67* Gesichtspunkt, Seite, Aspekt
to **assemble** *28T* montieren, zusammenbauen
assembly *16* Montage; **~ hall** *26T* Montagehalle
to **assess sth** *103* *(Zollgebühren usw.)* ansetzen, berechnen
assessment *11* Beurteilung, Bewertung, Einschätzung, Urteil
assessor *11* Betreuer/in, Gutachter/in
assignment *18* Auftrag, Aufgabe
to **assist sb** *79T* jdm helfen, jdn unterstützen
assistance *40* Hilfe, Unterstützung
associate, business ~ *63* Geschäftspartner/in
to **associate sth with sth** *77T* etw mit etw in Verbindung bringen
association *63P* Verband
to **assume: it is ~ed that …** *115* es ist davon auszugehen, dass …; **sb can be ~ed to do sth** *98* es kann davon ausgegangen werden, dass jd etw tut; **~ responsibility** *99* die Verantwortung übernehmen
assurance, quality ~ *18* Qualitätssicherung
to **assure: I ~ you …** *115T* ich versichere Ihnen, …
athletics *129* Leichtathletik
atmosphere *130* Atmosphäre
to **attach** *40* *(E-Mail:)* anhängen
attached, to **be ~ to sth** *15T* mit etw verbunden sein
attachment *55T* *(E-Mail:)* Anhang
attendee *57* Teilnehmer/in
attention *50* Aufmerksamkeit; *85* Beachtung; **for the ~ of** *85* zu Händen; to **bring sth to the ~ of sb** *113* jdn auf etw aufmerksam machen; to **draw sb's ~ to sth** *35T* jds Aufmerksamkeit auf etw lenken; to **grab sb's ~** *128* jds Aufmerksamkeit fesseln; **~ line** *84* Zeile „zu Händen"
attire *31* Kleidung
attitude (to sth) *77* Einstellung (zu etw)
to **attract: ~ sb** *46* jdn anlocken, jdn ansprechen, jdn anziehen; **~ sb to sth** *67* jdn zu etw locken
to **attribute sth to sb** *86* jdm etw zuschreiben
audience *29* Publikum
authority *98* Befugnis, Vollmacht
authorization *105* Ermächtigung, Vollmacht
to **authorize sb** *105* jdn ermächtigen, jdn bevollmächtigen
availability *8* Verfügbarkeit
available *37* erhältlich, verfügbar
average, below-~ *34* unterdurchschnittlich
to **avoid** *13* vermeiden
to **award sb sth** *64* jdm etw *(Preis usw.)* verleihen
aware, to **make sb ~ of sth** *33* jdn auf etw aufmerksam machen
awareness *71* Bewusstsein, Sensibilität; **brand ~** *68* Bekanntheitsgrad einer Marke

B

back, to **turn one's ~ on sb** *31* jdm den Rücken zuwenden
backdrop *69* Messewand
background *28T* Hintergrund; *71* Herkunft
backpack *89* Rucksack
balloon, gas ~ *24* Gasballon
bank, advising ~ *105* avisierende Bank; **negotiating ~** *105* negoziierende Bank; **paying ~** *105* ausführende Bank
bankrupt, to **go ~** *101T* Pleite gehen
bankruptcy *25* Konkurs
bar: ~ chart *52* Säulendiagramm; **~ table** *68T* Stehtisch
barbecue *90* Grill
bargaining, collective wage ~ *77* Tarifverhandlungen
barrier *24* Hindernis
base, customer ~ *86* Kundenstamm
based, to **be ~ in …** *13* seinen Sitz in … haben, in … sein
basic price *91T* Grundpreis
basis, on a daily ~ *131* täglich, jeden Tag
bath *35T* Badewanne
bathtub *35T* Badewanne
battery *114* Batterie; *126T* Akku; **~-powered** *109* Akku-, batteriebetrieben
beaker *67* Becher
bean, cocoa ~ *54* Kakaobohne
to **bear sth** *81* etw *(Risiko, Kosten)* tragen
because of sth *59* wegen etw
beginning, from the ~ *86* von Anfang an
behaviour *72* Verhalten, Benehmen
behalf, on ~ of sb *20* für jdn, in jds Namen; **on sb's ~** *93* für jdn
below: see ~ *132* siehe unten; **~-average** *34* unterdurchschnittlich
belt *38T* Band
bench, weight ~ *37* Hantelbank
beneficiary *105* Begünstigte/r
to **benefit sb** *33* jdm nützen
benefit *15T* Vorteil, Nutzen
benefits *pl* *8* Zusatzleistungen, Sozialleistungen
bespoke *68* maßgeschneidert
best, all the ~ *41* *(Brief:)* Viele Grüße
best-selling *72T* meistverkauft
beverage *70* Getränk
beyond, and ~ *46* und darüber hinaus
bill of exchange *103* Wechsel;
bill of lading (B/L) *82* Konnossement; **clean ~** *103* reines Konnossement; **foul ~** *103* unreines Konnossement
billion *24* Milliarde
birth, place of ~ *12* Geburtsort
bit, to **do one's ~** *77* seinen Beitrag leisten
bites *pl* *70* Häppchen
blackboard *19* Wandtafel
blank *105* leer
block release *6* Blockunterricht *(an der Berufsschule)*
blouse *9* Bluse
blue-collar workers *pl* *53* Arbeiter
board, to **come on ~** *56T* an Bord kommen; **~ of directors** *17T* Vorstand; **tourist ~** *129* Fremdenverkehrsamt
body *84* *(Brief:)* Haupttext; *91T* Gehäuse, Gestell; **~ (of a can)** *26T* Dosenrumpf, Dosenkörper; **~ language** *31* Körpersprache
booked up *81T* ausgebucht

to **boost sth** 45 etw ankurbeln, etw erhöhen
booth 32 (Messe-)Stand
bottom, to **get to the ~ of sth** 118T etw herausfinden; **~ line** 46T das, worauf es ankommt
bouncy castle 39 Hüpfburg
bowl, rice ~ 61P Reisschale
box-shaped 68 kastenförmig
to **brainstorm** 8 Ideen sammeln
branch 6 Niederlassung, Filiale
brand 24 Marke; **~ awareness** 68 Bekanntheitsgrad einer Marke; **~ name** 24 Markenname
branding 46T Markenbildung
to **break: ~ down** 59T *(Auto:)* eine Panne haben, liegen bleiben; **~ sth down** 45 etw aufschlüsseln, etw aufgliedern; **~ out** 24 ausbrechen
break, to **take a ~** 10T eine Pause machen; **lunch ~** 53 Mittagspause; **morning ~** 8T Frühstückspause
breakable 81T zerbrechlich
to **brew** 70 *(Tee, Kaffee:)* kochen
brewery 56 Brauerei
brewhouse, two-vessel ~ 105 Zweigerätesudhaus
brewing equipment 56 Brauanlage(n)
bricks and mortar outlet 46T stationäres Geschäft
brief 26T kurz, knapp; **product ~** 46 Produktbeschreibung
broadcast 50 (Radio-)Sendung
brochure 35T Broschüre, Prospekt; **glossy ~** 65T Hochglanzbroschüre
bubble, speech ~ 37 Sprechblase
budget 17T Etat, Budget
buffet 63P Büfett; **~ breakfast** 75T Frühstücksbüfett
built-in 91T eingebaut
bulk, in ~ 33 en gros, in großen Mengen; **~ order** 96T Großauftrag, Großbestellung
to **burn down** 106T niederbrennen
burner 91T Brenner, Flamme
business 120T Angelegenheit, Sache; **any other ~ (AOB)** 55T *(Tagesordnung:)* Verschiedenes; **core ~** 42 Kerngeschäft; **family ~** 8T Familienunternehmen; **terms** *pl* **of ~** 59 Konditionen; to **enter the railway ~** 24 ins Bahngeschäft einsteigen; to **take ~ away from sb** 24 jdm das Wasser abgraben; **~ acquaintance** 77T Geschäftsfreund/in; **~ administration** 11 Betriebswirtschaft; **~ arrangements** *pl* 60T Modalitäten; **~ associate** 63 Geschäftspartner/in; **~ card** 31 Visitenkarte; **~ objective** 43 Unternehmensziel; **~ partner** 24 Geschäftspartner/in; **~ trip** 8 Geschäftsreise; **~ venture** 24 Unternehmen, Geschäftsvorhaben
businessman 24 Geschäftsmann
buyer 11 Einkäufer/in; 39 Käufer/in
buying power 43 Kaufkraft
by the way 10T übrigens

C

to **calculate sth** 104 etw berechnen
calculation 96 Berechnung, Kalkulation
call, to **return a ~** 22T zurückrufen; to **take a ~** 20 ein Gespräch entgegennehmen
to **call: ~ on sb** 79 jdn besuchen, bei jdm vorbeischauen; **~ back** 20 zurückrufen; **~ a meeting** 66 eine Sitzung einberufen
to **calm down** 127T sich beruhigen
campaign 50 (Werbe-)Kampagne; **advertising ~** 45 Werbekampagne
can 26T (Konserven-)Dose; **~ body** 26T Dosenrumpf, Dosenkörper; **~ end** 26T Dosendeckel
can-making 78 Dosenherstellung
to **cancel** 63 *(Termin)* absagen; 99 *(Vertrag)* auflösen, annullieren; 115T stornieren
cancellation 99 *(Vertrag:)* Auflösung, Annullierung
candidate 125 Bewerber/in
canning 16 Konservenherstellung
capacity 101 Fassungsvermögen
capital 42 Kapital
caption 51 Bildunterschrift
carbon footprint 77 CO_2-Fußabdruck
care, to **handle sth with ~** 15 etw mit Vorsicht behandeln; to **take ~ of sth** 40 sich um etw kümmern, etw bearbeiten, etw erledigen
career 11 (berufliche) Laufbahn, Karriere; **~ prospects** *pl* 123 berufliche Perspektiven
carriage 80 Transport, Beförderung, Fracht; **contract of ~** 80 Beförderungsvertrag, Frachtvertrag; **main ~** 80 Hauptlauf; **post-~** 80 Nachlauf; **pre-~** 80 Vorlauf; **~ forward** 115T unfrei; **~ paid** 116 frachtfrei , franko
carrier 81 Spediteur, Reederei, Transportunternehmen
to **carry sth out** 113 etw durchführen
carton 102 Karton
case, in ~ 113T für den Fall, dass; falls; **in that ~** 20T in diesem Fall; **whatever the ~ may be** 114 wie dem auch sei; **worst-~ scenario** 59 schlimmster anzunehmender Fall; **~ study** 83 Fallstudie
cash 50T Bargeld; **~ discount** 102 Skonto; **~ with order (CWO)** 61P Vorkasse
cashier 45 Kassierer/in
casing 120T Gehäuse
cast iron 91T Gusseisen
castle, bouncy ~ 39 Hüpfburg
catalogue 33 Katalog; **~ price** 35T Listenpreis, Katalogpreis
catchphrase 51 Schlagwort, Slogan
to **catch sth** 20T etw verstehen, etw mitbekommen
category 47 Kategorie, Klasse
to **cater for sth** 70 für etw *(Veranstaltung usw.)* Speisen und Getränke liefern
catering 68 Verpflegung
cathedral 35T Dom, Kathedrale
cause, good ~ 49 gute Sache, guter Zweck
celebrity 50 Prominente/r; **~ endorsement** 49 Werbung mit Prominenten
cell (phone) *AE* 72T Handy
central station 50T Hauptbahnhof
CEO (Chief Executive Officer) 54 Vorstandsvorsitzende/r, Geschäftsführer/in
certificate 123 Zeugnis, Diplom; **insurance ~** 82 Versicherungsschein; **school leaving ~** 125 Schulabschluss; **~ of origin** 103 Ursprungszeugnis
chain 19 Kette; **supply ~** 43 Lieferkette
to **chair a meeting** 55T eine Sitzung leiten
chairman 24 Vorstandsvorsitzende/r
challenging 110 anspruchsvoll, fordernd
chamber of commerce 103 Handelskammer
champagne 117 Champagner
to **change hands** 33 den Besitzer wechseln
change of plan 40 Planänderung
channel 33 Kanal; **distribution ~** 33 Vertriebsweg, Vertriebskanal; **marketing ~** 43 Absatzweg, Vertriebskanal; **sales ~** 46T Absatzweg, Vertriebskanal; **television ~** 65T Fernsehsender
character 47 Zeichen
charcoal 90 Holzkohle
to **charge** 118 *(Preis:)* berechnen; 126 *(Akku)* aufladen; **~ sb sth** 91T etw *(Preis usw.)* von jdm verlangen; **~ a fee** 83 eine Gebühr verlangen
charge 70P Gebühr; 92 Kosten; **applicable ~es** *pl* 94 anfallende Gebühren; to **be in ~ of sth** 17 für etw zuständig/verantwortlich sein; **free of ~**

115T unentgeltlich, kostenlos; **packing ~** *60* Verpackungskosten; **taking in ~** *105* Übernahme
chargeable, sth is ~ at £20 *70* für etwas werden 20£ berechnet
charger *67* Ladegerät
charges *pl* *110* Gebühren, Kosten
chart *52* Diagramm; **bar ~** *52* Säulendiagramm; **flow ~** *19* Flussdiagramm; **organization ~** *16* Organigramm; **pie ~** *52* Tortendiagramm
chat *39* Plauderei, (informelles) Gespräch
to **check: ~ sth against sth** *57* etw mit etw abgleichen; **~ in** *75* sich anmelden, einchecken; **~ out** *75* sich abmelden, auschecken
check, credit ~ *77T* Bonitätsprüfung
check-out *45* Kasse
to **cheer sb on** *50T* jdn anfeuern, jdm zujubeln
child labour *77* Kinderarbeit
chronological *128* chronologisch
circle *25* Kreis
to **circulate sth** *55T* etw (an alle) verteilen
circumstances *pl* *99* Umstände
claim, to **make a ~** *77T* einen Anspruch / eine Forderung geltend machen
clarification *127* Klärung, Erläuterung
to **clarify** *96* klären, abklären; **~ sth** *127T* etw erläutern
clarity *25* Klarheit, Deutlichkeit
to **classify** *125* klassifizieren
clean bill of lading *103* reines Konnossement
to **clean sth up** *50T* etw säubern
to **clear: ~ up** *8T* aufräumen; **~ a space** *15T* einen Platz räumen
clearance, export ~ *80* Ausfuhrabfertigung; **import ~** *80* Einfuhrabfertigung; **~ sale** *117* Ausverkauf
clerk, export ~ *40* Außenhandelskaufmann/-frau
client *77T* Kunde/Kundin
clientele *51* Kundschaft, Klientel
to **climb** *52* ansteigen
climb *52* Anstieg
clinic *84* Klinik; **dental ~** *120T* Zahnklinik; **healthcare ~** *24* Klinik; **outpatient ~** *85* Ambulanz
to **clock in/out** *8T* ein-/ausstempeln
close, complimentary ~ *41* *(Brief:)* Schlussformel
closed *25* geschlossen; **semi-~** *69* halbgeschlossen; **~ wagon** *94* geschlossener Waggon
closely, to **look ~ at sth** *35T* sich etw genau ansehen
clothing *44* Kleidung; **~ industry** *11* Kleidungsbranche
CMR document *103* CMR-Frachtbrief
coat *13* Jacke, Mantel
cocoa bean *54* Kakaobohne
to **coincide with sth** *43* mit etw übereinstimmen, mit etw zusammenfallen
collar, blue-~ workers *pl* *53* Arbeiter; **white-~ workers** *pl* *53* Angestellte
to **collect sth** *81* etw abholen
collective wage bargaining *77* Tarifverhandlungen
colourful *29* bunt, farbenfroh
to **come** *37* *(Ware:)* erhältlich sein; **~ across** *30* wirken; **~ up** *54* bevorstehen; **~ up with sth** *51* sich etw einfallen lassen; **Something has ~ up.** *63T* Es/Mir/Uns ist etwas dazwischen gekommen.; **~ on board** *56T* an Bord kommen; **C~ to think of it ...** *8T* Wenn ich es mir recht/genau überlege ...
comfort and relaxation *110* angenehme Atmosphäre
to **comment** *56T* kommentieren, einen Kommentar abgeben
commerce *7* Handel, Wirtschaft; **chamber of ~** *103* Handelskammer
commercial: ~ director *16* kaufmännische/r Leiter/in; **~ invoice** *82* Handelsrechnung; **~ use** *35T* gewerbliche Nutzung, gewerblicher Gebrauch
to **commission sth** *68* etw in Auftrag geben
common, to **have sth in ~** *104* etw gemeinsam haben
to **communicate** *15T* kommunizieren
community, sense of ~ *15T* Gemeinschaftssinn
company, in-~ *7* betriebsintern; **parent ~** *28* Muttergesellschaft; **shipping ~** *79T* Reederei; **trading ~** *42* Handelsunternehmen; **training ~** *6* Ausbildungsbetrieb; **private limited ~ (Ltd)** *24* Gesellschaft mit beschränkter Haftung (GmbH); **public limited ~ (plc)** *24* Aktiengesellschaft (AG); **~ car** *8* Firmenwagen
compensation *113* Entschädigung
competition *61* Wettbewerb; **stiff ~** *59* harter Wettbewerb
competitive *59* konkurrenzfähig; *61P* *(Preis:)* günstig; **~ advantage** *110* Wettbewerbsvorteil
competitor *39* Wettbewerber/in, Konkurrent/in
to **complain** *57* sich beklagen, sich beschweren
complainant *113* Beschwerdeführer/in
complaint *56T* Reklamation, Beschwerde
compliant, to **be ~ with sth** *23* etw *(Norm usw.)* erfüllen, etw *(Vorschrift usw.)* einhalten
complimentary close *41* *(Brief:)* Schlussformel
to **comply with sth** *77* etw *(Norm usw.)* erfüllen, etw *(Vorschrift usw.)* einhalten
component *16* Bestandteil, Bauteil
compound *47* zusammengesetzt
computer studies *pl* *6T* Informatik
computerized *12* Computer-
to **concentrate (on sth)** *15T* sich (auf etw) konzentrieren
concerned, as far as sth is ~ *113* was etw betrifft
concerning sth *127T* etw betreffend
to **conclude: ~ sth** *26T* etw beschließen, etw beenden; **to ~** *56T* abschließend
conclusion *29* Schluss
condition *6* Bedingung; *79T* Zustand; **in good order and ~** *103* in einwandfreiem Zustand; **terms and ~s** *pl* *77T* Allgemeine Geschäftsbedingungen; **special ~s** *pl* *88* Sonderkonditionen
to **conduct sth** *8* etw durchführen
conference *52* Tagung, Konferenz; **~ centre** *74* Tagungszentrum, Kongresszentrum; **~ room** *26T* Besprechungsraum, Sitzungssaal
confident *130* selbstbewusst
confident(ly) *127T* selbstbewusst
to **confirm** *20* bestätigen
confirmation *84* Bestätigung; **~ of order** *100* Auftragsbestätigung; **subject to ~** *88* vorbehaltlich einer Bestätigung, freibleibend
confirmed, irrevocable and ~ documentary letter of credit *82* unwiderrufliches und bestätigtes Dokumentenakkreditiv
to **connect (to/with sth)** *20T* (mit etw) verbinden, (an etw) anschließen
connectivity *37* Anschluss, Anschlüsse, Verbindung
conscience *51* Gewissen
conscious, environmentally ~ *51* umweltbewusst
consequence *48* Folge, Konsequenz
consequently *42* dementsprechend, folgerichtig
to **consider sth** *46* etw in Betracht ziehen, über etw nachdenken, etw berücksichtigen

consideration, to take sth into ~ 77T etw in Betracht ziehen, etw berücksichtigen
to consign sth 105 etw übergeben
consignment 80 Sendung, Warensendung; groupage ~ 101 Sammelladung; ~ note 82 Frachtbrief
to consist of sth 111T aus etw bestehen
consistent(ly) 77T gleichbleibend, beständig, durchgehend
console 37 Konsole
constant, to remain ~ 52 gleich bleiben
constraint 65T Beschränkung
construction, road ~ 83 Straßenbau; ~ equipment 66T Baumaschinen
to consult with sb 58 mit jdm Rücksprache halten, sich mit jdm besprechen
consultant 15 Berater/in
consumer, end ~ 32 Endverbraucher/in; ~ electronics 6 Unterhaltungselektronik; ~ goods *pl* 33 Konsumgüter
contact 111T Ansprechpartner/in; point of ~ 43 Ansprechpartner/in, Anlaufstelle; ~ details *pl* 31 Kontaktdaten
container 120 Behälter; in shared ~ 94 in Sammelcontainer, als Beiladung
continued 86 anhaltend, kontinuierlich
continuous 125 ständig, kontinuierlich
contract 7 Vertrag; to enter into a ~ 77T einen Vertrag (ab)schließen, in einen Vertrag eintreten; supplier's ~ 59 Liefervertrag, Lieferantenvertrag; ~ of carriage 80 Beförderungsvertrag, Frachtvertrag; ~ of sale 98 Kaufvertrag; performance of a ~ 99 Vertragserfüllung, Durchführung eines Vertrags
contrast 72 Gegensatz; in ~ 15T im Gegensatz (dazu)
to contrast sth 53 etw (einander) gegenüberstellen, etw (miteinander) vergleichen
contribution, to make a ~ 126T einen Beitrag leisten
controlling, financial ~ 16 Controlling
convenience 110 Komfort; ~ store *AE* 11 *lang geöffneter Laden (oft mit Tankstelle)*
convenient 81 geeignet, zweckmäßig
convention centre 64 Tagungszentrum, Kongresszentrum
conventional 24 herkömmlich, konventionell
conversion rate 47 Umwandlungsquote, Konversionsrate
to convince sb of sth 89 jdn von etw überzeugen
cooking plate 91T Kochplatte
cooperation 23 Zusammenarbeit
co-operative 54 Genossenschaft, Kooperative
to coordinate 17 miteinander abstimmen, koordinieren
copy, hard ~ 55T Papierexemplar, Ausdruck
to copy sb in 113T *(E-Mail:)* jdn CC setzen
core business 42 Kerngeschäft
core time 58P Kernzeit
corner stand 66T Eckstand
corporate 67 Unternehmens-
correction 96T Korrektur
correctness 30 Richtigkeit
to correspond 51 entsprechen, korrespondieren
correspondence 125 Schriftverkehr, Korrespondenz; written ~ 23 Schriftverkehr
corridor 26T Flur, Gang
cost, at ~ price 8T zum Selbstkostenpreis; to cut ~s 78 Kosten senken; to return ~s 110 Kosten erstatten
cost-effectiveness 110 Wirtschaftlichkeit
costly 43 kostspielig, teuer
cotton, organic ~ 46 Bio-Baumwolle
council, works ~ 26 Betriebsrat
counter 68T Theke, Tresen
country of origin 77 Ursprungsland
countryside 75 Landschaft, ländliche Gegend
course 11 Studiengang
coursework 11 schriftliche Arbeit(en)
cover 70 Gedeck; 105 Umschlag; insurance ~ 75 Versicherungsschutz
to cover sth 27 etw *(Thema)* behandeln; 43 etw abdecken; 50 *(Medien:)* über etw berichten; 81 etw *(Kosten)* decken; 96T etw abdecken
coverage 91T Versicherungsschutz
covering 105 Deckung; seam ~ 28 Falzabdeckung, Bördeln; ~ letter 40 Anschreiben, Begleitschreiben
crafts *pl*, arts and ~ 86 Kunsthandwerk
to crash 24 abstürzen
crate, wooden ~ 106T Holzkiste
credit, (documentary) letter of ~ (L/C) 82 (Dokumenten-)Akkreditiv; documentary ~ transaction 103 Akkreditivgeschäft; ~ check 77T Bonitätsprüfung; ~ note 118 Gutschrift
crockery 117 Geschirr
crushed 132 eingedrückt
cubicle 15T Arbeitsplatz *(im Großraumbüro)*
cultural 71 kulturell
curing oven 28 Einbrennofen
currency 104 Währung; ~ sign 102 Währungssymbol
currently 35 momentan
customer, trade ~ 37 Gewerbekunde/-in, Großhandelskunde/-in; ~ base 86 Kundenstamm; ~ discount 97 Kundenrabatt; ~ loyalty 45 Kundenbindung, Kundentreue; ~ satisfaction 45 Kundenzufriedenheit
to customize sth 45 etw individuell anpassen
custom-made 47 individuell gefertigt
customs: ~ duty 81 Zollgebühr(en); ~ regulations *pl* 19 Zollvorschriften; export ~ entry 125 Ausfuhranmeldung
to cut: ~ sb out of sth 33 jdn aus etw heraushalten; ~ costs 78 Kosten senken
cutlery (set) 117 Besteck
CV (curriculum vitae) 123 Lebenslauf

D

daily 74 täglich; on a ~ basis 131 täglich, jeden Tag; ~ operations *pl* 19 Tagesgeschäft
data 14 Daten; to gather ~ 45 Daten erfassen; ~ projector 55T Beamer; ~ protection 128 Datenschutz
database 45 Datenbank
date of delivery 98 Lieferdatum
dated 90 (mit Datum) vom
day, open ~ 8T Tag der offenen Tür; time of ~ 52 Tageszeit; ~ release 6T *tagweise Freistellung zur beruflichen Weiterbildung;* ~-to-day update 50T täglicher aktueller Bericht
deadline 8T Frist, Fertigstellungstermin; to meet a ~ 8T eine Frist einhalten
deal 72T Geschäft, Abschluss; special ~ 50 Sonderangebot; We have a ~. 91T Abgemacht!
to deal: ~ in sth 86 mit etw handeln; ~ with sb 23 mit jdm umgehen; ~ with sth 17 sich um etw kümmern, sich mit etw befassen; 29 mit etw umgehen; 46T etw *(Thema usw.)* behandeln; 106 etw erledigen
to debit 105 *(Konto)* belasten, *(Geld)* abbuchen
debt, to be in ~ 11 Schulden haben, verschuldet sein; to get into ~ 11 sich verschulden
decaffeinated 70 koffeinfrei
decision, to take a ~ 25 eine Entscheidung treffen
declaration, tax ~ 110 Steuererklärung
to decorate sth 42T etw *(Innenraum)* gestalten

decrease *52* Abnahme, Rückgang
to **decrease** *52* abnehmen, zurückgehen
to **deduct** *118T* abziehen
defect *77T* Mangel; to **rectify ~s** *115* Mängel beheben
defective *98* mangelhaft
degree *7* Abschluss
delighted, to **be ~** *27* (hoch)erfreut sein, sich sehr freuen
delivery, date of ~ *98* Lieferdatum; **door-to-door ~** *91T* Haus-zu-Haus-Lieferung; **material ~** *26* Materialanlieferung; **terms** *pl* **of ~** *76* Lieferbedingungen; **~ period** *39* Lieferzeit
demand *61P* Nachfrage; to **be in great ~** *61P* stark nachgefragt sein
to **demonstrate sth** *38T* etw vorführen
demo(nstration) *39* Vorführung
dental clinic *120T* Zahnklinik
dented *120T* verbeult
department *8* Abteilung; **head of ~** *16* Abteilungsleiter/in; **~ store** *44* Kaufhaus
departure *74T* Abreise, Abflug
to **depend on sth** *15T* von etw abhängen; *126T* auf etw ankommen
depending on ... *7* je nach
depth *69* Tiefe
destination *26T* (Reise-, Fahrt-)Ziel, Zielort; **place of ~** *80* Bestimmungsort
destruction *50T* Zerstörung
to **determine sth** *18* etw festlegen, etw bestimmen
to **develop** *123* (sich) entwickeln
development manager *23* Entwicklungsleiter/in
to **devise sth** *49* etw entwickeln, etw ausarbeiten
to **diagnose** *79T* diagnostizieren
diagnosis, remote ~ *79T* Ferndiagnose
dial *133* *(Uhr:)* Zifferblatt
diameter *78* Durchmesser
to **dictate** *40* diktieren
digit *21* Ziffer
digital signage *45* digitale Außenwerbung
dimensions *pl* *69* Abmessungen
dining room *75T* *(Hotel:)* Speisesaal
dinner service *117* Tafelservice
diploma *11* Abschlusszeugnis
to **direct** *47* leiten, lenken
direct mail *33* Direktwerbung *(per Post)*
directions *pl* *55T* Wegbeschreibung; to **give ~** *27* den Weg beschreiben
director *23* Vorstandsmitglied; **financial ~** *23* Finanzvorstand; **managing ~** *16* Geschäftsführer/in; **board of ~s** *17T* Vorstand
to **disappoint sb** *113* jdn enttäuschen
disappointed *120T* enttäuscht
to **disclose sth** *44* etw preisgeben
discoloured *114* verfärbt
discount *8T* Rabatt, Skonto; **cash ~** *102* Skonto; **customer ~** *97* Kundenrabatt; **introductory ~** *61P* Einführungsrabatt; **quantity ~** *60* Mengenrabatt; **special ~** *42T* Sonderrabatt; **trade ~** *102* Händlerrabatt
to **discover sth** *114* etw feststellen
discrepancy *117* Unstimmigkeit, Diskrepanz
discrimination *77* Diskriminierung
dislike, likes and ~s *pl* *14* Vorlieben und Abneigungen
dismayed *116* bestürzt
dispatch *130* Versand; **advice of ~** *100* Versandanzeige
to **dispatch** *41* versenden
to **display sth** *55T* etw *(auf einem Bildschirm)* anzeigen; *86* etw ausstellen, etw zeigen
display, on ~ *34* ausgestellt, angeboten; **~ stand** *69* Präsentationsstand
disruption (to sth) *110* Störung (von etw)
dissatisfied *115T* unzufrieden
distance *77* Entfernung
to **distinguish** *115* unterscheiden
to **distribute sth** *33* etw vertreiben
distribution *46* Vertrieb; **~ channel** *33* Vertriebsweg, Vertriebskanal
distributor *90* Vertragshändler
to **divide sth (up)** *6* etw aufteilen
division of space *68* Raumaufteilung
DIY store *90* Baumarkt, Heimwerkermarkt
to **dock** *81T* festmachen
document: ~ of title *83* Dispositionspapier, Traditionspapier; **shipping ~s** *pl* *18* Transportpapiere, Versanddokumente
documentary: ~ credit transaction *103* Akkreditivgeschäft; **(irrevocable and confirmed) ~ letter of credit** *82* (unwiderrufliches und bestätigtes) Dokumentenakkreditiv
documentation *81* Papiere
domestic *77* im Inland
door-to-door delivery *91T* Haus-zu-Haus-Lieferung
dot *40* Punkt
downside *15T* Nachteil, Schattenseite
downstairs *26T* (nach) unten
to **draft** *55T* *(Text)* entwerfen, verfassen
draft *103* Tratte; to **draw a ~** *105* eine Tratte/einen Wechsel ziehen
drastic(ally) *53T* drastisch
draw, lucky ~ *39* Verlosung; **prize ~** *44* Verlosung
to **draw: ~ sb's attention to sth** *35T* jds Aufmerksamkeit auf etw lenken; **~ a draft** *105* eine Tratte/einen Wechsel ziehen
to **dress** *9* sich kleiden
dress *9* Kleid; **~ code** *8* Kleiderordnung
drill, electric ~ *61P* Bohrmaschine
drinks machine *8T* Getränkeautomat
to **drive sb away** *113* jdn vergraulen
drive *33* Fahrt *(mit dem Auto)*
driver *101T* Fahrer/in
driving licence *128* Führerschein
drone *24* Drohne
drop *52* Fall, Rückgang
to **drop** *52* fallen, zurückgehen
due *99* fällig; to **be ~ to do sth** *42* etw (in der Zukunft) tun sollen; **~ to** *57* aufgrund von, wegen;
duplicate, in ~ *105* in zweifacher Ausfertigung
durable *38T* haltbar, strapazierfähig; **~ goods** *pl* *43* Gebrauchsgüter
dustproof *108* staubdicht
duty *80* Zoll; *98* Aufgabe, Pflicht; **customs ~** *81* Zollgebühr(en); **heavy-~** *35T* strapazierfähig, für hohe Beanspruchung

E

ear: I'm all ~s. *91T* Ich bin ganz Ohr.
early shift *58P* Frühschicht
to **earn sth** *11* etw verdienen
earring *9* Ohrring
easily *91T* locker
eco-friendly *49* umweltfreundlich
economics *129* Wirtschaft
edition *85* Ausgabe
education, follow-up ~ *125* Weiterbildung
to **effect sth** *105* etw ausführen, etw tätigen, etw erwirken
efficient(ly) *15T* effizient
either *30* jedes *(von zweien)*; *62* eines *(von mehreren)*
electric drill *61P* Bohrmaschine
electricity generator *81* Generator
elevator *AE* *27* Aufzug, Fahrstuhl
emerging markets *pl* *86* Wachstumsmärkte, Schwellenmärkte
empire *24* Reich, Imperium
employment *128* Beschäftigung, Anstellung
to **enable sb to do sth** *43* jdm ermöglichen, etw zu tun
to **enclose** *84* *(Brief:)* beifügen
enclosure *84* *(Brief:)* Anlage
to **encourage sb** *8* jdn ermutigen, jdn ermuntern

end, can ~ 26T Dosendeckel; **~ consumer** 32 Endverbraucher/in; **~ of block stand** 66T Kopfstand
to **end up** 50T (irgendwo) landen
endorsement, celebrity ~ 49 Werbung mit Prominenten
engaged 20T *(Telefon:)* besetzt
engine, search ~ 46T Suchmaschine
engineering 20 Technik, Maschinenbau
to **enquire about sth** 36 sich nach etw erkundigen
enquiry 40 Anfrage
to **ensure sth** 23 für etw sorgen; 42 etw sicherstellen
to **entail sth** 17T etw mit sich bringen
to **enter: ~ a scheme** 7 an einem Programm teilnehmen; **~ the railway business** 24 ins Bahngeschäft einsteigen; **~ into a contract** 77T einen Vertrag (ab)schließen, in einen Vertrag eintreten
to **entertain sb** 87 jdn bewirten
enthusiasm 34 Begeisterung
enthusiastic 34 begeistert
entire 114 gesamte/r/s, ganze/r/s
entirely 50T völlig, ganz
entrance 26 Eingang
entry, export customs ~ 125 Ausfuhranmeldung
environmentally conscious 51 umweltbewusst
environmentally-friendly 46 umweltfreundlich
to **equip sth with sth** 38 etw mit etw ausstatten
equipment 14 Geräte, Ausstattung, Ausrüstung
equity 105 Billigkeit(srecht)
equivalent 80 Entsprechung, Übersetzung
ergonomic 22T ergonomisch
error 96 Fehler, Irrtum
to **establish** 77T festigen; **~ sth** 23 etw schaffen, etw festlegen
established 42 etabliert
estate agent 111T Immobilienmakler/in
ethical 77 ethisch, moralisch vertretbar
etiquette 71 Umgangsformen
to **evaluate sth** 91 etw auswerten, etw einschätzen, etw beurteilen; 110 etw einstufen
evaluation 64 Beurteilung, Evaluierung
even though 7 auch wenn
event 8T Veranstaltung
everyday 33 Alltags-
examination, final ~ 11 Abschlussprüfung
except for 21 außer
exception 81 Ausnahme
exceptional 64 außergewöhnlich
excess BE 75 *(Versicherung:)* Selbstbehalt
excessive 9 übermäßig, übertrieben
exchange, bill of ~ 103 Wechsel; **stock ~** 24 Börse
to **exchange sth** 76 etw austauschen
exclusive agreement 43 Exklusivvertrag
to **excuse: Excuse me.** 13 Verzeihung, Entschuldigung.
to **execute** 114 ausführen
exercise: ~ ball 37 Gymnastikball; **~ equipment** 44 Trainingsgeräte; **~ machine** 38 Trainingsgerät; **~ mat** 37 Fitnessmatte, Yogamatte
to **exhibit** 62 ausstellen
exhibition 125 Messe, Ausstellung; **~ centre** 26T Messezentrum; **~ hall** 66 Messehalle, Ausstellungshalle
exhibitor 86 Aussteller
existing 16 bestehend, existierend
to **expand** 59T expandieren; **~ sth** 19 etw ausweiten, etw erweitern; **~ rapidly** 59 schnell wachsen
expectation 113 Erwartung
expected, to **be ~ to do sth** 59 etw tun sollen
expenses *pl* 6 Kosten, Auslagen; **living ~** 6 Lebenshaltungskosten; **travel ~** 56T Reisekosten, Reisespesen
experience, job ~ 7 Berufserfahrung, praktische Erfahrung; **work ~** 18 Praktikum
experienced 122 erfahren
expertise 110 Fachwissen, Fachkenntnisse
expiration date 105 Verfallsdatum
explanation 7 Erläuterung
expo 68 Messe, Ausstellung
to **export** 26 exportieren, ausführen
export: ~ clearance 80 Ausfuhrabfertigung; **~ clerk** 40 Außenhandelskaufmann/-frau; **~ customs entry** 125 Ausfuhranmeldung; **~ licence** 81 Ausführgenehmigung
exporter 78 Exporteur, Ausführer
expression 20 Ausdruck
extent, to the ~ of sth 24 bis zu etw
external 23 extern
extrovert 34 extrovertierte Person
eye contact 31 Blickkontakt

F

to **face sb** 31 sich jdm zuwenden, jdn anschauen
face-to-face 126 persönlich
facilities *pl* 8 Einrichtungen, Anlage(n)
facility manager 111T Objektleiter/in, Gebäudeverwalter/in
fact, in ~ 13 genau genommen, tatsächlich, eigentlich; **~ sheet** 32 Informationsblatt
factor 46 Faktor
factory manager 20 Betriebsleiter/in, Werksleiter/in
fair 40 Messe; 64 mittelmäßig; **trade ~** 17T Fachmesse, Branchenmesse
faithfully, Yours ~ 41 *(Brief:)* Mit freundlichen Grüßen
family business 8T Familienunternehmen
fantastic 13 phantastisch, toll
fashion 100 Mode
faulty 114 mangelhaft, defekt
favour, in ~ of sb 105 zu jds Gunsten, zugunsten von jdm; to **be in ~ of sth** 58 für etw sein, etw befürworten
favourable 78 günstig; 90 positiv
feature 34 Merkmal, Eigenschaft
to **feature sth** 74 etw *(Merkmal usw.)* aufweisen
fee 11 Gebühr; to **charge a ~** 83 eine Gebühr verlangen; **rental ~** 66T Miete; **tuition ~s** *pl* 11 Studiengebühren
feedback 31 Reaktion(en), Rückmeldung(en)
to **feel: ~ free to do sth** 26T etw ruhig tun, gern etw tun können; **~ like sth** 8T Lust auf etw haben
field 17T Gebiet, Bereich, Feld; **~ research** 45 Feldforschung
figure 105 Ziffer
figures *pl* 53 Zahlen; **sales ~** 17T Umsatzzahlen, Verkaufszahlen
file number 105 Aktenzeichen
final: ~ examination 11 Abschlussprüfung; **~ grade** 11 Abschlussnote
to **finalize sth** 55T etw abschließen; 91T etw endgültig festlegen
finance 11 Finanz(en)
to **finance** 24 finanzieren
financial: ~ controlling 16 Controlling; **~ director** 23 Finanzvorstand; **~ report** 18 Finanzbericht; **~ services** *pl* 24 Finanzdienstleistungen; **~ stability** 77T Finanzstabilität; **~ year** 53T Geschäftsjahr
findings *pl* 76 (Untersuchungs-) Ergebnisse
fine: F~ by me. 46T Von mir aus gern.
finishing point 26 Endpunkt
fire 106T Brand
to **fire: ~ sb** 7 jdn entlassen; **~ away** 65T losschießen
firm 45 Firma; **~ handshake** 127T fester Händedruck; **~ offer** 69 verbindliches Angebot

first: ~ **aid** *129* Erste Hilfe; ~ **of all** *27* zuerst, zunächst
to **fit** *68* passen
fitted: ~ **with** *74* ausgestattet mit; ~ **kitchen** *47* Einbauküche
fixtures and fittings *pl 34* Armaturen, Zubehör
flashlight *67* Taschenlampe
flat *9* flach; *35* Wohnung
flat-packed *91T* zur Selbstmontage
to **flatten out** *52* sich abflachen
fleet *95* Fuhrpark, Flotte
flexibility *110* Anpassungsfähigkeit, Flexibilität
flexible *130* flexibel
flexitime *8* Gleitzeit
to **flick through sth** *126* etw durchblättern
floor tiles *pl 81* Bodenfliesen
flow chart *19* Flussdiagramm
flower *42T* Blume, Blüte
to **fluctuate** *52* schwanken
fluctuation *52* Schwankung(en)
fluent *125* *(Sprache:)* fließend
flute *117* Flöte
flyer *40* Faltblatt
focus *72* (inhaltlicher) Schwerpunkt
to **focus on sth** *15T* sich auf etw konzentrieren
focused *65T* gebündelt, konzentriert
folder *28T* Mappe, Ordner
folding *38T* Falt-, faltbar
folks *11* Leute
to **follow:** ~ **sth up** *113T* etw nachbereiten, in einer Sache nachfassen; **as follows** *20* wie folgt
follow-up education *125* Weiterbildung
food industry *74* Nahrungsmittelbranche
forced labour *77* Zwangsarbeit
foreign trade *6* Außenhandel; **management assistant in wholesale and** ~ *6* Kaufmann/-frau im Groß- und Außenhandel
fork *70* Gabel
to **form** *50* (sich) bilden
form, order ~ *39* Bestellformular
formal(ly) *13* formell, förmlich
formalities *pl 106* Formalitäten
forth, to **set** ~ *105* darlegen
to **forward sth** *114* etw weitersenden, etw verschicken
forward, carriage ~ *115T* unfrei
forwarder, freight ~ *59T* Spediteur, Spedition
forwarding, freight ~ **company** *125* Spediteur, Spedition; ~ **agent** *132* Spediteur, Spedition

foul bill of lading *103* unreines Konnossement
to **found sth** *24* etw gründen
frame *38T* Rahmen
framework *68* Rahmen
franchise *24* Konzession, Lizenz
frankly *111T* offen gesagt
free, for ~ *11* umsonst; to **be** ~ **to do sth** *77* etw tun dürfen; to **feel** ~ **to do sth** *26T* etw ruhig tun, gern etw tun können; ~ **of charge** *115T* unentgeltlich, kostenlos
freight *19T* Fracht; ~ **forwarder** *59T* Spediteur, Spedition; ~ **forwarding company** *125* Spediteur, Spedition
frequent(ly) *20* häufig
fresh *26T* frisch
to **freshen up** *55T* sich frisch machen
friendship *26T* Freundschaft
front desk *74* Rezeption
to **fulfil an order** *120* einen Auftrag abwickeln, eine Bestellung ausführen
full set *105* vollständiger Satz *(von Dokumenten)*
fully-integrated *78* vollintegriert
funds *pl*, **insufficient** ~ *105* mangelnde Deckung, unzureichende Mittel
furniture *8T* Möbel; **wooden** ~ *47* Holzmöbel; ~ **set** *92* (Möbel-)Garnitur
future prospects *pl 127T* Zukunftsperspektiven

G

to **gain sth** *7* etw erlangen, etw erwerben, etw gewinnen
gallery walk *25* Galerierundgang
garment *100* Kleidungsstück
gas balloon *24* Gasballon
gate *75T* Tor, Einfahrt
to **gather:** ~ **sth** *126* etw zusammenstellen; ~ **data** *45* Daten erfassen
general purpose *101* Allzweck-
generator, electricity ~ *81* Generator
generic *47* allgemein
gentleman *26T* Herr
gesture *31* Geste
to **get:** ~ **back to sb** *56T* jdn zurückrufen, sich (wieder) bei jdm melden; ~ **out of sth** *63T* um etw herumkommen; ~ **on with one's work** *15T* seine Arbeit machen; ~ **a message across** *25* eine Botschaft vermitteln
gift *86* Geschenk; **promotional** ~ *42T* Werbegeschenk
giveaway *67* Werbegeschenk
glance, at a ~ *53T* auf einen Blick
global market share *28T* Weltmarktanteil

glossy brochure *65T* Hochglanzbroschüre
to **go: Go ahead.** *8T* Nur zu! Na los!; ~ **a long way in sth** *86* viel zu etw beitragen, viel für etw tun
goal *11* Ziel; **strategy** ~**s** *pl 23* strategische Ziele, Geschäftsziele
good cause *49* gute Sache, guter Zweck
goodness, Thank ~**!** *106T* Gott sei Dank!
goods *pl 8T* Ware(n), Güter; **consumer** ~ *33* Konsumgüter; **durable** ~ *43* Gebrauchsgüter; **title to the** ~ *83* Eigentum(srecht) an den Waren
to **grab sb's attention** *128* jds Aufmerksamkeit fesseln
grade *11* Note; **final** ~ *11* Abschlussnote
to **grant sth** *79* etw gewähren, etw einräumen
graph *52* Diagramm, Kurve; **line** ~ *52* Liniendiagramm
graphic *25* Grafik
grateful *79* dankbar
ground floor *8T* Erdgeschoss
groupage consignment *101* Sammelladung
to **guarantee** *58* garantieren
guarantee *35T* Garantie; **lifetime** ~ *38T* lebenslange Garantie
guarantor *105* Bürge/Bürgin
guide *26T* Führer/in
to **guide** *29* leiten, führen
guided tour *26* Führung
guidelines *pl 23* Richtlinien
gym *74* Fitness-Studio; ~ **instructor** *38T* Fitnesstrainer/in
gymnastics *38T* Turnen, Gymnastik

H

habit *127T* Gewohnheit; to **get into the** ~ **of doing sth** *127T* sich daran gewöhnen, etw zu tun
to **hand:** ~ **sth in** *19T* etw einreichen, etw abgeben; ~ **over to sb** *31* an jdn übergeben; ~ **sth out** *67* etw austeilen, etw ausgeben; ~ **sth over** *81* etw übergeben
hand, to **change** ~**s** *33* den Besitzer wechseln; to **have sth on** ~ *43* etw zur Verfügung haben; to **shake** ~**s with sb** *127T* jdm die Hand geben; ~ **sanitizer** *67* Handdesinfektionsmittel
to **handle sth** *18* etw bearbeiten; *93* etw erledigen; ~ **sth with care** *15* etw mit Vorsicht behandeln
handling, rough ~ *133* unsanfte Behandlung
handout *29* Arbeitsblatt, Broschüre

handshake 51 Handschlag; firm ~ 127T fester Händedruck
to hang on: Hang on. 74T Einen Moment. Warte mal.
happy, to be ~ to do sth 28T etw gern tun
hard copy 55T Papierexemplar, Ausdruck
hardware 85 Geräte
hard-wearing 35T strapazierfähig
hard-working 126T fleißig
head: ~ of department 16 Abteilungsleiter/in; ~ office 42 Zentrale, Hauptsitz
heading 28 Überschrift, Rubrik
headline, to hit the ~s 24 Schlagzeilen machen
headquarters *pl* 64 Zentrale, Hauptsitz
health and safety 77 Arbeitsschutz
healthcare 25 Gesundheitswesen; ~ clinic 24 Klinik
heat 91T Hitze
heating 55T Heizung
heavy machinery 83 Schwermaschinen
heavy-duty 35T strapazierfähig, für hohe Beanspruchung
heel 9 *(Schuh:)* Absatz
to help oneself 37 sich bedienen
herbal tea 70 Kräutertee
to hesitate 35T zögern
heterogeneous 110 heterogen
to hide sth 15T etw verbergen
high-definition 85 hochauflösend
high-quality 86 hochwertig
high street 33 Einkaufsstraße
high-volume 43 großvolumig, Groß-
to highlight 30 hervorheben
hiking 88 Wandern
to hire sth 74 etw mieten
to hit: ~ a maximum 52 einen Höchstwert/-stand erreichen; ~ the headlines 24 Schlagzeilen machen
to hold: ~ up sb 13 jdn aufhalten; ~ the line 20T *(Telefon:)* am Apparat bleiben
holder 82 Inhaber/in; 91T Halter
honesty 46T Ehrlichkeit, Aufrichtigkeit
hospitality 70 Bewirtung
to host sb 59 jdn *(als Gast)* empfangen
hours *pl*, working ~ 8 Arbeitszeit(en)
human: H~ Resources (HR) 12 Personal(abteilung); ~ rights *pl* 77 Menschenrechte
humour 71 Humor
hurry 34 Eile
hyphen 40 Bindestrich, Minus

I

idea, No ~. 35T Keine Ahnung.
to identify 15 identifizieren, bestimmen
ignition 91T Zündung
illness 13 Krankheit
illustrated 29 bebildert, illustriert
imagination 87 Phantasie
immediate 89 direkt, sofortig
immediately 67 sofort, unverzüglich
implement, writing ~ 86 Schreibgerät
import: ~ clearance 80 Einfuhrabfertigung; ~ tax 93 Einfuhrzoll
importance 9 Bedeutung, Wichtigkeit
importer 80 Importeur, Einführer
impression 56T Eindruck
impressive 42 beeindruckend
to improve 45 verbessern
improvement 31 Verbesserung
to improvise 21 improvisieren
inch 101 Zoll *(ca. 2,54 cm)*
to include sth 68T etw einplanen
including sth 27 mit etw, einschließlich einer Sache
inclusive 40 einschließlich
in-company 7 betriebsintern
inconvenience 115T Unannehmlichkeiten
to inconvenience sb 63T jdm Umstände bereiten
Incorporated (Inc.) 106T GmbH
increase 52 Zunahme, Anstieg
to increase 52 zunehmen, ansteigen; ~ sth 47 etw steigern, etw erhöhen
increasingly 86 zunehmend
to incur 98 *(Kosten:)* anfallen
indeed 72T in der Tat, allerdings
independent(ly) 126T unabhängig
index card 30 Karteikarte
indication 40 Hinweis, Anzeichen
indirect 33 indirekt
individual training 110 individuelle Weiterbildung, Einzelschulung
indoor pool 74 Hallenbad
industrial management assistant 6T Industriekaufmann/-frau
industrialized country 11 Industrieland, -staat
industry, clothing ~ 11 Kleidungsbranche; food ~ 74 Nahrungsmittelbranche; trade ~ 128 Handelsbranche
infill panel 69 Ausfachung, Füllung
infrastructure, transport ~ 28T Verkehrsnetz
in-house 19T betriebsintern
initial: ~ order 61P Erstauftrag; ~ proposal 79 Erstvorschlag
initials *pl*, reference ~ 84 *(Brief:)* Zeichen
initially 78 zu Anfang, zunächst
to initiate sth 23 etw veranlassen
initiative, to take the ~ 126T die Initiative ergreifen
inside address 84 Innenadresse
to inspect sth 83 etw prüfen
inspection, visual ~ 133 Sichtprüfung
instantly 45 sofort
instead 106T stattdessen
instruction 21 Anweisung
instructor, gym ~ 38T Fitnesstrainer/in
insufficient funds *pl* 105 mangelnde Deckung, unzureichende Mittel
insulation, thermal ~ 111T Wärmedämmung
insurance 80 Versicherung; ~ in transit 80 Transportversicherung; terms *pl* of ~ 80 Versicherungsbedingungen; ~ certificate 82 Versicherungsschein; ~ cover 75 Versicherungsschutz; ~ policy 105 Versicherungspolice
to insure 81 versichern
integrated, fully-~ 78 vollintegriert
intelligence 71 Intelligenz
to intend to do sth 24 beabsichtigen, etw zu tun
to interact with sb 129 mit jdm kommunizieren
interaction 45 Austausch, Kommunikation
interest, out of ~ 106T interessehalber
interior 28 Innenbereich, das Innere
intermediate 11 mittlere/r/s
internal 23 intern
internship 11 Praktikum
to interrupt 15T unterbrechen, stören
interruption 72 Störung, Unterbrechung
interview 126 Vorstellungsgespräch
to interview sb 40 mit jdm ein Vorstellungsgespräch führen
interviewee 113 Befragte/r
introductions *pl* 11 Bekanntmachen, Vorstellen
introductory: ~ discount 61P Einführungsrabatt; ~ level 110 Einstiegsniveau
introvert 34 introvertierte Person
to invent sth 58P etw erfinden
inventor 24 Erfinder/in
inventory 14 Bestandsliste, -aufnahme, Inventar
to invest 25 investieren
investment 24 Beteiligung, Einlage; 101T Investition; return on ~ 110 Rendite, Ertrag
invitation 55T Einladung
to invite sth 30 zu etw auffordern, um etw bitten
inviting 77T verlockend
invoice 17 Rechnung; commercial ~ 82 Handelsrechnung; receipt of ~ 102 Rechnungseingang; ~ value 105 Rechnungswert

invoicing *125* Fakturierung, Rechnungsstellung
to **involve sth** *17T* etw beinhalten, etw umfassen
involved (in sth) *32* (an etw) beteiligt
iron, cast ~ *91T* Gusseisen
irrevocable and confirmed documentary letter of credit *82* unwiderrufliches und bestätigtes Dokumentenakkreditiv
island stand *66T* Blockstand, Inselstand
issue *56T* Problem; *77* Frage
to **issue** *103* *(Dokument)* ausstellen
it, That's ~. *8T* Das war's.
item *34* Artikel; *47* Punkt, Gegenstand; *56* Tagesordnungspunkt; **wear ~s** *pl* *38T* Verschleißartikel
itinerary *63* Reiseplan

J

jar *74* (Marmeladen-)Glas
jewellery *9* Schmuck
job: ~ advert(isement) *124* Stellenanzeige; **~ agency** *122* Arbeitsagentur, Arbeitsvermittlung; **~ description** *12* Stellenbeschreibung; **~ experience** *7* Berufserfahrung, praktische Erfahrung; **~ interview** *126* Vorstellungsgespräch; **~ offer** *8T* Stellenangebot; **~ opportunities** *pl* *123* Arbeitsmöglichkeiten; **~ profile** *18* Stellenprofil; **~ prospects** *pl* *8* berufliche Perspektiven; **~ title** *125* Stellenbezeichnung; **~ vacancy** *127P* offene Stelle
journey *13* Fahrt, Anreise
to **judge sth** *77T* etw beurteilen
to **jump at sth** *77T* sich auf etw stürzen
to **justify** *127P* rechtfertigen, begründen

K

keen, to **be ~ to do sth** *131* jdm liegt sehr daran, etw zu tun
to **keep: ~ to sth** *19T* sich nach etw richten, sich an etw halten; **~ up with sth** *59* mit etw Schritt halten; **~ sb waiting** *13* jdn warten lassen
Kenya *83* Kenia
kettle *96T* Wasserkocher
to **key sth in** *14* etw *(am Computer)* eingeben
keychain *67* Schlüsselbund
keyword *31* Stichwort; *47* Schlagwort
to **kid: You must be kidding!** *48* Das ist doch nicht dein/euer Ernst?
to **kill sb** *24* jdn töten
to **know:** to **let sb ~ sth** *40* jdm etw mitteilen, jdm Bescheid sagen

L

to **label** *27* bezeichnen, etikettieren
labelling *26* Bezeichnung, Etikettierung
labour, child ~ *77* Kinderarbeit; **forced ~** *77* Zwangsarbeit; **slave ~** *48* Sklavenarbeit; **~ price** *70P* Lohnkosten
lack (of sth) *126T* Mangel (an etw)
to **lack sth** *15T* etw nicht haben
lading, (clean/foul) bill of ~ *82* (reines/unreines) Konnossement
lady *26T* Dame
landline *126* Festnetz(telefon)
to **last** *48* halten
latest, at the ~ *20* spätestens
lathe *20* Drehbank, Drehmaschine
launch *65T* Start; *86* Eröffnung; **product ~** *48* Produkteinführung
to **launch sth** *24* etw starten, etw *(Unternehmen usw.)* gründen; *46* etw auf den Markt bringen
to **lay: ~ sth** *55T* etw herrichten, etw *(Tisch)* decken, etw *(Gedeck)* auflegen; **~ sth down** *23* etw festlegen
layout *26* Grundriss, Anordnung, Plan; *84* Gestaltung, Aufbau, Layout
lazy *46T* faul, träge
leaflet *35T* Merkblatt
least, last but not ~ *77T* zu guter Letzt
leather *100* Leder
to **leave a message** *20* eine Nachricht hinterlassen
legal adviser *55* Justiziar/in
to **let sb know sth** *40* jdm etw mitteilen, jdm Bescheid sagen
letter of credit (L/C) *82* Akkreditiv; **documentary ~ (L/C)** *103* Dokumentenakkreditiv
level, introductory ~ *110* Einstiegsniveau
to **level off** *52* sich einpendeln
liability *24* Haftung
liable *24* haftbar
licence, driving ~ *128* Führerschein; **export ~** *81* Ausführgenehmigung
licensed, to **be ~ to do sth** *23* etw (mit offizieller Genehmigung) tun
lid *26T* Deckel; *91T* Haube
life, to **be the ~ and soul of the party** *34* eine Stimmungskanone sein
lifetime guarantee *38T* lebenslange Garantie
lift BE *26T* Aufzug, Fahrstuhl
likes and dislikes *pl* *14* Vorlieben und Abneigungen
to **limit** *43* begrenzen, beschränken
limit *11* Beschränkung, Begrenzung; *48* (Ober-/Unter-)Grenze
limitation *65T* Begrenzung, Beschränkung
limited *77T* beschränkt, begrenzt
line, to **hold the ~** *20T* *(Telefon:)* am Apparat bleiben; **bottom ~** *46T* das, worauf es ankommt; **product ~** *46* Produktlinie; **production ~** *28* Fertigungslinie; **subject ~** *40* Betreffzeile; **~ graph** *52* Liniendiagramm; **~ manager** *6* (direkte/r) Vorgesetzte/r
link *43* Glied *(in einer Kette)*; *126T* Zusammenhang, Verbindung
to **link sth to sth** *67* etw mit etw verknüpfen, etw mit etw verbinden
linked to sth *47* in direktem Zusammenhang mit etw
listener *50T* Hörer/in
literature *91T* Informationsmaterial; **sales ~** *67* Verkaufsprospekte, Informationsmaterial; **~ rack** *68T* Prospektständer
litre *89* Liter
litter *50T* Müll, Abfall
living expenses *pl* *6* Lebenshaltungskosten
load *104* Ladung
to **load** *58* beladen, verladen
loaded up with sth *50T* mit etw beladen, voll mit etw
loading *80* Verladen, Verladung
lockable *68T* abschließbar, verschließbar
to **log in** *8T* sich einloggen
logistics *8T* Logistik
long-standing *77T* langjährig
long-term *11* langfristig
to **look: ~ into sth** *77T* etw prüfen; **~ sth up** *39* etw nachschlagen, etw nachlesen; **~ closely at sth** *35T* sich etw genau ansehen; **~ the part** *9* entsprechend (rollengerecht) aussehen
lorry *BE* *58* Lastwagen
loss *99* Verlust
loud *9* *(Farbe:)* grell, knallig, bunt
lounge *74* Gesellschaftsraum, Lounge
low-cut *9* tief ausgeschnitten
low-priced *59* preisgünstig
loyalty, customer ~ *45* Kundenbindung, Kundentreue; **~ card** *44* Kundenkarte
lucky draw *39* Verlosung
lunch break *53* Mittagspause

M

machinery *16* Maschinen, Geräte; **heavy ~** *83* Schwermaschinen
madam: Dear Sir or M~ *41* *(Brief:)* Sehr geehrte Damen und Herren,
magazine, trade ~ *85* Fachzeitschrift
magician *39* Zauberer/Zauberin
mail, direct ~ *33* Direktwerbung *(per Post)*; **~ order** *24* Versandhandel
main carriage *80* Hauptlauf

N

O

objective *23* Ziel; **business ~** *43* Unternehmensziel
obligation *10* Pflicht, Verpflichtung; **without ~** *88* unverbindlich, freibleibend; to **perform an ~** *98* eine Verpflichtung erfüllen
obligatory *23* obligatorisch, zwingend vorgeschrieben
to **observe** *72* beobachten
to **obtain sth** *18* etw erhalten, sich etw verschaffen
obviously *43* natürlich
to **occur** *87* *(Problem usw.:)* auftreten; **~ to sb** *127T* jdm einfallen
ocean *50T* Ozean, Weltmeer
off (work) *10T* frei; to **take time ~** *10T* sich frei nehmen
offer, firm ~ *69* verbindliches Angebot; **job ~** *8T* Stellenangebot; **official ~** *79T* offizielles Angebot; **qualification ~** *110* Fortbildungsmaßnahme; **special ~** *35T* Sonderangebot; to **have sth on ~** *37* etw im Angebot haben, etw anbieten
office, open-plan ~ *8* Großraumbüro; **~ management assistant** *12T* Bürokaufmann/-frau, Kaufmann/-frau für Büromanagement; **~ supplies** *pl* *86* Bürobedarf
official(ly) *8T* offiziell
often, every so ~ *113T* hin und wieder
old-fashioned *46T* altmodisch
Olympics *pl* *38T* Olympiade
to **omit: ~ sth** *96* etw weglassen; **~ to do sth** *118* es versäumen, etw zu tun
one: ~-to-one *110* Einzel-; **~-size-fits-all** *45* Einheits-, Standard-, 08/15-
open: ~ account *77T* offenes Zahlungsziel; **~ day** *8T* Tag der offenen Tür
opening *42T* Eröffnung
openness *66T* Offenheit
open-plan office *8* Großraumbüro
to **operate** *24* geschäftlich tätig sein; **~ sth** *17T* etw bedienen
operating theatre *85* Operationssaal
operation *42* Betrieb; **daily ~s** *pl* *19* Tagesgeschäft
operational *110* Betriebs-, Arbeits-
opinion, in my ~ *8* meiner Meinung nach
opportunity *125* Gelegenheit, Möglichkeit; **job ~ies** *pl* *123* Arbeitsmöglichkeiten
opposite *27* gegenüber; to **prove the ~** *115* das Gegenteil beweisen
optimization *47* Optimierung
option *44* Möglichkeit
order, bulk ~ *96T* Großauftrag, Großbestellung; **cash with ~ (CWO)** *61P* Vorkasse; **confirmation of ~** *100* Auftragsbestätigung; **initial ~** *61P* Erstauftrag; **mail ~** *24* Versandhandel; **minimum ~ quantity** *92* Mindestbestellmenge; **purchase ~** *43* Auftrag, Bestellung; **trial ~** *85* Probebestellung; **reverse ~** *128* umgekehrte Reihenfolge; **in good ~ and condition** *103* in einwandfreiem Zustand; to **be in ~** *15* in Ordnung sein; to **acknowledge an ~** *100* einen Auftrag bestätigen; to **place an ~** *35T* einen Auftrag erteilen, eine Bestellung aufgeben; **receipt of ~** *81T* Auftragseingang; **~ form** *39* Bestellformular; **~ number** *113T* Bestellnummer, Auftragsnummer; **~ situation** *56* Auftragslage
organic cotton *46* Bio-Baumwolle
organization chart *16* Organigramm
origin, certificate of ~ *103* Ursprungszeugnis; **country of ~** *77* Ursprungsland
otherwise, unless ~ stated *99* sofern nicht anders angegeben
out of interest *106T* interessehalber
outcome *59* Ergebnis, Resultat, Auswirkung(en)
outlet, bricks and mortar ~ *46T* stationäres Geschäft; **retail ~** *49* Einzelhandelsgeschäft
to **outline** *46T* skizzieren, darstellen
outpatient clinic *85* Ambulanz
output *52P* Produktion
oven, curing ~ *28* Einbrennofen; **microwave ~** *96T* Mikrowellenherd
overall *19* Gesamt-; **~ score** *31* Gesamtpunktzahl
to **overcharge sb** *117* jdm zu viel berechnen
to **overcome sth** *24* etw bewältigen, etw überwinden
overconfident *34* zu selbstsicher, übertrieben selbstbewusst
overexcited *34* überdreht, übertrieben begeistert
to **overload** *31* überladen
overnight *35T* über Nacht
overseas *42* im Ausland, in Übersee; **~ transactions** *pl* *23* Auslandsgeschäft
to **oversee sth** *19T* etw überwachen, etw beaufsichtigen
overtime *8* Überstunden
overview *26T* Überblick
to **owe: ~ sb sth** *118* jdm etw schulden; **sum owing** *118* Forderung
own, on one's ~ *122T* alleine
ownership *83* Eigentum, Eigentumsrecht

P

pace, work ~ *110* Arbeitstempo
pack *70* Paket
to **pack** *84* verpacken
package *77T* Paket
packaging *85* Verpackung
packing *56T* Verpackung; **~ charge** *60* Verpackungskosten; **~ list** *103* Packliste
to **paddle** *50T* paddeln
pale *51* blass, hell
palletized *100* auf Paletten, palettiert
panel *69* Platte, Tafel; *127T* Gremium; **infill ~** *69* Ausfachung, Füllung
paperwork *58* Unterlagen
parcel *132* Paket
parent company *28* Muttergesellschaft
part, on our ~ *115T* auf/von unserer Seite; **~ ... part** *34* teils ... teils; to **look the ~** *9* entsprechend (rollengerecht) aussehen; **spare ~** *26* Ersatzteil; **structural ~s** *pl* *95T* tragende Bauteile
part-time *11* Teilzeit
partial *110* teilweise; **~ shipment** *105* Teillieferung
participant *8* Teilnehmer/in
particular *34* bestimmt, speziell; **anything ~** *35* etwas Spezielles; **in ~** *28T* insbesondere; *126T* ausgerechnet, gerade
particularly *131* insbesondere; **Not ~.** *127T* Eigentlich nicht.
partition *15T* Trennwand
party *88* Partei; to **be the life and soul of the ~** *34* eine Stimmungskanone sein
to **pass: ~ sth on** *20* etw weiterleiten; **~ to sb** *81* auf jdn übergehen
past *50* vergangen, in der Vergangenheit; **~ sth** *66T* an etw vorbei
patience *71* Geduld
pay *13* Bezahlung, Gehalt
payable *104* zahlbar
paying bank *105* ausführende Bank
payload *101* Zuladung, Nutzlast
payment *18* Zahlung; **terms** *pl* **of ~** *61P* Zahlungsbedingungen
peak *52* Höchstwert, Höchststand
to **peak** *52* einen Höchstwert/-stand erreichen
pension scheme *23* Altersversorgung
per unit *91T* pro Stück
percentage *28* Anteil, Prozentsatz
to **perform: ~ sth** *39* etw aufführen; **~ an obligation** *98* eine Verpflichtung erfüllen

performance 18 Leistung; 99 Erfüllung, Durchführung (eines Vertrags)
permanent 6T unbefristet
permission 126T Erlaubnis
permitted 105 erlaubt, gestattet
personable 130 umgänglich, sympathisch
personal wealth 24 Privatvermögen
personality 15T Persönlichkeit
personnel 12 Personal, Mitarbeiter/innen; ~ file 12 Personalakte
Phillips screw 41 Kreuzschlitzschraube
Phillips screwdriver 41 Kreuzschlitzschraubenzieher
photocopy 14 Fotokopie
physical 77 physisch
to pick sth up 75 etw abholen
pie chart 52 Tortendiagramm
pile 126 Stapel, Haufen
pillow 75T Kopfkissen
to pin sth to sth 123 etw an etw heften
pine 47 Kiefer
pity, That's a ~. 63T Das ist schade.
to place: ~ an ad 65T eine Anzeige schalten; ~ an order 35T einen Auftrag erteilen, eine Bestellung aufgeben
place, to take ~ 59 stattfinden; meeting ~ 13 Treffpunkt; ~ of birth 12 Geburtsort; ~ of destination 80 Bestimmungsort
placement, work ~ BE 20 Praktikum
plant 18 Werk, Fabrik; 42T Pflanze
to plant sth 24 etw pflanzen
plate 71 Teller; cooking ~ 91T Kochplatte
pleasant 69 angenehm, nett
pleased, to be ~ to do sth 84 etw gern tun; sich freuen, etw zu tun
pleasure 56T Vergnügen; My ~. 94 Ganz meinerseits! Gern geschehen!; With ~. 95T Aber gerne!
point, finishing ~ 26 Endpunkt; starting ~ 26 Ausgangspunkt; ~ of contact 43 Ansprechpartner/in, Anlaufstelle; ~ of view 127P Sicht, Perspektive
to point: ~ to sth 31 auf etw deuten, auf etw zeigen; ~ out 115T darauf hinweisen(, dass ...); ~ sth out 38T auf etw hinweisen, auf etw aufmerksam machen
policy: ~ (on sth) 113 Richtlinien (für etw); insurance ~ 105 Versicherungspolice
polite(ly) 27 höflich
politics 13 Politik
pollution 50T Verschmutzung
port of shipment 80 Verschiffungshafen
portfolio 11 Arbeitsmappe
possession, to take ~ of sth 82 etw in Besitz nehmen
post 68 Säule, Pfosten; 126T Posten, Stelle
to post sb to ... 126T jdn nach ... versetzen
post-carriage 80 Nachlauf
to postpone 56 (nach hinten) verschieben
potential 17 möglich, potenziell
pottery 117 Keramik
power, buying ~ 43 Kaufkraft
practical 11 praktisch, Praxis-
pre-carriage 80 Vorlauf
to predict 45 vorhersagen
premises pl 15 Räumlichkeiten, Firmengelände
prepaid 105 im Voraus bezahlt
prepared, to be ~ to do sth 46T bereit sein, etw zu tun
to present sb sth 104 jdm etw (Dokument usw.) vorlegen
presentation 104 Vorlage (eines Dokuments)
presenter 30 Redner/in, Vortragende/r, Moderator/in
press 16 Presse
press-up BE 38T Liegestütz
price, to quote a ~ 88 einen Preis angeben/nennen; basic ~ 91T Grundpreis; catalogue ~ 35T Listenpreis, Katalogpreis; at cost ~ 8T zum Selbstkostenpreis; labour ~ 70P Lohnkosten; purchase ~ 98 Kaufpreis; recommended retail ~ (RRP) 46T unverbindliche Preisempfehlung (UVP); total ~ 96T Gesamtpreis; unit ~ 94 Stückpreis
pricing 16 Kalkulation; 43 Preise, Preisgestaltung; ~ strategy 48 Preisstrategie
primary research 45 Primärforschung
principle 82 Grundsatz, Prinzip
prior to sth 98 vor etw
priority 51 Anliegen, Priorität; 61P Vorrang
private limited company (Ltd) 24 Gesellschaft mit beschränkter Haftung (GmbH)
privately-owned 42 in Privatbesitz
privilege 44 Vergünstigung
prize draw 44 Verlosung
procedure 118 Vorgehen, Verfahren
process 19 Verfahren, Prozess
procurement 8T Beschaffung
producer 78 Produzent/in, Hersteller/in
product: ~ brief 46 Produktbeschreibung; ~ launch 48 Produkteinführung; ~ line 46 Produktlinie; ~ range 46 Sortiment; ~ hall 26T Fertigungshalle, Produktionshalle; array of ~s 86 Produktangebot
production: ~ line 28 Fertigungslinie; ~ manager 19 Produktionsleiter/in
productivity 10 Produktivität
profession 7 Beruf
professional 38T professionell
profit 24 Gewinn, Profit; to realize a ~ 43 einen Gewinn erzielen; ~ margin 17T Gewinnspanne
programme 39 Programm; 50T (TV-, Radio-)Sendung
progress 50T Fortkommen, Fahrt
to progress 127P vorankommen
project: ~ management 16 Projektleitung; ~ manager 19 Projektleiter/in
projector, data ~ 55T Beamer
to promote: ~ sb 18 jdn befördern; ~ sth 46T für etw werben, etw promoten
promotion 46T Werbung, Promotion; 125 Beförderung, Aufstieg
promotional 67 Werbe-; ~ gift 42T Werbegeschenk
prompt 36 Stichwort; ~ card 30 Moderationskarte
promptly 99 umgehend, unverzüglich, sofort
proposal 79 Vorschlag; initial ~ 79 Erstvorschlag
proposition, unique selling ~ (USP) 46 Alleinstellungsmerkmal
pros and cons pl 11 Argumente dafür und dagegen, Vor- und Nachteile
prospective 76 potenziell
prospects pl, career ~ 123 berufliche Perspektiven; future ~ 127T Zukunftsperspektiven; job ~ 8 berufliche Perspektiven
protection, data ~ 128 Datenschutz
to prove sth 86 sich als etw erweisen; 103 etw nachweisen; ~ the opposite 115 das Gegenteil beweisen
provider 110 Anbieter
public 25 Öffentlichkeit; ~ limited company (plc) 24 Aktiengesellschaft (AG)
to publish 45 veröffentlichen
punctual(ly) 56T pünktlich
punctuality 72 Pünktlichkeit
to purchase 43 kaufen
purchase 115 Kauf; ~ order 43 Auftrag, Bestellung; ~ price 98 Kaufpreis
purchasing 16 Einkauf; ~ director 90 Einkaufsleiter/in; ~ history 45 Kaufhistorie, Einkaufsverhalten; ~ manager 55 Einkaufsleiter/in
purpose 15T Zweck; general ~ 101 Allzweck-

to **put** *17T* formulieren, sagen; **~ sth aside** *34* etw zurücklegen; **~ sb off** *34* jdn abschrecken; **~ sb through** *20T* *(Telefon:)* jdn durchstellen; **~ a lot of thought into sth** *46T* intensiv über etw nachdenken; **~ sth at risk** *77T* etw gefährden; **~ sth to good use** *127T* etw sinnvoll nutzen; **~ your personal mark on sth** *15T* einer Sache seinen persönlichen Stempel aufdrücken

Q

qualification *11* Abschluss, Qualifikation; **school ~** *6* Schulabschluss; **~ offer** *110* Fortbildungsmaßnahme
to **qualify** *6* einen/den Abschluss machen; **~ for sth** *91T* zu etw berechtigen, für etw infrage kommen
quality: ~ assurance *18* Qualitätssicherung; **~ management** *16* Qualitätssicherung
quality-assured experts *pl* *110* qualifiziertes Fachpersonal
quantity *33* Menge, Anzahl; **minimum order ~** *92* Mindestbestellmenge; **~ discount** *60* Mengenrabatt
quarter *53T* Quartal
quarterly *53* vierteljährlich, Quartals-; **~ settlement** *101T* vierteljährliche Abrechnung; **~ statement** *117* Quartalsabrechnung
query *118* Frage, Rückfrage
to **query sth** *118* etw infrage stellen, etw anzweifeln
questionnaire *8T* Fragebogen
queue *50T* Warteschlange
quotation *78* Preisangebot, Angebot, Offerte
quote *91T* (Preis-)Angebot
to **quote a price** *88* einen Preis angeben/nennen

R

rabbit *24* Kaninchen
racing, motor ~ *24* Autorennen
rack, literature ~ *68T* Prospektständer
rail, by ~ *81T* mit der Bahn
to **raise sth** *68* etw steigern
range *38T* Sortiment; *60* Bereich, Spielraum; *74* Auswahl, Angebot; **wide ~** *26T* großes Angebot, breite Palette; **product ~** *46* Sortiment
to **range from ... to ...** *42* von ... bis ... reichen
ranging from ... to ... *43* von ... bis ...
to **rank** *77* einstufen, (in einer Rangliste) bewerten; **~ higher** *47* eine höhere Position einnehmen
ranking *77* Einstufung, Bewertung
rapidly, to **expand ~** *59* schnell wachsen
rarely *43* selten
rate, conversion ~ *47* Umwandlungsquote, Konversionsrate; **response ~** *65T* Rücklaufquote; **shipping ~** *93* Frachtsatz, Versandkosten
rating *64* Bewertung
to **react** *9* reagieren
to **realize: ~ sth** *50* sich über etw im Klaren sein, etw wissen; **~ a profit** *43* einen Gewinn erzielen; **I ~ that.** *121* Das ist mir bewusst.
to **rearrange sth** *62* etw *(Termin usw.)* verschieben
reason, to **give ~s for sth** *8* etw begründen
reasonable *48* vernünftig, angemessen
to **reassure sb** *87* jdn beruhigen
to **recalculate** *96T* neu berechnen
receipt *18* Beleg, Quittung; **~ of invoice** *102* Rechnungseingang; **~ of order** *81T* Auftragseingang
received, to **be well ~** *86* (großen) Zuspruch finden
reception *55T* Empfang, Rezeption
receptionist *75* Empfangsmitarbeiter/in
recognized *7* anerkannt
recommendation *45* Empfehlung
recommended retail price (RRP) *46T* unverbindliche Preisempfehlung (UVP)
record *24* Schallplatte; *113T* Aufzeichnung, Protokoll; *121* Datensatz
recording *19* Aufzeichnung, Aufnahme; **~ studio** *25* Tonstudio
records *pl* *118* Unterlagen, Aufzeichnungen
to **recover** *53T* sich erholen
to **recruit** *18* *(Personal)* einstellen
recruitment *126T* Einstellung, Anwerbung *(von Personal)*; **~ agency** *124* Personalvermittlung
to **rectify defects** *115* Mängel beheben
recycling centre *50T* Wertstoffhof
reduction *59T* Nachlass, Preissenkung, Reduzierung
redundancy *23* (betriebsbedingte) Kündigung
ref. *54* Unser Zeichen
to **refer to sth** *81* auf etw zurückgreifen, etw zu Hilfe nehmen
referee *128* Referenz(geber/in)
reference *77T* Referenz; **with ~ to** *69* mit Bezug auf, bezugnehmend auf; **~ to sth** *89* Verweis auf etw, Bezug auf etw; **~ initials** *pl* *84* *(Brief:)* Zeichen; **~ number** *125* Aktenzeichen, Kennziffer
to **refresh** *52* auffrischen
refreshment *13* Erfrischung
refundable, tax-~ *110* steuerlich absetzbar
regarding *69* betreffend
regard: R~s, Best R~s *38* *(Brief:)* Mit freundlichen Grüßen
regional director *23* Regionalleiter/in
to **register sth** *113* etw melden, etw zum Ausdruck bringen; **~ sth with sth** *65T* etw bei etw anmelden
registration *64* Anmeldung
regulations *pl* *77* Vorschriften; **customs ~** *19* Zollvorschriften
to **reimburse sb** *113* jdm Geld zurückzahlen, jdn entschädigen
reimbursement *113* Rückerstattung
to **reject sth** *72* etw ablehnen, etw abweisen; *99* etw zurückweisen, etw beanstanden
to **relate: ~ to sth** *112* sich auf etw beziehen; **~ sth to sth** *127T* etw auf etw beziehen
relationship *45* Beziehung
relaxation, comfort and ~ *110* angenehme Atmosphäre
release, block ~ *6* Blockunterricht *(an der Berufsschule)*; **day ~** *6T* *tageweise Freistellung zur beruflichen Weiterbildung*
to **release sth** *106T* etw freigeben
relevant (to sth) *47* wichtig (für etw), relevant (für etw)
reliability *77* Zuverlässigkeit
reliable *83* zuverlässig
to **remain constant** *52* gleich bleiben
remainder *79T* Rest
remaining *10T* übrige/r/s
to **remind sb (of sth)** *55T* jdn (an etw) erinnern
reminder function *126T* Erinnerungsfunktion
to **remit** *118* *(Geld)* überweisen
remote diagnosis *79T* Ferndiagnose
remotely *79T* aus der Ferne
to **rent** *66* mieten
rent *6* Miete
rental, store ~ *43* Ladenmiete; **~ fee** *66T* Miete
to **replace sth** *114* etw ersetzen
replacement *113T* Ersatz
reply (to sth) *41* Antwort (auf etw)
to **reply (to sth)** *41* (auf etw) antworten, (etw) beantworten
to **report: ~ sth to sb** *17T* jdm etw melden; **~ to sb** *17* jdm unterstehen; **~ back** *44* Bericht erstatten
to **represent** *46T* repräsentieren, vertreten, darstellen
representative *27* Vertreter/in; **sales ~** *39* (Handels-)Vertreter/in

service, after-sales ~ 39 Kundendienst; **dinner ~** 117 Tafelservice; **financial ~es** *pl* 24 Finanzdienstleistungen; **tea ~** 118 Teeservice; **train ~** 25 Zugbetrieb
session 110 Unterrichtseinheit
to **set: ~ sth up** 15T etw einrichten, etw aufbauen; 24 etw *(Unternehmen usw.)* gründen; 62 etw *(Termin usw.)* vereinbaren; **~ forth** 105 darlegen
set 128 vorgegeben, starr, fest; **full ~** 105 vollständiger Satz *(von Dokumenten)*; **cutlery ~** 117 Besteck; **furniture ~** 92 (Möbel-)Garnitur
settlement, quarterly ~ 101T vierteljährliche Abrechnung
set-up 15T Anordnung, Einrichtung, System
setoff rights *pl* 105 Aufrechnungsrechte
sexual 77 sexuell
shabby 111T heruntergekommen, schäbig
to **shake hands with sb** 127T jdm die Hand geben
shape 68 Form, Gestalt
shaped, box-~ 68 kastenförmig
share 24 Aktie; **market ~** 28 Marktanteil
shared, in ~ container 94 in Sammelcontainer, als Beiladung
shareholder 24 Aktionär/in
shell scheme stand 68 Systemstand
shift 110 Schicht; **early ~** 58P Frühschicht; **~ work** 8 Schichtarbeit
to **ship** 18 versenden, verschicken
shipment 17 Sendung; **partial ~** 105 Teillieferung; **port of ~** 80 Verschiffungshafen
shipping 77 Versand; **~ agent** 92 Spediteur; **~ company** 79T Reederei; **~ documents** *pl* 18 Transportpapiere, Versanddokumente; **~ rate** 93 Frachtsatz, Versandkosten
shortlisted, to **be ~** 126 in die engere Auswahl kommen
short-term 24 kurzfristig
shoulder 71 Schulter
to **show sb around** 26 jdn herumführen
show, trade ~ 67 Fachmesse
shower 35T Dusche; **~ enclosure** 35T Duschkabine
showroom 26 Ausstellungsraum, Verkaufsraum
shuttle 74 Zubringer
shy 127T schüchtern
(at) sight 105 (bei) Vorlage
to **sign** 55T unterzeichnen
sign (of sth) 104 Anzeichen (von etw)
signage, digital ~ 45 digitale Außenwerbung
signal strength 126T Signalstärke
signature 84 Unterschrift; **~ block** 84 Signatur
significant(ly) 59 deutlich
signpost 30 Wegweiser
silence 71 Schweigen, Stille
simplified 82 vereinfacht
simply, to put it ~ 17T vereinfacht gesagt
since 114 seitdem
sincerely, Yours ~ 41 *(Brief:)* Mit freundlichen Grüßen
sir: Dear S~ or Madam 41 *(Brief:)* Sehr geehrte Damen und Herren,
to **sit back** 70 sich zurücklehnen
site 17T Standort, Gelände; **on ~** 28T vor Ort
situated, to **be ~** 42 sich befinden
situation, order ~ 56 Auftragslage
size, one-~-fits-all 45 Einheits-, Standard-, 08/15-
sketch 69 Skizze
to **sketch sth out** 25 etw (vor)zeichnen
skirt 9 Rock
slave labour 48 Sklavenarbeit
slide 28 *(Präsentation:)* Folie
slight(ly) 127T geringfügig, etwas
slitter 28 Schneidemaschine, Schlitzer
slotted screw 41 Schlitzschraube
slotted screwdriver 41 Schlitzschraubenzieher
smart 8 *(Kleidung:)* schick
smoke alarm 114 Rauchmelder
smoke-free 74 rauchfrei
snack 74 Imbiss
social media *pl* 45 soziale Medien
socializing 128 Ausgehen
socially-responsible 46 sozial verantwortlich
sole trader 24 Einzelunternehmer/in
solid 35T massiv, solide
solution 68 Lösung
to **solve** 26T lösen
solvency 77T Zahlungsfähigkeit
to **sort sth out** 96 etw klären, etw regeln
sorted, to **get sth ~** 120T etw klären, sich um etw kümmern
soul, to **be the life and ~ of the party** 34 eine Stimmungskanone sein
source 77T Quelle
to **source sth** 42 etw *(Waren usw.)* beschaffen
spa 64 Wellnessbereich
space travel 24 Raumfahrt
space-saving 71 raumsparend
spacecraft 24 Raumschiff
spacious 15 geräumig
spare part 26 Ersatzteil
sparkling water 70 Sprudelwasser
to **speak: Speaking.** 20T *(Telefon:)* Am Apparat.; **technically ~ing** 24 genaugenommen
special: ~ conditions *pl* 88 Sonderkonditionen; **~ deal** 50 Sonderangebot; **~ discount** 42T Sonderrabatt; **~ offer** 35T Sonderangebot
specialist 26T Fachmann/-frau; 44 Fachgeschäft
speciality 28T Spezialität
to **specialize in sth** 44 sich auf etw spezialisieren
specialty 64 Besonderheit
specific 45 bestimmte/r/s; 47 genau, bestimmt, spezifisch
specifications *pl* 19 technische Daten, Spezifikationen; 68 Vorgaben
to **specify sth** 105 etw (genau) angeben
spectacular 24 spektakulär
speech bubble 37 Sprechblase
to **spell** 40 buchstabieren
spelling 30 Rechtschreibung; 120 Schreibweise
to **split** 104 teilen; **~ sth** 7 etw aufteilen
to **sponsor sb** 50T jdn sponsern
sports equipment 37 Sportartikel
sportswear 44 Sportbekleidung
spreadsheet 123 Tabellenkalkulation, Tabelle
square: ~ foot 64 Quadratfuß *(ca. 0,09 qm)*; **~ metre** 68T Quadratmeter
stability, financial ~ 77T Finanzstabilität
staff, member of ~ 23 Mitarbeiter/in; **waiting ~** 70 Servierkräfte
stage 127T Phase, Abschnitt
stained 132 fleckig
stainless steel 91 Edelstahl
stairs *pl* 26 Treppe, Treppenhaus
stamp 44 Briefmarke; 86 Marke, Stempel
stand 35 (Messe-)Stand; **corner ~** 66T Eckstand; **display ~** 69 Präsentationsstand; **end of block ~** 66T Kopfstand; **island ~** 66T Blockstand, Inselstand; **row ~** 66T Reihenstand; **shell scheme ~** 68 Systemstand
standard 7 Maßstab, Norm; to **be up to ~** 132 den Anforderungen entsprechen
standardized 123 genormt
standby 8T Bereitschaft
starting point 26 Ausgangspunkt

to **state** *40* angeben, erklären, sagen, darlegen; **unless otherwise ~ed** *99* sofern nicht anders angegeben
state-of-the-art *28T* auf dem neuesten Stand der Technik, hochmodern
statement *99* Erklärung; *117* Abrechnung; **quarterly ~** *117* Quartalsabrechnung
station *50T* Bahnhof
stationary *46* ortsgebunden, ortsfest, stationär
stationery *86* Schreibwaren
statistics *28T* Statistik(en)
statutory *115T* gesetzlich vorgeschrieben
to **stay on** *8T* bleiben, dableiben
stealth advertising *49* heimliche Werbung, Schleichwerbung
steel *47* Stahl; **stainless ~** *91* Edelstahl
sticky notes *pl* *67* Haftnotizen
stiff competition *59* harter Wettbewerb
to **stimulate sth** *86* etw beleben, etw ankurbeln
stock, from ~ *96T* ab Lager; **in ~** *35T* vorrätig, auf Lager, lieferbar; **while ~s last** *35T* solange der Vorrat reicht; **~ exchange** *24* Börse
stool *68T* Hocker
stop *26T* Station, Halt
storage *78* Lagerung; **~ space** *43* Lagerfläche; *68T* Stauraum
store rental *43* Ladenmiete
straight *59T* direkt; **~ away** *101T* sofort
strategy *45* Strategie; **marketing ~** *44* Vermarktungsstrategie; **pricing ~** *48* Preisstrategie; **~ goals** *pl* *23* strategische Ziele, Geschäftsziele
strength *77T* Stärke; **signal ~** *126T* Signalstärke
to **strengthen** *110* stärken
to **stress sth** *71* etw betonen
to **stretch to sth** *91T* sich auf etw einlassen, jdm bis auf etw entgegenkommen
strict *8T* streng
structural parts *pl* *95T* tragende Bauteile
structure *30* Aufbau, Struktur
to **structure** *7* aufbauen, strukturieren
study *45* Untersuchung, Studie; **case ~** *83* Fallstudie
sturdy *102* stabil, robust
stylish *74* elegant, stilvoll
subject: ~ line *40* Betreffzeile; **~ matter** *110* Materie, Unterrichtsstoff; **~ to confirmation** *88* vorbehaltlich einer Bestätigung, freibleibend
to **submit sth** *88* etw einreichen, etw abgeben
subsidiary *20* Niederlassung
to **subsidize** *8* subventionieren, bezuschussen
substantial *79* erheblich, beträchtlich
sub-total *95* Zwischensumme
suit *9* Anzug; Kostüm; **trouser ~** *9* Hosenanzug
to **suit: ~ sb** *63T* jdm passen; **~ sb/sth** *51* (zu) jdm/etw passen; **S~ yourself.** *35T* Wie Sie wollen. / Wie du willst.
suitability *34* Eignung
suitable *13* geeignet, passend
sum owing *118* Forderung
to **sum up: to ~** *10T* zusammenfassend (gesagt)
superior *72* Vorgesetzte/r
to **supervise sth** *17T* etw beaufsichtigen, etw betreuen, etw überwachen
supervision *125* Aufsicht, Kontrolle
supervisor, training ~ *12* Ausbildungsleiter/in
supplement *123* Zusatz, Ergänzung
supplier *8T* Zulieferer, Lieferant/in, Anbieter; **~'s contract** *59* Liefervertrag, Lieferantenvertrag
supplies *pl*, **medical ~** *84* Sanitätsartikel; **office ~** *86* Bürobedarf
supply chain *43* Lieferkette
to **supply: ~ sth** *19* etw liefern, etw bereitstellen; **~ sb with sth** *90* jdm etw liefern
to **support** *15T* unterstützen; *31 (Argumentation)* untermauern
support *49* Unterstützung; *125* Betreuung
to **suppose** *74T* vermuten, annehmen, glauben
to **surf the internet** *24* im Internet surfen
surfboard *50T* Surfbrett
surplus *133* überschüssig
surprised *10T* überrascht, erstaunt
surprising(ly) *35T* erstaunlich
to **surround sth** *66T* etw umgeben
surroundings *pl* *64* Umgebung
survey *8* Umfrage
suspicion *77* Verdacht
sustainability *46T* Nachhaltigkeit
sustainable *77* nachhaltig
to **swap** *39* tauschen
sweetcorn *78* Zuckermais, Süßmais
to **swipe a card** *45* eine Karte durchziehen
to **switch sth off** *72T* etw ausschalten, etw abschalten
swivel chair *22T* Drehstuhl

T

tableware *117* Geschirr
tag, name ~ *55T* Namensschild
tailor-made (to sth) *110* individuell (auf etw) zugeschnitten
to **take: ~ sb on** *125* jdn einstellen, jdn übernehmen; **~ care of sth** *40* sich um etw kümmern, etw bearbeiten, etw erledigen; **~ place** *59* stattfinden; **~ sth seriously** *26T* etw ernst nehmen; **~ business away from sb** *24* jdm das Wasser abgraben
taking in charge *105* Übernahme
tally list *15* Abhakliste, Strichliste
tap *35T* Wasserhahn; **mixer ~** *35T* Mischbatterie
target group *45* Zielgruppe
to **target sb** *45* jdn ins Visier nehmen
targeted advertising *49* gezielte/zielgruppengenaue Werbung
tax *23* Steuer(n); **import ~** *93* Einfuhrzoll; **value added ~ (VAT)** *96T* Mehrwertsteuer (MwSt.); **~ declaration** *110* Steuererklärung; **~-refundable** *110* steuerlich absetzbar
tea service *118* Teeservice
teapot *117* Teekanne
technical term *39* Fachbegriff
technically speaking *24* genau genommen
technician *20* Techniker/in
technique *34* Technik, Methode
television channel *65T* Fernsehsender
template *88* Vorlage
temporary *49* vorübergehend, vorläufig
tenant *111T* Mieter
to **tend to do sth** *43* dazu neigen, etw zu tun
term *118* Begriff; **technical ~** *39* Fachbegriff
terminal *80* Terminal
terms *pl* *19* (Vertrags-)Bedingungen; **~ and conditions** *pl* *77T* Allgemeine Geschäftsbedingungen; **~ of business** *59* Konditionen; **~ of delivery** *76* Lieferbedingungen; **~ of insurance** *80* Versicherungsbedinungen; **~ of payment** *61P* Zahlungsbedingungen
territory *43* Gebiet, Territorium
test flight *24* Testflug
testimonial *49* Erfahrungsbericht
text (message) *8T* SMS
to **text sb** *8T* jdm eine SMS schicken
theatre, operating ~ *85* Operationssaal
theoretical *7* theoretisch, Theorie-
therefore *59* daher, folglich
thermal insulation *111T* Wärmedämmung
thermostatic mixer *35* Thermostat

thermostatically controlled 35T per Thermostat geregelt
thickness 37 Stärke, Dicke
to **think: Come to ~ of it ...** 8T Wenn ich es mir recht/genau überlege ...
thoroughly, to **agree ~ with sb** 56T voll und ganz einer Meinung mit jdm sein
thought 46T Gedanke(n); to **put a lot of ~ into sth** 46T intensiv über etw nachdenken
three-piece 78 dreiteilig
throughout ... 7 in ganz ...
to **throw sth away** 50T etw wegwerfen
thus 110 auf diese Weise, so
tidy, neat and ~ 15T sauber und ordentlich
tie 9 Krawatte
tile 102 Fliese; **floor ~es** *pl* 81 Bodenfliesen
time, for the ~ being 35 einstweilen, fürs Erste; **in (good) ~** 19 rechtzeitig; **on ~** 19T pünktlich; **core ~** 58P Kernzeit; **transit ~** 92 Laufzeit; **part-~** 11 Teilzeit; to **take ~ off (work)** 10T sich frei nehmen; **~ of day** 52 Tageszeit; **~ savings** *pl* 110 Zeitersparnis
to **time sth** 110 etw zeitlich abstimmen
timeless 35 zeitlos
timeline 24 Zeitachse, Zeitschiene
title 15 Titel, Überschrift; **job ~** 125 Stellenbezeichnung; **~ to the goods** 83 Eigentum(srecht) an den Waren; **document of ~** 83 Dispositionspapier, Traditionspapier
tone 51 Farbton
to **tone up** 38T *(Muskeln:)* in Form bringen, kräftigen
tool 26T Werkzeug, Instrument
top 9 Oberteil
total price 96T Gesamtpreis
tote bag 67 Tragetasche
touch, to **get in ~ with sb** 62 sich bei jdm melden, sich mit jdm in Verbindung setzen; to **be in ~** 91 sich melden
tour 27 Rundgang; **guided ~** 26 Führung
tourist board 129 Fremdenverkehrsamt
towel 75T Handtuch
toy 86 Spielzeug
to **track** 19T verfolgen
trade 40 Gewerbe, Branche; 46 Handel; **foreign ~** 6 Außenhandel; **~ customer** 37 Gewerbekunde/-in, Großhandelskunde/-in; **~ discount** 102 Händlerrabatt; **~ fair** 17T Fachmesse, Branchenmesse; **~ industry** 128 Handelsbranche; **~ magazine** 85 Fachzeitschrift; **~ show** 67 Fachmesse; **~ union** 77 Gewerkschaft
trader 59 Händler/in; **sole ~** 24 Einzelunternehmer/in
trading: ~ company 42 Handelsunternehmen; **~ partner** 72 Handelspartner/in
traditional 46T traditionell, hergebracht
traffic 47 Verkehr
to **train** 7 eine Ausbildung machen
train service 25 Zugbetrieb
to **train to be a ...** 6 eine Aubildung zum/zur ... machen
trainee 6 Auszubildende/r, Lehrling
traineeship 126T Ausbildung, Lehre
trainer 8 Ausbilder/in
trainers *pl* 9 Turnschuhe, Sportschuhe
training, vocational ~ 7 Berufsausbildung; **~ company** 6 Ausbildungsbetrieb; **~ course** 6 Ausbildung; **~ supervisor** 12 Ausbildungsleiter/in
trampoline 37 Trampolin
transaction 82 Geschäft, Vorgang, Transaktion; **documentary credit ~** 103 Akkreditivgeschäft; **overseas ~s** *pl* 23 Auslandsgeschäft
transcript 121 Mitschrift
to **transfer sth** 95 etw übertragen
transferable 103 übertragbar
transformation 64 (grundlegende) Veränderung, Wandel
transit, in ~ 91T beim Transport; **insurance in ~** 80 Transportversicherung; **~ time** 92 Laufzeit
transparency 29 (Overhead-)Folie, Dia
transport, mode of ~ 80 Beförderungsart, Verkehrsmittel; **sea ~** 93 Seetransport; **~ infrastructure** 28T Verkehrsnetz
transportation 78 Transport
transshipment 105 Umladung
travel expenses *pl* 56T Reisekosten, Reisespesen
traveller 52 Passagier, Fahrgast
treadmill 37 Laufband
to **treat sb** 77 jdn behandeln
trial order 85 Probebestellung
triple 46T dreifach
to **trouble sb** 63 jdm Umstände bereiten
to **troubleshoot** 79T Fehler suchen, Fehler beheben
trouser suit 9 Hosenanzug
truck waybill 103 Lastwagenfrachtbrief
to **trust** 100 hoffen(, dass)
try, to **give it a ~** 106T es versuchen
to **try sth out** 35 etw ausprobieren
tuition fees *pl* 11 Studiengebühren
turn, to **be one's ~** 19 an der Reihe sein
to **turn: ~ sth into sth** 26T etw zu etw machen, etw in etw umwandeln; **~ one's back on sb** 31 jdm den Rücken zuwenden
turnover 28 Umsatz
two-vessel brewhouse 105 Zweigerätesudhaus
to **type in sth** 118T etw eingeben, etw eintippen
typically 43 normalerweise

U

unable, to **be ~ to do sth** 56 etw nicht tun können
unavailable, to **be ~** 20T *(Telefon:)* nicht zu sprechen sein
unconditional(ly) 98 vorbehaltlos, uneingeschränkt
unconventional 49 unkonventionell
to **undercut sb** 24 jdn unterbieten
to **underline** 51 unterstreichen
underscore 40 Unterstrich
uninviting 15T wenig einladend
union 52 Gewerkschaft; **trade ~** 77 Gewerkschaft
unique 49 einzigartig; **~ selling proposition (USP)** 46 Alleinstellungsmerkmal
unit 52P Einheit, Stück; **per ~** 91T pro Stück; **~ price** 94 Stückpreis
unknown 24 unbekannt
unless otherwise stated 99 sofern nicht anders angegeben
unlimited 24 unbeschränkt, unbegrenzt
to **unload** 58 entladen
unloading 80 Entladung, Löschen
unpaid 10T unbezahlt
unsatisfactory 116 unzulänglich
unusual 50T ungewöhnlich
to **unwrap sth** 34 etw auspacken
up, to **be ~ and running** 79T in (laufendem) Betrieb sein; to **be ~ to standard** 132 den Anforderungen entsprechen
update: ~ (on sth) 40 aktuelle Informationen (zu etw), aktueller Überblick (über etw); **day-to-day ~** 50T täglicher aktueller Bericht
to **update sth** 32 etw aktualisieren
to **upload** 11 hochladen
upstairs 27 (nach) oben
up-to-date 66 aktuell, auf dem neuesten Stand
urgent(ly) 20T dringend
use, to **put sth to good ~** 127T etw sinnvoll nutzen
user-friendly 38T benutzerfreundlich

V

vacancy 127P offene Stelle
valid 35T gültig
validation 105 Bestätigung
validity 101 Gültigkeit

valuables *pl* 68T Wertsachen
value 104 Wert; invoice ~ 105 Rechnungswert; ~ for money 77T (preis)günstig; ~ added tax (VAT) 96T Mehrwertsteuer (MwSt.)
varied 122T vielfältig
various 114 mehrere
to vary 11 variieren, sich unterscheiden
VAT (value added tax) 96T MwSt. (Mehrwertsteuer)
vehicle 68 Fahrzeug
vendor 77T Anbieter, Verkäufer
venture, business ~ 24 Unternehmen, Geschäftsvorhaben
venue 40 Veranstaltungsort
vessel 91 Schiff; two-~ brewhouse 105 Zweigerätesudhaus
via 92 per, mittels, über
to video sth 50 etw (auf Video) filmen
view 13 Aussicht, Blick; ~ (of sb/sth) 72 Auffassung, Bild (von jdm/einer Sache); in ~ of sth 59 angesichts von etw; point of ~ 127P Sicht, Perspektive
viewer 47 Zuschauer/in, Betrachter/in
viral, to go ~ 50 sich (im Internet) rasend schnell verbreiten
virtual 46T virtuell
visible 9 sichtbar
visual: ~ aids *pl* 31 visuelle Hilfsmittel; ~ inspection 133 Sichtprüfung
visual(ly) 25 visuell
visualization 68 Visualisierung
visuals *pl* 29 visuelles Hilfsmittel
vocational: ~ college 7 Berufsschule, Berufsfachschule; ~ school 6 Berufsschule; ~ training 7 Berufsausbildung
voicemail 20 Mailbox
volume of sales 53T Umsatzvolumen
voluntary 115 freiwillig
volunteer 38T Freiwillige/r
voucher 87 Gutschein
voyage 24 Reise, Fahrt

W

wage bargaining, collective ~ 77 Tarifverhandlungen
wagon, closed ~ 94 geschlossener Waggon
to wait: to keep sb ~ing 13 jdn warten lassen
waiting staff 70 Servierkräfte
wall panel 68 Wandplatte
war 105 Krieg
warehouse 33 Lager; ~ manager 55 Lagerleiter/in
warmth 15T Wärme
to warn sb 106T jdm (etw) sagen, jdn vorwarnen
warranty 77T Gewährleistung; ~ period 115 Gewährleistungszeit
washbasin 35T Waschbecken, Waschtisch
to waste 45 verschwenden, vergeuden
waterproof 108 wasserdicht
waterway 50 Wasserstraße
way, by the ~ 10T übrigens; this ~ 26T hier entlang; one ~ or another 106T so oder so; to go a long ~ in sth 86 viel zu etw beitragen, viel für etw tun
waybill, air ~ 82 Luftfrachtbrief; truck ~ 103 Lastwagenfrachtbrief
weakness 77T Schwäche
wealth, personal ~ 24 Privatvermögen
wear items *pl* 38T Verschleißartikel
to weigh 89 wiegen
weight bench 37 Hantelbank
welcome, You're ~. 8T Bitte (sehr). Gern geschehen.
welcoming 66T einladend
welding machine 28 Schweißmaschine
well-established 46T bewährt, fest etabliert
well-stocked 74 gut sortiert
wheelchair 75T Rollstuhl
while stocks last 35T solange der Vorrat reicht
white-collar workers *pl* 53 Angestellte
to wholesale 80 en gros handeln
wholesale 6 Großhandel; management assistant in ~ and foreign trade 6 Kaufmann/-frau im Groß- und Außenhandel
wholesaler 6 Großhändler
wide range 26T großes Angebot, breite Palette
windproof 89 winddicht
wine list 70 Weinkarte
winner 10T Sieger/in
wish, Best ~es 41 *(Brief:)* Mit freundlichen Grüßen
wooden: ~ crate 106T Holzkiste; ~ furniture 47 Holzmöbel
wording 59 Formulierung
to work: ~ alongside sb 26T mit jdm arbeiten; ~ sth out 16 etw berechnen, etw ausrechnen; ~ sth out 42T eine Lösung für etw finden, etw erarbeiten
work, administrative ~ 125 Verwaltungstätigkeiten; shift ~ 8 Schichtarbeit; ~ and costs 98 Arbeit und Kosten; off ~ 10T frei; to take time off ~10T sich frei nehmen; to get on with one's ~ 15T seine Arbeit machen; ~ experience 18 Praktikum; ~ pace 110 Arbeitstempo; ~ placement *BE* 20 Praktikum; ~ schedule 110 Arbeitsablauf
workforce 28T Belegschaft, Arbeitskräfte
working: ~ conditions *pl* 6 Arbeitsbedingungen; ~ hours *pl* 8 Arbeitszeit(en)
workplace 9 Arbeitsplatz
works council 26 Betriebsrat
workshop 30 Werkstatt
workwear 132 Arbeitskleidung
to worry 63T sich Sorgen machen; Don't ~. 63T Keine Sorge.
worst-case scenario 59 schlimmster anzunehmender Fall
worth 24 wert
to wrap sth up 56T etw abschließen, etw zum Abschluss bringen
wrapped 34 verpackt
writing, in ~ 8T schriftlich, in Schriftform; ~ implement 86 Schreibgerät
written 99 schriftlich; ~ correspondence 23 Schriftverkehr

XYZ

X-ray machine 120 Röntgengerät

Basic trade vocabulary (German–English)

Firmenorganisation – Company organization

Aktiengesellschaft (AG)	public limited company (plc) *BE*; open corporation *AE*
Aktie	share
Aktionär/in, Teilhaber/in	shareholder
Einzelunternehmer/in	sole proprietor/trader
Gesellschaft mit beschränkter Haftung (GmbH)	limited company (Ltd) *BE*; closed corporation *AE*
Kommanditgesellschaft (KG)	limited partnership
Personengesellschaft, offene Handelsgesellschaft (OHG)	(general) partnership

Firmenabteilungen – Company departments

Buchhaltung	Accounts (department)
Einkauf(sabteilung)	Purchasing (department)
Forschung(s-) und Entwicklung(sabteilung)	Research and Development (department, R&D)
Geschäftsführung, Vorstand	board (of directors)
Lager(halle)	warehouse
Marktforschung(sabteilung)	Market Research (department)
Personal(abteilung)	Human Resources (department, HR)
Rechnungswesen	Finance (department)
Rechtswesen	Legal department
Rezeption, Empfang	reception
Verkauf(sabteilung), Vertrieb	Sales (department)
Vertrieb	Distribution (department)
Verwaltung	administration
Zentrale	head office, headquarters

Mitarbeiter/innen – Members of staff

Abteilungsleiter/in	head of department
Arbeitgeber/in, Unternehmer/in	employer
Arbeitnehmer/in, Beschäftigte/r	employee
Arbeitsplatz	workplace
Ausbildung	training
Buchhalter/in	accountant
Groß- und Außenhandelskaufmann/-frau	management assistant in wholesale and foreign trade
Empfangsmitarbeiter/in	receptionist
Gehalt	salary
Geschäftsführer/in	managing director (MD), chief executive officer (CEO)
Handelsvertreter/in	sales representative
Kollege, Kollegin	colleague
Lehre	apprenticeship
Manager/in	manager
Personal	staff
Persönliche/r Assistent/in	personal assistant (PA)
Qualifikation, Abschluss	qualification
Sekretär/in	secretary

Bürotätigkeiten – Office activities

etw ausrichten	to take a message
Berichte schreiben	to write reports
Briefe beantworten	to reply to letters
Mitteilungen, Vermerke, Notizen	to write memos
ein Telefongespräch annehmen	to answer the telephone
Textverarbeitung	word processing
Überstunden machen	to work overtime
Unterlagen, Schriftstücke	paperwork
etw weiterleiten	to forward sth

Geschäftsbriefe – Commercial correspondence

Absatz	paragraph
Absender	sender
Adresse	address
anhängen (*E-Mail*)	to attach sth
Anhang (*E-Mail*)	attachment
Anlage(n)	enclosure (enc)
Anrede	salutation
Antwort	reply
beifügen (*Brief*)	to enclose
Betreff(zeile)	subject (line)
Briefkopf	letterhead
Datum	date
Einschreiben	registered mail/post
Empfänger/in	addressee
Entschuldigungsschreiben	letter of apology
Mit den besten Wünschen	Best wishes
Mit freundlichen Grüßen	Yours faithfully
Mit freundlichen Grüßen	Yours sincerely
Mit freundlichen Grüßen, Viele Grüße	Best wishes, Regards
Mit herzlichen Grüßen	Best wishes, Cordially *AE*
Schlussformel	complimentary close
Unterschrift	signature
Zeichen	reference (ref)
zu Händen	attention (attn)

Besprechungen/Präsentationen – Meetings/ presentations

Abwesenheit	absence
Bericht	report
Einladung	invitation
Liniendiagramm	line chart
Protokoll	minutes *pl*
eine Rede halten	to make a speech
Säulendiagramm	bar chart
die Sitzung leiten	to take the chair / to be in the chair
stattfinden	take place
Tagesordnung	agenda
Tagesordnungspunkt	item on the agenda
teilnehmen	to participate
Teilnehmer/in	participant
Termin	date
Tortendiagramm	pie chart
Verschiedenes	any other business (AOB)
Vortrag	talk; lecture
vortragen	to report; to state
X-Achse	x-axis
Y-Achse	y-axis

Dienstreisen – Business trips

absagen	to cancel
Anforderung	requirement
Anschlussflug	connecting flight
Ausstellung	exhibition
etw besuchen, an etw teilnehmen	to attend sth
Bitte, Anfrage	request
einfacher Flug	one-way flight
Hin- und Rückflug	return flight
Messe	(trade) fair
Passagier/in	passenger
Reservierung, Buchung	reservation
stornieren	to cancel
Termin	appointment
Unterkunft	accommodation
verschieben	to postpone

Geschäftspartner und Händler – Business partners and traders

Einzelhändler/in	retailer
Exporteur	exporter
Großhändler	wholesaler
Importeur	importer
Käufer/in	buyer
Klient/in	client
Konkurrent/in, Konkurrenz	competitor
Konkurrenz	competition
Kunde, Kundin	customer, client
Lieferant	supplier
Spediteur	carrier; forwarding agent; freight forwarder
Verkäufer/in	seller

Geschäftsvorgänge – Business transactions

Anfrage	enquiry
Angebot, Kostenvoranschlag	quotation
Auftrag, Bestellung	order
einen Auftrag erteilen	to place an order
einen Auftrag erledigen	to fill an order
Auftragsbestätigung	acknowledgement/ confirmation (of an order)
einen Auftrag bestätigen	to acknowledge an order
Bestellformular	order form
Bestellnummer	order number
Erhalt, (Waren-)Eingang	receipt (of goods)
Folgeauftrag	repeat order
Lieferbedingungen	terms of delivery *pl*
liefern	to deliver
Lieferung	delivery
Muster	sample
Probeauftrag	trial order
Reklamation, Beschwerde	complaint
eine Reklamation bearbeiten/regulieren	to adjust a complaint
Sendung	consignment
Umsatz	turnover
Verkäufe, Umsatz	sales *pl*
Versandanzeige, Versandmitteilung	advice of dispatch
Versandpapiere	shipping documents *pl*
versenden	to ship
versenden, absenden	to dispatch
Vertrag	contract
Ware(n), (Lager-)Bestand	stock
Zahlungsanzeige	advice of payment
Zahlungsbedingungen	terms of payment *pl*

Zahlung – Payment

Dokumente gegen Akzept	documents against acceptance
Dokumente gegen Zahlung	documents against payment
Dokumentenakkreditiv	documentary letter of credit
fällig, ausstehend	overdue
Konto, Kreditkonto	account
letzte Mahnung	final demand
Mahnung	reminder
MwSt = Mehrwertsteuer	VAT = value added tax
Nicht(be)zahlung	non-payment
Rabatt, Nachlass	discount
Rate	instalment
Rechnung	bill, invoice
Skonto, Barzahlungsrabatt	cash discount
überweisen	to remit, to transfer
Überweisung, Zahlung	bank transfer, remittance
Vorauszahlung, Vorkasse	cash in advance
Wechsel	bill of exchange
zahlbar bei Lieferung, per Nachnahme	cash on delivery (COD)

Irregular verbs

be – was/were – been	sein
become – became – become	werden
begin – began – begun	anfangen, beginnen
break – broke – broken	brechen
bring – brought – brought	bringen
build – built – built	bauen
burn – burnt/burned – burnt/burned	(ver)brennen
buy – bought – bought	kaufen
catch – caught – caught	fangen
choose – chose – chosen	wählen
come – came – come	kommen
cost – cost – cost	kosten
cut – cut – cut	schneiden
do – did – done	tun, machen, erledigen
draw – drew – drawn	zeichnen
dream – dreamt – dreamt	träumen
drink – drank – drunk	trinken
drive – drove – driven	fahren
eat – ate – eaten	essen
fall – fell – fallen	fallen
feed – fed – fed	füttern, ernähren
feel – felt – felt	(sich) fühlen, empfinden
fight – fought – fought	kämpfen
find – found – found	finden
fit – fit/fitted – fit/fitted	passen
fly – flew – flown	fliegen
forget – forgot – forgotten	vergessen
get – got – got (*AE* gotten)	bekommen, erhalten
give – gave – given	geben
go – went – gone	gehen, fahren
grow – grew – grown	wachsen
hang – hung – hung	hängen
have – had – had	haben
hear – heard – heard	hören
hide – hid – hidden	(sich) verstecken
hit – hit – hit	schlagen, aufprallen auf
hold – held – held	halten, festhalten
keep – kept – kept	behalten
know – knew – known	kennen, wissen
lay – laid – laid	legen
lead – led – led	führen, leiten
learn – learnt/learned – learnt/learned	lernen
leave – left – left	abfahren, verlassen, weggehen
let – let – let	lassen
lose – lost – lost	verlieren
make – made – made	machen
mean – meant – meant	meinen, bedeuten
meet – met – met	treffen
pay – paid – paid	bezahlen
put – put – put	setzen, stellen, legen
read – read – read	lesen
ride – rode – ridden	reiten, fahren
ring – rang – rung	klingeln, anrufen
rise – rose – risen	(an)steigen
run – ran – run	laufen, rennen
say – said – said	sagen
see – saw – seen	sehen
sell – sold – sold	verkaufen
send – sent – sent	senden, schicken
shake – shook – shaken	schütteln
set – set – set	setzen, stellen
show – showed – shown	zeigen
shut – shut – shut	schließen
sing – sang – sung	singen
sit – sat – sat	sitzen
sleep – slept – slept	schlafen
smell – smelt/smelled – smelt/smelled	riechen
speak – spoke – spoken	sprechen
spell – spelt/spelled – spelt/spelled	buchstabieren
spend – spent – spent	ausgeben, verbringen
stand – stood – stood	stehen
steal – stole – stolen	stehlen
swim – swam – swum	schwimmen
take – took – taken	nehmen
teach – taught – taught	unterrichten, beibringen
tear – tore – torn	(zer)reißen
tell – told – told	sagen, erzählen
think – thought – thought	denken
throw – threw – thrown	werfen
understand – understood – understood	verstehen
wake – woke – woken	wecken
wear – wore – worn	tragen (Kleidung)
win – won – won	gewinnen
write – wrote – written	schreiben

Acknowledgements

S. 6: Shutterstock/kosmos1115; **S. 8.1:** Shutterstock/Viktor Gladkov; **S. 8.2:** Shutterstock/Monkey Business Images; **S. 9.1:** Shutterstock/ostill; **S. 9.2:** Shutterstock/Flashon Studio; **S. 9.3:** Shutterstock/Viktor Gladkov; **S. 9.4:** Shutterstock/Wisiel; **S. 9.5:** Fotolia/Michael A; **S. 9.6:** Fotolia/sanneberg; **S. 9.7:** Fotolia/ulianna19970; **S. 9.8:** Shutterstock/Kopytin Georgy; **S. 11.1:** Shutterstock/Billion Photos; **S. 11.2:** Shutterstock/Dan Kosmayer; **S. 12.1:** Shutterstock/Djomas; **S. 12.2:** Fotolia/Photozi; **S. 12.3:** Shutterstock/PR Image Factory; **S. 12.4:** Fotolia/contrastwerkstatt; **S. 12.5:** Shutterstock/UncleOles; **S. 12.6:** Shutterstock/g-stockstudio; **S. 14.1:** Shutterstock/Andrey_Popov; **S. 14.2:** Shutterstock/Konstantin Chagin; **S. 14.3:** Shutterstock/Monkey Business Images; **S. 14.4:** Shutterstock/ESB Professional; **S. 14.5:** Shutterstock/Stock-Asso; **S. 14.6:** Fotolia/contrastwerkstatt; **S. 15.o:** Shutterstock/ESB Professional; **S. 15.1:** Fotolia/ProstoSvet; **S. 15.2:** Shutterstock/Africa Studio; **S. 15.3:** Shutterstock/MSSA; **S. 15.4:** Fotolia/magneticmcc; **S. 15.5:** Fotolia/electriceye; **S. 15.6:** Fotolia/morganka; **S. 17:** Shutterstock/Africa Studio; **S. 18.1:** Shutterstock/Dmitry Kalinovsky; **S. 18.2:** Shutterstock/stockfour; **S. 18.3:** Shutterstock/create jobs 51; **S. 18.4:** Shutterstock/Moon Light PhotoStudio; **S. 19.1:** Shutterstock/BalLi8Tic; **S. 19.2:** Shutterstock/Rido; **S. 24/25:** interfoto e.k./Danita Delimont/Julien McRoberts; **S. 25+26:** Oxford Illustrators; **S. 28.A+C–F:** mit freundlicher Genehmigung der Cantec GmbH & Co. KG, Essen; **S. 28.B:** Shutterstock/Bananaboy; **S. 28.u.re:** Shutterstock/Nattanan Zia; **S. 30:** Shutterstock/ESB Professional; **S. 32.1:** Shutterstock/ESB Professional; **S. 32.2:** Fotolia/niroworld; **S. 32.3:** Fotolia/rcfotostock; **S. 32.4:** Shutterstock/Concept Photo; **S. 32.5:** Fotolia/WavebreakMediaMicro; **S. 32.6:** Fotolia/georgejmclittle; **S. 33:** Shutterstock/Photobac; **S. 34:** Shutterstock/g-stockstudio; **S. 35.1:** Fotolia/Roman Samokhin; **S. 35.2:** Shutterstock/evru; **S. 37.A:** Fotolia/Konstantin Shevtsov; **S. 37.B1:** Shutterstock/Печать; **S. 37.B2:** Shutterstock/Scanrail1; **S. 37.C:** Shutterstock/Kitch Bain; **S. 37.D:** Shutterstock/Joyce Vincent; **S. 37.E:** Shutterstock/Serghei Starus; **S. 37.F:** PE-Redskaber A/S, Gram, Dänemark; **S. 37.G:** Shutterstock/Value ho; **S. 37.H:** shutterstock/Maksym Bondarchuk; **S. 46:** Shutterstock/Anna Stacey; **S. 47:** Shutterstock/chombosan; **S. 48:** Shutterstock/Phil Date; **S. 49:** Shutterstock/Anna Stacey; **S. 50:** Shutterstock/AleksOrel; **S. 51:** Shutterstock/Roman Sigaev; **S. 56:** Shutterstock/Africa Studio; **S. 61:** Shutterstock/F8 studio; **S. 62:** Shutterstock/Rawpixel. com; **S. 67.B1:** Fotolia/mariesacha; **S. 67.B2:** Shutterstock/Jiri Hera; **S. 67.B3:** Shutterstock/Coprid; **S. 67.B4:** Shutterstock/Artem Kovalenco; **S. 70.1:** Shutterstock/marilyn barbone; **S. 70.2:** Shutterstock/Konstantin Kopachinsky; **S. 70.3:** Shutterstock/Natalia Kirichenko; **S. 70.4:** Shutterstock/Serghei Starus; **S. 71:** Shutterstock/creativesunday; **S. 72.1–4:** Yang Liu Design, Berlin; **S. 75.1:** Shutterstock/leungchopan; **S. 75.2:** Shutterstock/Lisa F. Young; **S. 75.3:** Shutterstock/Rehan Qureshi; **S. 76.1:** Shutterstock/AlexHliv; **S. 76.2:** Fotolia/naum; **S. 76.3:** Shutterstock/welcomia; S. 76.4: Fotolia/rcfotostock; **S. 78:** Shutterstock/amphaiwan; **S. 83:** Fotolia/ake1150; **S. 88:** Shutterstock/Alexander Ishchenko; **S. 89:** Shutterstock/VecFashion; **S. 94.1+2:** Shutterstock/veryulissa; **S. 94.3+4:** shutterstock/Zdenka Darula; **S. 95:** Shutterstock/vdimage; **S. 98:** Shutterstock/Florin Burlan; **S. 100:** Shutterstock/pavalena; **S. 101:** shutterstock/Differr; **S. 106:** Shutterstock/Weredragon; **S. 110.1+2:** Shutterstock/Leremy; **S. 114:** Shutterstock/SpeedKingz; **S. 117.1:** Shutterstock/Boleslaw Kubica; **S. 117.2:** Shutterstock/Madarakis; **S.120:** Shutterstock/Daniel M Ernst; **S. 122.1:** Fotolia/Bojan; **S. 122.2:** Shutterstock/F8 studio; **S. 122.3:** Shutterstock/CREATISTA; **S. 124.1:** Shutterstock/Christopher Hall; **S. 124.2:** Fotolia/thanksforbuying; **S. 124.3:** Shutterstock/Douglas Freer; **S. 124.4:** Shutterstock/Sinseeho; **S. 127:** Shutterstock/Michal Kowalski; **S. 150:** Fotolia/spanishjohnny72